The Age of Transition
The Archaeology of English Culture 1400–1600

The Age of Transition
The Archaeology of English Culture 1400–1600

*Proceedings of a conference hosted by the Society for Medieval Archaeology and the
Society for Post-Medieval Archaeology at the British Museum, London,
14–15th November 1996*

Edited by

David Gaimster and Paul Stamper

The Society for Medieval Archaeology Monograph 15
Oxbow Monograph 98
1997

Published by
Oxbow Books in association with the Society for Medieval Archaeology
and the Society for Post-Medieval Archaeology

© Oxbow Books, 1997

ISBN 1 900188 55 4

This book is available direct from
Oxbow Books, Park End Place, Oxford OX1 1HN
(Phone: 01865-241249; Fax: 01865 794449)

and

The David Brown Book Company
PO Box 511, Oakville, CT 06779
(Phone: 860-945-9329; Fax: 860-945-9468)

*Front cover: **The Holy Family at a Meal*** *painted by Jan Mostaert between c.1495 and 1500. The scene depicts the increasing formalisation of dining habits and diversity of ceramic (stoneware), pewter and wooden tableware in use within a northern European urban household of the early 16th century (Wallraf-Richartz Museum, Cologne, inv. WRM471; courtesy of the Rheinisches Bildarchiv, Cologne).*

*Back cover: Polychrome maiolica tile painted with the figure of Lucretia stabbing herself, probably made in Antwerp, South Netherlands, c.1520. Part of the pavement laid in the Chapel of The Vyne, Hampshire, a mansion built by William Sandys between c.1500 and 1520 (from B. Rackham, **Early Netherlands Maiolica**, London, 1926).*

Printed in Great Britain by
The Short Run Press, Exeter

Foreword

The conference proceedings presented here represent the outcome of the first joint conference between the Society for Medieval Archaeology and the Society for Post-Medieval Archaeology. These two leading period societies have a pivotal role in stimulating research in their respective areas, or 'periods' of interest, in defining new research agendas, and in promoting a wider awareness of current issues in European historical archaeology. In coming together in 1996 for a conference focussing upon the theme of the medieval to post-medieval transition – a subject which has hitherto been ill-defined, and which is poorly represented in archaeological literature – the two societies have taken a step which is logical by examining in detail an important area of common interest, which is stimulating and provocative, and which is absolutely essential if we are properly to understand the forces at work in shaping the culture of the English.

The papers in this volume are a testament to the outstanding success of the conference in dealing with the question of what constitutes a medieval to post-medieval 'transition'. Some of the country's most eminent authorities, together with visiting scholars from continental Europe, have approached the question from a range of different viewpoints – those of the archaeologist, the historian, the art historian, the architectural historian – to present a variety of evidence in a cohesive and readable format. The result is a credit to the vision of the conference organisers, David Gaimster and Paul Stamper, whose efforts have been well-rewarded, and of the defining roles of the two societies which they represent.

The Age of Transition serves as a model of co-operation between two of the foremost period societies, and highlights the importance of a joint approach to an area of common interest. This volume will remain an important work of reference for many years to come and will serve as the standard against which future research into the subject will be measured.

David Barker
President, Society for Post-Medieval Archaeology

Martin Biddle
President, Society for Medieval Archaeology

Contents

Introduction

David Gaimster and Paul Stamper

And thus we do spend the Sabbath day in good and godly exercises, all done in our vulgar tongue, that each one may hear and understand the same... (William Harrison, *The Description of England*, 1587).[1]

Traditionally in England, as in most European Protestant countries, the Reformation marks a fault line between the Middle Ages and the modern world. Equally, the arrival of Continental Renaissance culture or the Discovery of the New World have been regarded as yardsticks for the cultural transformation of early modern England. As in historical writing, so in archaeology, the date of 1500 continues to form a rigid division in terms of the research interests and professional organisation. Recent statements by the Society for Medieval Archaeology and the Society for Post-Medieval Archaeology have only served to reinforce the mutual exclusivity created by the c.1500 divide: the former body ceasing its interest at the 'impact of the Renaissance and the cultural changes of the 16th century',[2] the latter 'accepting the assumption that there is something distinctive about the years between the impact of the Renaissance and Reformation at one end and the onset of the Industrial Revolution at the other'.[3] However, as Paul Courtney notes in his discussion of the periodisation problem (Chapter 9), such a rigid boundary can only obscure, not enlighten, the true nature of the transition between medieval and post-medieval society. With the pressure on to justify the allocation of resources in each field, there has been little desire to challenge this orthodoxy or to promote a better understanding of the nature and pace of change.

Medieval and post-medieval archaeology are relatively new disciplines in Britain, the foundation of period societies in both fields taking place just over 40 and 30 years ago respectively. The agreement of a demarcation line set at c.1500 can be seen partly as a product of political necessity in the context of a long struggle for government funding and recognition among the archaeological community. The rigid division reflects the need felt by both Societies to carve out distinctive academic and political identities for their respective disciplines. However, the traditional schism contrasts squarely with current thinking, needs and priorities in British field archaeology. With the majority of resources in the historic period going into the investigation of multi-period settlements and sites, whether towns, villages, fortifications or churches, it is becoming increasingly clear that the two Societies must develop a new agenda, one geared to exploring longer-term developments, and one more sensitive to the variable rate of change across time and space.[4] It is no coincidence that English Heritage has recently identified the medieval to early modern transition as a priority for further research and resourcing.[5] Moreover, both period disiplines share the same general methodology, particularly with respect to the integration of historical evidence, and generate the same sorts of questions about society. As we write, calls for the formalisation of a new 'historical archaeology' for the Middle Ages and the early modern period continue to intensify across Europe and North America.[6] These developments were responsible, in part, for the calling of this first joint conference of the Society for Medieval Archaeology and the Society for Post-Medieval Archaeology on the subject of the transition between the medieval and early modern periods.

The aim of the meeting was to explore the contribution of archaeology – in its widest sense – to fundamental questions of continuity and change in English society between the 15th and 16th centuries. These proceedings are intended as a review of the state of research across a wide cross-section of subject areas – from royal palaces to gentry houses and urban tenements, from villages to fortifications, and from pottery to personal seals, dress and diet. It is hoped that they will go some way towards redefining the focus of archaeological research into late medieval and early modern culture, encouraging a pluralist approach to the period and its sources, and helping to dissolve some of the more entrenched academic divisions which have so obscured it, notably between archaeologists and historians and between medievalists and post-medievalists. Medieval and, in particular, later archaeology has been criticised all too often in the past for accepting a complementary role to documentary history, a failing often described as the 'handmaiden-of-history' syndrome.[7] This conference was designed to put material culture at the top of the research agenda, primarily because only archaeology – even for this period – offers the opportunity to examine change at all levels of society as opposed to only among elite groups. Collectively these papers establish a new framework for the study of cultural transition in early modern England, one which challenges the traditional divisions between medieval and post-medieval archaeology. As a survey of the current state of research these proceedings are intended as a contribution to the wider historical debate.

———

There are old men yet dwelling in the village where I remain, which have noted three things to be marvellously altered in England within their sound remembrance; and three other things too-too much increased. One is the multitude of chimneys lately erected.... The second is the great (although not general) amendment of lodging.... The third thing they tell of is the exchange of vessel, as of treen platters into pewter, and wooden spoons into silver or tin.... And as they commend these, so ...they speak also of three things that are grown to be very grievous unto them, to wit: the enhancing of rents...; the daily oppression of copyholders....The third thing they talk of is usury,..now perfectly practiced almost by every Christian... (William Harrison, *The Description of England*, 1587).[8]

As one 16th-century witness, William Harrison, rector of Radwinter, Essex (1559–93), rightly observed, some changes were for the better, some were for the worse. In virtually each of the case-studies presented here, it is also important to note that the rate and extent of development was not uniform, and that tradition loomed as large as revolution in lives of ordinary men and women of the time. It has been demonstrated recently, for instance, that although the break with Rome was indeed profound, the pre-Reformation liturgy, ritual and imagery remained central to lay religion into the 1540s and beyond.[9] On the other hand, it is hard to avoid the evidence for a number of major innovations which transformed the meaning and quality of life for large sections of the population. Although some changes of the period c.1400–1600 were sudden, momentous and distinctive, others were less so, including some which represent the culmination of a much longer period of change, if not evolution. Other forces were only just beginning to gain momentum by 1600 and did not manifest themselves fully until later in the 17th century.

As well as considering the effects of individual innovations, this collection of papers turns the spotlight on to the underlying dynamics, processes and effects of change in early modern England. Avoiding the sterile debate on which date or what constitutes 'medieval' or 'modern', virtually all the case-studies consider the compositional nature of transition and inform with original evidence the general and global trends such as the rise of capitalism, secularism, individualism, materialism and increasing social mobility. Several papers deal with the impact of specific innovations, including the reconfiguration of personal space within the home or the influence of Continental Renaissance culture on building, the domestic interior and personal adornment, one effect being to increase the division between polite and popular culture. Others consider the impact of particular technological achievements such as the invention of gunpowder which revolutionised fortification design, the discovery of the New World and the expansion of maritime trade which affected dietry habits across Europe or the invention of the printing press which formed a vehicle for Reformation. In keeping with such a wide range in subject matter, the case-studies draw on an impressive array of physical and historical evidence and assimilate the results of buildings, landscape, artefact and ecofact analysis with information derived from contemporaneous documentary and representational sources. Whatever label we attach to it, it is clear that the archaeology of early modern England is evolving as a mature and distinctively multi-disciplinary discipline.

The first group of essays affirm some of the fundamental themes and issues of the 'Age of Transition'. Hugh Tait sets out to remind us of the magnitude of change in the mentality of Englishmen over the two hundred years which traditionally divide the Middle Ages and the modern world (Chapter 1). The visual and emotional contrasts of the Age are illustrated eloquently by representations of the monarchs Richard II (1377–1399) in the Wilton Diptych and Elizabeth I (1588–1603) in the 'Three Goddesses Panel' (Figs 1.1, 1.2). The writer singles out a further metaphor of transition, namely Coverdale's *Great Bible* of 1539 which, written in English, democratised access to the Written Word and helped to spread the message of Henrician Reform. Paul Courtney, in contrast, avoids individual events or innovations and emphasises the importance of recognising longer-term processes in English culture over the course of the late Middle Ages (Chapter 2). He identifies the origins of acquisitive, consumersist behaviour as a mid 14th-century phenomenon, a trend traditionally associated with the 16th century. Similarly, like the Industrial Revolution, the roots of the Renaissance in England can be traced back a long

way into the medieval period. Frans Verhaeghe, offering a Continental perspective, continues on this theme and questions the validity of attributing the 'transitional' label exclusively to the period c.1400–1600 when so many of the changes which manifested themselves at this time can be linked with earlier medieval developments (Chapter 3). The traditional Marxist model of transition from feudalism to capitalism during the 15th to 16th centuries underplays the magnitude of previous change. After all, the Burgundian Netherlands became an urbanised, cosmopolitan and materialist society well before the 15th century. Helmut Hundsbichler of the Institut für Realienkunde des Mittelalters und der Frühen Neuzeit (Institute for the Study of Material Things of the Middle Ages and early modern period), based in Krems, Austria, provides a further Continental perspective on our understanding of change and innovation in early modern culture, both adding support to the long-term view and questioning the lack of methodological and theoretical refinement in previous studies of the more recent past. In a thought-provoking article he stresses not only the importance but also the problems of multi-disciplinary research in historical archaeology (Chapter 4). Like Tait, the writer also emphasises that an understanding of the medieval to early modern transition and its material 'reality' depends not only on the cross-reference of archaeological and documentary sources but also on an appreciation of contemporary mentalities.

As so many of the contributors, Christopher Dyer advocates a longer-term view of the 15th and 16th centuries (Chapter 5). In his case study of peasants and farmers he cautions that developments in the early modern countryside must be seen against a background of commercialisation in the 13th century and demographic crisis in the 14th century. As in any instance of transition, particularly in the countryside, there was always much continuity. Likewise, as Richard Morris emphasised in a paper given at the conference but not included here, the Reformation was not so much a break with the past, but a metamorphosis, with the Roman Catholic tradition in worship, funerary tradition and benefaction detectable well into the Jacobean age.

On specific innovations, one group of papers, although diverse in subject matter, investigates the material evidence for the arrival of Continental Renaissance culture in early 16th-century England. Phillip Lindley explores the stylistic and functional revolution in tomb-sculpture and the influence of Italians such as Pietro Torrigiano on indigenous sculptors (Chapter 6). Simon Thurley, meanwhile, examines Henry VIII's new palace of Whitehall on which so much excavation has taken place since the 1930s and the extent to which its plan, function and context represented a radical metamorphosis from the traditional late medieval form (Chapter 7). The physical separation of private residence from the machinery of government within the same complex put Whitehall in the vanguard of change in royal residential planning. Tudor palaces form the key for studying innovation in the architectural ornament of aristocratic residences during the 1530s (Chapter 8). Maurice Howard reviews the introduction of decorative terracotta as a medium by which Continental-style antique ornament, then in use at royal sites, was adapted for the houses of the courtier class as a vehicle for social competition.

A third clutch of papers examines the spatial reorganisation of the home at various levels of society during the 15th and 16th centuries. Quite profound changes in the configuration of the the gentry house are identified by Nicholas Cooper (Chapter 9). The multiplication and increasing diversity of rooms during the 16th century reflects the decline of late medieval hierarchical structures and a new emphasis on privacy and personal distinction in the home. Likewise, in the towns, John Schofield describes the increasing partition of houses over the course of the 15th century (Chapter 10), a trend which reflects the emerging need for privacy, the functional division of working and living spaces and the changing priorities of new classes of inhabitants, including professional merchants and artisans along with the urban gentry. Finally, Matthew Johnson in his case-study of vernacular housing in the English countryside (Chapter 11), argues that the reorganisation of space within the houses of the socially middling classes reflects the increasingly complex and sophisticated mentality of their owners, who intimate with the changing constitution of the early modern world. The final collection of studies on the transformation of English

society during the 15th to 16th centuries concerns the impact of individual technological innovations and cultural developments on diverse categories of material culture. Jonathan Coad considers the revolution in fortification design and the growth of a specialist navy as a result of the introduction of gunpowder and effective heavy ordinance (Chapter 12). In their study of ceramic evidence for the transformation of the household, David Gaimster and Beverley Nenk emphasise the role of large-scale immigrant communities in south-east England who imported not only new commodities (stoneware, maiolica vessels and tiles, stove-tiles, hearth bricks and floor-tiles) but also new lifestyles in which these goods were used (Chapter 13). The imports had an immediate and profound effect on native production, frequently stimulating potters to compete with the imports. The new elasticity of the English ceramic market and the multiplicity and multidimensionality of products in circulation during the 15th and 16th centuries are characterised as revolutionary and distinctive from earlier instances of innovation. Moreover, the enhanced status and widespread social distribution of ceramics in early modern England emphasise the role of the medium as an index of cultural and behavioural change in the English household of the period. One of the most important sources of evidence for the expansion of maritime trade and consequent dietary change is provided by the rich archaeobotanical remains recovered from ports in the south-east. In his survey of the inner London evidence, John Giorgi identifies a series of exotic plants which demonstrate the increasing intensity of commercial contact with the Far East, North Africa and North America during the 16th century (Chapter 14). Finally, John Cherry analyses the effects of religious, economic and cultural change on personal seals and heraldic objects (Chapter 17). Focusing on the Great Seal and the influence of the Italian Renaissance on seal design, Cherry concludes that transition in the use of heraldry and seals was both simple and subtle. At one level it replaced the depiction of saints and on another became an instrument of secular and royal propaganda. Once again, the medium forms an index of changing mentalities and attitudes in early modern England.

Being so closely linked with personal taste and

expression, our final group of study-materials – tailored clothing and dress-fittings – have always been in a state of transition (Chapters 15–16). For this reason, it has been difficult for our contributors, Kay Staniland and Geoff Egan with Hazel Forsyth respectively, to identify specific innovations in dress fashion and accessories of the early modern period. Ironically, many significant changes in design occured before the 15th century, the 'tailoring revolution' of the 14th century being a case in point. One development can be identified immediately in the archaeological record, however: namely the introduction of cheaply-made copper-alloy buckles and wound-wire jewellery designed to attract a much broader spectrum of 16th-century society. Thus dress accessories for the period demonstrate a wide variety of fashionable self-expression and the emergence of popular products for a much wider constituency of consumers. Commodification appears to be another, but not exclusive, feature of the 'Transitional' period in England.

The success of the 1996 Age of Transition conference and the rapid turn-around of these conference proceedings is in no small measure a reflection of the support and encouragement given to its editors by its contributing authors and by fellow officers and members of the Society for Medieval Archaeology and the Society for Post-Medieval Archaeology. In addition David Gaimster and Paul Stamper would like to thank Dr Robert Anderson, Director of the British Museum for hosting the Meeting and for welcoming delegates; Neil Stratford, Keeper of Medieval and Later Antiquities at the Museum, for hosting the conference reception in the post-medieval *Europe* gallery; Mark Woolcott and Cathy Marsh of the same Department for providing organisational support; Paul Drury (English Heritage), Tim Wilson (Ashmolean Museum, Oxford) and Dr Dora Thornton (BM) for chairing sessions; Dr Steven Driscoll of Glasgow University Archaeological Research Division for managing the finances of the conference; Shropshire County Council Archaeology Unit for administrative support; and David Brown and Val Tomlin at Oxbow Books, Oxford, for ensuring that this volume was processed and published in time for the 1997 Medieval Europe conference. Furthermore, the two Societies wish to

acknowledge the generosity of the British Academy in awarding a Conference Grant to cover the costs of Continental speakers and of the British Museum for providing an ideal venue and conference reception. And finally, the editors would like to express their personal debt of gratitude to the twenty contributors to this volume, particularly for producing written versions of their paper at such speed and enabling us to keep to our ambitious publication schedule.

In the Notes and Bibliographies to the papers which follow the place of publication is London, unless otherwise indicated.

Notes

1. William Harrison, *The Description of England*, 1587 (edited by G. Edelen), reprinted Dover Publications, New York, 1994.
2. 'Archaeology and the Middle Ages. Recommendations by the Society for Medieval Archaeology to the Historic Buildings and Monuments Commission for England', *Medieval Archaeology*, 31 (1987), 1–12.
3. *Research Priorities for Post-Medieval Archaeology*, Society for Post-Medieval Archaeology (1988), i.
4. For a discussion of the variable pace of transition in different parts of Britain see I.A. Crawford's seminal paper on the Scottish experience in the first edition of *Post-Medieval Archaeology*, 1 (1967).
5. *Frameworks for Our Past. Policies for Our Archaeological Past 1979–1999*, English Heritage (1990), 43; *English Heritage Archaeology Division Research Agenda*, English Heritage (1997), 45.
6. Orser 1996, 190–194.
7. Austin 1990 among others.
8. As note 1.
9. Duffy 1992.

Bibliography

Austin, D. 1990, 'The 'proper study' of medieval archaeology' in D. Austin & L. Alcock eds., *From the Baltic to the Black Sea*

Crawford, I.A. 1967, 'The Divide between Medieval and Post-Medieval in Scotland', *Post-Medieval Archaeology*, 1, 84–89

Duffy, E. 1992, *The Stripping of the Altars. Traditional Religion in England 1400–1580*, New Haven and London

Orser, C.E., Jr. 1996, *A Historical Archaeology of the Modern World*, New York and London

1   The Great Divide?

Hugh Tait

Few in this audience will have escaped the testing experience of sitting down with an object (or an excavated fragment) with the intention of writing a short note to demonstrate, firstly, how some of its characteristics stem from the past and, secondly, how other features anticipate the future. Underlying these attempts to establish how things fit into a sequence of developments, based on our knowledge of what went before and what came after, is our recognition that change tends to be an ever-present factor.

This exercise, when applied to any specific historical period, will enable the historian to claim that the latter is '*an* age of transition'. However, if every period – like every individual life – can be shown to be, to a greater or lesser extent, in a state of transition, why was this conference on 'the archaeology of English culture 1400–1600' given a title that singles out these two hundred years from all other periods and identifies it as '*The* Age of Transition'?

The organisers of this Conference, by introducing this exaggerated claim into the title, have implicitly acknowledged the true magnitude of the change – a change so fundamental that the historian is still able to retain, with complete justification, those familiar labels of convenience, 'medieval', 'modern' and 'the great divide', in spite of the considerable continuity in many basic crafts and their products. What happened in those two hundred years would, without doubt, mean that anyone living in England around 1400 would have experienced a culture very different from that prevailing in the decades around 1600.

Among the most visually-telling expressions of this great difference are two exceptionally well-documented portrayals of English sovereigns: King Richard II (reigned 1377–1399) in the Wilton Diptych[1] and Queen Elizabeth I (reigned 1558–1603) in the 'Three Goddesses' Panel.[2] Both are small, intimate paintings and, in this context, both have a special significance because they were almost certainly commissioned (and, in a sense, created) by the two monarchs, themselves.[3]

The Wilton Diptych is now thought to have been painted a few years before Richard II (aged 32) was murdered and, in it, the King is shown in late medieval tradition wearing the crown but *kneeling* and being recommended to the Virgin and Child, apparently standing in a meadow in Heaven. The King's three presenters are his patron saint (St John the Baptist) and two English royal saints (St Edmund, the last King of East Anglia, martyred by the Danes in A.D. 870, and St Edward the Confessor, the last of the Anglo-Saxon line of kings, who died in January, 1066). So, whatever else this painting may be – and the debate about its half-hidden meanings has not yet been closed – it is a clear visual expression of religious devotion and of the sacred nature of kingship.

By contrast, Elizabeth's allegorical panel has no religious content. The Queen in full majesty is depicted not only wearing the crown but also carrying the orb and sceptre; she is seen – not kneeling – but advancing in a most commanding manner towards – not three saints – but three goddesses from Classical

Fig. 1.1 *Richard II (reigned 1377–1399) and Three Saints: the interior of The Wilton Diptych, executed by an unknown artist using oak panels, gold and silver leaf, water and mordant gilding, and the egg tempera technique of painting; probably c.1395 (Courtesy of the National Gallery, London).*

mythology. In this conceit, Elizabeth would seem to be cast in the role of Paris faced with the choice between Juno, Minerva and Venus, but there the resemblance ends, for this is no puny mortal but a ruler who can put these goddesses to flight, being already possessed of all their virtues, and more. Indeed, the original frame, which has survived with this picture, bears a Latin inscription[4] that leaves no room for doubt, as a contemporary translation made clear:

> 'Pallas was keen of brain, Juno was queen of might,
> The rosy face of Venus was beauty shining bright,
> Elizabeth then came
> And, overwhelmed, Queen Juno took to flight,
> Pallas was silenced, Venus blushed for shame.'

This painting (dated 1569) was recorded in the Royal Collection as early as 1600, just three years before the peaceful death of Elizabeth I (aged 69). It contains one further statement that is, again, in complete contrast with the religious sentiments expressed in the Wilton Diptych. Unambiguously, the Queen confounds the three goddesses – not in some heavenly, flower-bedecked meadow nor, even, on the imagined slopes of Mount Olympus – but here in England, under the walls of one of the Queen's favourite royal residences, Windsor Castle. Indeed, no earlier painted view of it is known.

The differences between these two portrayals of English monarchy, separated by nearly 200 years, speak for themselves. They are products of two

Fig. 1.2 *Elizabeth I (reigned 1558–1603) and Three Goddesses: a panel painting in its original inscribed frame, signed by the monogrammist HE and dated 1569; recorded in the Royal Collection in 1600 (By gracious permission of H.M. The Queen).*

different cultures and, whereas the terms 'medieval' and 'Gothic' can properly be used when speaking of the Wilton Diptych, the historical and art-historical labels, 'Renaissance' and 'Mannerism', can be most appropriately applied in any discussion of the Queen's allegorical panel.

A similar profound contrast can be found within the Kingdom of Scotland. The portrayal of King James III in the famous altarpiece painted for Trinity College Church, Edinburgh, in the 1470s by the great Flemish artist, Hugo van der Goes (died 1482), is in the medieval tradition.[5] The King, who is depicted wearing the crown, again kneels, while his presenter (St Andrew) towers over him. Indeed, the sacred nature of kingship is here emphasised as St Andrew

is actually shown supporting the crown on the King's head. The scene, set within an ecclesiastical building, is an expression of religious devotion that is echoed on the other wing of this altar-piece, in which James III's Queen, Margaret of Denmark, is seen bedecked in jewels but kneeling with a prayerbook open in front of her. She is dwarfed by her saintly supporter in armour for, despite her elevated rank, this Queen remains an imperfect mortal.

No such sentiments are expressed in the double standing portrait of James VI of Scotland (crowned in 1567) and his Queen, Anne of Denmark, which was engraved by Johan Wiriex[6] soon after James had inherited the English throne upon the death of Elizabeth I in 1603 and been proclaimed King James

a   b

Fig. 1.3a–b *James III of Scotland (reigned 1460–1488) supported by St Andrew, and (opposite) his consort, Margaret of Denmark, supported by St Cnut: interior of the two wings of the alterpiece painted for Trinity College Church, Edinburgh, by Hugo van der Goes (died 1482); now on loan to the National Gallery of Scotland (By gracious permission of H.M. The Queen).*

of the world, to the opening up of minds, with the Renaissance's preoccupation with the tradition of Antiquity (rather than Christianity) and with the recognition of the urgent need for the reform of the Church by both humanists, like Erasmus, and the leaders of Protestantism. The invention of printing and woodcut illustration, the transformation of music and vocal polyphony and, in particular, the use of the vernacular language in place of Latin and French were some of the major contributions that gave added momentum and enriched the transforming process.

By 1500, the language of the English court of the founder of the new dynasty, the Tudors, was no longer French and his second son, Henry VIII (reigned 1509–1547), was to extend the process yet further after he had made himself Supreme Head of the Church in England in 1534, successfully brought about the Dissolution of the monasteries, and so radically changed the teaching at the universities that it marked the end of medieval scholasticism.

Even Henry VIII's collection of pictures reflected something of this turmoil; it contained at least three with anti-papal subjects, of which one was painted by Girolamo da Treviso and is still preserved in the

Fig. 1.4 James VI of Scotland and I of England (died 1625) and his Queen, Anne of Denmark: an engraving by Johan Wiriex executed shortly after the King's accession to the English throne in 1603 (Courtesy of the Victoria and Albert Museum, London).

I of England (reigned 1603–1625). The King's standing pose is expressive of a successful military commander; his helmet is just behind him but he still wears the breast-plate of his armour and a large sword, while grasping the baton in his right-hand in the manner of a classical Roman ruler. His consort, attired in court dress and jewellery, stands expressionless and, in place of a prayerbook, she holds a fan and a lace kerchief.

The truly momentous events that filled those intervening years and changed attitudes in a fundamental way are well-known. They ranged from the opening up of new global horizons, with the discovery of direct sea contact between the continents

Fig. 1.5 An Anti-papal Allegory belonging to Henry VIII (reigned 1509–1547); panel painting in grisaille by Girolamo da Treviso, who arrived in England in 1538, four years after the Act of Supremacy had established the Sovereign as head of the Church of England (By gracious permission of H.M. The Queen).

Royal Collection.[7] The propagandist element in this painting is explicit, since it is painted in grisaille and the four standing figures are identified by name (in gold letters) as the four Evangelists and the two female figures lying beside the prostrate body of the Pope are labelled 'Avarice' and 'Hypocrisy'. As this Italian artist came to England in 1538 and died six years later, while serving as a military engineer at Henry VIII's siege of Boulogne in 1544, it is curious that this picture does not seem to have entered the Royal Collection until after the 1542 Inventory had been compiled; it is, however, listed in the more wide-ranging Inventory of 1547 (following the King's demise).

As early as 1536 and 1538, *Injunctions* had been authorised by the King, requiring that the Pater Noster, the Articles of Faith and Ten Commandments should be taught *in their mother tongue* and that, in each church, there should be installed a copy of the Bible *in English* so that all parishioners could have easy access 'and read it'. For that reason, Coverdale was engaged in printing in Paris at great haste the so-called '*Great Bible*', which was finally ready in 1539.[8] However, there were unforeseen consequences and, within three years, it had been decided that universal access to the Bible in English was creating 'a diversity of belief' and leading to 'strange and contradictory doctrines'. As a result, the Act of 1543 withdrew this right to read the Bible in English unless the readers were 'noblemen, gentlemen and merchant householders' – and even they had to read it *privately*. Others, such as women, artificers, apprentices, and so on, were forbidden.

So, the introduction of policies that might create a climate in which the individual's freedom of the mind could flourish, was not without obstacles. Progress was slow but the changed England of c. 1600 was the England of Shakespeare, of Marlowe and Spenser, of Dowland and Byrd – undoubtedly, a different culture from c. 1400 and, some would say, more civilised.

Vasari, the great Renaissance historian of art who died in 1574, tried to explain why Florence had been the place where men excelled in the arts. The first of his reasons was: '*The spirit of criticism: the air of Florence making minds naturally free and not content with mediocrity*'.[9] This statement could

Fig. 1.6 *Richard Haydocke's engraved title-page for his book on the Arts published in Oxford in 1598 (Courtesy of the British Museum, London).*

equally be a partial definition of a civilised society. Certainly, England around 1600 was experiencing a remarkable concentration of intellectual energy and competitive spirit, allied to a desire to create works of originality and enduring beauty. To illustrate how great a transformation had taken place in English society, despite its many imperfections, one has only to look at the life of Richard Haydocke, the earliest English writer on art.[10]

Haydocke's '*Tracte containing the Artes of Curious Painting, Carving and Building*' was published in Oxford in 1598. It contains his translation of Giovanni Paolo Lomazzo's *Trattoria dell'Arte de la Pittura*, first published in Milan in 1584. Richard Haydocke's family were small country gentry, owning a modest estate at Greywell, in Hampshire, for about a century before his birth in 1570. His parents, James and Margaret, sent him to school at Winchester and, at 18, he matriculated at New College, Oxford, where within three years he took his B.A. Then, he 'travelled for some time beyond the seas', but was certainly back in Oxford by 1597 (if not before) and was completing his translation of Lomazzo for his book. Being an amateur artist, himself, Richard Haydocke both designed and engraved the title-page, incorporating (at the bottom) a small self-portrait bust; he also based five of his illustrative plates on drawings by Dürer, whose treatise on the proportions of the human figure he clearly knew well. Furthermore, in his Preface which contains a generous appreciation of the artistic talents of Nicholas Hilliard, the Queen's limner and miniaturist, Haydocke makes it clear that his aim is to improve English taste and patronage so that is will encourage (and reward) English artists who are gifted.

In the same year that his book was published, Richard Haydocke started to read for his degree of Bachelor of Medicine, which he took, after three years, in 1601. So, Haydocke was apparently putting into practice the new Renaissance doctrine, as expressed in Castiglione's *Il Cortegiano* (1528; translated into English in 1561), that a knowledge of the theory and practice of the arts is an essential element in learning, and learning is a fundamental part of 'nobility'. Richard Haydocke, like an increasing number of similarly cultivated Elizabethans, represents the fundamental change that had taken-place in English cultural life within those past two centuries.

Notes

1. Gordon 1993 includes (pp. 88–91) a full bibliography. See also an essay therein on 'Richard II: image and reality' by Caroline M. Barron. The Wilton Diptych had entered Charles I's Collection before 1639, but probably not earlier than 1632; its history between 1399–1639 is undocumented.

2. Lloyd 1991, no. 9, where the artist's monogram HW and the date 1569 (lower right corner of the panel) are accepted as original but 'the attribution of the painting is unresolved'.

3. The two oak panels of the Wilton Diptych are hinged and each panel measures approximately 47.5 × 29.2

cm; consequently, when opened to the full extent, its maximum width is approximately 58.5 cm. The Queen Elizabeth Allegorical panel measures 70.8 × 84.5 cm (approximately 28 × 33 in).

4. IVNO POTENS SCEPTRIS ET MENTIS ACVMINE PALLAS
   ET ROSEO VENERIS FVLGET IN ORE DECVS
   AD FVIT ELIZABETH IVNO PERCVLSA REFVGIT
   OBSTVPVIT PALLAS ERVBVITQ VENVS
   The translation is from Groos 1981, 46–7.

5. Panofsky 1953; Thompson and L. Campbell, 1974.

6. Victoria and Albert Museum, reg. no. E. 3890–1960; reproduced in Barkley, 1982, 33.

7. Pouncey 1953, pp. 208–211; Lloyd 1991, no. 6, with bibliography and size (68 × 84.4 cm) (p. 56).

8. For a fuller discussion of the printing of English translations of the complete Bible (from the 'Coverdale' Bible of 1535' to the 'Sixth Great Bible' of 1541) and the further intervention of the King himself in May, 1541, when any church failing to install a copy by 1 November was threatened with a fine of 40s. per month, see Tait 1985, figs 1–26, and specifically pp. 44–5.

9. Vasari, 1550, 1568, under 'Pietro Perugino, painter, (1446–1523)'. *N.B.* The best edition (in Italian) remains that edited by G. Milanesi 1878–85.

10. Hind 1952, 32–33; 231–35; Corbett & Lightbown 1979, 67–78; Auerbach 1961, 198 ff; Hard 1940.

Bibliography

Auerbach, E. 1961, *Nicholas Hilliard*

Barkley, H. 1982, *Likenesses in Line*

Corbett, M. and Lightbrown, R. 1979, *The Comely Frontispiece*

Gordon, D. 1993, *Making and Meaning: The Wilton Diptych*, The National Gallery, London

Groos, G.W. (ed.) 1981, *The Diary of Baron Waldstein: a traveller in Elizabethan England*

Hard, F. 1940, 'Richard Haydocke and Alexander Browne: Two half-forgotten Writers on the Art of Painting, *Publications of the Modern Language Association of America*, 55, no. 3

Hind, A.M. 1952, *Engraving in England in 16th–17th Centuries. A descriptive catalogue: Pt. 1, The Tudor Period*, British Museum

Lloyd, C. 1991. *The Queen's Pictures*, National Gallery

Panofsky, E. 1953, *Early Netherlandish Painting*, Cambridge, Mass.

Pouncey, P. 1953, 'Girolamo da Treviso in the Service of Henry VIII', *The Burlington Magazine* 95, 208–211

Tait, H. 1985, 'The girdle prayer book or "Tablett": an important class of Renaissance jewellery at the court of Henry VIII', *Jewellery Studies*, Journal of the Society of Jewellery Historians, vol. 2, 29–58

Thompson, C. and Campbell, L. 1974, *Hugo van der Goes and the Trinity Panels in Edinburgh*

Vasari, G. 1550, *The Lives of the most excellent Architects, Painters and Sculptors* (1st edition, Florence, 1550, 2nd enlarged edition, Florence, 1568)

2   The Tyranny of Constructs: some thoughts on periodisation and culture change

Paul Courtney

"In the continuum of human societies, the vibrations between molecule and molecule spread out over so great a span that understanding of a single moment, no matter what its place in the chain of development, can never be attained merely by contemplation of its immediate predecessor."   Marc Bloch (1966, 248)

In a seminal paper of 1974 entitled 'The tyranny of a construct: feudalism and historians of medieval Europe' the American scholar Elizabeth Brown questioned the usefulness of feudalism as a concept. She drew attention to the heterogeneous nature of medieval lordship in Western Europe, both in time and space, and noted the insidious influence of post-medieval lawyers on our perception of medieval institutions. Brown ended her article by suggesting that other beloved '-isms' of medievalists such as manorialism, scholasticism and humanism might also crumble under objective scrutiny.[1] More recently, Susan Reynolds has launched an even more extensive and damning critique of the 'fief' and 'vassalage', the pair of concepts at the centre of most non-Marxist definitions of feudalism.[2] For most of us the term 'feudal', despite its imprecision, remains too useful as short-hand to be totally abandoned; while for Marxists and fellow-travellers, feudalism has always had a distinct set of meanings centred on the idea of a mode of production in which lords used their domination of the tenurial and juridical fabric to coerce surplus from a dependant peasantry.[3] Nevertheless, Brown's critique was a timely reminder that historians rarely lend the same critical rigour to wider conceptual frameworks that they daily apply to the minutiae of evidence.

Perceptions of Transition

Traditional forms on the other hand, may contain the spirit of the coming age. Nothing is more erroneous than to identify classicism and modern culture.' Jacob Huizinga (1924, 318)

In addressing change across one of the most persistent fault lines in historical writing, namely that between the 15th and 16th centuries, this conference is arguably long overdue. Both continuity and the true origins of change are often hidden by rigid period demarcations. A visit to any university library or academic book shop will reveal serried ranks of historical works beginning and ending in 1500. Many such works begin by arguing that this date marks a period of major change but often do so by contrasting rigorous research of the period under study with what is clearly a vague, even mythologised, impression of the adjoining period.

In their search to understand the world human beings have a fundamental need to categorise it into convenient parcels. Standard periodisations represent such parcels, but there is always an inherent danger that they become paradigms which restrict and inhibit analysis. In many cases they originate with an 18th- and 19th-century world view that saw human history in a series of steps, for example, from barbarism to civilisation or feudalism to capitalism. The most awkward and arbitrary unit of historical writing must surely be the century (long, short or regular). One wonders to what extent our perception of history would be altered if the birth of Jesus Christ was 40 or 50 years earlier and the progression of centuries so displaced.

Even Leopold von Ranke, father of 19th-century professionalised history, recognised that each generation writes its own history.[4] Like other later historians, such as Geoffrey Elton, von Ranke's attempts to answer this problem by meticulous study of the sources were doomed to failure. His own brand of divinely ordered, nationalist history was no less value-laden than those he criticised.[5] Our view of history is also shaped, though less obviously, by past perceptions which enter into the generalised historical memory. Two of the greatest fault lines in history as perceived by both professional scholars and the general public are the Industrial Revolution and the Renaissance. I wish first to examine some aspects of the Industrial Revolution. This is not so strange in a conference on the end of the Middle Ages as it offers many useful analogies especially given the better historical evidence and in particular the more widespread application of quantification. Furthermore the notion of the Industrial Revolution has widely influenced approaches to the early modern period. Examples include the widespread search for so-called proto-industrial roots and the dominance of supply-led models, centred on technological innovation and investment, as explanations for economic and social change.

For most of the 19th century there was little interest in the Industrial Revolution. It was too recent a phenomenon, and the big questions of the day were those of the origins of constitutional democracy and Empire. However, in the 20th century the Industrial Revolution has become one of the central pillars of the popular historical imagination and was at the heart of the extraordinary growth of economic history as a major subject in the post-year wars. In some ways the notion of the British Industrial Revolution seems to have supplanted the notion of Empire as the great achievement of our island in popular consciousness. It was a more pragmatic and modernistic gift to the world than our three centuries as colonial rulers which we erased from our national consciousness in an act of collective denial in the post-war period.

The debate over whether the Industrial Revolution represents a period of rapid and cataclysmic change or a slow and long drawn out transformation dates back to the first decades of the 20th century.[6] This debate took a new twist in the 1980s with the publication of new calculations of economic growth, notably by Crafts, which indicated slow economic growth rates throughout the 18th and early 19th centuries.[7] However, as a regional historian I have a great deal of sympathy for the reaction of such economic historians as Maxine Berg and Pat Hudson. They have suggested that the aggregate figures hide a series of regional and sectoral revolutions throughout the period 1700–1830.[8] Furthermore, they suggest that the Industrial Revolution was more than the sum of its parts in representing an enormous shift in the fundamental nature of both the economy and society. This view would appear to be supported by Mark Overton's recent book in which he argues the case for the period 1750–1850 being the only post-medieval era in which real growth in productivity merits the description of an agricultural revolution. As he points out, in 1700 80 per cent of the population worked in agriculture compared with only 20 per cent in 1850, a dramatic social as well as economic transformation.[9]

Not only did the new aggregate growth figures cause problems with the notion of an Industrial Revolution but also with the Consumer Revolution of the mid 18th century as classically formulated by Neil McKendrick and, in America, by Thomas Breen.[10] Inventories in Britain run out by the 1730s, but much longer series exist in some other countries, notably the U.S.A. Quantitative study there, as in Britain, failed to find evidence for the American consumer revolution, stressing steady long-term consumer growth.[11] There are, however, problems with inventories in that they do not include capital expenditure on dwellings and such consumables as food and drink. Furthermore, cultural change may be expressed in terms of product replacement rather than real growth in consumer expenditure. Shammas has moreover suggested that what we may be seeing in the mid 18th century is a shift to expenditure on cheaper and less durable goods.[12] Cissie Fairchild's study of 18th-century Paris revealed not only a growing demand for middle-class luxuries sold in shops but a parallel market dominated by street peddlers selling what she terms 'populuxe' goods: umbrellas, snuff boxes, game-boards and rosaries.[13]

One of the problems with the Industrial Revolution is that it has been in many of its classic forms a largely Anglo-centric concept. A trend of recent years has been to place it more in the context of general economic and consumer growth in north-western Europe.[14] Early industrialisation was a regionally located phenomenon whether in England, France or Belgium. Another important trend has been to recognise the financial and commercial roles of cities in what has often been seen as essentially a rural phenomenon.[15] One of the most interesting contributions in recent years has been the Dutch historian Jan de Vries's concept of the 'industrious revolution'.[16] De Vries argued, on the basis of probate inventories, that the mid 17th century saw marked consumer growth on both sides of the Atlantic. Furthermore he went on to suggest that this phenomenon was related to a shift in the household economies of a wide spectrum of the populace. Most notably, women and children became more involved in wage labour in order to purchase the new consumer goods, products of colonialism and innovation. This is an important model in that it presents possibilities of linking material culture and economic behaviour. It also emphasises that explanations of economic change need to look at consumption by the masses as well as supply-led factors such as middle-class investment and innovation. An archaeological illustration of this phenomenom is probably provided by Andre van Holk's analysis of the numerous excavated dry-land wrecks of the drained Dutch polder. His work on the artefact assemblages suggests a shift in the 17th century from all-male crews to boats run by families.[17]

The notion of a 'medieval' period was born with the Renaissance. It in effect applies to the whole 'dark' period between the end of Classical antiquity and the supposed rebirth of classical civilisation in the 15th and 16th centuries. There are obvious problems with the Renaissance schema, for instance, it ignores the long life of many Classical influences throughout the medieval period and the classically inspired, though non-secular, 'renaissance' of the 12th century. In the late 18th and 19th centuries there were two competing views of the medieval period. One, particularly associated with Catholic scholars, and in England with high Anglicanism, saw the Middle Ages as a romantic golden age. It was the source of Gothic architecture and of William Morris's idealised medieval craftsmen farmers. This tradition of 'Catholic romanticism' can still be recognised today in the work of the of the 'Toronto school' of historians, associated with Father Prof. Raftis of the Pontifical Institute of Medieval Studies. The Institute's work on English court rolls offers a vision of medieval society based on co-operation rather than class conflict.[18] However, the dominant trend of 19th-century thought saw the Renaissance as the origin of a modern humanistic society despite the so-called 'revolt of the medievalists' early this century who tried to trace many of the roots of civilisation back to the medieval period.[19] In Protestant countries emphasis was also put on the Reformation as the dawning of a new age. In Britain, as Walter Ferguson long ago pointed out, the Renaissance formed only part of a package centred on the Tudor monarchy.[20] It is no accident that we have no national museum of the Renaissance (only a gallery in the British Museum) to parallel that in the beautiful 16th-century chateau of Écouen on the northern outskirts of Paris.

In many respects the Protestant, empire-building Tudors can be seen as the real initiators of the Whig version of history, culminating in a monarchist though democratic (at least if you were male and white) empire. The Middle Ages was widely seen as a period of Catholic barbarism as exemplified on the scholarly front by G.G. Coulton's polemic 1920s book, *The Medieval Village*. This deliberately set out to refute romanticised notions of the pre-Reformation past: 'Nothing is to be gained by looking back, except the eternal lesson of thanks to those who set us a glorious example of struggle for better things'.[21] The patronising attitude of even Victorian liberals to Catholicism is exemplified in the Elizabethan adventure story, *Westward Ho*! This novel, written by the Christian-socialist reformer Charles Kingsley, is peopled by brave, English Protestant adventurers fighting Spanish Catholics portrayed as cruel, hypocritical, moral cowards.[22] Certainly, the general image of the Middle Ages as barbaric has had a lasting impact on popular imagination long after its roots have been generally forgotten. The adjective 'medieval' still carries derogatory overtones of barbarism, for instance when used in debates on capital and corporal punishment.

Even today the 16th century is the first period when historical figures take on a three-dimensional character, though this may be due as much to Alexander Korda and the B.B.C drama department as our education system. The Tudors still have a prominent place in the National Curriculum for schools. That most beloved character of the British Middle Ages who ran around Sherwood forest with an American accent and green tights was of course fictional. Even Henry V, the victor of Agincourt and archetypal English hero, is largely known through the Renaissance vision of Shakespeare: 'God for Harry! England and St George'.[23]

The academic debate has continued in a different form from time to time, for instance the Marxist historian Perry Anderson took the redoubtable historians George Sayles and Henry Loyn to task for stressing English constitutional continuity from the late Anglo-Saxon period.[24] However, the modern divide between medieval and early modern historians is perhaps more an institutionalised than an ideological one, though they have often been divided in terms of their interests and approaches. There are certainly discontinuities in the sources. The 16th century sees the arrival of vernacular sources in increasing numbers and a knowledge of Latin is no longer an essential requirement for anyone wishing to do primary research on documents. Even the medieval sources which continue into the 16th century, such as minister's accounts and court rolls, undergo changes in content which reflect the decline of 'feudal' institutions. The new sources of the 16th century clearly reflect real changes in the institutions of state and church. Jack Goody and Matthew Johnson have drawn our attention to the evidence for changing mentalities implied by documents such as inventories, listing possessions.[25] However, changing sources while themselves indicative of change do not necessarily reflect transformation across the entire spectrum of human activity.

Despite the never totally convincing attempt of some scholars, notably Eric Kerridge, to see the 16th century as a period of agricultural revolution, agrarian historians have been less prone than others to see a fault-line around 1500.[26] This perhaps reflects the less violent nature of change seen through estate accounts and manorial court records. Marxists have always tended to see the period between the crisis of the Black Death and the crisis of the 17th century as a period of transition.[27] For non-Marxists too, the demographic crisis of the Black Death and the ensuing decline in feudal institutions has been the major turning point. However, if one reviews the actual range of published agrarian studies, the 1500 fault-line is still a formidable dividing point. Campbell and Overton's recent study of Norfolk agriculture from c.1250–1850 is a notable exception.[28]

Not surprisingly in the period of Thatcherite economics and Ralph Nader, markets and consumption have played a key role in the preoccupations of economic historians since the 1970s. More significantly, medievalists have become theoretically closer in approach to their early modernist and even industrial period colleagues than in the past. This has tended to emphasise the dynamism and innovation of the medieval economy and portray the peasants as active consumers and producers for the market. Examples of the new work include John Langdon's study of the spread of horse traction in the high Middle Ages and Chris Dyer's work on peasant and small town consumption patterns.[29] It has even been suggested that the peasant as well as lordly consumption played a causative role in the landscape reorganisation of the late Saxon period which saw the creation of villages and common fields.[30] It has given fresh life to the debate over the relative roles of lords and peasants as driving forces in the medieval economy.

The recent 'Feeding the City' project has indicated how pre-Black Death London affected the agrarian activity of a wide region reminiscent of Fisher's 1935 model for London's food market in the period 1540–1640.[31] This has even led Bruce Campbell to reflect on the structural similarities between the agrarian economy of 1300 and 1600.[32] Urban historians have been more prone to see the 16th century as a real turning point, perhaps reflecting their greater interest in institutional change and the Reformation. There has also been an emphasis on economic growth after late medieval decline and the widespread urban crises of the 1520s, such as that vividly portrayed by Charles Phythian Adams's book, *Coventry: Desolation of a City*.[33]

Archaeologists have perhaps been less conscious of the divide. Certainly many post-medievalists are also medievalists, either by primary training or economic necessity. There are, however, great discontinuities in the evidence which effectively rend asunder the archaeology of the periods regardless of any theoretical model. By about 1400 in British towns as disparate as London, Lincoln and Monmouth, vertical build-up of deposits, the bread and butter of high medieval archaeology, had ceased. Whereas the ground floors of 12th-century houses survive as cellars, one enters a 15th-century house at much the same level today as when it was built (Figs 2.1 & 2.2). In the short-term, economic crisis may have played a part, but one of the more significant long-term causes is probably a change to more permanent building methods.[34] This change in the stratigraphic formation process means that there is a much poorer survival of archaeological evidence. Activity deposits near the surface are easily destroyed by time or by initial demolition and clearance of archaeological sites. Post-medievalists are very reliant on structures which survive above ground or which cut into medieval deposits. Apart from monastic drains abandoned unemptied at the Dissolution, the main source of closely dateable artefact assemblages in towns are provided by wells, the relatively few rubbish pits and especially stone-lined cesspits. The latter are usually associated with high status dwellings, and as they were regularly emptied the fills of excavated examples are often associated with house clearance deposits prior to demolition.

Fig. 2.1 *Ground floor of 12th-century house preserved as a cellar in Guildhall Lane, Leicester, photographed in 1861. This cellar has been recently rediscovered (Courtesy of Leicestershire Records Office).*

Fig. 2.2 *Late-medieval timber houses, since demolished, in Thornton Lane, Leicester. The far building was demolished c.1872 (Courtesy of Leicestershire Records Office).*

Fig. 2.3 *Part of the rich assemblage found in a cesspit at 16 Tunsgate, Guildford, deposited c.1702–14 (Courtesy of Guildford Museum).*

They are thus a rich source of often closely dateable artefact assemblages and environmental evidence (Fig. 2.3). However, they offer a socially restricted view of urban life and appear to be concentrated in the late 17th and early 18th century, though neither in numbers or richness do they parallel the urban *beerputten* (cesspits) of the Low Countries, emblems of the 'embarrassment of riches' in the Dutch Golden Age.[35]

In rural archaeology we are very dependant upon deserted, and to a lesser extent, shrunken, settlements. However, the pattern of desertion is by no means uniform either chronologically or regionally. Even within regions desertion was often not random. In the Midlands, for example, sites on the upland wolds were more prone to late medieval desertion than their larger, richer and possibly earlier-founded neighbours in the river valleys.[36]

Consumers in Transition

Yt is all wayes sene now a days
That money makythe the man
Anonymous 15th-century jingle
(cited by Thrupp 1948, 317)

In the final section of this paper I wish to examine some aspects of consumption in the later Middle Ages. Competitive consumption was not an invention of the later period. The late Romanesque urban stone houses of which numerous fragments survive in cities such as Prague and Ghent indicate considerable patrician expenditure.[37] The stone-built, patrician tower-houses of Flemish towns suggest emulation of the aristocratic castle. As early as the late 12th century documents in Ghent record 'high houses with towers', while crenellations are indicated by iconographic sources.[38] These examples remind one of the towerhouses of 16th-century English towns and John Stow's disapproval of two London merchants, one a lord mayor, for building houses overlooking their peers.[39] Even in the small town of Monmouth in south-east Wales, remote from the economic heartland of Europe, excavations have revealed 13th-century Italian enamelled glass in a masonry cesspit associated with what appears to be an all-stone merchant's house.[40] The London waterfront excavations have shown a richness of material things in the high Middle Ages not always recognizable on more typical urban sites.[41] The metal toys would appear to be typical of the late-medieval growth in consumer objects.[42] However, the series begins in the early 14th century, a period of economic crisis. This raises the question of whether their appearance was consumer-driven or an example of active product promotion by producers to compensate for a declining market in other goods, a process very evident in the post-medieval small metals trade.[43]

The new evidence for economically active peasants in the high Middle Ages needs to be balanced against the severe restrictions of seigneurial control and exaction and the fact that many held plots of a size that could barely have fed their families even in good times.[44] However, at Raunds (Northants.), the subject of a major landscape survey in the 1980s, an active land market developed before the Black Death. The minor manorial complex in the outlying settlement of West Cotton was abandoned in the mid 13th century and replaced by a number of peasant tenements with storage rooms and malting kilns/corn dryers.[45] This is an early example of the type of complex more commonly associated with the 15th century and indicative of more commercially orientated production for the market.[46]

I have cited the above examples merely to indicate that the mid 14th century should not become a new chronological fracture and that the roots of acquisitive, and competitively consumerist, behaviour are very long. Nevertheless, the post-Black Death period is widely seen as a period of consumer growth although as far as I am aware no one has talked of a consumer revolution as they have for every century from the 16th to the 20th. The late medieval period in Britain saw a retreat from direct demesne farming. Agricultural production compensated for a falling population by producing less wheat and more luxury products, notably meat and barley. The latter presumably indicates increased social drinking. The leasing of the demesnes and a rising land market (made possible by the conversion of labour services to money rents) allowed the more enterprising peasants to build up estates. Some members of the new peasant elite had even joined the gentry in the 16th century. There is also good evidence for improved purchasing power among wage labourers. Archaeological and architectural evidence suggests improved standards of housing in the late Middle Ages both in the countryside and towns. The 15th and early 16th century is the first period from which urban houses survive in number or lasted long enough to appear in historic prints and photographs.[47] Continental scholars have had little hesitation in linking the downward diffusion of consumer goods in late-medieval towns with rising standards of living.[48]

However, this leads right into the very English debate over the late medieval urban decline, a controversy which no general assessment of culture change in Britain in the period 1400–1600 can ignore. The general thesis is that there was not only demographic contraction in English towns in the late Middle Ages, associated with the plague-driven mortality crisis of the 14th century, but also widespread economic decay and crisis. Cloth towns like

Coventry and Colchester certainly grew in the late 14th century but afterwards suffered decline.[49] By contrast, Chris Dyer has suggested that middling towns which developed specialisms such as Waldron's saffron and Walsall's lorimery (horse-bits etc.) may have expanded their markets and prospered at the same time as rural markets and larger towns declined.[50] London has generally been assumed to have prospered regardless, due to its stranglehold on the import/export trade. The evidence of the urban housing stock has been used as an argument against the decline, but the pro-decline school has countered with the argument that factors other than economic fortune may govern patterns of expenditure and consumption.[51] Critics of the urban-decline concept, among whom I would include myself, have suggested that the concept of decline masks a more complex restructuring and that urban standards of living may have risen.[52] However, the anecdotal nature of much of the evidence, whether documentary or archaeological, will ensure that this continues to be an area of fierce debate.

I wish to briefly examine an area I have researched in detail, Monmouthshire in south-east Wales.[53] This was an area of marcher lordship, discrete territories where lords were particularly strong. The urban hierarchy was flat with no equivalent to the English county town and rural markets and fairs were virtually unknown. Indeed I have argued that this pattern, created in the Norman and Angevin periods, had a long lasting impact on economic and cultural development in Wales, evident even in the period of industrialisation. Responses to the 14th-century crisis were varied. Trellech, with a specialised upland economy based on iron and woodland products, collapsed dramatically and ceased to be a borough by the 16th century. Chepstow seems to have shrunk to judge by topographic evidence. It is hardly surprising given its strong trading connections with Bristol that it was in crisis in the 1520s when the great port suffered from a realignment in the English wool trade towards the London-Rouen axis. However, despite its apparent stagnation until the 19th century, the 1540s taxation records indicate that Chepstow had an urban elite hardly paralleled by every other Monmouthshire town put together, reminding us of the social complexity even within

individual towns. By contrast other towns like Newport show few signs of contraction while Abergavenny seems to have doubled in size in the later Middle Ages, although the exact chronology of expansion is uncertain. Like Colchester this may have been due to expansion in the wool trade, though it later had an important role funnelling consumer goods to mid Wales. Nevertheless, whether or not its growth was prolonged it continued to maintain its new position as the county's largest town until the 19th century despite failing to become the county town in 1536.

It thus seems that we are seeing the creation of the early modern urban hierarchy not in the 16th century but the 14th and 15th. This can probably be ascribed to the disruptive impact of the demographic crisis, breakdown of 'feudal' control (by both lords and towns) and an initial shift to more regionalised trading patterns. An archaeological example of shifting trading patterns is the total displacement in 15th-century Monmouthshire of locally-produced ceramics by Malvernian wares from Worcestershire. The best parallel I have seen for this general picture of economic realignment is in Steven Epstein's recent work on late medieval Sicily.[54] It seems likely that similar forces were at work across north-west Europe. However, as Epstein points out, there are considerable variations in the market pattern of late-medieval Europe which reflect not only patterns of consumption but differing political frameworks.[55] Marcher Wales was not lowland England with its more diffuse and intermixed patterns of lordship; nor is there much evidence in Wales for the urban guilds whose regulations may have stifled entrepreneurship in larger English towns. Hopefully regional studies such as that now being undertaken on the east midlands by Birmingham and Leicester Universities will shed more light. It is too soon to offer a definitive answer to the urban decline debate. Nevertheless, an understanding of urban fortunes and consumption is one of the greatest necessities if we are to understand the economic and social base of cultural change in this period.

Recent work on the Renaissance has tended to break down some of the barriers between students of high and low culture. There has been more emphasis on the economic and social under-pinning of the

Renaissance and its diverse regional nature even within Italy. Scholars have also pointed to the indigenous contributions to the Renaissance in both northern and central Europe and the way in which Classical culture was variously appropriated by different cultures and social groups.[56] The peasant dance is an image well known to archaeologists through the friezes of 16th-century Raeren jugs.[57] Pieter Bruegel the Elder's paintings, The Peasant Dance and The Wedding Dance of the 1560s, appear at first glance to be Gothic in character. However, Margaret Sullivan has recently argued that these paintings depended on their audience's knowledge of Classical satire, for example Juvenal, in their depiction of 'the fools of the world about to be overtaken by death and time'.[58] Certainly, Peter Burke has argued that the increased hostility of elites to popular culture was a widespread feature of early modern Europe.[59]

The hybrid nature of the Renaissance has also been stressed with German masons working in Bohemia and the 16th-century Italian sculptor Giovanni de Bologna, alias Jean de Boulogne, having been born in Douai, then in the Spanish Netherlands (now NE France).[60] The great Flemish towns and fairs, for example, acted as meeting points not only between the cultures and economies of north and south but between the conspicuous consumption of the Burgundian court and a rich merchant elite who provided much of its economic base.[61] Over 1,000 Hanseatic merchants have been identified in Bruges between 1360 and 1390. At the formal entry into the city in 1440 by Duke Philip the Good 136 Hanseatics rode next to 150 Italians and many Spaniards.[62]

The Burgundian Netherlands were an important source for English fashions in the late Middle Ages. Important commercial ties were highly significant for the transfer of influences from the German/ Flemish/Dutch urban, beer drinking culture.[63] Additionally, the Burgundians were allies of the English in the Hundred Years War. French and Burgundian influence can be seen in the elaborate material culture revealed by the incomplete inventories of John, Duke of Bedford (d. 1435). These indicate that, in addition to his acquisitions from the French crown and nobility, he was an important patron of goldsmiths, embroiderers and makers of manuscripts.[64] Bedford

was perhaps exceptional in that he was Regent of France as well as being married to Anne of Burgundy. However, his brother, Humphrey of Gloucester could boast the largest secular library in England with five to six hundred volumes, though his employment of Italian secretaries is a reminder that English culture received influences from more than one country.[65] The Anglo-Burgundian alliance was terminated by the treaty of Arras in 1435 but more cordial relations resumed with the marriage of Margaret of York to Charles the Bold in 1468. Simon Thurley has documented the impact of the Burgundian court on changes in English courtly etiquette and architecture in the second half of the 15th century.[66] From the reign of Henry VIII, continental influences became more obvious but then it was the glittering court of Francis I of France which provided the premier model for Renaissance fashion in northern Europe.

Like the Industrial Revolution, the Renaissance now appears to be a much more diverse phenomenon with roots deep in the medieval period. However, this is not to dispute that it represents a cultural shift of enormous significance. There are still many problems associated with it. One major line of scholarship by German scholars has been the significance of court culture. At the turn of the century Werner Sombart suggested that there might be a link between the luxury spawned by court life and the growth of capitalist production.[67] He saw the papal court at Avignon in the 14th century as the first modern court in which luxury played an explicit part in the lives of a leisured and cultured elite. Sombart's work attracted the particular ire of Fernand Braudel, who saw court culture as an aberrant form with little relevance to the bourgeois world of commerce.[68] Some support for Sombart's general thesis, if not his chronology, can be seen in George Duby's argument that the growth of the great northern towns in the 11th and 12th centuries was fuelled by the aristocracy's demand for luxury goods.[69] It seems likely, though, that bourgeois and court cultures evolved in a symbiotic manner from an early date. The early patrician elites of the 12th century appear to have been derived from the ranks of the rural landed classes rather than, as once suggested by Pirenne, the ranks of transient merchants.[70] Lords always had strong ties with towns; for instance, in Leicester the abbey rented a stone hall to various rural knightly families from at least the 13th century.[71] In the 14th and 15th centuries successful merchants aspired to join the ranks of the gentry.[72]

An important contribution of the exiled German sociologist Norbert Elias was to emphasise the political use of material culture by court society. He pointed out that courtiers were compelled to make extravagant expenditure on luxuries, even to the point of bankruptcy, as a means of social assertion. Elias also researched etiquette books over the centuries. This led him to suggest that the growth of manners or 'civilised' behaviour was rooted in changing social and political patterns. In particular, he argued that the social instability of the later Middle Age promoted manners as a means of distinguishing new or insecure elites. Emulation by those below constantly eroded social distinctions and thus acted as a constant spur to increasing refinement.[73] Recent scholarship influenced by Elias includes Chandra Mukerji's study of French aristocratic gardens and Stephen Mennell's comparative history of English and French cuisine.[74] Mennell came to the conclusion that the widespread influence of courtly *haute cuisine* in France was related to its distinctive political and social structures rather than Catholicism's supposedly liberal attitude to luxury. Other research, for example Martin Hall's study of Dutch cuisine in the 18th-century Cape colony, has shown how elites may also appropriate, and thus make safe, elements of low culture.[75] Yet, not withstanding the importance of courts as originators of both aristocratic and bourgeois fashion, any general model of socio-cultural change needs to address all sections of society.

By the later Middle Ages new goods were starting to transform the world of the everyday. Scholars, such as Graham Dawson and David Gaimster, have drawn attention to the ceramic revolution of the mid 15th century which saw the arrival of a wide variety of new specialised ceramic forms from the Rhineland and Low Countries.[76] This was an example of both cultural change and the wider trading patterns of the late Middle Ages. Examples of the new continental imports are found across the country, often in remote areas such as the Welsh uplands. Sixteenth- century deserted upland sites in Wales have produced some interesting examples of Renaissance artefacts in what

at first glance appear to be artefact-poor sites. Hafod y Nant Criafolen in the Brenig Valley (Denbighs.) produced sherds from a north French, Martincamp flask and a (?Spanish) maiolica vessel as well as part of a pistol. Excavations at Beil Bedw (Radnors.) recovered the rim of a (?Netherlandish) *façon de Venise* beaker.[77] The pistol and glass are probably better regarded as emblematic badges of status than as purely functional. As Welsh freemen, the patriarchs of these settlements would have regarded themselves as gentlemen though they would not have been recognised as such by their English counterparts. One wonders if new goods and consumerism played a role in encouraging the breakdown of the traditional systems of kindred and transhumance barely touched by centuries of Anglo-Norman lordship.

It is often stated that one of archaeology's main contributions is its ability to study the poor unrecorded by documents. Yet, the discipline has singularly failed to do this in late medieval and early-modern Britain. This is probably more due to the rescue-led nature of archaeological excavation rather than survival of evidence. Indeed, some of the best preserved archaeology in the period belongs to the poor. Despite Derek Keene's seminal 1975 overview, the urban suburbs have not received the attention they deserve, not least because the archaeology has often escaped the worst devastation of Victorian cellaring so dominant in many urban cores.[78] Not all suburbs were impoverished. Leicester's north suburb was industrial in character, its eastern suburb, the bishop's fee, was wealthy but the towns' poor were concentrated outside the southern gate. It was no coincidence that the southern suburb was the only one demolished by the Parliamentarian defenders in 1645 in order to shorten their over-stretched defences.[79] In the countryside we are losing abandoned squatter settlements to development at an alarming rate with virtually no archaeological response. We still know very little of the impact of new consumer goods on the poorer sections of society or the lower part of that historians catchall the 'middling sort'. Lorna Wetherill's recent major study of British material culture from probate inventories almost certainly underestimates the downward penetration of such items as ceramics in the 17th century.[80] Such goods seem to be far better represented in the American inventories, perhaps reflecting the high value placed on all objects in the early days of colonialism when replacement was far from easy.[81]

In the latter part of this paper I have tried to bring out some key problems upon which historians and archaeologists might collaborate. It is an area of study bedevilled by both the difficulties of the evidence and by the artificiality of institutional bounds between specialists and periods. However, it is also a period of enormous potential in which we are only just beginning to see the promise of new approaches. Also the importance of combining both a regional and an inter-regional, pan-European perspective cannot be over-emphasised. It is not the study of regions in themselves but the similarities, contrasts and connections between them which shed most light. I will end by paraphrasing Umberto Eco's brilliant metaphor on the role of theory.[82] We must remember that such key constructs as feudalism, the Middle Ages, the Renaissance and the late medieval urban decline are all conceptual ladders for enabling us to climb from one level of understanding to the next. However, having climbed to the next level we must be prepared to discard the ladder or else it becomes our master rather than our tool, stifling rather than aiding creativity.

Notes

1. Brown 1974.
2. Reynolds 1994.
3. Anderson 1974, 182–96.
4. Von Ranke 1925, 52.
5. See Krieger 1977 and Burke 1988. For useful general critiques of the 'positivist' school of history, which manage to avoid the abyss of total relativism, see Steadman Jones 1972 and Appleby *et al.* 1994.
6. Cannadine 1984.
7. Crafts 1985.
8. Berg & Hudson 1992.
9. Overton 1996, 8.
10. McKendrick 1982; Breen 1983 and 1986.
11. See De Vries 1993 for a useful summary as well as the other articles in Brewer & Porter (eds) 1993. See also Courtney (P.) 1996.
12. Shammas 1993, 191.
13. Fairchild 1993.
14. O'Brien & Keyder 1978; Pollard 1981; Berg 1991a; De Vries 1993.
15. De Vries 1984; Hohenberg & Lees 1985.
16. De Vries 1993 and 1994.
17. Paper given at 'Artifacts from Wrecks' conference, Cardiff 1994: conference publication forthcoming, (ed.) M. Redknap.
18. See Hilton 1976, 28–9, and Razi 1979 for critiques by the 'Birmingham school'.
19. Ferguson 1948, 329–85.
20. *Ibid.* 268–75.
21. Coulton 1925, 394.
22. Kingsley 1855.
23. Shakespeare, Henry V.
24. Anderson 1974, 159: fn 9.
25. Goody 1986, and Johnson 1996, 196–8.
26. Kerridge 1967.
27. Hilton 1976.
28. Campbell & Overton 1993.
29. Langdon 1986; Dyer 1989 and 1994.
30. Dyer 1995; Courtney, forthcoming.
31. Campbell *et al.* 1993; Fisher 1935.
32. Campbell 1988, 90.
33. Phythian Adams 1979.
34. Vince 1991–2.
35. For examples of excavated British urban cesspits see Alvey 1973 and Courtney 1994. For Dutch urban cesspits see Carmiggelt *et al.* 1987; Clevis & Kottman 1989 and Thijssen 1991.
36. Fox 1989.
37. Büttner & Meissner 1982, 11–37; Laleman & Raveschot 1991.
38. *Ibid.* 168 and pls 89 & 148 and Laleman & Raveschot 1994, 203. For other illustrations of crenellated, stone houses (now destroyed) see Fockema Andreae & Ter Kuile 1948, 362–3 and pls 183 (Leiden, Neths.) and 191 (anonymous town); as well as the example, in the Markt of Oudenaarde (Belgium), recorded on a 1747 military model in Les Invalides, Paris: Lille Museums 1989, 122–3 and Hoebecke 1965, pls VI and VIII: 32b.
39. Kingsford 1908, i, 133 and 151.
40. 61–3 Monnow St. excavation: information from Steve Clarke (Monmouth Archaeology Soc.). Glass report by John Clark (Museum of London).
41. Egan & Pritchard 1991.
42. Egan 1996.
43. Berg 1991b, 183–90; Courtney (Y.C.) 1996, *passim.* See also Munro 1991 on the early 14th-century Flemish textile industry.

44. Dyer 1989a, 109–50.
45. Windell *et al.* 1990.
46. Astill 1983, 233–4.
47. See Dyer 1989a and Britnell 1996.
48. Hasse 1979. A similar process is evident in the countryside, see Dyer 1989a, 173–4 and 205–7.
49. Phythian Adams 1979, and Britnell 1986.
50. Dyer 1989b, 325–6.
51. See Platt 1990, 263–7 on the debate over buildings and decline.
52. See Dyer 1991, and Britnell 1996, 155–78.
53. Courtney 1994.
54. Epstein 1992 and 1993. See also Howell and Boone 1996.
55. Epstein 1994, 473–7.
56. For recent views of the Renaissance see Burke 1986 and 1987; Chartier (ed.) 1989; Porter & Teich (eds) 1992; Hale 1993; Kaufman 1995, and Jardine 1996. For changes in popular culture see Burke 1994.
57. Kohnemann 1994.
58. Sullivan 1994.
59. Burke 1994; see also Muchembled 1985, and Ginzburg 1980.
60. See Kaufmann 1995, 74–95 on Bohemia.
61. Huizinga 1924; Prevenier & Blockmans 1985; Nicholas 1992.
62. Vandewalle 1995, 43.
63. Gaimster 1993; Gaimster *et al.* (eds) 1988; Kistemaaker & Vilsteren 1994; Barron & Saul 1995.
64. Stratford 1993.
65. Weiss 1957, 22–70.
66. Thurley 1993, 11–24.
67. Sombart 1967.
68. Braudel 1981, *passim.* See also Mukerji 1993, 439–40.
69. Duby 1974, 168–80 and 211–56.
70. Hibbert 1953.
71. Bodleian Library (Oxford), Laud Ms 625 fos. 97^v, 178^v and 189^r. See also Flemming 1993 on the late Saxon period.
72. Horrox 1988, and Thrupp 1948, 234–87.
73. Elias 1969 and 1978. See also Mennell 1992. The 'trickle-down' theory of social emulation is derived from the work of Simmel 1904.
74. Mukerji 1993, and Mennell 1985.
75. Hall 1992, 390–6.
76. Dawson 1979, microfiche; Gaimster 1993, and Barton 1992.
77. Allen 1979, and Courtney 1991.
78. Keene 1975.
79. Courtney 1992.
80. Wetherill 1988, 193. For contrasting views see Shammas 1990, 299, and Glennie 1995, 173.
81. See Horn 1994, 293–333 for the hard material conditions faced by many early colonists in eastern America.
82. The theory as ladder allegory was given by Eco in a journalistic interview, the source of which I have long since forgotten.

Bibliography

Allen, D. 1979, 'Excavations at Hafod y Nant Criafolen, Brenig Valley, Clwyd, 1973–4', *Post-Medieval Archaeology* 13, 1–59

Anderson, P. 1974, *Passages from Antiquity to Feudalism*

Appleby, J., Hunt, L. & Jacob, M. 1994, *Telling the Truth about History*, New York

Alvey, R.C. 1973, 'A cesspit excavation at 26–28, High Pavement, Nottingham', *Trans. Thoroton Soc.* 77, 53–72

Astill, G.G. 1983, 'Economic change in later medieval England: an archaeological review', in Aston, Coss, Dyer & Thirsk (eds), 217–47

Aston, M., Austin, D. & Dyer, C. (eds), *The Rural Settlements of Medieval England: Studies Dedicated to M.W. Beresford and J.G. Hurst*, Oxford

Aston, T.H., Coss, P.H., Dyer, C. & Thirsk, J. (eds) 1983, *Social Relations and Ideas: Essays in Honour of R.H. Hilton*, Cambridge

Barley, M.W. (ed.), 1975, *The Plans and Topography of Medieval Towns in England and Wales*

Barron, C.M. & Saul, N. (eds) 1995, *England and the Low Countries in the Late Middle Ages*

Barton, K. 1992, 'Ceramic changes in the western European littoral at the end of the Middle Ages: a personal view', in Gaimster & Redknap (eds), 246–55

Berg, M. (ed.) 1991a, *Markets and Manufacture in Early Industrial Europe*

Berg, M. 1991b, 'Commerce and creativity in eighteenth-century Birmingham', in Berg 1991a, 173–204

Berg. M. & Hudson, P. 1992, 'Rehabilitating the Industrial Revolution', *Econ. Hist. Rev.* 45, 24–50

Blackburn, R. (ed.), 1972, *Ideology in Social Science: Readings in Critical Social Theory*

Bloch, M. 1966, *French Rural History: An Essay on its Basic Characteristics* (1st French edn 1931)

Braudel, F. 1981, *Civilization and Capitalism 15th-18th Century, vol. 1. The Structures of Everyday Life*

Breen, T. 1983, 'Baubles of Britain: the American and consumer revolutions of the eighteenth century', *Past and Present* 119, 73–104

Breen, T. 1986, 'An empire of goods; the anglicisation of Colonial America, 1690–1776', *J. of British Studies* 25, 467–99

Brewer, J. & Porter, R. (eds) 1993, *Consumption and the World of Goods*

Britnell, R.H. 1986, *Growth and Decline in Colchester, 1300–1525*, Cambridge

Britnell, R.H. 1996, *The Commercialization of English Society 1000–1500*, (2nd edn), Manchester

Brown, E.A.R. 1974, 'The tyranny of a construct: feudalism and historians of medieval Europe', *American Hist. Rev.* 79, 1063–88.

Burke, P. 1988, 'Ranke the Reactionary', *Syracuse Scholar* 9, 25–30

Burke, P. 1986, *The Italian Renaissance: Culture and Society in Italy*, 2nd edn

Burke, P. 1987, *The Historical Anthropology of Early Modern Italy: Essays on Perception and Communication*, Cambridge

Burke, P. 1994, *Popular Culture in Early Modern Europe*, (2nd edn)

Büttner, H. & Meissner, G. 1982, *Town Houses of Europe*, New York

Campbell, B.M.S. 1988, 'Towards an agricultural geography of medieval England', *Agricultural Hist. Rev.* 36, 87–98

Campbell, B.M.S. (ed.) 1991, *Before the Black Death: Studies in the 'Crisis' of the Early Fourteenth Century*, Manchester

Campbell, B.M.S., Galloway, J.A., Keene, D. & Murphy, M. 1993, *A Medieval Capital and its Grain Supply: Agrarian Production and Distribution in the London Region c.1300*

Campbell, B.M.S. & Overton, M. 1993, 'A new perspective on medieval and early modern agriculture: six centuries of Norfolk farming c.1250 – c.1850', *Past and Present* 141, 38–105

Cannadine, D. 1984, 'The present and the past in the English Industrial Revolution 1880–1980', *Past and Present* 103, 131–9

Carrmiggelt, A., Van Gangelen, H., Kortekaas, G. & van Zeist, W. 1987, *Uitgeput Huisraad: Twee Groninger Beerputten in Historisch-Archeologisch Perspectif*, Groningen

Chartier, R. (ed.) 1989, *A History of Private Life, vol. 3, Passions of the Renaissance*, Cambridge (Mass.)

Clevis, H. & Kottman, J. 1989, *Weggegooid en Teuggevonden: Aardewerk en Glas uit Deventer Vondstcomplexen 1375–1750*, Vechtstreek

Coulton, G.G. 1925, *The Medieval Village*, Cambridge

Courtney, P. 1991, 'A native Welsh settlement: excavations at Beili Bedw, St. Harmon (Powys)', *Bull. Board Celtic Studies* 38, 233–54

Courtney, P. & Courtney, Y.C. 1992, 'A siege examined: the Civil War archaeology of Leicester', *Post-Medieval Archaeology* 26, 47–89

Courtney, P. 1994, *Medieval and Later Usk: Report on the Excavations at Usk 1965–1976*, Cardiff

Courtney, P. 1996, 'In small things forgotten: the Georgian world view, material culture and the consumer revolution', *Rural History* 7i, 87–95

Courtney, P. forthcoming, 'Raunds and its region', in Parry (ed.)

Courtney, Y.C. 1996, *British Public House Tokens c.1830 to c.1920: Material Culture in the Industrial Age*. University of Wales, Cardiff, unpublished Ph.D thesis

Crafts, N.F.R. 1985, *British Economic Growth during the Industrial Revolution*, Oxford

Dawson, G.J. 1979, 'Excavations at Guy's Hospital 1967', *Research Volume of the Surrey Archaeol. Soc.* 7, 27–65 (and microfiche)

Demelon, P., Galinié, H. and Verhaeghe, F. (eds) 1995, *Archéologie des Villes dans le Nord-Ouest del'Europe (VIIe–XIIIe siècle)*, Douai

De Vries, J. 1984, *European Urbanisation 1500–1800*

De Vries, J. 1993, 'Between purchasing power and the world of goods; understanding the household economy in early modern Europe', in Brewer and Porter (eds), 85–132

De Vries, J. 1994, 'The industrial revolution and the industrious revolution', *J. of Economic History* 54, 249–70

Duby, G. 1974, *The Early Growth of the European Economy: Warriors and Peasants from the Seventh to Twelfth Century*, Cornell

Dyer, A. 1991, *Decline and Growth in English Towns 1400–1600*

Dyer, C. 1989a, *Standards of Living in the Later Middle Ages: Social Change in England c.1200–1520*, Cambridge

Dyer, C. 1989b, 'The consumer and the market in the later Middle Ages', *Econ. Hist. Rev.* 42, 356–76: reprinted in Dyer 1994, 257–81

Dyer, C. 1994, *Everyday Life in Medieval England*

Dyer, C. 1995, 'On the trail of the village revolution', *British Archaeol.* 5 (June), 8–9

Egan, G. & Pritchard, F. 1991, *Medieval Finds from Excavations in London, vol. 3. Dress Accessories c.1150 – c.1450*

Egan, G. 1996, *Playthings from the Past: Lead Alloy Miniature Artifacts c.1300–1800*

Elias, N. 1978, *The Civilising Process, vol. 1, The History of Manners*, (German edn 1939), Oxford

Elias, N. 1969, *The Court Society*, Oxford

Epstein, S.R. 1992, *An Island for Itself: Economic Development and Social Change in Late Medieval Sicily*, Cambridge

Epstein, S.R. 1993, 'Town and country: economy and institutions in late medieval Italy', *Econ. Hist. Rev.* 46, 453–77

Epstein, S.R. 1994, 'Regional fairs, institutional innovation and economic growth in later medieval Europe', *Econ. Hist. Rev.* 47, 459–82

Fairchilds, C. 1994, 'The production and marketing of populuxe goods in eighteenth-century Paris', in Brewer and Porter (eds), 228–48

Ferguson, W.K. 1948, *The Renaissance in Historical Thought: Five Centuries of Interpretation*, Cambridge (Mass.)

Fisher, F.J. 1935, 'The development of the London food market, 1540–1640', *Econ. Hist. Rev.* 5, 46–64

Flemming, R. 1993, 'Rural elites and urban communities in late Anglo-Saxon England', *Past and Present* 141, 3–37

Fockema Andreae, S.J. & Ter Kuile, E.H. 1948, *Duizend Jaar Bouwen in Nederland, deel. 1, De Bouwkunst van de Middeleeuwen*, Amsterdam

Fox, H.S.A. 1989, 'The people of the wolds in English settlement history', in Aston, Austin & Dyer (eds), 77–101

Gaimster, D.R.M. 1993, 'Cross-channel ceramic trade in the late Middle Ages: archaeological evidence for the spread of Hanseatic culture to Britain', in Gläser (ed.), 251–60

Gaimster, D.R.M. & Redknap, M. (eds) 1992, *Everyday and Exotic Pottery from Europe c.650–1900: Studies in Honour of John G. Hurst*, Oxford, 246–55

Gaimster, D.R.M., Redknap, M. & Wegner, H-H. (eds) 1988, *Zur Keramik des Mittelalters und der beginnenden Neuzeit im Rheinland*, Oxford

Ginzburg, C. 1980, *The Cheese and the Worms: the Cosmos of a Sixteenth-Century Miller*, Baltimore

Gläser, M. (ed.), *Archäologie des Mittelalters und Bauforschung im Hanseraum: eine Festschrift für Günter P. Fehring*, Rostock

Glennie, P. 1995, 'Consumption within Historical Studies', in Miller (ed.), 164–203

Goody, J. 1986, *The Logic of Writing and the Organisation of Society*, Cambridge.

Hale, J. 1993, *The Civilization of Europe in the Renaissance*

Hall, M. 1992, 'Small things and the mobile, conflictual confusion of power, fear and desire', in Yentsch and Beaudry (eds) 1992, 374–400

Hasse, M. 1989, 'Neues Hausgerät, neue Häuser, neue Kleider. Eine Betrachtung der städtischen Kultur im 13. und 14. Jahrhundert sowie ein Katalog der metallenen Hausgeräte', *Zeitschrift für Archäologie des Mittelalters* 7, 7–83

Hibbert, A.B. 1953, 'The origins of the medieval town patriciate', *Past and Present* 3, 15–27

Hilton, R.H. 1976, 'Introduction', in R.H. Hilton (ed.) 1976, *The Transition from Feudalism to Capitalism*, 9–30

Hoebecke, M. 1965, 'Audenarde', in *Plans en Relief des Villes Belges: Levés des Ingénieurs Militaires Français -XVIIe- XIXe Siècle*, (Centre Pro Civitate), Brussels, 263–98

Hohenberg, P.M. & Lees, L.H. 1995, The Making of Urban Europe, 1000–1994, (2nd edn), Cambridge (Mass.)

Horn, J. 1994, *Adapting to a New World: English Society in the Seventeenth-Century Chesapeake*, Chapel Hill

Horrox, R. 1988, 'The urban gentry in the fifteenth century', in Thomson (ed.), 22–44

Howell. M. & Boone, M. 1996, 'Becoming early modern in the late medieval Low Counties', *Urban History* 23, 300–24

Huizinga, J. 1924, *The Waning of the Middle Ages*, New York (Penguin 1955 ed.)

Jardine, L. 1996, *Worldly Goods: a New History of the Renaissance*

Johnson, M. 1996, *The Archaeology of Capitalism*, Oxford

Kaufmann, T.D. 1995, *Court, Cloister and City: the Art and Culture of Central Europe 1450–1800*

Keene, D. 1975, 'Suburban growth', in Barley (ed.), 71–82

Kerridge, E. 1967, *The Agricultural Revolution*.

Kingsford, C.L. (ed.) 1908, *John Stow, A Survey of London*, 2 vols., Oxford

Kingsley, C. 1855, *Westward Ho! or the voyages and adventures of Sir Amiyas Leigh, knight, of Burrough, in the county of Devon in the reign of her glorious majesty Queen Elizabeth*

Kistemaker, R.E. & van Vilsteren, V.T. (eds) 1994, *Beer! The Story of Holland's Favourite Drink*, Amsterdam

Kohnemann, M. 1994, *Raerener Bauerntänze*, Raeren

Krieger, L. 1977, *Ranke: the Meaning of History*, Chicago

Laleman, M.C. & Raveschot, P. 1991, *Inleiding tot de Studie van de Woonhuizen in Gent. Periode 1100–1300. De Kelders*, Brussel

Laleman, M.C. & Raveschot, P. 1994, 'Maisons patriciennes médiévales à Gand (Gent), Belgique', in Demelon, Galinié & Verhaeghe (eds), 201–6

Langdon, J. 1986, *Horses, Oxen and Technological Innovation: the Use of Draught Animals in English Farming from 1066 to 1500*, Cambridge

Lille Museums 1989, *Plans en Relief: Villes Fortes des Anciens Pays-Bas Français au XVIIIe S.*, (Catalogue, Musée des Beaux-Arts), Lille

McKendrick, N. 1982, 'Commercialisation and the economy', in McKendrick, Brewer & Plumb (eds), 9–194

McKendrick, N. Brewer J. and Plumb, J.H. 1982, *The Birth of a Consumer Society: The Commercialisation of Eighteenth-Century England*

Mennell, S. 1985, *All Manners of Food: Eating and Taste in England and France from the Middle Ages to the Present*, Oxford

Mennell, S. 1992, *Norbert Elias: an Introduction*, Oxford

Miller, D. (ed.) 1995, *Acknowledging Consumption: A Review of New Studies*

Muchembled, R. 1985, *Popular Culture and Elite Culture in France 1400–1750*, Baton Rouge

Mukerji, C. 1993, 'Reading and writing with nature: a materialist approach to French formal gardens', in Brewer & Porter (eds), 439–61

Munro, J.H. 1991, 'Industrial transformations in the north-west European textile trade, c.1290 – c.1340: economic progress or economic crisis?', in Campbell (ed.), 110–48

Nicholas, D. 1992, *Medieval Flanders*

O'Brien, P.K. & Keyder, C. 1978, *Economic Growth in Britain and France, 1780–1914: Two Paths to the Twentieth Century*

Overton, M. 1996, *Agricultural Revolution in England: the Transformation of the Agrarian Economy 1500–1850*, Cambridge

Parry, S. (ed.) forthcoming, *The Raunds Area Survey*

Phythian Adams, C.V. 1979, *Desolation of a City: Coventry and the Urban Crisis of the Later Middle Ages*, Cambridge

Platt, C. 1990, *The Architecture of Medieval Britain: A Social History*, New Haven

Pollard, S. 1981, *Peaceful Conquest: The Industrialization of Europe, 1760–1970*, Oxford

Porter, R. & Teich, M. (eds) 1992, *The Renaissance in National Context*, Cambridge

Prevenier, W. & Blockmans, W. 1985, *The Burgundian*

Netherlands, Cambridge

Razi, Z. 1979, 'The Toronto school's reconstitution of medieval peasant society: a critical view', *Past and Present* 85, 141–57

Reynolds, S. 1994, *Fiefs and Vassals: the Medieval Evidence Reinterpreted*, Oxford

Shammas, C. 1990, *The Pre-industrial Consumer in England and America*, Oxford

Shammas, C. 1993, 'Consumption from 1550 to 1800', in Brewer & Porter (eds), 177–205

Simmel, G. 1904, 'Fashion', *International Quarterly* 10, 130–55

Sombart, W. 1967, *Luxury and Capitalism*, (German edn, 1913), Ann Arbor

Steadman Jones, G. 1972, 'History: the poverty of empiricism', in Blackburn (ed.), 96–105

Stratford, J. (ed.) 1993, *The Bedford Inventories: the Worldly Goods of John, Duke of Bedford, Regent of France (1389–1435)*

Sullivan, M.A. 1994, *Bruegel's Peasants: Art and Audience in the Northern Renaissance*, Cambridge

Thijssen, J. 1991, *Tot de Bodem Uitgezocht: Glas en Ceramiek uit een Beerput de 'Hof van Batenburg' in Nijmegen, 1375–1850*, Nijmegen

Thomson, J.A.F. (ed.) 1988, *Towns and Townspeople in the Fifteenth Century*, Stroud

Thrupp, S.L. 1948, *The Merchant Class of Medieval London (1300–1500)*, Ann Arbor

Thurley, S. 1993, *The Royal Palaces of Tudor England: Architecture and Court Life 1460–1547*, New Haven

Vandewalle, A. 1995, 'Medieval trade centre', in *Bruges and Zeebrugge: the City and the Sea*, (Lloyds List), 32–43

Vince, A. 1991–2, 'Late medieval Lincoln – a suitable case for treatment?', *Lincoln Archaeol.* 4, 41–6

von Ranke, L. 1925, *Das politische Gesprach und andere Schriften zur Wissenschaftslehre*, Halle

Weatherill, L. 1988, *Consumer Behaviour and Material Culture in Britain 1660–1760*

Weiss, R. 1957, *Humanism in England during the Fifteenth Century*, (2nd edn), Oxford

Windell, D., Chapman, A. & Woodiwiss, J. 1990, *From Barrows to By-pass. Excavations at West Cotton, Raunds, Northamptonshire*, Northampton

Yentsch, A.E. & Beaudry, M.C. (eds) 1992, *The Mystery and Lore of Historical Archaeology: Essays in Honor of James Deetz*, Boca Raton

3   The Archaeology of Transition: a Continental view

Frans Verhaeghe

Introduction

Human history has always been marked by almost continuous change which occasionally affected society in fundamental ways. Therefore, periods of transition are not altogether uncommon and as change also marks most if not all forms of material culture, it is not surprising that processes and phenomena of change – including innovation – have been the subject of some debate in theoretical archaeology from the late 70s onwards.[1] But for many reasons, the topic seems to have raised relatively little systematic interest among archaeologists of medieval and later times. This is particularly true in the case of what is perceived to be one of the major phases of change of the past millennium, generally called the transition from the Middle Ages to Modern Times and identified with the period from 1400 to 1600 (at least in the Western world). The British Museum conference itself illustrates the point, being among the first to try and consider the archaeological evidence for the British Isles in a more systematical way.

The present paper was commissioned to provide a general look at the archaeological evidence for this transition in continental north-western Europe. This poses several major problems.

First, there is the sheer complexity of the subject and the multitude of aspects to be taken into consideration, covering the broad spectrum of society and behaviour and ranging from royal palaces and country houses to monasteries, castles, urban houses and rural dwellings, not to forget all the other components of material culture, including landscapes, spatial organisation, burial, vernacular and religious architecture, the arts, fittings, furnishings and other domestic utensils, ceramics, glass, metal objects, food and diet, seals, heraldry, dress, fashion, textiles, techniques, gardens and botany, sciences and many others. On another level, communities, mentalities, lifestyles and – more importantly – the changing meanings of all these things and the possible perceptions and manipulations of the material world that may lie behind them should equally be taken into account. Furthermore, considering that the past is a whole which consists of continuously interacting components and phenomena, it can be argued that the paper should also take an explicitly interdisciplinary approach, including historical and art historical debates as well as the results of the rapidly expanding field of building archaeology (*Bauforschung*), the work on 'popular culture',[2] folklore and many others. And lastly, the paper should also range from the Atlantic Ocean to the Baltic Sea and try and identify and explain both the regional differences within that area and the general pattern of 'transition' from feudalism to capitalism. Together with the limited space available, the sheer mass of data and the complexity of the subject in effect preclude a detailed discussion of the many categories of objects and topics involved.

Other difficulties result from the relatively recent emergence of continental medieval and later archaeology as adult disciplines and from their current status and state of development as reflected in the literature. They help to understand not only the already mentioned lack of explicit interest in theoretical work and broader issues but also the continuing emphasis on description, cataloguing and categorising. It can be argued that to a large extent, both disciplines are driven not so much by questions regarding broader issues but rather by external circumstances such as rescue work – particularly in urban contexts – and others. In these conditions, the attention more often than not goes to the more pressing tasks such as basic data gathering and identification, description and dating as in the case of ceramics.[3] But however worthwhile and indeed essential to further research, these tasks do not in themselves constitute the ultimate goal of archaeological work. The situation is compounded by the development of specialisms which, however unavoidable, do tend to fragment our knowledge, perceptions and understanding of the material past through emphasising specific classes of objects. Ceramics, glass and a few others constitute cases in point and the situation often leads to these classes of objects being effectively isolated from one another as well as from other disciplines.

Equally detrimental is that many archaeologists still regard medieval and particularly later archaeology as complementary in a very simplistic way to 'traditional' history and art history, thus subjugating their work to agendas set by other disciplines.[4] But this means that the specific nature and dynamics of archaeological sources as well as the intricate links between the individual components of the past material world, people and society are largely neglected. The same is true in the case of the possible life-trajectories of medieval and later individual objects and classes of objects in terms of culture and commodification.[5]

As a result of all this, medieval and later changes and transitions seem to have been approached in a rather pragmatic way, i.e. through identifying changes in specific categories or even types of objects and explaining them mainly in function of general historical developments. There are of course notable exceptions as in the case of early medieval archaeology, American historical archaeology and individual approaches[6] which have gone much

further in analysing and interpreting the archaeological evidence regarding phases and processes of change in terms of human behaviour. In contrast and in a very general way, however, continental medieval and later archaeology in north-western Europe has yet to consider the evidence for the changes which occurred between 1400 and 1600 in a systematic way and to try and explain these changes.

The present paper cannot hope to encompass the many and often complex issues involved, to consider in some detail the many categories of objects and phenomena concerned or to try and interpret the nature of the transition between 1400 and 1600. Therefore, it can only offer a somewhat 'impressionistic' approach, using a few examples as simple illustrations and suggesting a few avenues of research.

A few questions

To try and identify and interpret the characteristics of the changes which affected the material world from the late Middle Ages to Modern Times begs many thorny questions: what is change and what is transition? Which changes are detectable in the archaeological record for the period in question and how? What do they have in common and which types of broader phenomena may they reflect? Behind these questions lie other, even more difficult ones related to social history and to the nature and dynamics of material culture and its interactions with humans, not to forget those concerning the many different ways material remains can be interpreted. None of this can be discussed in any detail here but it may be useful to mention briefly that I look upon material culture as a dynamic and interactive – not a passive – component of the past (and present). As such, the material world is influenced and even manipulated by humans and human behaviour but simultaneously it also influences and thus changes – or freezes – not only human behaviour and perceptions of the world but also later material culture itself. This may be seen as related to the new – i.e. non-deterministic – Darwinian approaches in recent archaeology[7] with an emphasis on how humans and the material world they (partly) create are mutually embedded. Some of the other questions have to be addressed however briefly because the proposed answers have a direct bearing on the general approach used in the present paper.

The crucial question is of course how we are to understand the notion 'transition' and which changes allow us to characterise a phase as a period of transition. Basically, transition can be taken to mean the gradual change from one state to another, these states being fundamentally different from one another. Put otherwise, it is both a gradual phenomenon and a break. When applied to the period 1400 to 1600, the notion reflects the differences between the Middle Ages and the post-medieval period and implies these differences to be of a fundamental nature. In fact, it also reflects the traditional – historical and art historical – perception of the evolution of the past millennium, which is itself largely based on a general assessment of only part of the evidence, be it art or written sources which are both of them somewhat biased socially. This perception of a break between medieval and later times is not totally devoid of ideological implications: the impact of late medieval humanism with its new emphasis on Antiquity and antique values, critical approaches and the individual[8] eventually led to the mainly 18th-century idea of the Renaissance as opposed to the Middle Ages ('the period in between'), thus not only creating a link with Antiquity but also characterising the medieval period as a 'dark age'. The strongly qualitative overtones speak for themselves. And to make matters worse, this perception has become institutionalised, notably in research and training (e.g. in most universities) and even elsewhere (as any visit to the history section of a bookshop will show). This in turn has long affected further work – often adversely – and still does.

On the whole, the historical literature seems generally more interested in what distinguishes Modern Times from the Middle Ages than in paying attention to what links both periods and how the process of transition is to be characterised. Archaeologists sometimes also follow this road. Even when drawing attention to the role of enduring structures and insisting on the long roots of the changes leading to the 18th-century world, Matthew Johnson[9] mainly emphasises the differences between medieval and later times and on the 'new' world and 'new' perceptions thereof.

As a means of categorising time more easily as well as to mark the end of the Middle Ages and to characterise the 'new' nature of post-medieval times, the literature tended to refer to a crucial date (e.g. 1492, 1517, c.1450, etc.). In themselves, such dates are of limited practical value, particularly where archaeological remains are concerned: finds can rarely be linked to such precise events. More important is the attention paid to new phenomena and social, socioeconomic or sociocultural frameworks, among them the flowering of Humanism, the emergence of Protestantism, the advent of new forms of art, the changing socioeconomic environment, the decline of feudalism and the growth of capitalism, the emergence of states, the spread of printing, the arrival of new commodities. Even notions such as 'consumer revolution' – mainly for the late 17th and 18th centuries – have been used[10] In a more global sense and with explicit reference to the main objectives of the archaeology of the new, post-medieval times, Charles E. Orser Jr[11] has emphasised the notions of global colonialism, Eurocentrism, capitalism and modernity, though without neglecting other changes or without loosing sight of the need for a more holistic approach. Others[12] have drawn suitable attention to the new, post-medieval perceptions and manipulations of the material world while at the same time emphasising particular phenomena such as increasing and even systematic commodification, growing literacy, the emergence of the individual or the new approaches to ordering people and the (material) world. And on another level, David Gaimster[13] and others[14] have pointed at a 'Post-Medieval Ceramic Revolution' in the period 1450–1550.

There is of course much in favour of all these approaches. But on the whole, the literature also reflects a tendency to contrast late 17th- and 18th-century situations with the 15th-century one, rather than focusing on the range of changes from the 12th, 13th or 14th century onwards. Put otherwise, the Braudelian long term (*longue durée*) perspective does not figure prominently in the debate. At the same time, contrasting the extremes of an evolution helps to understand why the emphasis generally lies on the notion of a rift – the Great Divide – between medieval and later times. Remarkably enough, this seems combined with an almost evolutionist approach which does allow for the increasing complexity of society. Many studies also seem to favour the identification of a 'prime mover' and monocausality rather than adopting the multicausal complex interaction model proposed by a number of more recent social and cultural anthropologists.[15]

The fact that society grew increasingly complex in what is now frequently called Early Modern Times can hardly be denied. But whether this is really a typical feature of that period only remains debatable. It can indeed be argued that the medieval world equally went through numerous changes, some of them being quite fundamental such as the emergence of new urban societies, networks and cultures, and most if not all of them leading to greater complexity in terms of society and social stratification, economy and social and cultural behaviour. This constitutes yet another good reason to pay at least as much attention to what survived from the medieval period (and if possible why) as to what changed and why.

This leads us to the problem of change and the dynamics of change. Processes (in the post-processual sense of the word) of change are a rather delicate subject in archaeological research. Some types of changes are of course readily detectable in the archaeological record, among them morpho-logical ones, the emergence of new objects (includ-ing buildings and even landscapes), the growing importance of some goods, the disappearance of others and new associations of objects. But identify-ing the many possible meanings of such changes as well as the possible manipulations and societal developments behind them remains a matter of multiple 'transformations' (in the sense used by Clarke 1978), approaches and interpretations which are themselves dependent on the kinds of questions asked. So far, the archaeological literature relevant in the present context has mainly emphasised the simpler types of changes while at the same time being somewhat biased towards specific categories of objects such as ceramics, glass, fortifications and strongholds, and – to a lesser extent – (mainly urban) buildings. This in turn is a result both of the state of medieval and later archaeology (cf. above) as well as of the changing patterns of waste disposal and formation processes of the archaeological record[16]

As to more penetrating explanations, only a few north-western European archaeological studies[17] have gone much further than the more or less simplistic registration of changes and general comments in terms of new fashions, technological developments (particularly in terms of progress), new contacts and exchange networks, and/or new wealth. But such comments do not really explain *why* the changes occurred, why they occurred at this particular point in time and what they may mean in terms of possible new forms of behaviour and perception.

Much more could be said about changes and the processes of change for which archaeology has yet to develop suitable conceptual tools.[18] But one point cannot be neglected here. It is that change does not necessarily mean *fundamental* change. An archae-ologically detectable change such as an apparently new type of object may of course result from totally new perceptions of the world and new ways of manipulating it. Nor can it reasonably be argued that such changes occurred in a societal and behavioural void. But any change may also represent a fairly simple, in some cases even more or less logical development from earlier situations or objects. Similarly, they may represent developments which had a relatively short lifespan which in turn limited their role and impact on society in the longer term. Examples of this are provided by the changes in dress and dress accessories which are often limited to a generation and which recur regularly within the period discussed here: taken individually, they do not necessarily reflect totally 'new' perceptions of society and of the world. The situation is of course different when series of such changes coincide in time: in those circumstances, they may reach a kind of critical mass which does influence society as a whole or major components thereof. In this respect, the situation is akin to what has been proposed in terms of catastrophe or chaos theory, which in turn could well be a suitable way to try and look at the archaeological evidence for the transition from medieval to later times.

All this may also be true of associations of objects, of technological developments,[19] of topographical developments and even of institutional or societal developments – as with networks – and of perceptions of the (material) world. Such changes may eventually become fundamental in that they reach a critical point of no return but that does not imply their being fundamental *per se* nor their being the result of new perceptions of the world and new manipulations thereof. Such changes may result from mechanisms set in motion – and possibly inadvertently – long before the period under discussion. Therefore, suitable attention should be paid to the long term and to the conditions in which changes – taken both individually and as a complex – occurred.

All this of course requires and deserves a much more detailed discussion which cannot be included here. It may also seem that these comments are leading to a denial of the notion 'age of transition' itself. The points I want to emphasise, however, are:

a. looking at the archaeological evidence for the period from c.1400 to c.1600 in terms of an 'age of transition' requires looking both at what was new on the one hand and at what endured or what was set in motion in earlier times on the other;

b. more attention should be paid to the notion of 'gradual development' within the concept of transition and the discussion should not be limited to or over-emphasise what was 'new';

c. each change detected in the archaeological record should be looked at both individually and in terms of its possible relations to other changes in order to try and interpret them in terms of fundamental and significant change.

Unfortunately and for complex reasons, it would seem that continental western European archaeology is still a fairly long way off from being able to make encompassing statements concerning the 'age of transition'. Still, a few examples may help to illustrate some of the points mentioned earlier.

A few examples

Because of the state of development and present dynamics of medieval and later archaeological work in continental north-western Europe as well as because of the limited space available, only a few specific examples can be discussed here. They concern a few particular categories of objects in specific regions and are intended as illustrations for the points suggested in the previous paragraph.

The first case is that of the development of ceramic production and consumption and in the Low Countries, particularly in Flanders. It relates to what has been characterised as the 'Post-Medieval Ceramic Revolution' of the period 1450–1550 in England, which has been described as the 'introduction of a new and more sophisticated range of ceramic products both from abroad and from the native industries, the latter heavily influenced by the continental import wares [and which together] satisfied the changed cultural requirements of the period'.[20]

At first sight, something comparable may be observed in 16th-century Flanders and the Netherlands. By c.1550, the overall picture of the common, domestic pottery had also changed significantly when compared to the earlier, mainly 14th-century one. The local, partially glazed red wares had become predominant, having replaced the formerly omnipresent grey, reduced and unglazed wares almost completely by the second half of the 15th century in western Flanders and by c.1530 elsewhere. Simultaneously, other developments equally had become obvious: the regional differences between the common wares produced locally had become far less pronounced; the range of domestic ceramic objects with more or less specialised functions had been expanded considerably, including now not only cooking and tablewares but also others types of objects; the number of ceramic objects in the individual household seems to have been expanded significantly, judging from the increasing number of individual objects yielded by contexts of this period; new quality or luxury items such as the maiolicas became more widespread and were now also produced in north-western Europe; and imported Rhenish stonewares were now a fairly common feature on the average table. Taken together, all this seems quite a change when compared to the 14th-century situation and to characterise the overall picture succinctly, it can be said to reflect phenomena of specialisation, standardisation, growth of number of material goods and – taking into account that these wares were produced by specialised potters for marketing purposes – aspects of commodification. All of these can be interpreted as indications of emerging capitalism.[21]

But it can reasonably be argued that all this was the end result of a slow and gradual process which started around 1200 or even somewhat earlier. At that time, Flemish and Dutch potters started producing glazed redwares alongside grey ones, using the same kilns and raw materials. In some areas and notably in West Flanders, the redwares already constituted almost half of the common domestic pottery by 1350. In the 15th century, the greywares went through a process of degradation and demise: the group still included a few jugs and the occasional drinking vessel, but the bulk of it consisted of large storage jars and water pitchers. Other objects were simple feeding boxes and sewer tubes, the latter already appearing in the 14th century. A perhaps somewhat simplified picture is that of the grey wares moving from the living quarters to the kitchen, then to the cellar and the courtyard and finally underground before becoming totally extinct.

Probably, this development can be explained in part by technical aspects, the glazing of the objects requiring an oxidising firing, which in turn leads to red fabrics instead of grey ones. But this glazing also entailed (slightly?) higher costs and required a higher degree of specialisation on the part of the potters. Therefore, the gradual ousting of the unglazed and coarser grey wares may well point to improving standards of living.

It is also of interest to note that the emerging redwares of the late 12th and 13th centuries seem to have broken through with two major groups: specialised objects such as skillets and tripod cauldrons (*Grapen*) on the one hand and highly decorated jugs on the other. The latter were themselves to some extent the (mainly) Flemish response to presumably French (Normandy and/or Paris) imports and would in turn trigger the emergence of other, autochthonous versions of this kind of product in different parts of the Low Countries (*e.g.* in Brabant) and elsewhere (possibly in Denmark and in northern Germany). Small amounts of these wares were traded across the North Sea to England, Scotland and Scandinavia, but the distribution pattern suggests that there was little if any interest in them in those areas which had

their own version of highly decorated objects.[22] Thus, these highly decorated wares reflect processes of active competition as early as the late 12th or early 13th century. The *Grapen* are equally interesting in this respect: basically, they are copies of the metal cauldrons[23] and represent aspects of competition across the boundaries within the artisanal world, while at the same time reflecting early processes of commodification, of 'popularisation' of more expensive objects and perhaps of improving living standards. From the mid 14th century onwards and well into the 15th and early 16th century and later, a similar development occurred when the Flemish potters dropped the production of highly decorated jugs but still used the decoration techniques to copy metal ewers, basins, chafing dishes, lavabos and other objects. It was not an important part of the production but it recurred regularly and it always presented the same features: the objects generally belong to the sphere of non-essential utensils and the decoration techniques used earlier for the highly decorated jugs allowed the potters to provide a probably somewhat cheaper but also distinct and colourful alternative to the metal models which became more common at the time.[24] The pattern was occasionally repeated with another 13th- to early 16th-century product of these potters: some of the glazed and highly decorated ceramic finials seem to copy stone and metal models known from the buildings of that time (e.g. pinnacles).[25]

All this is borne out by the Rhenish stonewares, particularly the Siegburg products. From c.1300 onwards, these grew continuously more popular and after c.1350 were also joined by other stoneware imports from the Raeren-Langerwehe-Cologne region. Arriving in large numbers, partly as a result of the large-scale production organisation in the Rhineland and of the main trading routes along the Rhine and the road from Cologne to Antwerp, these functionally specialised tablewares replaced the autochthonous quality drinking and serving vessels, the highly decorated jugs, by the early to mid 14th century and went on to become more or less common features of the domestic table of the 15th century, ending up as common drinking vessels by the mid 16th century (as shown by the peasant scenes by Pieter Bruegel the Elder and by many if not most archaeological assemblages of the same period).[26] Very occasionally, Flemish potters would try and copy stoneware forms. But lacking suitable clays to manufacture a product which could compete directly with the Rhenish stonewares, they abandoned this market. One interesting exception deserves to be mentioned here. The Flemish and Dutch potters were well acquainted with the use of a rich green lead-glaze which had been very much a trademark of the highly decorated jugs, particularly in West Flanders. From the mid 14th century onwards, the potters would regularly use the technique to refire and glaze Siegburg stoneware jugs.[27] Here again, emerging patterns of fairly complex forms of competition can be detected.

The gradual functional specialisation of the vessel forms and its corollaries, increasing numbers of mutually exclusive object-types and growing import-ance of ceramic objects within the households also is a process which started well before 1400, as shown by many an archaeological complex, including production ones.[28] In addition, by the early 15th century, many object-types seem to have acquired a more specialised form which will endure until well into the 16th–17th centuries and even later. After c.1500–1550, new vessel-forms did occasionally appear but in many cases, they were a more or less logical development of earlier forms.[29]

Another new development was the breakthrough of the majolicas, with autochthonous productions starting in Antwerp and spreading rapidly through the Low Countries and further north in the early 16th century. However, tin-glazed tiles were already produced locally – by specialised and possibly itinerant artisans – before 1300, the 14th and 15th centuries saw the arrival first of some Italian maiolicas and later of more numerous Iberian ones, and some maiolicas may already have been produced in the Low Countries in the 15th century as in the case of the so-called 'altar vases'. There seems to be little doubt about the nature of these new quality wares: most of them belong in the sphere of con-spicuous consumption and there is some evidence that the Italian specialists attracted by the major market that Antwerp represented considered them-selves to be artists rather than craftsmen, a fact supported by display items such as tile-pictures and

by the use of themes copied from prints and paintings. It is, however, also worth noting that in the 16th and 17th centuries, the maiolicas went through the same cycle as other, earlier classes of ceramics: after a phase of being items of conspicuous consumption, they gradually became more widespread socially until they would be replaced by the full-fledged delftwares and other products.[30] In passing, it may also be noted that the decoration techniques and the decoration patterns used on the maiolicas did of course reflect the new tastes and perceptions of the world, but at same time, we should forget neither that these constitute a logical development from earlier Mediterranean ones nor that some of the local highly decorated wares of the 13th and 14th centuries also had anthropomorphic, zoomorphic or heraldic ornaments.

Another interesting case is that of the late 16th-century and later slipwares, a truly north-western European trend with many productions from the Low Countries and northern France to Germany, occa-sionally also including objects which were clearly influenced by Bernard de Palissy's products.[31] In the Low Countries, there may well have been a strong link with between the 13th- and 14th-century highly decorated wares and some of the 14th- and 15th-century highly decorated products (including slip-ware dishes) mentioned earlier: the basic tools and techniques are the same. What did change signific-antly were the forms and particularly the decoration patterns. For Germany, things seem somewhat different as these slipwares do not have direct medieval forebears. But as Hans-Georg Stephan[32] has shown, these groups seem to emerge fairly suddenly as fully developed products, which makes it possible that external influences were involved. Whatever the case, it is the decoration which changes both in technology and in terms of motives and it is here that one sees the stronger influences of changing times, be it that some part was probably played by cross-European diffusion and new or rather expand-ing – because comparable ones existed before 1400 – networks (including migrant potters as in the case of some English slipwares or the Werra-type slip-wares produced at Enkhuizen in the Netherlands).[33] Similar phenomena seem to characterise the German stonewares, with the emergence of 16th-century highly decorated items. The whole suggests a growing importance of multi-coloured objects for display. This was not, however, a totally new phenomenon but it did now acquires a new importance. The trend is also visible in the case of the decorated stove-tiles, which follow the introduction of a new heating system, itself an innovation which belongs in what is called here the 'age of transition'.[34]

This very rapid and somewhat simplified overview of the 12th- to 17th-century pottery production in the Low Countries and particularly in Flanders suggest that quite a few changes detectable in the pottery of the period 1400 to 1600 were in fact strongly linked with developments and trends set in motion well before the 15th century. This is certainly true in the case of the technological developments and of the dynamics of production, consumption and even standardisation and commodification. Some vessel forms seem to have reached their fundamental shape by the 15th century or even before. Similarly, at least in some areas, the pottery was then already produced by specialised craftsmen working for a market.

It is not that changes did not occur or that the late 16th- and early 17th-century pottery scene was identical to the medieval one. A few new forms and certainly new decoration patterns reflecting new tastes and fashions testify to that. Nor can the role of the dramatically expanding global networks and of colonialism be neglected as demonstrated by clay pipes or by the influences of Oriental imports on late majolicas and delftwares. The development of individualised sets of ceramic tablewares (combined with tablewares in other materials), itself linked with the emergence of the new fashion of individualised and formalised dining customs[35] is another example, be it that dishes and plates already occurred in the 14th century and that Ruth E. Mohrmann[36] has recently argued that the basic conditions for early modern table- and eating-culture were established by the early 14th century. And the growing emphasis on ceramic tablewares as opposed to kitchenwares and thus on display, documented for England by David Gaimster[37] and others, seems equally to occur in north-western Europe as shown by the rapidly growing success of and demand for quality products such as delftwares and slipwares.

But when looking at a broader chronological framework, it would appear that from the 12th to the 18th century we are also confronted with recurrent cycles of categories of pottery emerging, growing successful and declining, often through a process of 'popularisation', before being replaced with other, newer products. Other phenomena such as the gradually growing number of ceramic objects or the important role played by new imports which often triggered both new consumer demands and competitive behaviour on the part of the potters are equally well documented from at least the 12th century onwards. And the same holds true for the patterns of social emulation and gradually increasing standards of living[38] which sustained the cycles mentioned earlier. At the same time, this implies that not only social and behavioural factors were at play but also functional and economic ones.

On the whole, it would seem that the notion 'Post-Medieval Ceramic Revolution' has to be qualified in the case of the Low Countries ceramic scene (and probably also in other parts of continental northwestern Europe). It may well be that this is to some extent linked with the fact that the Low Countries and particularly Flanders were a strongly urbanised society from the 12th and 13th centuries onwards: this context may have been conducive to the early emergence of the social and economic impulses which contributed to the general picture given.[39] Whatever the case, the Flemish and Low Countries pottery scene suggests both that linking the notion 'age of transition' to the phase 1400–1600 may be somewhat problematic in some respects, that the mechanisms set in motion well before the 15th century played an important part in later developments and that regional differences have to be taken into account.

Ceramics should of course not be discussed in total isolation from other categories of 'mobile' objects, i.e. the other smaller, physically more or less easily transferable commodities, nor for that matter should they stringently be divorced from the 'immobile' material world of buildings, settlements, landscapes and environments with which they are so intricately intertwined. Unfortunately, the archaeological evidence for the other categories of 'mobile' objects often is still too sketchy to allow for more general interpretations. Glass vessels constitute a case in point. A fair number of late medieval and later have been published and for some regions, our knowledge of the chronotypology of glass vessels has progressed significantly.[40] The literature does convey the impression of developments to some extent comparable to those noted in the case of ceramics: gradually increasing numbers of glass vessels with a significant peak in the latter part of the 16th century and probably reflecting changes in living standards and life-styles; increasing diversification of object-types; technological refinements and shifts, at least in part induced by external influences (e.g. the development of the *façon de Venise* glass). Craft specialisation and other phenomena such as increasing commodification and patterns of social emulation combined with shifts in fashion equally seem at work in the 16th and 17th centuries. But again, these trends may at least in part be due to mechanisms set in motion well before the 15th century and notably from the 13th century onwards when glass tableware rapidly becomes a commodity present in most contexts which can be associated not only with the wealthy but also with somewhat less wealthy – though definitely not poor – households.

Metal objects and particularly kitchen utensils and tablewares also remain somewhat of a problem, notably because of the continuous curation through re-use of the materials. The written sources (notably probate inventories) and iconographic evidence suggest their number to be growing consistently and becoming part of 'middle class' and even less wealthy households. In urban England, however, the trend may have started as early as the mid 14th century,[41] while on the Continent, new technologies significantly increased the output and consumption of such commodities from the late 12th or early 13th century onwards.[42] The copying of metal objects by potters and more notably the *Grapen* or tripod cooking-pots mentioned earlier, documented from the late 12th or 13th century onwards in some regions, equally points to the rise of the success of metal cooking utensils and other metal objects from that time onwards.

The situation is more difficult to assess in the case of (mainly metal) dress accessories which have yet to be studied more systematically. A wealth of late medieval and later finds has been made available in numerous site reports and catalogues but notwithstanding a few encompassing works on specific kinds of objects such as medieval buckles[43] or jewellery,[44] it seems still somewhat early to risk overall interpretations. Through time, such objects did of course change, reflecting new fashions and thus new visions of the world. It is not, however, impossible that at least in some cases the cycles of change had a relatively short life-span and that their succession reflects to some extent logical and normal developments linked to the need for new forms of display. In this respect, the continental situation seems comparable to the English one.[45] Thus, it is conceivable that an overall social and cultural change is not the only factor involved. The phenomenon of fashion seems to have emerged as early as the 12th century and therefore we may again be confronted with changes which had very long roots.

Another interesting field is that of furniture, a subject still far too much neglected by archaeology basically because the excavated evidence is rather limited. Furniture is, however, important, particularly as it can be and is used to order – physically and mentally – domestic and public space. What the mainly historical and iconographical evidence seems to reflect is a slow increase in number of furniture items, combined with a gradual diversification and specialisation of objects which took the world away from the much simpler and very utilitarian medieval situation. The pattern is comparable to that reflected by ceramics, be it that it comes later in the 15th and mainly 16th century and that there were important differences depending on the social class involved. But again, the picture is chequered one: in 17th-century northern Germany and Brabant, for instance, the simple medieval removable table is still very much the rule as it also is even in mid 16th-century elite circles which often tended to be somewhat conservative.[46]

Many other categories of objects also reflect patterns of change while a few new ones (e.g. clay pipes) appeared and others disappeared or were replaced by new media (e.g. pilgrim signs), the world of 'mobile' objects growing increasingly diversified and complex. In the case of categories of objects which already existed before c.1400, the picture generally appears to be one of increasing numbers and sometimes growing diversification, often combined with changing morphological details and/or changing decoration.

Our second case belongs in the sphere of the 'immobile' material world and concerns the physical, social and behavioural world of towns. As towns and urban buildings may be seen as physical and spatial expressions of society and social networks as well as of particular economic and functional circumstances (notably industry and trade) or even technological developments, they should reflect fundamental changes affecting society as a whole. The bulk of the information on this topic is provided by the rapidly growing archaeological and architectural analysis of standing building remains (*Bauforschung*) and by retrogressive historical geography and building history rather than by archaeology in its traditional form, i.e. excavations. This may well mean that it is still somewhat early in the day to reach definitive conclusions where some aspects such as fittings and furnishings are concerned. Equally important, very little effort has yet been spent on interpretative work. But some points may be noted.

It can hardly be denied that in some parts of the Low Countries – particularly the strongly urbanised regions of the old County of Flanders and the Duchy of Brabant – and of the neighbouring regions, conspicuous changes can be observed in the physical urban fabric of Early Modern Times. New fortifications, influenced by developments in Italy, followed the emergence of new military technologies and the increasing use of towns as *points d'appui* for emerging states and 'national' policies. Eventually, they transformed the outward appearance of towns in drastic ways. New public and private buildings, adapted to the new tastes and new perceptions of social representation and space, appeared. At least from the 15th century onwards, the role of the municipal authorities grew more pronounced and they encroached more and more on the private domain through devising and implementing all kinds of regulatory measures concerning street frontages, building materials, etc.[47] In combination with shifting centre and periphery patterns (illustrated by the gradual decline of Bruges and the emergence of

Antwerp as a new 'world' centre in the 16th century), expanding international trade networks and new patterns of exchange led to new industries and new spatial patterns of specialised production (as in the case of new types of textiles in Flanders and in Brabant).[48] The sociocultural domain – strongly linked with urban culture – witnessed all kinds of changes from new art forms and types of architectural and interior decorations over printing, cartography and literacy (at least in some circles) to religion and social behaviour, up to and including a gradual shift to greater intimacy, a growing isolation of private life as opposed to public life and eventually also new forms of social intermingling (notably operas and coffee houses).[49] Much of this corresponds with some of the patterns discussed by Matthew Johnson.[50]

But in terms of really fundamental change, the 16th- to (early) 18th-century urban picture may well have been much more complex than a superficial glance at the evidence suggests. Underneath all these apparently dramatic changes, at least as many older and more particularly medieval mechanisms were still at work and in many respects, medieval situations continued to dominate the physical and ideological urban world until well into the 18th century and sometimes even later. Thus, for instance, the new fortifications occasionally influenced the internal structure and fabric of the town centre, but their impact mainly concerned – and was sometimes even limited to – the outer quarters and suburbs.[51] Similarly, there are earlier, 13th- and 14th-century examples of municipal authorities intervening more and more in private construction ventures, notably through incentives for the use of more durable and fire-proof building materials such as roof tiles, brick and stone instead of wood.[52] Another illustration is the topography, overall layout and general spatial organisation of the urban cores. In many if not most cases, the overall pattern of streets and even of plots seems to have come into being well before the 'age of transition' and more often than not changed little before 1800 or even later. This is not too surprising as a costly infrastructure is not as rapidly replaced or changed as 'mobile' equipment such as for instance kitchen utensils, tablewares, dress or furniture. Furthermore, a number of monuments such as churches, urban castles (e.g. the Gravensteen in

Ghent or the Steen in Antwerp) or some public buildings and squares (e.g. the Belfry and market square in Bruges), all of them endowed with strong traditional, sociocultural and even sociopolitical values, continued to dominate and structure their immediate and less immediate surroundings. Sometimes, the spatial organisation of these zones hardly changed. Even if caution is required when it comes to studying the earlier, pre 12th-century urban topographies, there is good reason for historians and historical geographers to combine 19th-century cadastral plans and retrogressive analysis to try and reconstruct the later medieval ones. In the case of Bruges, the fairly detailed topographical maps by Jacob van Deventer (c.1555) and Marcus Gerards (1562), other 16th- to 18th-century plans or even the late 15th- or early 16th-century 'Painted Plan' illustrate the point when confronted to more recent situations. Bruges may be somewhat exceptional as it lost much of its demographic and economic impetus after the 13th century. The late 13th-century town wall reflected the optimism of the period: it encompassed a much larger area than the actual town centre. But the 14th-century crisis and the later development of the economic situation stopped the growth of the town and the largely open and unbuilt 'urban' space around the town centre would not be filled in until the 19th century.[53] In growth centres such as Antwerp, things were somewhat different. New quarters did emerge, sometimes as a result of proto-capitalistic or capitalistic ventures combined with explicitly urbanistic designs of a new nature as exemplified by the interventions of *entrepreneurs* such as Guy van Schoonbeke.[54] But such developments hardly touched the older, 10th- to 12th-century urban core around the 10th-century stronghold, parts of which survived well into the 19th and even 20th century.[55]

As to individual and private buildings – and notwithstanding the new houses of part of the urban elite – many (late) medieval ones survived well into the 18th and even 19th centuries, as shown not only by a few which still survive but also by the many examples drawn and documented by 19th-century artists. Quite a few of these even retained their wooden street frontages notwithstanding earlier municipal directives tending to replace wood with

stone and brick as building materials. There are numerous examples of all this for quite a few towns.[56] The evidence also shows the process of process of 'petrification', the conversion from wood to stone, of the urban world to have been a gradual and long process. The phenomenon started in the 11th and 12th centuries (or somewhat later in other regions such as the Baltic) and probably reflected both social emulation concerns and practical ones (comfort, durability, safety, etc.) on the part of the urban elite. Slightly later, in the 13th and 14th centuries, safety concerns (fire hazard) grew more important from the point of view of the municipal authorities and more often than not the pattern of 'petrification' was one of the less visible common walls between individual houses being built in stone of brick while the street frontages and floors were constructed of wood.[57] In many cases, this is the situation which survived until well into the 18th and 19th centuries.

Post-medieval private buildings show quite a few regional variations throughout Europe as well as variations which can be correlated with the social standing and/or wealth of the inhabitants. The occupational diversity (different crafts) and even the overall type and nature of the town (harbour towns, regional markets, etc.) also played a part. The present state of the question makes it difficult to identify and assess possible overall patterns of change, even if it would appear that a few general traits are common to the area from Flanders to the Baltic regions. Among these are the constant densification of the built areas, the gradual alignment along more regular street frontage lines and a trend towards aligning the gables along the street. A number of patrician's houses had another overall organisation with different functional components (with in a few cases a tower-like structure) arranged around a central courtyard closed off from the street. This may be seen as an element of closure as defined by Matthew Johnson[58] but it is combined with an element of social display and many if not most other houses[59] the actual living quarters remained oriented towards the street. Another overall trait may well be that of a gradually increasing functional specialisation and diversification, which in turn contributed to the eventually almost complete infilling of the plots and the expansion of the buildings in both the horizontal and vertical planes. Some (merchants') houses also had warehouses at the back, a development which sometimes started in the 14th century or even earlier and continued to influence the spatial organisation of the plots until well into the 17th century and even later (as for instance in Amsterdam). On the whole, the major area of regional variations seems to have been that of interior and particularly exterior decoration.[60] In the case of adoption of external influences and fashions, autochthonous adaptation with strong influences from older, local traditions, more or less seems to have been the general pattern. To some extent, this even applies to the process of conversion from wood to stone: some of the early to mid 16th-century houses in Antwerp – though at the time a highly dynamic town open to all kinds of innovations – have street frontages which were are basically stone copies of wooden models.[61]

Again, however, many of these developments which eventually shaped the early modern urban environment started well before the 15th century.[62] Quite a few of the post-medieval houses retained their medieval core while new ones of the time were in fact the logical development of general types which first appeared in the 13th or 14th centuries. The same applies to many of the building plots and their spatial organisation. New plot layouts – often following encompassing and systematic reorganisations of space – appeared in the 12th and 13th centuries and lived on into fairly recent times or still survive. In other cases, larger block-shaped plots known in the 11th to 13th centuries – and often with a centrally placed (patrician's) house – were split up through speculation or heritage settlements and were eventually converted into smaller and narrower units, the successor(s) of the earlier house moving to the street frontage.[63]

The medieval *substratum* even continued to influence the urban world of the 16th to 18th centuries in many other, archaeologically as yet less directly tangible respects and notably in the fields of social and economic control, the organisation of production and the social structures and institutions (e.g. the guilds).[64] In some cases, even late 18th-century urban sociotopographies reveal the strong lingering influence of situations which started developing as early as the 12th and 13th centuries.

Ghent offers a nice example of this. A cluster analysis of the spatial distribution of the population in 1799, based on social, professional and demographic variables, revealed a somewhat concentric pattern of 'intellectual' and well-to-do inhabitants in the old centre, intertwined with zones (streets) of more down-to-earth economic and commercial activities and surrounded by areas with inhabitants of somewhat lower status.[65] Interestingly enough, the central 'higher-status' areas coincide largely with the area where from the late 11th to early 14th century, powerful and wealthy patricians built their rather imposing stone houses, known as *stenen*.[66]

What all this seems to suggest is that on many levels – both communal and individual ones – the urban environments of the period 1400 to 1600 and later reflected the logical continuation of trends which started to emerge in the 13th or even 12th century. Christopher R. Friedrichs'[67] vision of a town which 'in many fundamental ways [...] remained remarkably stable' in the period from 1450 to 1750 is certainly not contradicted by the archaeological evidence known to date.

Other components of the 'immobile' material world such as rural settlement patterns, rural buildings, castles and landscapes should not be neglected in the debate on the changes which occurred between 1400 and 1600 but for practical reasons, they have to be left aside in the present paper. It is, however, worth noting that in all these fields, changes – some of them apparently quite fundamental – did occur in the period under consideration. But at the same time, the links with the medieval and particularly 12th- to 14th-century situations always remained very strong and in some cases this may have been a deliberate strategy. The gradually changing functional and social nature of castles is an example of this, the general picture being one of the emphasis shifting from defensibility combined with social display to social display combined with residential requirements and considerations related to comfort. The evolution is at least in part linked with the developments in the field of military technology, tactics and strategy but has strong social overtones. This is fairly well documented for the Low Countries and Germany and seems also valid for other north-western European regions.[68] Belonging in the sphere of the social and/or economic elite, castles seem to have been fairly open to new architectural developments and tastes. But they always retained the social display functions which they had acquired through the Middle Ages. And the links with the Middle Ages were often – consciously or otherwise – materialised in all sorts of ways. In Flanders, a nice example is provided by the moats around many 16th-, 17th- and 18th-century *maisons de plaisance* and castles of the (lower) nobility or the new *burgher* elite with aspirations to nobility. Essentially derived from the moat around the 11th- and 12th-century motte-and-bailey castles, moats were strongly 'popularised' from the late 12th and 13th century onwards and were – to some extent unconsciously – used by many freeholders and larger farms to reflect and make visible a higher social status which they rightly or wrongly believed to have or aspired to. The moat would retain this 'hidden' function until well into the 18th and even 19th centuries and in a few cases, the new 'modern' castles built on or immediately next to an older castle site would even retain the by then abandoned and sometimes even unbuilt motte as a symbol of power and long and well-established roots.[69] From the (late) 15th and more particularly from the 16th century onwards, the moat would in fact often be combined with new perceptions of the social and physical world – and notably with Palladio's principles of *belezza* and *magnificenzia* as well as with new interest in and perceptions of nature – in the new *maisons* and *jardins de plaisance* built in the neighbourhood of Antwerp by wealthy merchants.[70] The latter clearly saw such *maisons* as an investment but also as a means of positioning themselves socially and coming closer to their perception of themselves as 'landed gentry'. This in turn is not in itself a totally new phenomenon: already in the 13th century, cases are known of wealthy *burghers* moving into the rural world as an investment of both an economic and a social nature[71] and this in turn again emphasises the strong impact of basically medieval developments, behavioural patterns and perceptions, be it that these were now translated in (partly) new physical forms.

Something similar may also apply to other aspects of the rural world where phenomena such as restructuring (including patterns of new concentrations of holdings such as those documented for England; see

Dyer in the present volume) are known historically. In the case of Belgium, the pattern is one of strong regional variations depending on local conditions as well as on complex economic long-term and short-term trends. But the smaller holding often remained predominant (at least in some areas and well into the 17th century) and the conversion from direct to indirect exploitation started well before the 15th century.[72] Archaeological fieldwork still has a long way to go to help and document these patterns.

In some respects, however, a little more is known. An example is provided by Lampernisse, a rural area in the coastal polders between Veurne and Diksmuide. The archaeological and historical analysis revealed that the plot and overall plot-pattern came into being in the 12th to 14th centuries, in part as the result of an intensification of agriculture combined with the creation of new freeholders' farms which often took the form of moated farmsteads. Many if not most of these farms located on rather marginal soils disappeared after the mid 14th-century crisis and part of the land was integrated into those holdings that survived. But the plots and their spatial organisation did hardly change and their 12th- to 14th-century layout survives to this day.[73] The polder area may be somewhat special in that its exploitation required the creation of a suitable system of drainage ditches which served as field boundaries and represented a substantial investment in terms of work, effort and money. It is therefore understandable that they were not replaced in later times. But comparable situations also occur elsewhere in Flanders, demonstrating the strong lingering influences of medieval situations and developments on the later and even present-day landscape.[74]

A few provisional conclusions

Though this was not my original intention, the present rather impressionistic survey of some of the (archaeological) evidence for part of continental north-western Europe has ended up by almost deliberately emphasising not so much the changes which manifested themselves during the 1400 to 1600 'age of transition', but rather the very strong links with earlier medieval situations and phenomena. It is not that changes or indeed even fairly fundamental transformations did not occur, quite to the contrary. Rather, it is the result of the present state of research combined with the fact that quite a few developments in the period 1400 to 1600 and even later appear to have strong and long medieval roots.

As to the present state of (archaeological) research, it seems clear that the relevant archaeological evidence still seems too patchy and even biased – in terms of basic categories of objects as well as of social representativity of this evidence – to allow for sweeping interpretations concerning the nature, dynamics and meanings of an overall transformation of society at all social and behavioural levels. In addition, continental north-western European archaeology to a certain degree still has to come of age and reflect seriously and actively on the kind of questions involved in the present debate as well as on the nature and *Aussagekraft* of the present and future data. In practice, this also means that while continuing gathering of primary data and descriptive work of a chronotypological type remain among the immediate priorities, more attention should also be paid to question-driven research. This implies that we need a better balance between fieldwork of a rescue type and inductive fieldwork and research. Equally important in view of the specific nature of material culture and of archaeological evidence, is that this kind of work should refer to but not let itself be blindly dominated by the historical debate. At the same time, we would do well to try and break down the more or less institutionalised conceptual and practical barriers between the different disciplines such as history, anthropology, art history, archaeology and others because the material world we are focusing on is the melting pot in which all conceivable human actions (and non-actions) are combined with all conceivable environmental factors in a dynamic and permanent interaction.

At present, a suitable way of providing a general assessment of the limited evidence extant is perhaps to look at it briefly in terms some of the fundamental changes discussed by Matthew Johnson[75] and Charles E. Orser Jr.[76] The more obvious of these include closure, commodification, and the role of consumers, expanding (trade) networks and – on a somewhat higher level – capitalism and much of what

these phenomena entail in terms of behavioural patterns. As far as can be seen now, the continental evidence does not contradict the interpretations proposed by Johnson or Orser, be it that the latter tend to emphasise the later 17th- and more particularly 18th-century situations. The same seems to be valid in the case of the major question which is of course the one related to the growth of late medieval and early modern capitalism and the decline of medieval feudalism, particularly as possibly reflected in the material evidence. This cannot be discussed in any detail here.[77] On the whole, the archaeological evidence does not contradict the picture of the growing importance of capitalist approaches to and manipulations of the material world but it remains hard to document such a development in concrete archaeological detail in north-western Europe. Furthermore, this process too may well have been more convoluted, affecting different social and socio-economic groups – and therefore also their material world – in different ways and even at different speeds. It is also worth noting that historians such as Richard H. Britnell[78] have argued convincingly that the essentially Marxist model used to characterise the 15th- and early 16th-century situation as the transition from feudalism to capitalism is not altogether to be trusted in that it 'seriously misrepresents the magnitude of earlier change'.[79]

It can indeed be shown that in quite a few cases the developments detectable in the finds had very long roots and were the logical result of processes set in motion long before the 15th century and often even in the 12th and 13th centuries. This not only applies to down-to-earth developments such as technological ones but also to perceptions and manipulations of the material world, including public and private space, landscape and settlements.

As far as the 'mobile' material culture is concerned, the most notable changes from the 15th century onwards seem to be increasing diversification and increasing numbers of objects, both phenomena being of course related (e.g. through a combination of progressive functional specialisation, increasing commodification, growing consumers' demands, and other factors). New categories of objects equally appeared following either the expansion of trade and other networks or improving standards of living (at least for part of the population). But the archaeological evidence extant also suggests that quite a few of these developments started well before the 15th century. All this could mean that the fundamental change was not necessarily an exclusively qualitative one but basically also a quantitative one which in turn led to increasing complexity and only then to more fundamental qualitative change. To some extent, this may possibly be seen in terms of the chaos of catastrophe theory, which would in turn perhaps help to explain why some of the processes involved seem to have had such a long life-cycle.

In the case of the 'immobile' components of the material world, change is equally undeniable but often seems to have come about much more slowly, notwithstanding such obvious and incisive developments as new urban fortifications or public and private buildings, the latter with a gradually increasing emphasis on privacy though still with a lot of attention for social display. But here too, many developments show strong links with mechanisms set in motion in much earlier times some of them may well have been somewhat less fundamental than is generally perceived (e.g. new decorations as opposed to new buildings). In passing, it is worth noting that in the 'immobile' world comprehensive and fundamental change often seems to have come about more slowly than changes in the world of 'mobile' goods or commodities, which means that future work should also pay attention not only to the correlation between major categories of objects but also to their specific dynamics.

When preparing the present paper and looking through mounds of publications, the overall impression gained – the word is important – is that while many changes are detectable in the material world of the period 1400 to 1600, quite a few of them were not really fundamental in nature and this in turn made me question the propriety of the term 'age of transition' for the two centuries concerned. I also gained the impression that much more fundamental (and quicker?) changes occurred in the 12th–13th century on the one hand and in the 18th century on the other, which made me wonder whether it would not be more suitable to think of the period from the 12th to the 18th century as the real 'age of transition' between the medieval and the modern world. It also made me wonder whether the undeniable and obvious changes visible in the *apparent* material world (art, architecture, elements of spatial organisation, etc.) and manipulations thereof in the 15th and 16th centuries – however important – are somewhat overrated as compared to many more down-to-earth and clearly very gradual developments. It remains to be stressed, however, that all this is still very much in the speculative stage as the archaeological database for continental north-western Europe – particularly for post-medieval times – remains at best still very limited.

Notes

1. For some recent examples, see van der Leeuw & McGlade (eds) 1997; van der Leeuw & Torrence (eds) 1989; Kühnel (ed.) 1986; Lemonnier (ed.) 1993.
2. E.g. Burke 1978; 1992; Muchembled 1978; 1988.
3. Mellor 1994 for England.
4. Austin 1990; Champion 1990.
5. Appadurai 1986; Kopytoff 1986.
6. E.g. Johnson 1993; 1996; Orser 1996.
7. Maschner (ed.) 1996; Teltser (ed.) 1995.
8. Nauert 1995.
9. Johnson 1996, 20 ff. and 206.
10. E.g. Weatherill 1988; different contributions in Brewer & Porter (eds) 1993 and in Bermingham & Brewer (eds) 1995.
11. Orser 1996, 57–88; Orser & Fagan 1995.
12. E.g. Johnson 1996; Jardine 1996.
13. Gaimster 1993; 1994, 287 ff.
14. E.g. Barton 1992.
15. E.g. Claessen & van de Velde 1985; Claessen 1996.
16. See also Courtney in this volume.
17. E.g. Johnson 1993; 1996; Sinclair 1987.
18. See different contributions in van der Leeuw & McGlade (eds) 1997.
19. Cf. Lemonnier 1992; *idem* (ed.) 1993.
20. Gaimster 1994, 287; see also Barton 1992.
21. E.g. Verhaeghe 1987; 1988; Janssen 1983; see also Johnson 1996.
22. Verhaeghe 1983; 1987; 1989.
23. Cf. Drescher 1968; 1982.
24. Verhaeghe 1989; 1989a; 1989b; 1991; 1992; Gaimster & Verhaeghe 1992.

25. Verhaeghe 1986; 1989.
26. Verhaeghe 1987; 1989.
27. Verhaeghe 1989; Hurst *et al.* 1986.
28. E.g. at Utrecht, c.1400; Bruijn 1979.
29. Verhaeghe 1988.
30. Verhaeghe 1988; Dumortier 1986; 1988; 1995; Dumortier & Oost 1989.
31. E.g. Stephan 1987; 1992; Burhenne *et al.* (eds) 1991; Blazy *et al.* 1986; Hurtrelle 1991; see also Hurst *et al.* 1986.
32. Stephan 1987; 1992.
33. Gaimster 1994, 291; Hurst *et al.* 1986, 154 ff.; Bruijn 1992.
34. See also Gaimster 1994, 292 ff. for England.
35. Mennell 1985; Hundsbichler 1984 1990; Moulin 1988; Zischka *et al.* (eds) 1993.
36. Mohrmann 1996, 168.
37. Gaimster 1994.
38. Dyer 1989.
39. Chapelot 1987.
40. E.g. Henkes 1994 for the Netherlands.
41. Dyer 1989.
42. Drescher 1986.
43. E.g. Fingerlin 1971.
44. E.g. Lightbown 1992; Hackenbroch 1979.
45. See Egan in this volume.
46. Boccador 1988; Ottenjann 1985; Kreisel 1981.
47. E.g. Tijs 1993 for Antwerp; see also De Jonge in press.
48. Soly 1991.
49. Soly 1991; see also many other contributions in Van der Stock (ed.) 1991.
50. Johnson 1996.
51. Ryckaert 1993.
52. E.g. in Bruges; Ryckaert 1984.
53. Ryckaert 1991.
54. Soly 1977; Tijs 1993.
55. See different contributions in Voet *et al.* (ed.) 1978; Oost (ed.) 1982.
56. For Antwerp, see Tijs 1993; for Bruges, see Ryckaert 1991.
57. Verhaeghe 1994.
58. Johnson 1996.
59. As with a number of mid 16th-century houses in Antwerp: Tijs 1993.
60. Tijs 1993; Griep 1992; Meischke 1969; Temminck Grolle 1963.
61. Tijs 1993.
62. Verhaeghe 1994.
63. Verhaeghe 1994.
64. Soly 1991 for Flanders and Brabant; see also Friedrichs 1995.
65. Vanneste 1987, 157, quoted by Baetens & Blondé 1991, 60–2.
66. Laleman & Raveschot 1991.
67. Friedrichs 1995, 331–2.
68. E.g. Doperé & Ubregts 1991; Janssen *et al.* (eds) 1996; Hotz 1979.
69. Verhaeghe 1977; 1981; 1986a.
70. Baetens 1991.
71. E.g. Boone 1996.
72. Verhulst 1990.
73. Verhaeghe 1977; 1986a; Dewilde *et al.* 1995.
74. Verhulst 1995.
75. Johnson 1996.
76. Orsler Jr 1996.
77. See Courtney in the present volume.
78. Britnell 1993; 1993a, 233–6.
79. See also Coward 1995.

Bibliography

Appadurai, A. 1986, 'Introduction: commodities and the politics of value', in Appadurai (ed.) 1986, 3–63

Appadurai, A. (ed.) 1986, *The social life of things. Commodities in cultural perspective*, Cambridge

Austin, D. 1990, 'The 'proper study' of medieval archaeology', in Austin & Alcock (eds) 1990, 9–42

Austin, D. & L. Alcock (eds) 1990, *From the Baltic to the Black Sea. Studies in medieval archaeology*, One World Archaeology, 18

Baetens, R. 1991, 'La "Belezza" et la "Magnificenza": symboles du pouvoir de la villa rustica dans la région anversoise aux temps modernes', in Baetens & Blondé (eds) 1991, 159–79

Baetens, R. 1996, 'Le rôle d'Anvers dans la transmission de valeurs culturelles au temps de son apogée', in *La ville et la transmission des valeurs culturelles ...*, 37–72

Baetens, R. & Blondé, B. 1991, 'Wonen in de stad : aspecten van de stedelijke wooncultuur', in Van der Stock (ed.) 1991, 59–70

Baetens, R. & Blondé, B. (eds) 1991, *Nouvelles approches concernant la culture de l'habitat. New approaches to living patterns. Colloque international/ International Colloquium, 24–25.10.1989.* Turnhout

Barnard, A. & Spencer, J. (eds) 1996, *Encyclopedia of social and cultural anthropology*

Barton, K.J. 1992, 'Ceramic changes in the Western European littoral at the end of the Middle Ages. A personal view', in Gaimster & Redknap (eds) 1992, 246–255

Bermingham, A. & Brewer, J. (eds) 1995, *The consump-*

tion of culture 1600–1800. Image, object, text

Blazy, S., Dilly, G., Hurtrelle, J. & Jacques, A. 1986, *Terres vernissées du XVIIe–XIXe siècle dans les musées du Nord-Pas-de-Calais*, Lille

Boccador, J. 1988, *Le mobilier français du moyen âge à la renaissance*. Saint-Just-en-Chaussée

Boone, M. 1996, 'La terre, les hommes et les villes. Quelques considérations autour du thème de l'urbanisation des propriétaires urbains', in *La ville et la transmission des valeurs culturelles ...*, 153–73

Brewer, J. & Porter, R. (eds) 1993, *Consumption and the world of goods*

Britnell, R.H. 1993, *The commercialisation of English society, 1000–1500*

Britnell, R.H. 1993a, 'Commerce and capitalism in Late Medieval England: problems of description and theory', *Journal of Historical Sociology*, 6, 359–76

Bruijn, A. 1979, *Pottersvuren langs de Vecht. Aardewerk rond 1400 uit Utrecht*, Rotterdam

Bruijn, A. 1992, *Spiegelbeelden. Werra-Keramiek uit Enkhuizen 1605*, Zwolle

Burke, P. 1978, *Popular Culture in Early Modern Europe*

Burke, P. 1990, 'Popular culture reconsidered', in Jaritz (ed.) 1990, 181–91

Champion, T.C. 1990, 'Medieval archaeology and the tyranny of the historical record', in Austin & Alcock (eds) 1990, 79–95

Chapelot, J. 1987, 'Aspects socio-économiques de la production, de la commercialisation et de l'utilisation de la céramique, in Chapelot *et al.* (eds) 1987, 167–78

Chapelot, J., Galinié, H. & Pilet-Lemière, J. (eds) 1987, *La céramique (Ve-XIXe s.). Fabrication-Commercialisation-Utilisation. Actes du premier colloque international d'archéologie médiévale (Paris, 4–6 octobre 1985)*

Claessen, H.M. 1996, 'Evolution and evolutionism', in Barnard & Spencer (eds) 1996, 213–18

Claessen, H.J.M. & van de Velde, P. 1985, Social evolution in general. Chapters 1, 9 and 16 in H.J.M. Claessen, P. van de Velde & M.E. Smith (eds), *Development and decline. The evolution of sociopolitical organisation*, South Hadley, MA, Bergin & Harvey

Clarke, D.L. 1978, *Analytical archaeology*, 2nd edition

Coward, B. 1995, *Social change and continuity in Early Modern England, 1550–1750*

Davey, P.J. & Hodges, R. (eds) 1983, *Ceramics and trade. The production and distribution of later medieval pottery in north-west Europe*, Sheffield

De Jonge, K. in press. "Stedebouwkundige aspecten". Verwoesting als motor voor de beheersing van de stedelijke ruimete in de Zuidelijke Nederlanden tot in

de 18de eeuw, in *Verwoesting en wederopbouw van steden in België – Destruction et reconstruction urbaines en Belgique. Colloque international – Internationaal Colloquium. Spa, 10–12 sept. 1996.* S.l. [Bruxelles – Brussel]: Gemeentekrediet van België – Crédit Communal de Belgique (*Collection Histoire, série in 8*)

Dewilde, M., Ervynck, A., Strobbe, M. & Verhaeghe, F. 1995, 'Lampernisse: protecting a landscape of major archaeological and environmental value', in M. Cox, V. Straker & D. Taylor (eds), *Wetlands: archaeology and nature conservation. Proceedings of the International Conference Wetlands: Archaeology and Nature Conservation, held at the University of Bristol, 11–14 April 1994*, 218–28

Doperé, F. & Ubregts, W. 1991, *De donjon in Vlaanderen. Architectuur en wooncultuur*, Brussel & Leuven

Drescher, H. 1968, 'Mittelalterliche Dreibeintöpfe aus Bronze. Bericht über die Bestandsaufnahme und den Versuch einer chronologischen Ordnung' in J.G.N. Renaud, (ed.), *Rotterdam Papers. A contribution to medieval archaeology. Teksten van lezingen, gehouden tijdens het Symposium voor "Middeleeuwse Archeologie in oude binnensteden" te Rotterdam, Schiedam en Delft van 21 t/m 24 maart 1966*, Rotterdam, 23–33

Drescher, H. S.d. [1982], 'Zu den bronzenen Grapen des 12.-16. Jahrhunderts aus Nordwestdeutschland', in J. Wittstock (ed.), *Aus dem Alltag der mittelalterlichen Stadt. Handbuch zur Sonderaustellung vom 5. Dezember 1982 bis 24. April 1983 im Bremer Landesmuseum*, Bremen: Bremer Landesmuseum (*Hefte des Focke Museums*, 62): 157–74

Drescher, H. 1986, 'Zum Guss von Bronze, Messing und Zinn "um 1200"', in H. Steuer (ed.), *Zur Lebensweise in der Stadt um 1200. Ergebnisse der Mittelalterarchäologie. Bericht über ein Kolloquium in Köln vom 31. Januar bis 2. Februar 1984*. Köln & Bonn: Dr. R. Habelt GmbH (*Zeitschrift zur Archäologie des Mittelalters, Beiheft* 4) 389–404

Dumortier, C. 1986, 'Het atelier van de Antwerpse geleyerspotbacker Franchois Frans (16de eeuw)'. *Mededelingenblad van de. Nederlandse Vereniging van Vrienden van de Ceramiek*, 125, nr. 5, 3–37

Dumortier, C. 1987, 'Les faïenciers italiens à Anvers au XVI siècle. Aspects historiques', *Faenza*, 73, nr. 4–6, 161–72

Dumortier, C. 1988, 'Les ateliers de majolique à Anvers (1508–1585)', *Bulletin van de Antwerpse Vereniging voor Bodem- en Grotonderzoek*, 1988, nr. 1, 23–38

Dumortier, Cl. 1995, 'Italian influence on Antwerp maiolica in the 16th and 17th century', in P. Vincenzini (ed.), *The ceramics cultural heritage. [Colloquium*

Firenze, 06–07.1994]. Firenze: Techna Srl., 769–76

Dumortier, C. & Oost, T. 1989, 'Un atelier de majoliques installé à Anvers vers 1600', *Bulletin M.R.A.H. – Bulletin K.M.K.G.*, 60, 203–16

Dyer, C. 1989, *Standards of living in the later Middle Ages. Social change in England c.1200–1520*. Cambridge

Fingerlin, I. 1971, *Gürtel des hohen und späten Mittelalters*. München & Berlin: Deutscher Kunstverlag (*Kunstwissenschaftliche Studien*, XLVI)

Friedrichs, Ch.R. 1995, *The Early Modern city 1450 – 1750*. London & New York

Gaimster, D.R.M. 1993, 'Cross-Channel ceramic trade in the late Middle Ages: archaeological evidence for the spread of Hanseatic culture to Britain', in Gläser (ed.) 1993, 251–60

Gaimster, D. 1994, 'The archaeology of post-medieval society, 1450–1750: material culture studies in Britain since the War' in B. Vyner (ed.), *Building on the past. Papers celebrating 150 years of the Royal Archaeological Institute*. London: The Royal Archaeological Institute, 283–312

Gaimster, D. & Redknap, M. (eds) 1992, *Everyday and exotic pottery from Europe, c. 650–1900. Studies in honour of John G. Hurst*, Oxford

Gaimster, D.R.M. & Verhaeghe, F. (with a contribution by M.J. Hughes). 1992, 'Handles with face-masks: a cross-Channel type of late medieval highly decorated basin', in Gaimster & Redknap (eds) 1992, 303–23

Gläser, M. (ed.) 1993, *Archäologie des Mittelalters und Bauforschung im Hanseraum. Eine Festschrift für Günter P. Fehring*. Rostock: Konrad Reich Verlag (*Schriften des kulturhistorischen Museums in Rostock*, 1)

Griep, H.-G. 1992, *Kleine Kunstgeschichte des deutschen Bürgerhauses*, Darmstadt: Wissenschaftliche Buchgesellschaft

Hackenbroch, Y. 1979, *Renaissance jewellery*. München: Sotheby Parke Bernet, Verlag C.H. Beck

Henkes, H.E. 1994, *Glas zonder glans. Vijf eeuwen gebruiksglas uit de bodem van de Lage Landen. 1300–1800*. S.l. [Rotterdam]: Coördinatie Commissie van Advies inzake Archeologisch Onderzoek binnen het Ressort Rotterdam (*Rotterdam Papers*, 9)

Hotz, W. 1979, *Kleine Kunstgeschichte der deutschen Burg*. Darmstadt: Wissenschaftliche Buchgesellschaft [4th edition]

Hundsbichler, H. 1984, 'Nahrung', in H. Kühnel (ed.), *Alltag im Spätmittelalter*. Graz: Verlag Styria, 196–231

Hurtrelle, J. (with the collaboration of Ph. Knobloch) 1991, *Potiers du Pays de Montreuil et de Dèsvres. Les plats décorés*. S.l. [Berck-sur-Mer] (*Nord-Ouest Archéologie*, 4)

Hurst, J.G., Neal, D.S. & van Beuningen, H.J.E. 1986, *Pottery produced and traded in north-west Europe 1350–1650*. Rotterdam: Stichting 'Het Nederlandse Gebruiksvoorwerp' (*Rotterdam Papers*, VI)

Janssen, H.L. 1983, 'Later medieval pottery production in the Netherlands', in Davey & Hodges (eds), 121–85

Janssen, H.L. Kylstra-Wielinga, J.M.M. & Olde Meierink, B. 1996, *1000 jaar kastelen in Nederland. Functie en vorm door de eeuwen heen*. Utrecht: Uitgeverij Matrijs

Jardine, L. 1996, *Worldly goods. A new history of the Renaissance*, London & Basingstoke

Jaritz, G. (ed.) 1990, *Mensch und Objekt im Mittelalter und in der frühen Neuzeit. Leben – Alltag – Kultur*. Wien: Verlag der Österreichischen Akademie der Wissenschaften (*Veröffentlichungen des Instituts für mittelalterlicher Realienkunde Österreichs*, 13)

Johnson, M. 1993, *Housing culture. Traditional architecture in an English landscape*

Johnson, M. 1996, *An archaeology of capitalism*, Oxford

Kopytoff, I. 1986, 'The cultural biography of things: commoditization as process', in Appadurai (ed.) 1986, 64–91

Kreisel, H. 1981, *Die Kunst des deutschen Möbels. I. Von den Anfängen bis zum Hochbarock*, München

[Kühnel, H. (ed.)]. 1986, *Alltag und Fortschritt im Mittelalter. Internationales Round-Table-Gespräch, Krems an der Donau, 1. Oktober 1984*. Wien: Verlag der Österreichischen Akademie der Wissenschaften (*Veröffentlichungen des Instituts für mittelalterliche Realienkunde Österreichs*, 8)

Laleman, M.C. & Raveschot, P. 1991, *Inleiding tot de studie van de woonhuizen in Gent. Periode 1100–1300. De kelders*. Brussel: Kon. Academie voor Wetenschappen, Letteren en Schone Kunsten van België (*Verhandelingen van de Kon. Academie voor Wetenschappen, Letteren en Schone Kunsten van België*, 53, nr. 54)

Lemonnier, P. 1992, *Elements for an anthropology of technology*. Ann Arbor (Michigan, USA): Museum of Anthropology, University of Michigan (*Anthropological Papers, Museum of Anthropology, University of Michigan*, 88)

Lemonnier, P. (ed.) 1993, *Technological choices. Transformation in material cultures since the Neolithic*, London

Lightbown, R.W. 1992, *Mediaeval European jewellery*.

With a catalogue of the collection in the Victoria & Albert Museum

Maschner, H.D.G. (ed.) 1996, *Darwinian archaeologies*, New York & London

Meischke, R. 1969, *Het Nederlandse woonhuis van 1300–1800*, Haarlem

Mellor, M. 1994, *Medieval ceramic studies in England. A review for English Heritage*

Mennell, S. 1985, *All manners of food: eating and taste in England and France from the Middle Ages to the present*, Oxford

Mohrmann, R.-E. 1996, 'Tischgerät und Tischsitten nach Inventaren und zeitgenössischen Bildern', in Wiegelmann & Mohrmann (eds) 1996, 167–78

Moulin, L. 1988, *Les liturgies de la table. Une histoire culturelle du manger et du boire*, Antwerpen & Paris

Muchembled, R. 1978, *Culture populaire et culture des élites dans la France moderne (XVe–XVIIIe siècles). Essai*, Paris

Muchembled, R. 1988, *L'invention de l'homme moderne*, Paris

Nauert, Ch.G. 1995, *Humanism and the culture of Renaissance Europe*, Cambridge

[Oost, T. (ed.)]. S.d. [1982], *Van nederzetting tot metropool. Archeologisch-historisch onderzoek in de Antwerpse binnenstad. Volkskundemuseum, 3 december 1982 - 17 april 1983*, S.l. [Antwerpen]: Stad Antwerpen, Oudheidkundige Musea

Orser, Ch.E. 1996, *A historical archaeology of the modern world*, New York & London

Orser, Ch.E. & Fagan, B.M. 1995, *Historical archaeology*, New York

Ottenjann, H. 1985, 'Möbel des spätmittelalters und der frühen Neuzeit als Indikator für kulturelle Beziehungen zwischen Stadt und Land', in C. Meckseper, (ed.), *Stadt im Wandel. Kunst und Kultur des Bürgertums in Norddeutschland 1150–1650. Ausstellungskatalog. Band 3. Aufsätze*, Stuttgart & Bad Cannstatt: Edition Cantz, 531–43

Ryckaert, M. 1984, 'Brandbestrijding en overheidsmaatregelen tegen brandgevaar tijdens het Ancien Régime', in *L'initiative publique des communes en Belgique. Fondements historiques (Ancien Régime) – Het openbaar initiatief van de gemeenten in België. Historische grondslagen (Ancien Régime. 11e colloque international – 11de internationaal colloquium. Spa, 1–4 sept., 1982. Actes – Handelingen*, S.l. [Bruxelles – Brussel]: Gemeentekrediet van België – Crédit Communal de Belgique (*Collection Histoire, série in 8 ,* 65), 247–56

Ryckaert, M. 1991, *Historische stedenatlas van België.*

Brugge. S.l. [Brussel]: Gemeentekrediet van België

Ryckaert, M. 1993, 'Stad, tijd en landschap', in E. Taverne & I. Visser (eds), *Stedebouw: de geschiedenis van de stad in de Nederlanden van 1500 tot heden*, Nijmegen

Sinclair, T. 1987, 'All styles are good, save the tiresome kind'. An examination of the pattern of stylistic changes occurring among silver candlesticks of the eighteenth century (1680–1780), in I. Hodder (ed.), *The archaeology of contextual meanings*, Cambridge: Cambridge University Press (*New Directions* in Archaeology), 39–54

Soly, H. 1977, *Urbanisme en kapitalisme in de 16de eeuw. De stedebouwkundige en industriële onderneming van Guy van Schoonbeke*. Brussel: Gemeentekrediet van België (*Historische Uitgaven Pro Civitate, Series in-8*, 47)

Soly, H. 1991, 'Economische en sociale structuren: continuïteit en verandering' in Van der Stock (ed.) 1991, 30–44

Stephan, H.-G. 1987, *Die bemalte Irdenware der Renaissance in Mitteleuropa. Ausstrahlungen und Verbindungen im gesamteuropäischen Rahmen*, München: Deutscher Kunstverlag (*Forschungshefte herausgegeben vom Bayerischen Nationalmuseum München*, 12)

Stephan, H.-G. 1992, *Keramik der Renaissance im Oberweserraum und an der unteren Werra. Beiträge der Archäologie zur Erforschung der Sachkultur der frühen Neuzeit*, Köln: Rheinland-Verlag GmbH & Bonn: Dr. R. Habelt GmbH (*Zeitschrift für Archäologie des Mittelalters, Beiheft* 7)

Teltser, P.A. (ed.) 1995, *Evolutionary archaeology. Methodological issues*, Tucson & London

Temminck Groll, C.L. 1963, *Middeleeuwse stenen huizen te Utrecht en hun relatie met die van andere noordwesteuropese steden*, 's-Gravenhage: Martinus Nijhoff

Tijs, R. 1993, *Tot Cieraet deser stadt. Bouwtrant en bouwbeleid te Antwerpen van de middeleeuwen tot heden. Een culturrhistorische studie over de bouwtrant en de ontwikkeling van het stedebouwkundige beleid te Antwerpen van de 13de tot de 20ste eeuw.* Antwerpen

van der Leeuw, S.E. & Mcglade, J. (eds) 1997, *Time, process and structured transformation in archaeology*, London & New York

van der Leeuw, S.E. & Torrence, R. (eds) 1989, *What's new? A closer look at the process of innovation*

Van der Stock, J. (ed.) 1991, *Stad in Vlaanderen. Cultuur en maatschappij 1477–1787*, Brussel

Vanneste, D. 1987, *De pre-industriële Vlaamse stad: een*

sociaal-economische survey. Interne differentiatie te Gent en te Kortrijk op het einde van de 18de eeuw, Leuven (Acta Geographica Lovaniensia, 28)

Verhaeghe, F. 1977, De middeleeuwse landelijke bewoningssites in een deel van Veurne-Ambacht. Bijdrage tot de middeleeuwse archeologie, S.l. [Gent], doct. diss., ms

Verhaeghe, F. 1981, 'Moated sites in Flanders. Features and significance', in T.J. Hoekstra, H.L. Janssen & I.W.L. Moerman (eds), Liber Castellorum. 40 variaties op het thema kasteel, Zutphen: De Walburg Pers, 98–121

Verhaeghe, F. 1983, 'Low Countries medieval pottery imported into Scotland: notes on a minor trade. The third Gerald Dunning Lecture', Medieval Ceramics, 7, 1983, 3–43

Verhaeghe, F. 1986, 'Quelques épis de faîtage produits par les potiers flamands (13e–15e siècles)', in D. Deroeux (ed.), Terres cuites architecturales au moyen âge. Musée de Saint-Omer. Colloque des 7–9 juin 1985. Arras (Mémoires de la Commission départementale d'Histoire et d'Archéologie du Pas-de-Calais, XXII²), 108–56

Verhaeghe, F. 1986a, 'Les sites fossoyés du moyen âge en basse en moyenne Belgique: état de la question', in M. Bur (ed.), La maison forte au moyen âge. Actes de la Table ronde de Nancy – Pont-à-Mousson des 31 mai - 3 juin 1984, Paris: Editions du C.N.R.S., 55–86

Verhaeghe, F. 1987, 'La céramique en Flandre (XIIIe–XVe siècle): quelques aspects de l'évolution et de la concurrence', in Chapelot et al. (eds) 1987, 203–25

Verhaeghe, F. 1988, 'Post-medieval pottery research in Flanders and in the Waasland', in F. Verhaeghe F. & M. Otte (eds), Archéologie des Temps Modernes. Actes du Colloque international de Liège (23–26 avril 1985), Liège: Service de Préhistoire (E.R.A.U.L., 26), 227–326

Verhaeghe, F. 1989, 'La céramique très décorée du Bas Moyen Age en Flandre', in G. Blieck (ed.), Travaux du Groupe de Recherches et d'Etudes sur la Céramique dans le Nord-Pas-de-Calais. Actes du colloque de Lille (26–27 mars 1988). S.l. [Lille & Berck-sur-Mer]: C.R.A.D.C. (Nord-Ouest Archéologie, numéro hors-série), 19–113

Verhaeghe, F. 1989a, 'Middeleeuwse tuitkannen: metaal, ceramiek en ambachtelijke competitie', Westvlaamse Archaeologica, 5, nr. 3, 65–83

Verhaeghe, F. 1989b, 'Ewers and ewers. An aspect of competition between artisans', in [S. Myrvoll, S. (ed.)], Archaeology and the urban economy. Festschrift to Absjorn E. Herteig, S.l. [Bergen]: Historisk Museum & Universitetet i Bergen (Arkeologiske

Skrifter fra Historisk Museum, 5), 199–228

Verhaeghe, F. 1991, 'An aquamanile and some thoughts on ceramic competition with metal quality goods in the Middle Ages', in E. Lewis (ed.), Custom and ceramics. Essays presented to Kenneth Barton, Wickham: APE, 25–61

Verhaeghe, F. 1992, 'Light in the darkness: a ceramic lantern', in Gaimster & Redknap (eds) 1992, 167–76

Verhaeghe, F. 1994, 'L'espace civil et la ville. Rapport introductif', in P. Demolon, H. Galinié & F. Verhaeghe (eds), Archéologie des villes dans le Nord-Ouest de l'Europe (VIIe-XIIIe siècle). Actes du IVe Congrès International d'Archéologie Médiévale (Douai, 1991). Douai, Société Archéologique de Douai (Archaeologia Duacensis, 11 Maison des Sciences de la Ville de l'Université de Tours, 7), 145–90

Verhulst, A. 1990, Précis d'histoire rurale de la Belgique, Bruxelles: Editions de l'Université Libre de Bruxelles

Verhulst, A. 1995, Landschap en landbouw in middeleeuws Vlaanderen, S.l. [Brussel]: Gemeentekrediet van België

La ville et la transmission ... 1996. La ville et la transmission des valeurs culturelles au Bas Moyen Age et aux Temps Modernes – Die Städte und die Übertragung von kulturellen Werten im Spätmittelalter und in die Neuzeit – Cities and the transmission of cultural values in the Late Middle Ages and Early Modern Period. Actes – Abhandlungen – Records. 17e colloque internati onal – 17. Internationales Kolloquium – 7th International Colloquium, Spa, 16–19.V.1996, Bruxelles/Brussels: Crédit Communal de Belgique (Crédit Communal, Série in-8°, 96)

Voet, L., Verhulst, A., Asaert, G., De Nave, F., Soly, H. & Van Roey, J. 1978, De stad Antwerpen van de Romeinse tijd tot de 17de eeuw. Topografische studie rond het plan van Virgilius Bononiensis, 1565. S.l. [Brussel]: Gemeentekrediet van België (Historische Uitgaven Pro Civitate, Reeks in-4°, 7)

Weatherill, L. 1988, Consumer behaviour and material culture in Britain 1660–1760

Weatherill, L. 1994, 'The meaning of consumer behaviour in late seventeenth- and early eighteenth-century England', in Brewer & Porter (eds) 1993, 206–27

Wiegelmann, G. 1996, 'Thesen und Fragen zur Prägung von Nahrung und Tischkultur im Hanseraum', in Wiegelmann & Mohrmann (eds) 1996, 1–21

Wiegelmann, G. & Mohrmann, R.-E. (eds) 1996, Nahrung und Tischkultur im Hanseraum, Münster & New York

Zischka, U., Ottomeyer, H. & Bäumler, H. (eds) 1993, Die anständige Lust. Von Esskultur und Tafelsitten, München

4   Sampling or Proving 'Reality'? Co-ordinates for the evaluation of historical/ archaeology research

Helmut Hundsbichler

Originally I was invited to give a historical overview to this conference. The result is both a rather theoretical and a rather personal paper. Philosophy of history, historical anthropology and the theories of communication and daily life have contributed essential stimulations. My contribution represents the actual stage of reflection upon myself or, as to say, an 'archaeology of myself', which I have synthesised during the 23 years of my tenure as historian at the Institute where I work.[1] I want to draw in some of our Institute's experiences to exemplify certain problems of research into transition.

History and Transition

Since its beginning, our Institute has tried to follow, to adapt and to spread the most advanced model of historical research, the paradigm of the *Annales*.[2] Some years ago we extended the upper chronological limit of our interests from 1520 to 1620. The thesis behind this extension is also relevant for the organizers of the Transitions conference: the change from 'medieval' to 'early modern' material culture could not have proceeded as abruptly or as fundamentally as a rigid periodisation of history would perhaps suggest. In my opinion the analysis of the late medieval conditions allows us to unfold what was probably the crucial mechanism to stimulate the 1400 to 1600 transition.

In the 'traditional' medieval view everything which works or looks according to its intended purpose reveals God's plan and existence. The appropriate term is 'beautiful', and material things – fine arts, music or science – could serve as media for the purpose of visualising such 'beauty': unequalled joinery, a qualified scientific treatise or cultivated nature as well as, for example, consummate architecture or heavenly music or a 'beautiful' painting (Fig. 4.1). The 'beauty' of a late medieval painting was not defined by criteria of aesthetic delight or attraction or entertainment but exclusively by the intensity of religious didacticism and by the spirituality evoked in the observer's mind.[3]

The idea to associate 'beauty' with God followed a strictly conservative purpose: to show that God had created a perfect world. But the accent upon 'beauty' brought about something like a creeping inflation: the media required to visualize 'beauty' were challenged continuously and became more and more refined in the course of time. This way the originally conservative intention was infiltrated slowly by the perpetual steps of innovation, until the model overturned and promoted innovation as a constitutive principle to praise the 'beauty' of God. Nonsuch Palace[4] is an example for the final stage of that process, but its name may also serve as metaphor for the intention's flow: the means which were originally intended to praise God have been increasingly instrumentalised to enhance the prestige of self-admiring individuals. The intention to create 'beautiful' things yielded to the intention to create 'nonsuch' things. In this way transition could take its course wherever it was possible in order to

Fig. 4.1 *Medieval paintings combine religion and daily life, symbols and things, mentality and reality, past and present with one another. St Elizabeth demonstrates Christian Charity in a panel painting of c.1500 in the parochial church of Laufen (Bavaria) (Photograph: Institut für Realienkunde, Krems, Austria).*

- associate high perfection to an attitude or an action or a thing, or
- demonstrate accurate performance, or finally
- perhaps only to stimulate this intention.

Such change appears in many manifestations during the 1400–1600 period of transition. Most

indicatively, for instance, in 16th-century Germany the quality of craftsmen's work reached heights which have never been achieved before or thereafter.[5] Concerning that mechanism, the prerequisite to understand the 1400 to 1600 transition is to understand the conditions at the late medieval status of the process. In particular the fundamental change from 'beautiful' to 'non-such' would mean that the setting for material culture transition was not material culture itself, but mentality.[6] The understanding of transition, therefore, depends basically on understanding a changing medieval mentality. The German philosopher Hans Blumenberg has analyzed this field and found that the mental stimulus which initiated the dawning of modern times was the legitimation of curiosity.[7] Thereby curiosity, which was regarded as sinful since early Christianity (*curiositas*), became an ideal for the education of European noblemen during the 17th century (*curiosité*).[8]

To demonstrate the influence of mentality on material culture I refer to a diagram which was developed by Ewald Kislinger, a Byzantine scholar from Vienna.[9] In the research of material culture, things are only the smallest units to be considered, and not at all an exhaustive aspect of human life (Fig. 4.2). They can only be fully understood in correlation to a person. The scene for this correlation is daily life which is strongly coherent with structures and mentalities. And within this highly complex context, structures and mentalities re-influence daily life and persons and things. This correlation shows

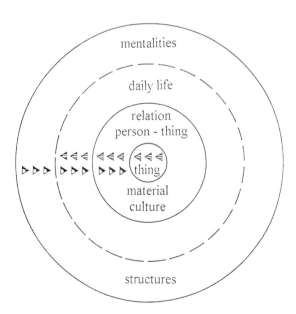

Fig. 4.2 *The correlation things and mentalities – mentalities and things (After Hundsbichler 1991, 93, fig. 3).*

that the field of material culture research may not at all be restricted to the mere study of things but demands a multi- and/or inter-disciplinary approach (the *sciences humaines* in the words of the *Annales*-school).[10]

Everybody is familiar with both the boom in publications on medieval topics and the subsequent wave of interest in the early modern period – but on the other hand it is comparatively hard to find books which focus on the 15th and 16th centuries,[11] much less on the question of transition. One reason may be that the process of change and innovation began before 1400 and continued after 1600. In addition, periodisations may follow diverging criteria.[12] One of the few who regarded transition from the Middle Ages to early modern times as a coherent period was Egon Friedell writing in the 1920s. In his view, which I strongly support, two traumatic events in the history of continental Europe were decisive: the Black Death and the Thirty Years' War. In this way he identified the period 1347–1618 as one of transition, one which corresponds closely to the scope of this conference.[13]

In the field of material culture and daily life, no systematic research on the 1400–1600 transition is being conducted in the German speaking countries today. However, at least three groups of scholars have made contributions to this subject. They can be characterised as follows:

1) The first is represented by a complex of discipline subdivisions which is summarised under the German term *Volkskunde* (folk-life studies). In my opinion, the main merit of this branch has been to introduce advanced methods in the broad sense which include the context of things and functions, of individuals and culture, of innovation and continuity.[14] Unfortunately the research of German *Volkskunde* rarely covers the 15th century. With regard to a process such as transition it should be mentioned that in 1969 Hermann Bausinger published a set of criteria which show that change in material culture is much more probable than constancy.[15]

2) As the second group I mention our Institute, founded by the Austrian Academy of Sciences. On the one hand the Institute offers a unique data-bank of Central European pictorial sources to support studies of daily life and material culture of the period

between 1200 and 1620. The upper chronological limit indicates that we are conscious of the process of transition. On the other hand we propagate both appropriate methodical access and a theoretical framework and thus are sometimes criticised for not doing enough 'practical' work. As the Institute's former field of activities concerned the late medieval period, only a few of our biennial conferences considered the transition between 'the Middle Ages and the early modern period'. With this being a rather too general chronological definition,[16] none of the conference proceedings touch diachronic aspects of their topics nor questions of transition in the narrower sense.

3) The third and (at least in Germany) by far the largest and accordingly most important group are the archaeologists. It must be emphasised that medieval archaeologists, following the stratigraphic continuity, were the first who consequently started to include the early modern period. On the one hand they may be characterised by introducing new methods, activities and results. On the other hand Wolfgang Seidenspinner, representing the advanced level of modern *Volkskunde*, pointed out a considerable theoretical void facing medieval archaeologists in Germany.[17] This failing splits German speaking archaeologists into two quite different parties.

To the more 'narrow-minded' group it appeared controversial[18] when I started a similar discussion on the relation between historical and archaeological research in 1989.[19] They claim essential differences between archaeological and historical research, and I do not.[20] In my opinion it only matters to become aware of the congruences. To some extent this is a problem of terminology or, in a wider context, a problem of communication. An effort to avoid that sterile dualism is integrated into my article: I naturally include 'the' archaeologist, whenever I mention 'the' historian, and whatever I postulate for historians, I do equally for archaeologists. This is not a random priority claim for history but an expression of the fact that there does not exist a more universally valid term than *historia*[21] which is the most common denominator for a wide range of 'different' disciplines. In that sense, at least in my opinion, interdisciplinarity is a fundamental part of

my contribution (although I put no special emphasis on it):[22] it is possible to consider history in many ways. On the one hand, none of them is sufficient, on the other hand nobody will ever be able to cover all of them. However, the many and different disciplines which help to consider history should regard the attribute 'historical' not simply in its chronological meaning or as term to separate a certain discipline,[23] but particularly as a theoretical challenge. Even the Austrian geologists who proved that the Great Flood was a real event 9,950 years ago had to organise their scientific thought according to historical principles.[24] Whoever is doing research into the past should feel obliged to think in the way of historians. This is not an arrogant demand of learned historians. It apparently is the basic principle to make multi-disciplinary views of the past comparable/compatible and to discuss/improve them seriously.[25]

What I want to point out, therefore, is our access towards history and our handling of history. Searching for historical reality is much more than gathering records or describing things and even more than explaining the past. In that sense we also have to regard in what way the 'historian' him/herself is integrated both into history and into the process of historical re-view: history continuously took/takes place as *histoire totale*. Each historical process was starting 'then' (whenever and wherever a certain subject of actual re-view came into being) and is ending currently 'now', with every single breath of a re-viewing historian. Each of us thus represents one of innumerous individual ends of that process: historical re-view necessarily divides the broad stream of universal history into separate strings which depend on the view, the knowledge and the experience of individuals who are 'looking back'. And, moreover, the historical process is not complete with 'final' results, as every update of knowledge and experience are a repercussion on the individual researcher and changes his/her mind, personality and previous views.[26] Whoever has burnt their tongue will become more cautious henceforth in eating or drinking hot things. And a final and generalising conclusion would suggest that fire/heat/energy have the power to transform things.

With respect to historical reality, this processual circle is more important than results in the narrower sense. The historical process modifies former questions and/or opinions and initiates new ones. New knowledge, of course, does not change history. It only reveals what we have not seen of history before. This way the processuality of historical research brings about a continuous rewriting of history.[27] Even sensational results and breathtaking findings are only preliminary. Consequently the historian should accommodate the intensity of his/her efforts more properly: after history has taken place, it can be revealed and discovered, making sense of historical realities by interaction with history. But the reality of the past cannot be proved, because it is a processual sequence of unrepeatable, unique, individually determined precedences, each of which has the character of a sample.

In that sense all of us are looking upon the same history, which (as I have said) can be done in different ways and with accordingly different results. Peter Ustinov recently wrote in an Austrian newspaper that it is the same thing with reality and the chandelier in a ballroom: everybody can see it – but constantly from another perspective. So it makes no sense to propagate a certain or only one or even 'the' method to study a historical period such as transition or a historical aspect such as material culture. John Moreland expressed this with a lovely metaphor: the 'looking-glass of possibilities'.[28] It is very important though not to over estimate or to misinterpret the plurality of methodologies. That plurality is not a matter of arbitrariness or boundlessness, but on the contrary the result of considerable limitations which occur if we want to find historical reality.[29] There always remains a huge gap between the authentic reality of history and our facilities to reveal and to discover and to understand that reality. These limitations originate from:

– the character of the sources
– the disposition of the researchers (of ourselves)
– the character of historical research

1st limitation: the character of the sources

What we call sources – texts, pictures or things – were originally intended to convey intentions, not history: they came into being as media, and historical

research should aim to utilise them as media. None of the sources was created to answer the questions of our research. They never answer exhaustively, and they never answer in our language. Medieval pictures are a case in point (Fig. 4.1). Almost exclusively their purpose was religious didacticism. They intended to show the connection of daily life and salvation, but they do this in a genuine way: reassuming the words of the Bible or the legends of Saints, they transpose historical events into current actuality, and they emphasise metaphoric realities, and they may combine a number of contents within one single scene. The example shown in Figure 4.1, for instance, simultaneously visualises four issues of the seven exhortations to practice Christian charity (to give food to those who are hungry; to give drinks to those who are thirsty; to give shelter to those who are travelling; to support those who are sick). Thus the sampling of things depends on the religious meaning of the picture. Moreover, historical sources (including pictures and archaeological material) are neither historical reality nor the results of historical research. Having the character of media they require appropriate decoding and interpretation. The sources represent a considerably reduced number of traces of that former context. Therefore they offer only a small fraction of information about the past.

Considering material culture, the basic requirement if we are to understand and to interpret the sources is to look for the authentic context of things within daily life and daily use.[30] That context is, in addition to 'the' thing itself, determined by an individual person, by a certain situation and by certain qualities (Fig. 4.3). Depending on the natural plurality of individuals, things, situations and qualities, the correlations among those contextual determinants correspond to an infinite plurality. Daily life, therefore, does not represent 'a' certain reality, but simultaneously consists of innumerable, diverse and different individual realities next to each other. And the closer we utilise the 'looking glass of possibilities', the more we will find non-simultaneous realities existing simultaneously.[31] For example, religious thought lost its predominance in the course of transition period, but it neither disappeared nor lost its validity.

The limited access towards historical reality can

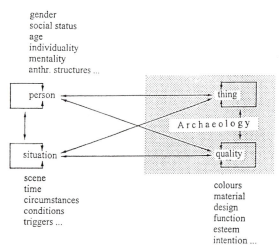

gender
social status
age
individuality
mentality
anthr. structures ...

scene
time
circumstances
conditions
triggers ...

colours
material
design
function
esteem
intention ...

Fig. 4.3 *The context of things within daily life and daily use: a matter of plurality. After Jaritz 1989, 13, graph 1, and Tauber 1992, 725, fig. 1.*

be confirmed very impressively in the case of archaeological sources: 'As it has been beautifully expressed more than once, an archaeologist is working with a sample (what he has excavated) of a sample (what has survived) of a sample (what has been deposited) of a sample (the material culture) of the past.'[32] Anyhow, this represents four levels filtering the validity of evidence and information. In addition, every artefact which has passed into the ground by this means has lost its connexion with the reality of daily life (the authentic context). Therefore, what archaeologists excavate was actually worn out and discarded.[33] And finally, it is the genuine characteristic of excavations that they destroy what remains of the authentic context.[34] Equally drastic words would be appropriate for written sources or pictures.[35] Only a synthesis of things, written evidence and pictures may claim an adequate degree of probability, as they also in 'real' life form a unified, coherent context. Such a view shows that it is with the sources that multi-discipinarity originates.[36] But source-embracing multi-disciplinarity can be misunderstood and misused within material culture research, at least in German speaking countries. The misunderstanding is based on the intention to verify mono-disciplinary evidence (for example that of an archaeologist) by gathering so called 'parallels' from other kinds of sources.[37] This is a misguided intention. It makes no sense to confirm the same result by more and more equivalent evidence. Normally you will find different answers (different 'realities') if you ask the same question amongst different types of sources: the colours of cloths which are listed in late medieval probate inventories, for example, have quite another frequency than those represented in paintings.[38] And only around ten per cent of the medieval belt buckles studied in German museums by Ilse Fingerlin are comparable to the contemporaneous ones excavated in Switzerland.[39] So the intention should be turned the other way round: calculating with different answers, the questions to be asked must not be pre-fabricated, but should be accommodated to the character and the structure and the 'power'[40] of the sources concerned. Take for instance a painting of c.1430 originating from Salzburg, which apparently shows a kitchen (Fig. 4.4): you will more easily recognise the architectural context of this detail if you are familiar with a corresponding element in the archaeological evidence (Fig. 4.5), although the archaeological evidence originates from a quite distant place (the so-called Husterknupp in Nordrhein-Westfalen) and from quite a distant time (400 years before).[41] Or the other way round, if the archaeological evidence should have occurred first: the example from Salzburg could help to define the open niche in front of the house as the kitchen. In this way sources are permitted to illuminate each other in an interactive way through the comparison of structures.[42]

In conclusion we can say though the limits of reality cannot exceed the degrees of reality as far as they are represented by the sources. Historical reality in the discriminate sense of Leopold Ranke ('*wie es eigentlich gewesen*') is an illusion: it neither exists as 'the' method of historical research nor as 'the' historical reality, and it is highly advisable to write or at least to think the term 'reality' in quotation-marks. There does not appear an immediate access to history, which means, that historical reality in the strict sense is beyond the historian's range.[43]

Fig. 4.4, left *The kitchen is evident, but additional evidence is necessary to imagine the entire house. illumination from Schondoch's 'History of the French Queen': The discovery of the repudiated queen (detail). Salzburg, around 1430. Vienna, National Library, cod. 2675*, fol. 7ᵛ (Photograph: Institut für Realienkunde, Krems, Austria).*

Fig. 4.5, above *An entire house is 'reconstructed', but additional evidence is necessary to define a detail like the niche in its front. Reconstruction of house number 3, motte Husterknupp (Nordrhein-Westfalen), 11th century (From Fehring 1986, 48, Fig. 5).*

2nd limitation: the disposition of ourselves

Another and probably the most important fact which necessarily leads to a plurality of realities is the individuality of the reviewing historians. This phenomenon originates from our self-centred, egocentric disposition. That is not a reproach which anybody can repudiate, because egocentricity is an anthropological constant. It is determined on the genetic level, and it is the pre-condition anyway to recognise the environment.[44] In consequence this means that egocentricity also influences our research into (historical) reality. Any research can be clearly defined as a continuous confrontation of own and foreign positions. For the historian the research into history is quite the same as a confrontation with a foreign, unknown culture. This is easily comprehensible for everyone who has learned by experience,

how much knowledge is necessary to understand, for example, a historical picture.[45]

The historian's foreignness with history and his/her distance from history can be characterised by the position of an 'observer'. The 'cultural filters' of the outsider prevent that immediate understanding, which would be characteristic for an insider and 'participant', who has much more background information and a higher competence.[46] Therefore, our historical sensitivity depends to a high degree on our consciousness and handling of egocentricity. Apparently it would be an accurate compensation to integrate the theory of foreignness more concisely into the framework of historical methods.

To evaluate potential prejudices of historians towards historical reality we should consider the wide spectrum of general attitudes towards foreigness: there are considerable contrasts between

- – fascination and fear
- – tolerance and dominance
- – awareness and repression
- – recognising and marvelling at the foreign
- – sensitivity and voyeurism
- – insight and lack of understanding
- – acceptance and arrogance
- – the spirit of partnership and expropriation
- – respect and occupation or even destruction of the foreign

The metaphor 'foreigness' illustrates clearly, that for the comprehension of reality there always exists a wide spectrum between quite different points of view, that is between one's own and the foreign one. They can be so completely opposite that they even may exclude each other. This statement is fully in accord with firm insights of psychology and philosophy. I quote my compatriots Paul Watzlawick, Fritz Wallner and Karl Popper: an absolute reality does not exist. There are only subjective, sometimes totally contradictory, concepts of reality, which are assumed to coincide with 'the true' reality.[47] We must not assume that a certain view of history could be confirmed or proved to be true or that any series of historical records could ever be interpreted in only one way.[48] For the same reason our questions towards history and the results of our historical research depend to a very high degree on ourselves: on our individual interests, intentions, mentalities, levels of knowledge and points of view.

If the historian derives his/her questions from the context of present time and individual knowledge and actual interests, he/she is providing the historical sources with an additional meaning, which was not conscious to or interesting for the contemporaries. This happens above all if criteria and definitions of nowadays are utilised, although such a view naturally was not relevant during history. A book, for instance, was quite a different thing for a monk of the 11th century than it was for Gutenberg, and it became quite another thing for the time after Gutenberg than it was for himself. Other examples would be topics such as beauty or gender or mobility or the differentiation in living space in the early modern period or consumption rates in the food supply, and an endless

list of others – not to forget transition. Here we find a phenomenon which constitutes the value of history: a meaning or a sense or a message is not implicitly inherent to history but depends exclusively on human reflection,[49] i.e. on a person who finds a meaning or sense or message (after he/she has burnt the tongue, to refer to the example quoted above). Insofar we can note a 'power' of sources.[50] Apparently this is a crucial point, because that additional meaning is determined individually and therefore never will match individually determined authentic context. Here we arrive at the third limitation of our access towards history.

3rd limitation: the character of historical research

If it is the intention of historical research to clarify the former, the authentic, the foreign reality, it seems to be the historian's main task to decode history and to free it from its foreignness (in German: *entfremden*). But this is a deceptive and unattainable aim. As we have seen it is not possible to define or to touch historical reality, and thus history must remain foreign, remote. Nobody can enter the past, so to say, and if so, this would literally mean turning back in time and either re-absolving a 1:1 copy of history or changing history after the event, which is not possible.[51] The unbridgeable distance is the main characteristic of history and remains the fundamental phenomenon of historical research.

The foreign and distant and irreversible history allows access only by means of mediation.[52] Such mediation takes place on three levels: the primary media consist of the sources. The second and the actually creative step of mediation is constituted by human investigation, interpretation and reflection. And the final step of mediation is the dissemination of results through lectures, publications, graphs, pictures and photographs, exhibitions, data-banks, CD-ROMs, theatre, sculptures, films, music and so on.

Remember here two other excellent metaphors. For Barbara Tuchman history is 'a distant mirror'.[53] And Karl Popper introduced the metaphor of a spotlight to characterise the situation of the historian in relation to history: the spotlight is fixed in a certain position and lights up only a sector of that dark context which we actually would like to illuminate in total.[54] The German historian Hans-Werner Goetz utilises a similar image to point out the characteristic individuality of the historian's view (Fig. 4.6). The historical view results from a number of sources which were focused and, so to say, processed in the historian's mind.[55]

The image shown in Figure 4.6 may be modified to visualise an additional observation of highest importance: the essential difference between multi-disciplinarity and inter-disciplinarity. It is important to distinguish them clearly,[56] because too often what is called inter-disciplinarity would be actually multi-disciplinarity. A multi-disciplinary concept is characterised by a series of different disciplines represented by different persons, whilst in the case of inter-disciplinarity there exists an 'interface' of disciplines which coincides with the mind of one individual person (Fig. 4.7). This is no more an additional, but a processual concept.[57]

Despite many potential deficiencies (including the inevitable subjectivism, the individual pre-occupations and the possibilities of error which may originate from a pleasure seeking use of media), the interpreter's part is of crucial importance in mediating history.[58] The historian has to communicate with an actual existing, but not concrete partner. This is a one-sided and genuinely mental communication. It demands sensitive and respectful partnership, with tolerance towards the foreign, and it should avoid authoritarian or colonial overtones. And the result of such a mental communication, of course, is a mental one and not a material one: historical research never constitutes real history, but 'only' the images and views of history in the historian's mind. Such images and views are evidently not historical realities, but present realities, and until the historian makes them public by imparting media, they exist only as virtual realities. Even the most elaborate 'reconstruction' or 'copy' or 'replica' represents a present and not a historical reality. Thus historical research does not constitute the past: it only constitutes a certain presence of the past.[59] I will illustrate this with a 'reconstruction', which an Austrian ethnologist derived from a deed written in 1303 to divide a house:[60] Although the house no longer exists,

critical analysis of the document allowed him to 'imagine' its interior structure (Fig. 4.8).

This example shows the creative aspect in the mediating work of the historian. This creative aspect led David Austin to the metaphoric role of archaeologists (and in my sense I add historians) as 'poets'. Based on individual interpretation and depending on the plurality of imparting media, every archaeologist/historian would be able to elaborate his/her singular 'text' about history.[61] I agree with David, but my own favourite and perhaps more universal metaphor for the archaeologist/historian is the term *homo faber* (in the sense of the 'maker').[62]

I especially like this metaphor because of its implicit ambiguity: it points to favourable as well as to alarming characteristics, and this way it demands an ethical responsibility from historians. If the historian first of all 'makes' virtual reality, this facility can (but should not) become a drug for the 'maker' or a means of power towards his/her customers. Furthermore, if the reality of the past is unattainable for historians, it cannot consequently be the real aim of historical research to regard, describe or to explain merely the past. The sense of history actually involves learning.[63] Learning depends on understanding, which has quite another quality in addition to simply describing: it means creating a relationship between two distant contexts, the principle of which is shown in Figures 4.6 & 4.7. This is the most decisive activity in the creative work of the historian, and it does not get under way without that repercussion which we have discussed above. The means of understanding historical contexts and learning by history is that of a 'translation', as Fritz Wallner has shown: to understand the 'foreign' meaning of a historical precedence it has to be mentally transplanted into a well-known context. This way experience illuminates that distant and 'foreign' historical context. Or *vice versa*, after a formerly distant and 'foreign' context has been understood it may illuminate actual experience. Thus the means of such understanding and 'translation' is the 'alienation' of experience (in German: *Verfremdung*).[64] It is quite the same process as the understanding of a metaphor or a proverb or a joke or the Bible, and even everyday conversation follows the same principle. Another example was that of the

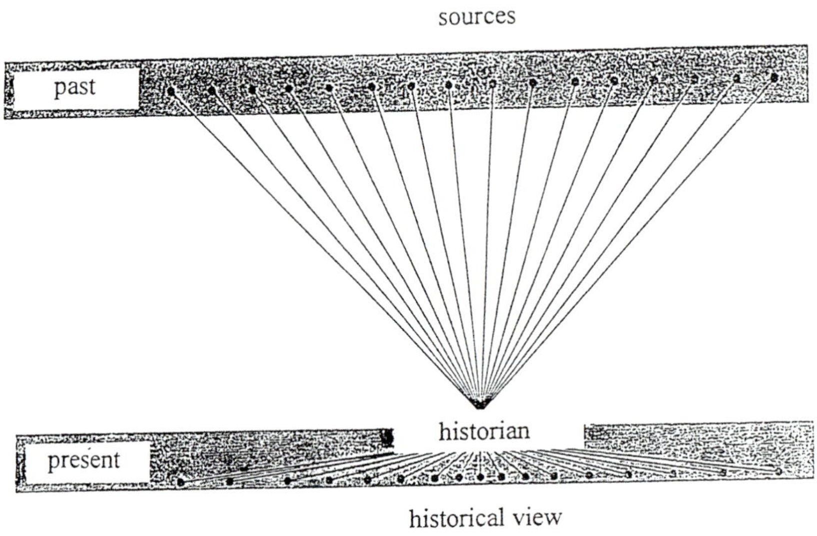

sources

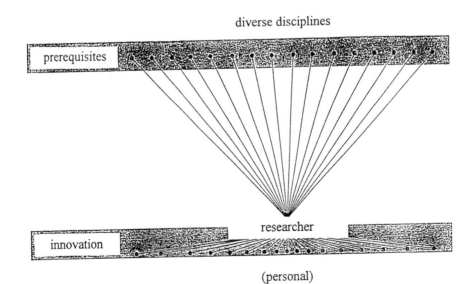

Fig. 4.6 *The individuality of historical view. After Goetz 1993, 22, fig. 3.*

diverse disciplines

Fig. 4.7 *The individuality of interdisciplinarity (a 'translation' of Fig. 4.6 by means of 'alienation').*

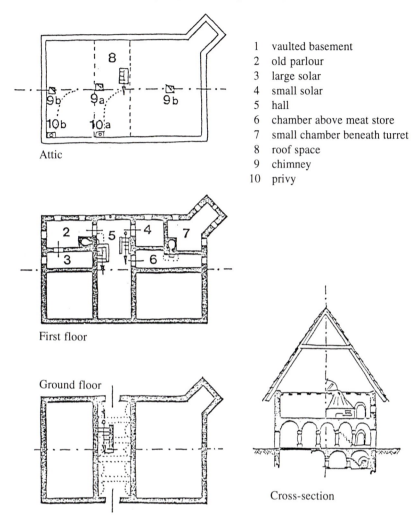

1 vaulted basement
2 old parlour
3 large solar
4 small solar
5 hall
6 chamber above meat store
7 small chamber beneath turret
8 roof space
9 chimney
10 privy

Attic

First floor

Ground floor

Cross-section

Fig. 4.8 The historian/archaeologist as 'homo faber': 'Reconstruction' of a medieval house based on a written source. The example demonstrates the creative aspect of the historian's work. After Moser 1975, 281.

burnt tongue, and one more was given just above by the 'alienation' of Figure 4.6 (the historian's view) to demonstrate the proper character of interdisciplinarity (Fig. 4.7).

The aspect of learning shows that historical research does not mean a one-way ticket back to the past, but rather improves present knowledge and individual experience and thus substantiates the future. The sense of historical research is fulfilled whenever the historian realises the example of him/ herself or his/her actual interests and problems in the 'distant mirror' of a historical precedence.[65]

Conclusion

I will conclude by trying to demonstrate that reciprocity of 'translation'/'alienation' and by examining my favourite picture of c.1500: the foolish scholar, whom Sebastian Brant introduced as the prototype symbol of 111 further variations of distorted, foolish intentions (Fig. 4.9). A fool is Brant's professor for evident reasons. He accumulates a treasury of books for promoting his image, but in fact they are useless: instead of reading and understanding them he prefers to defend them from

Fig. 4.9 *The foolish scholar representing the archetype of the* homo faber's *distorted intentions.* Von unnutzen buchern *['about useless books'], woodcut, illustrating the initial chapter of Sebastian Brant's 'Narrenschiff'. Albrecht Dürer, c.1494. From Lemmer 1986, 7.*

flies.[66] He is not conscious of his responsibility and the sense of his research. Thus he estimates lowest material criteria (number and cleanliness of books) higher than criteria of quality (communication, understanding). This way we can recognise that the foolish professor is a timeless reminder of the *homo faber's* potential deficiencies: a 'distant mirror' of habits which may unwittingly direct the research of present historians into inefficiency.[67]

Perhaps some of the ideas which I have communicated here may also appear rather foolish, or let us say sophisticated, theoretical, ivory-towered. But as far as I have learned by my own experience they are useful and necessary in reminding us of the 'maker's' potential autocracy in historical/archaeology research and thus help to uncover the manifold power of reality.

Notes

1. For the research of that Institute see Hundsbichler 1982; *idem* 1997a; for methods applied see Jaritz 1989; a bibliography of the Institute's publications: Zwanzig Jahre 1992.
2. Le Goff *et al.* 1978; Burke 1990; Middell & Sammler 1994; an additional list of titles in Raulff 1987, 15, fn. 2. It may be mentioned here that this model was originally initiated by the German historian Karl Lamprecht c.1900 (Fuhrmann 1987, 271 f.).
3. Cf. Jaritz 1989, 71–92; Assunto 1982; Eco 1987.
4. Biddle, forthcoming.
5. Friedell 1976, 327 ff.
6. Cf. Borst 1973; Gurjewitsch 1980; Graus 1987; Dinzelbacher 1993; Kortüm 1996.
7. Blumenberg 1988.
8. Müller 1984, 252.
9. Kislinger 1987; cf. Hundsbichler 1991, 92 ff.
10. Hundsbichler 1996.
11. For instance: La Famiglia 1986; Ertzdorff 1989.
12. Cf., for instance, Meckseper 1985; Bitterli 1986.
13. Friedell 1976, first published in 1927.
14. Gerndt 1997; cf. also Wernhart 1986.
15. Bausinger 1969; cf. Hundsbichler 1986; Pounds 1997.
16. The topics involved were the relatives persons – things; pilgrimage and daily life; communication and daily life; cf. *Veröffentlichungen* 13, 14, and 15 = Sitzungsberichte 568, 592, and 596.
17. Seidenspinner 1986/7; cf. also Hundsbichler 1991; Tauber 1991b, 7–12; *idem* 1992, 701–10; *idem* 1996.
18. Cf. Scholkmann 1997, in press.
19. Hundsbichler 1991.
20. *Idem* 1996, 11–15; cf. Schnapp 1996.
21. Le Goff 1990, 52.
22. For this aspect, cf. Hundsbichler 1996, 20 ff.; *idem* 1998, in press; Kocka 1987; Wallner 1990, *passim*.
23. Cf., for example, the pleonastic term 'historische Archäologie' in Germany.
24. Tollmann & Tollmann 1991 (with summary in English on pp. 2–5); *idem* 1993.
25. Hundsbichler 1996, 11 ff.
26. The process of learning, see also below ('translation', 'alienation', understanding). I tried to illustrate this aspect by a flow chart: see Hundsbichler 1996, 13, Fig. 1, and *idem* 1997, in press, Fig. 5.
27. Raulff 1986.
28. Moreland 1997, in press.
29. Cf. Pernoud 1979, 132–54 (Geschichte, Vorstellungen und Phantasie).
30. See Jaritz 1989, 13 ff. (with references).

31. Hundsbichler 1996, 15 ff.
32. Janssen 1990, 404.
33. Steuer 1997, in press.
34. Fehring 1987, 49.
35. Cf. Hundsbichler 1997, in press.
36. *Idem* 1991, 87.
37. Cf., for example, Steffens 1979, 171; Mittler & Werner 1989; cf. also the request not to prove reality which was discussed above.
38. Jaritz 1984a.
39. Remark of Werner Meyer discussing Jaritz 1984b, 39.
40. Cf. note 50.
41. Hinz 1991.
42. For such efforts within the discipline *Volkskunde*, see Reichmann 1976, 44 ff. ('*wechselseitige Erhellung*' by considering things as well as the meaning of their names, the method of '*Wörter und Sachen*'); Wiegelmann 1967, 10 ff. (three variations of the so called '*Analogieschluß*', a critical comparative exchange of information between different manifestations of the same phenomenon, if normal methods don't work); see also below concerning 'translation', 'alienation'.
43. Heintel 1960; Brunner 1995; Steuer 1997, in press; Moreland 1997, in press.
44. Greverus 1972; Schäffter 1991; Hundsbichler 1993.
45. Cf. once again Fig. 1; fn. 3; fn. 46.
46. Jaritz 1989, 71 ff. (following Michael Baxandall).
47. Watzlawick 1992, 21; cf. Wallner 1990, 39–57.
48. Popper 1995, 183 ff.
49. *Ibid.* 189 ff.
50. Cf. Freedberg 1989 (concerning pictures).
51. Heintel 1960.
52. Hundsbichler 1997, in press.
53. Tuchman 1978.
54. Popper 1995, 175.
55. Goetz 1993, 22.
56. Cf. Wallner 1990, 18–27; Hundsbichler 1996, 20 ff.; *idem* 1998, in press.
57. Wallner 1993, 5.
58. Hundsbichler 1996, 19 ff.; *idem* 1997, in press.
59. Steuer 1997, in press; Schnapp 1996, 11–38.
60. Moser 1975.
61. Austin 1997, in press.
62. See, Hundsbichler 1996, 23 ff.
63. Knape 1984, 238–400 (Historie als literarischer Terminus technicus vom 15. bis 17. Jahrhundert).
64. Wallner 1990, *passim*.
65. Cf. Settis 1986.
66. See Lemmer 1986, 7.
67. Wallner 1990, 49–80; Hundsbichler 1996, 23 ff.

Bibliography

Alltag und Fortschritt 1986, 'Alltag und Fortschritt im Mittelalter', *Veröffentlichungen* 8 = *Sitzungsberichte* 470, Wien

Alltag und Sachkultur 1984, 'Die Erforschung von Alltag und Sachkultur des Mittelalters. Methode – Ziel – Verwirklichung', *Veröffentlichungen* 6 = *Sitzungsberichte* 433, Wien

Assunto, R. 1982, 'Die Theorie des Schönen im Mittelalter', *dumont Taschenbücher* 117, Köln

Austin, D. 1997, 'Private and Public: An Archaeological Consideration of Things', in Vielfalt 1997, in press

Bausinger, H. 1969, 'Zur Algebra der Kontinuität', in Bausinger & Brückner 1969, 9–30

Bausinger, H. and Brückner, W. (eds) 1969, *Kontinuität? Geschichtlichkeit und Dauer als volkskundliches Problem*, Berlin

Biddle, M. forthcoming, *Excavations at Nonsuch Palace*

Bitterli, U. 1986, *Alte Welt – neue Welt. Formen des europäisch-überseeischen Kulturkontakts vom 15. bis zum 18. Jahrhundert*, München

Blaschitz *et al.* 1992, Blaschitz, G., Hundsbichler, H., Jaritz, G., and Vavra, E. (eds), *Symbole des Alltags – Alltag der Symbole. Festschrift für Harry Kühnel zum 65. Geburtstag*, Graz

Blumenberg, H. 1988, 'Die Legitimität der Neuzeit', *suhrkamp taschenbuch wissenschaft* 24, Frankfurt/M.

Borst, A. 1973, *Lebensformen im Mittelalter*, Frankfurt/ M.

Brunner, K. 1995, 'Fiktion der Wirklichkeit', in Wallner, F. G. and Schimmer, J. (eds) 1995, *Wissenschaft und Alltag. Symposionsbeiträge zum Konstruktiven Realismus*, Wien

Burke, P. (ed.) 1990, *The French Historical Revolution. The Annales School, 1929–89*, Cambridge

Dinzelbacher, P. (ed.) 1993, 'Europäische Mentalitätsgeschichte. Hauptthemen in Einzeldarstellungen', *Kröners Taschenausgabe* 469, Stuttgart

Eco, U. 1987, *Arte e bellezza nell'estetica medievale*, Milano

Ertzdorff, X. v. (ed.) 1989, *Romane und Novellen des 15. und 16. Jahrhunderts in Deutschland*, Darmstadt

La Famiglia 1986, 'La famiglia e la vita quotidiana in Europa dal '400 al '600', *Pubblicazioni degli archivi di stato, saggi* 4, Roma

Fansa, M. (ed.) 1996, 'Realienforschung und Historische Quellen', *Archäologische Mitteilungen aus Nordwestdeutschland, Beiheft* 15, Oldenburg

Fehring, G.P. 1986, 'Städtischer Hausbau in Norddeutschland von 1150 bis 1250', in Steuer 1986, 44–61

Fehring, G.P. 1987, *Einführung in die Archäologie des Mittelalters*, Darmstadt

Freedberg, D. 1989, *The Power of Images: Studies in the History and Theory of Response*, Chicago

Friedell, E. 1976, *Kulturgeschichte der Neuzeit. Die Krisis der europäischen Seele von der schwarzen Pest bis zum Ersten Weltkrieg*, vol. 1, München, 57–408 (Erstes Buch: Von der schwarzen Pest bis zum Dreißigjährigen Krieg)

Fuhrmann, H. 1987, *Einladung ins Mittelalter*, München

Gerndt, H. 1997, 'Studienskript Volkskunde. Eine Handreichung für Studierende', *Münchener Beiträge zur Volkskunde* 20, 3rd ed., Münster, New York, München, Berlin

Goetz, H.-W. 1993, 'Proseminar Geschichte: Mittelalter', *Uni-Taschenbücher* 1719, Stuttgart

Graus, F. (ed.) 1987, 'Mentalitäten im Mittelalter. Methodische und inhaltliche Probleme', *Vorträge und Forschungen* 35, Sigmaringen

Greverus, I.-M, 1972, *Der territoriale Mensch. Ein literaturanthropologischer Versuch zum Heimatphänomen*, Frankfurt/M.

Gurjewitsch A. J. 1980, *Das Weltbild des mittelalterlichen Menschen*, München

Heintel, E. 1960, 'Wie es eigentlich gewesen ist. Ein geschichtsphilosophischer Beitrag zum Problem der Methode der Historie', in *Erkenntnis und Verantwortung. Festschrift für Theodor Litt*, Düsseldorf, 207–30

Hinz, H. 1991, 'Husterknupp', in *Lexikon des Mittelalters*, vol. 5, München, Zürich, 236 f.

Hundsbichler, H. 1982, 'Approaches to the Daily Life in the Middle Ages. Methods and aims of the Institut für mittelalterliche Realienkunde Österreichs', *Medium Aevum Quotidianum* 1, 11–25

Hundsbichler, H. 1986, 'Innovation und Kontinuität als Determinanten von Alltag und Fortschritt', in *Alltag und Fortschritt* 1986, 65–81

Hundsbichler, H. 1991, 'Perspektiven für die Archäologie des Mittelalters im Rahmen einer Alltagsgeschichte des Mittelalters', in Tauber 1991a, 85–99

Hundsbichler, H. 1993, 'Eigenwelten und das Fremde', in Bericht über den 19. Österreichischen Historikertag 1992, *Veröffentlichungen des Verbandes Österreichischer Historiker und Geschichtsvereine* 28, Wien, 361–64

Hundsbichler, H. 1996, 'Sachen und Menschen, Alltag und Geschichte. Faust und die Erkenntnis der Realität', in Fansa 1996, 11–28

Hundsbichler, H. 1997, 'Sachen und Menschen. Das Konzept Realienkunde', in *Vielfalt* 1997, in press

Hundsbichler, H. 1988, 'Interdisziplinarität und (spätmittelalterlicher) Alltag', *Medium Aevum Quotidianum*, in press

Janssen, H.L. 1990, 'Medieval Culture and the Problem of the Historical Interpretation of Archaeological Evidence: the Example of the Town of 's-Hertogenbosch', in *Mensch und Objekt* 1990, 397–438

Jaritz, G. 1984a, 'Bürgertestamente als Quellen zur Erforschung städtischer Lebensformen des Spätmittelalters', *Jahrbuch für Geschichte des Feudalismus* 8, 249–64

Jaritz, G. 1984b, 'Mittelalterliche Realienkunde: Quellenbefund und Quelleninterpretation', in *Alltag und Sachkultur* 1984, 33–44

Jaritz, G. 1989, *Zwischen Augenblick und Ewigkeit. Einführung in die Alltagsgeschichte des Mittelalters*, Wien, Köln

Kislinger, E. 1987, 'Notizen zur Realienkunde aus byzantinischer Sicht', *Medium Aevum Quotidianum* 9, 26–33

Knape, J. 1984, 'Historie in Mittelalter und früher Neuzeit. Begriffs- und gattungsgeschichtliche Untersuchungen im interdisziplinären Kontext', *Saecvla spiritalia* 10, Baden-Baden

Kocka, J. (ed.) 1987, *Interdisziplinarität. Praxis – Herausforderung – Ideologie*, Frankfurt/M.

Kortüm, H.-H. 1996, *Menschen und Mentalitäten. Einführung in Vorstellungswelten des Mittelalters*, Berlin

Le Goff et al. 1978, Le Goff, J., Chartier, R., and Revel, J. (eds), *La nouvelle histoire*, Paris

Le Goff, J. et al. 1990, Le Goff, J., Chartier, R., and Revel, J. (eds), *Die Rückeroberung des historischen Denkens. Die Grundlagen der Neuen Geschichtswissenschaft*, Frankfurt/M.

Le Goff, J. 1990, 'Neue Geschichtswissenschaft', in Le Goff et al. 1990, 11–61

Lemmer, M. (ed.) 1986, 'Sebastian Brant, Das Narrenschiff', *Neudrucke deutscher Literaturwerke, Neue Folge* 5, 3rd ed., Tübingen

Meckseper, C. (ed.) 1985, *Stadt im Wandel. Kunst und Kultur des Bürgertums in Norddeutschland 1150–1650*, 4 vols., Stuttgart, Bad Cannstatt

Mensch und Objekt 1990, Mensch und Objekt in Mittelalter und früher Neuzeit. Leben – Alltag – Kultur, *Veröffentlichungen* 13 = *Sitzungsberichte* 568, Wien

Middell, M. and Sammler, S. (eds.) 1994, *Alles Gewordene hat Geschichte. Die Schule der Annales 1929–1992*, Leipzig, 40–60

Mittler, E. and Werner, W. (eds) 1989, *Codex Manesse. Wörter – Bilder – Sachen. Die Welt des Codex Manesse. Ein Blick ins Mittelalter*, Heidelberg

Moreland, J., 'Through the Looking Glass of Possibilities. Understanding the Middle Ages', in *Vielfalt* 1997, in press

Moser, O. 1975, 'Die Räume eines Villacher Bürgerhauses um 1300', *Carinthia I* 165, 269–82

Müller, J.-D. 1984, '*Curiositas* und *erfarung* der Welt im frühen deutschen Prosaroman', in Grenzmann, L. and Stackmann, K. (eds), Literatur und Laienbildung im Spätmittelalter und in der Reformationszeit (*Germanistische Symposien-Berichtsbände* 5) Stuttgart

Patzelt, W.J. 1987, *Grundlagen der Ethnomethodologie. Theorie, Empirie und politikwissenschaftlicher Nutzen einer Soziologie des Alltags*, München

Pernoud, R. 1979, *Überflüssiges Mittelalter? Plädoyer für eine verkannte Epoche*, Zürich, München

Popper, K.R. 1995, 'Über Geschichtsschreibung und über den Sinn der Geschichte', in *idem* (ed.), *Alles Leben ist Problemlösen. Über Erkenntnis, Geschichte und Politik*, 5th ed., München, Zürich,173–205

Pounds, N.J.G., 'The Multiplicity of Things', in *Vielfalt* 1997, in press

Raulff, U. (ed.) 1986, 'Vom Umschreiben der Geschichte', *Wagenbachs Taschenbücherei* 131, Berlin

Raulff, U. (ed.) 1987, 'Mentalitäten-Geschichte', *Wagenbachs Taschenbücherie* 152, Berlin

Reichmann, O. 1976, *Germanistische Lexikologie*, Stuttgart

Schäffter, O. 1991, *Das Fremde. Erfahrungsmöglichkeiten zwischen Faszination und Bedrohung*, Opladen

Schnapp, A. 1996, *The Discovery of the Past. The Origins of Archaeology*

Scholkmann, B. 1997, 'Sachen und Menschen. Der Beitrag der archäologischen Mittelalter- und Neuzeitforschung', in *Vielfalt* 1997, in press

Seidenspinner, W. 1986/7, 'Mittelalterarchäologie und Volkskunde. Ein Beitrag zur Öffnung und zur Theoriebildung archäologischer Mittelalterforschung', *Zeitschrift für Archäologie des Mittelalters* 14/15, 9–48

Settis, S. 1986, 'Die Zeitmaschine. Über den Umgang mit Geschichte', in Raulff 1986, 147–53.

Sitzungsberichte, Sitzungsberichte der Österreichischen Akademie der Wissenschaften, philosophisch-historische Klasse

Steffens, H.-G. 1979, 'Der mittelalterliche Alltag nach zeitgenössischen Miniaturen', *Rotterdam Papers II: A Contribution to Medieval Archaeology*, Rotterdam, 171–5

Steuer, H. (ed.) 1986, 'Zur Lebensweise in der Stadt um 1200. Ergebnisse der Mittelalter-Archäologie', *Zeitschrift für Archäologie des Mittelalters, Beiheft* 4, Köln, Bonn

Steuer, H., 'Archäologie und Realität mittelalterlichen Alltagslebens', in *Vielfalt* 1997, in press

Tauber, J. (ed.) 1991a, 'Methoden und Perspektiven der Archäologie des Mittelalters', *Archäologie und Museum* 20, Liestal

Tauber, J. 1991b, 'Aspekte zu Möglichkeiten und Grenzen einer Archäologie des Mittelalters', in Tauber 1991a, 7–30

Tauber, J. 1992, 'Symbole im Alltag aus der Sicht der Archäologie. Ein Annäherungsversuch', in Blaschitz *et al.* 1992, 701–31

Tauber, J. 1996, 'Archäologische Funde und ihre Interpretation', in Fansa 1996, 171–87

Tollmann, E. and A. 1991, 'Der Sintflut-Impakt. The Flood impact', *Mitteilungen der österreichischen geologischen Gesellschaft* 84, 1–61

Tollmann, E. and A. 1993, *Ich habe die Sintflut erlebt*, München

Tuchman, B. 1978, *A Distant Mirror – The Calamitous 14th Century*, New York

Veröffentlichungen, Veröffentlichungen des Instituts für Realienkunde des Mittelalters und der frühen Neuzeit

Vielfalt 1997, *Die Vielfalt der Dinge*. Neue Wege zur Analyse mittelalterlicher Sachkultur, *Veröffentlichungen* 17 = *Sitzungsberichte*, Wien, in press

Wallner, F. 1990, 'Acht Vorlesungen über den Konstruktiven Realismus', *Cognitive Science* 1, Wien

Wallner, F. 1993, 'Die Geisteswissenschaften – eine Herausforderung', *Wissenschaftliche Nachrichten* 98/April, 4–6

Watzlawick, P. 1992, 'Wie Wirklich ist die Wirklichkeit? Wahn – Täuschung – Verstehen', *Serie Piper* 174, 21st ed., München

Wernhart, K. R. (ed.) 1986, 'Ethnohistorie und Kulturgeschichte. Ein Studienbehelf', *Böhlau-Studien-Bücher, Aspekte der Ethnologie* 1, Wien, Köln

Wiegelmann, G. 1967, Alltags- und Festspeisen. Wandel und gegenwärtige Stellung, *Atlas der deutschen Volkskunde, Neue Folge, Beiheft* 1, Marburg

Zwanzig Jahre 1992, 'Zwanzig Jahre Institut für Realienkunde', *Medium Aevum Quotidianum* 25, 63–95

5   Peasants and Farmers: rural settlements and landscapes in an age of transition

Christopher Dyer

The 15th and 16th centuries are famous as the era of 'enclosures', and for generations of historians, from Marx to Brenner, the birth of agrarian capitalism has been associated with this period.[1] Under feudalism, it was argued, peasants worked in egalitarian village communities in which subsistence needs were the main aim of production. Lords lived by extracting labour services and rents from their peasant tenants, many of whom were serfs. This society was destroyed by market forces in the age of transition. Peasants were either evicted or deprived of their land and depressed into agricultural labourers. The old village communities in which dozens of families made a living were replaced by a few farms, and the common fields were carved up into efficient enclosures. The gentry have often been identified by historians as the driving force behind this process, as they have a reputation for being especially ambitious and flexible. They transformed their own estates, and extended their influence by acquiring the lands of the monasteries after the Dissolution. This initiated a process which culminated in the 'agricultural revolution' in the 18th and 19th centuries.

Recent enquiries have shifted the emphasis away from the cataclysmic effects of enclosures, and change is seen as rooted in developments within rural society. The structure of the family is thought to have had a strong influence on the economy by encouraging individual initiative and responsibility. Studies of rural communities have traced the emergence of the 'middling sort' who moulded social behaviour through such mechanisms as the poor law.

Mentality, including attitudes towards wealth, status and consumption, receives more attention. Research into the economy has included a new preoccupation with productivity, on modest holdings as well as larger farms.[2] The organisation of production remains a key issue, and here settlement archaeology and landscape history can make a major contribution.

Evidence from documents, excavation and the landscape will be used here to show that there was a significant move towards capitalist farming, even in the earlier part of the period of transition, between 1400 and 1540. However, in line with recent research, less importance will be assigned to enclosures and the role of the gentry, and alternative paths of development will be considered.[3] In particular, this essay explores four themes. Firstly, the 'transitions' of our period could only take place after the commercial growth of the 13th century, an important example of medieval dynamism. Secondly, the changes of the 15th and 16th centuries involved the creation of new units of production, sometimes by replacing a whole village with a single farm, but more often by amalgamating holdings into larger units, and by leasing demesnes to form new tenant farms. This could lead to the reorganisation of the land, not just by consolidation and enclosure, but also occasionally by subdivision. These changes were not confined to nucleated villages and open field systems, but had their effects in every type of settlement and rural landscape. The third and related argument, while recognising the varied role of landlords who promoted change both directly and indirectly, also shows that many initiatives came from among the peasants, some of whom acquired land, produced marketable surpluses, and adopted the role of entrepreneurs. And fourthly, lest we exaggerate the impact of these individual activities, or under-estimate the strength of the old institutions, it has to be acknowledged that this period saw a flourishing of the village community.

During the 15th and 16th centuries entrepreneurs were operating in the countryside who can be described as capitalists. Capitalism is always difficult to define, but here the term includes production primarily for the market, investment in fixed assets such as buildings, employment of wage labour, orientation towards profit, and a willingness to make innovations. The scale of production had to be sufficiently great to yield both profits and funds for further investment.[4] While capitalist enterprises defined along these lines can be identified in our period, they were not functioning within a 'capitalist system', and the full financial, commercial and industrial infrastructure was not to emerge for another two centuries. Very high levels of agri-cultural productivity, for example, were not achieved until the second half of the 18th century.[5]

The foundations for all subsequent developments lay in the expansion of commerce in the long 13th century (c.1180–1310), when the numbers of towns probably tripled, from c.200 to c.650; the proportion of people living in towns doubled from 10 per cent to almost 20 per cent; and the amount of money in circulation increased eight-fold, from £125,000 to £1,100,000.[6] This is to some extent based on the formal records of institutions, which enable us to count the numbers of boroughs, tenants with burgage plots, chartered markets, and mint output; the assurance that there were changes in the real world comes from topography and archaeology. The substance behind the charters and tax lists is proved by the hundreds of planned towns with their numer-ous plots and wide market places, or the abundance of structures and small finds from urban excavations. The growth of the pottery industry is an especially striking feature of the period, with an increase in the number of production centres, and in the volume and variety of their output. Confirmation that the use of money was extended comes from the reported finds

of single coins, which suggest that more cash was circulating in the decades around 1300 than at any other time in the Middle Ages.[7]

The rural participation in the 13th-century trade boom is best known from the manorial accounts, which show lords selling quantities of grain, wool, livestock, dairy produce and hay. Peasant involve-ment is reflected in their payments of rents and taxes in cash, which was mainly obtained from sales of produce. Indeed, calculations of grain output and consumption lead to the conclusion that peasants sold a higher proportion of their crops than did the lords.[8] This meant that male peasants drove carts containing grain and animal products to market towns, and women sold ale to their neighbours brewed from surplus barley. Peasants were the principal suppliers to the market of fruit, vegetables, flax, hemp, honey, wax, poultry and other small scale but cumulatively valuable products. To these crops should be added the goods deriving from rural industries, in which peasants participated as part-time workers, extracting coal and metal ores, and making cloth, iron work, pottery, charcoal and woodland products.[9]

Finds from village excavations reveal the peasants as consumers, who bought and used pottery, and a wide range of metal implements, fittings and orna-ments. Fish bones from inland village sites show that the inhabitants were not entirely self sufficient in food. Although the finds are not closely datable and often not clearly stratified, sites which seem to have begun in the 12th century, leaving meagre traces of the early phases of occupation, and were abandoned in the early or mid 14th, are likely to be reflecting in their small finds the goods acquired during the long 13th century.[10] The changes in the construction of peasant houses, indicated both by the stone founda-tions excavated on village sites from Cornwall to Northumberland, and the standing peasant houses in the south midlands dated by dendrochronology to the late 13th and early 14th centuries, must also be connected with craft specialisation in that period.[11] The closely distributed markets and small towns by c.1300 gave all sections of the rural population ready access to local centres of exchange.[12]

The importance of this period lies not just in the establishment of trading institutions and networks, but also in the permanent changes in ways of life and outlook. The recessions of the 15th century may have reduced prices and the opportunities for trade, but everyone continued to buy and sell, and to presume that labour, rent, land and produce had cash values. Indeed, in this period industry in the countryside expanded. The material culture of village sites, judged from building techniques and small finds, went through no radical change between c.1300 and the mid 16th century. Without the 'commercial revolution', the subsequent development of rural capitalism would be inconceivable.

Commercialisation coincided with sustained demographic growth in the 13th century, but in some regions by c.1320 the population went into decline, and this tendency became universal with the Black Death of 1348–9 and subsequent epidemics. After a long period of reduced numbers of people throughout the 15th century and into the early 16th, rapid growth after c. 1540 was not sustained, and the level of population of c.1300 was not reached again until the 18th century.[13] The changes in rural society and landscape in 1400–1540 were influenced by the low levels of population, but were not entirely conditioned by them. It is rightly said that that villages shrank, that holdings grew in size, and that peasants obtained better conditions of tenure, including lower rents, because people were scarce and land plentiful. But that does not explain why there were such large differences between regions and villages, all of which were initially experiencing similar population losses. Nor does it explain why, when population recovered in the late 16th century, many of the larger holdings persisted.

The restructuring of landholding involved two processes (which were sometimes connected): the amalgamation of tenements, and the farming of demesnes.

The putting together of multiple holdings, known to contemporaries as engrossing, is revealed in all types of settlement by using a combination of evidence. Beginning with areas of dispersed settlement it could take the form of the shrinkage of a hamlet, even down to a single dwelling, which has been demonstrated from documentary evidence in the case of the complex and shifting settlement pattern of Hartland (Devon). Here the hamlet of

Brownsham with fourteen farms at its height was reduced to eight in 1365 and three in 1566. Similar evidence, from an account roll rather than a rental, shows the loss of houses and farms in the Cornish manor of Helston in Kirrier, where in 1486 the single tenant at Carnebone could be said to hold 'the whole vill', in fact absorbing into his own hands two other adjacent abandoned farmsteads.[14] In the same county field work at Brown Willy on Bodmin Moor has shown that a hamlet of six houses was replaced in the 14th century by two new farmsteads. The medieval hamlet had cultivated blocks of land on the hillside, divided into narrow strips (2.2m – 2.7m wide) which were dug with spades. By the 18th century both this land and the surrounding moor had been divided into rectangular enclosed fields belonging to three farms.[15]

The same engrossing tendency is found in the woodlands of the west midlands, where single houses or hamlets still stand, but adjoining them lie the earthworks of abandoned medieval holdings, or pottery scatters indicating the sites of houses abandoned between the 14th and 17th centuries. Sometimes there may have been simply two or three holdings merged into one, but in more complex cases like Sledge Green in Pendock (Worcs.) or Temple Broughton (Worcs.) there had been a combination of abandonment of houses leading to the amalgamation of holdings, and subsequent new building, which can give the modern hamlet a more compact appearance than its medieval predecessor.[16] Straggling green edge settlements are especially characteristic of East Anglia, and they can be located by field walking on the now extensively cultivated fields. In the parishes of Hales and Loddon (Norfolk) at Stubbs Green and Spot Common extensive scatters of 13th- and 14th-century pottery suggest the presence of a number of houses in that period, but both settlements shrank down to a single concentration of pottery marking the site of a farmstead occupied within the period 1400–1600.[17]

There have been insufficient excavations of hamlets and isolated farmsteads outside the southwest. However, large scale work has been done at Westbury by Shenley (Bucks.), which like many woodland villages in the midlands, belongs to the type of dispersed settlement known as the 'inter-

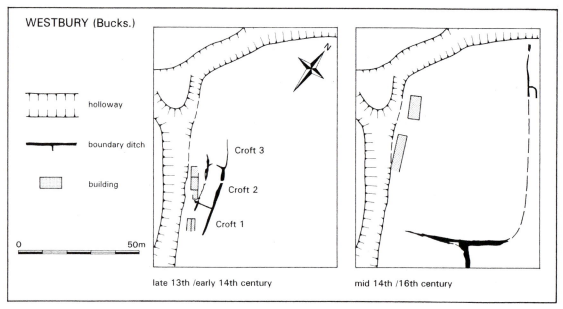

Fig. 5.1 *Excavation plans of part of the deserted settlement at Westbury (Bucks.), showing the absorption of three small crofts into a single larger holding (Ivens et al. 1995, 89–103, courtesy of Buckinghamshire Archaeological Society).*

rupted row', in which houses, singly or in groups, were interspersed with parcels of agricultural land. The excavators have called the plots of land on which houses and other buildings stood 'crofts', though others prefer the term 'tofts'. Crofts numbered 1 and 2 were apparently laid out in the 13th century, and number 3 was added a little later. Croft 3 then expanded to take over its two neighbours, and during the 14th, 15th and 16th centuries a single dwelling (which was periodically rebuilt) occupied the space which had previously contained three (Fig. 5.1). In another part of the settlement to the east four previously separate crofts were taken in a similar process into two adjacent 'farms' which were occupied from c.1400 to c.1540.[18]

The tendency for peasant holdings to be grouped together, by which not just the houses and surrounding closes (the tofts and crofts) were acquired by a single tenant, but also the attached lands in the fields, is sometimes treated as the 'natural' result of population decline. In fact acquiring new land, even if it was going cheap or lying vacant through the death or departure of the previous tenant, resulted

from deliberate decision making and conscious planning. The transfer might be a matter of agreement between peasants – in effect a sale, recorded in the manor court rolls as a surrender by the outgoing tenant *ad opus* (for the use of) the incoming tenant.[19] Land transactions could be bound up with other changes in the lives of the tenants – in connection with a retirement agreement by which the new holder agreed to maintain his elderly predecessor for life, or as part of a marriage contract. The granting of the tenancy would be a matter of formal legal procedures, either the issuing of a charter in the case of a free holding, or attendance at the manor court to register the surrender and the admission of the new holder for a customary tenement. Some cash would be paid to an outgoing tenant, and at least a nominal sum as an entry fine or relief to the lord. Some peasants attempted to take over land without observing the formalities, but this would lead to repeated reminders by the lord to comply with the rules. Casual unregistered occupation of land did happen, but gave no security of tenure or protection from eventual seizure by someone with a better claim.[20]

The practicalities of occupying newly acquired land could not be evaded, because there was no point in taking it over unless it was to be worked or stocked. Tenants of multiple holdings had to make difficult decisions about the maintenance of buildings. Keeping them in repair involved unnecessary expense if there was a house, barn and byre on the main tenement. A building on the second tenement might be useful for agricultural purposes, like the dwelling that is sometimes recorded as turned into accommodation for animals, a conversion which has also been observed in excavations of deserted villages.[21] And a house could be profitably sublet. But the most practical solution was to demolish the buildings and sell the materials, or just to allow them to decay, which then led to trouble in the manor court (in the case of customary tenures), with a succession of repair orders, amercements (fines of money), threats of large penalties or even eviction.[22] The lords looked back to the good old days when they had numerous separate holdings, each occupied by rent-paying tenants, and the decay of the housing stock made the return to such a situation unlikely.

The houses and lands that fell vacant did not have to be taken on by neighbours as part of multiple holdings, and it was common enough for them to lie empty and unused, or at least for the uncultivated strips or fields to be added to the common grazing shared by the remaining peasants. On Dartmoor, for example, the land would return to moorland, not of course to revert to 'waste' in the modern sense, but to become part of the rough grazing exploited by the surrounding settlements. Abandoned land might be added to the demesne, though this would depend on whether the parcels of the holding lay adjacent to the lord's land.

The best excavated evidence for engrossing comes from work on deserted villages. At West Whelpington (Northumberland) after a Scottish raid in c.1320, the village was comprehensively reorganised in a process that may have taken a century, with fewer households than in the 13th century, and went through further restructuring in the 17th century. But most of the examples seem to relate to piecemeal abandonment of individual houses, and amalgamations initiated by individual tenants. Often the excavator reports simply a series of desertions of single properties. At Barton

Blount (Derbys.) three crofts were apparently abandoned in the late 14th and early 15th centuries, and a fourth in the late 15th. Two or three crofts at Great Linford (Bucks.) were deserted in the 15th century, while most of their neighbours continued in occupation until the 17th century.[23]

When buildings are seen to be falling into disuse we tend to use negative language – the settlement is seen to be decaying or shrinking, and very often this was the first stage of a process of total desertion. But the documents show it in a different light. The great majority of villages were reduced in size at some time between c.1340 and 1520, not just those which were eventually to be completely 'lost'. The records describe the site of the collapsed buildings as a toft, but the empty plot in the village was firmly attached to its land in the fields, so it remained a valuable asset, in most cases rented out to a villager who still occupied a house on another holding. Rentals would often describe the resulting multiple tenement in such terms as 'John Smyth holds a messuage and a yardland and a toft and a yardland' and record a rent for the 'abandoned' holding similar to or only a little lower than one headed by an intact 'messuage'. Even when the 'toft and yardland' is said to be 'lying in the lord's hands', apparently unoccupied, we find in manorial accounts that it was being rented out to a tenant, rather informally and often from year to year.[24] In other words, the positive side of the apparent devastation or disuse is the continued use of the land in the fields. Indeed, while holdings in a decaying settlement might be embarrassments to the lord, which he hoped to be able to pass on to a reluctant tenant cheaply and for a short term, we can find in some healthier villages lively competition among tenants anxious to acquire them. The lord was able to charge quite high entry fines, and the would-be purchaser can be found offering substantial sums of money to the outgoing tenant.[25]

The material evidence can show that the engrossing tenant was operating on a large scale. At Hangleton (Sussex) a 15th-century farm occupied the site of a number of buildings constructed in the 13th century. The tenant of the new holding must have been working the land of perhaps four predecessors.[26] In the Yorkshire wold village of Cowlam, excavation shows two crofts being merged into one

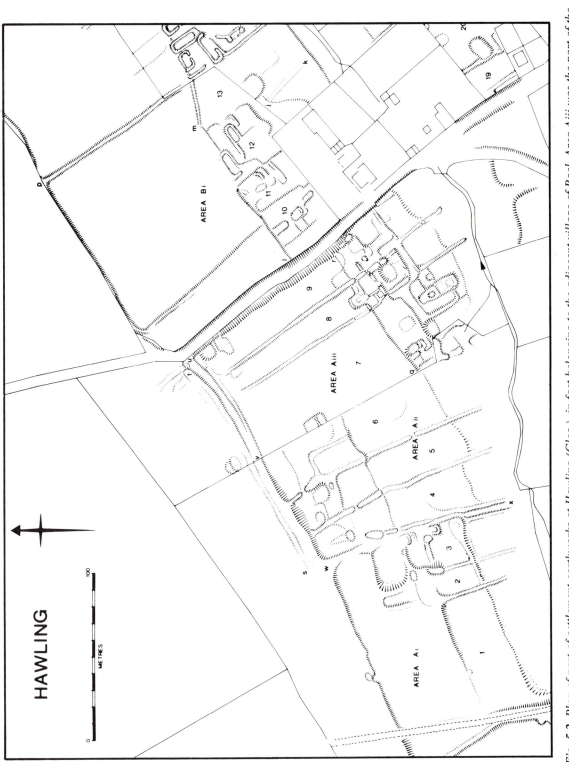

Fig. 5.2 *Plan of part of settlement earthworks at Hawling (Glos.), in fact belonging to the adjacent village of Roel. Area Aiii was the part of the village known in the Middle Ages as Coppethrop, which appears on modern maps as Cockrup. The substantial buildings at the south end of toft no. 7 are likely to have belonged to Henry Chandeler. The toft is clearly double the width of its neighbours (plan by J. Bond and C. Lewis, published*

at the end of the Middle Ages. The new holding was provided with an impressive range of buildings which remained in occupation into the 17th century. A will from the village shows that in 1579 a single tenant called William Milner had 16 oxgangs, probably more than 200 acres, while his predecessors before 1400 would usually have held no more than two oxgangs.[27] In exceptional circumstances the archaeological evidence can be matched precisely to a named individual tenant. At the village of Roel (Glos.), manorial court rolls record the activities of Henry Chandeler, who by 1400 had accumulated five holdings, about 150 acres, and allowed buildings to decay. He was a typical 'kulak', an acquisitive tenant who caused trouble to his neighbours with his trespassing animals, and by putting excessive numbers of sheep to pasture on the common. By good chance we are told in the court rolls that his buildings lay in a part of the village called 'Coppethrop', and in the modern field bearing that name the grassed-over foundations of a complex of buildings larger than the usual peasant houses can still be seen (Fig. 5.2). Such well-documented examples help to strengthen the interpretation of the material evidence from other deserted villages sites where in a last phase the settlement seems to have been dominated by a wealthy tenant. At North Marefield in Leicestershire earthwork remains of a prominent group of buildings occupied a large section of the village, and adjacent ridge and furrow had been enclosed with banks and ditches into paddocks.[28]

Henry Chandeler's agricultural activities seem to have concentrated on sheep grazing, and most engrossers were inclined to use land as pasture because keeping animals required less labour and gave better returns in the market than the grain cultivation favoured by their predecessors. However, the most striking complex of excavated buildings apparently occupied by an engrossing tenant was that of the 15th century at Caldecote (Herts.), in which a dwelling house was dwarfed by two large barns, suggesting large scale arable farming, which might be linked to the influence of London's demand for grain (Fig. 5.3).[29] Earthwork evidence sometimes supports the same observation that shrinkage of a village did not always lead to the conversion of fields to pasture. On the site at Stretton Baskerville

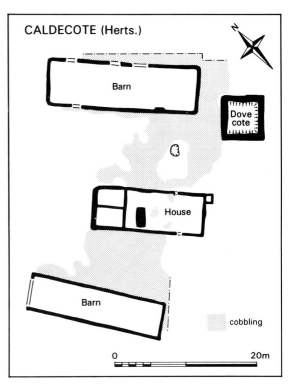

Fig. 5.3 *Plan of group of buildings excavated at Caldecote (Herts.). Instead of the usual single barn, 15m long, this late medieval house is associated with two barns each 20m long and capable together of storing the crops from 160 acres. The stone built dovecot may have given its owner status as well as a source of meat and cash (plan by G. Beresford, see note 29).*

(Warwicks.) the deserted tofts of one part of the village were at some time overploughed with well-marked ridge and furrow, as if when houses were abandoned their sites for a time were incorporated into the village arable.

Most material evidence for the accumulation of large holdings has been gathered from deserted village sites where earthworks can be planned and buildings excavated. The process has, however, left its mark on the topography of still inhabited villages. Abandoned house sites now often used as paddocks lie interspersed among the existing dwellings, and in a regularly planned village some modern plots which appear to be double the conventional width are likely to owe their origin to the merging of once separate crofts. Such double plots are clearly visible on the 1755 map of Hawling (Glos.), the village adjoining Roel mentioned above, for which the late medieval records contain abundant references to tenants with two yardlands.[30]

We can conclude then that the engrossing tenants, sometimes called 'yeomen' in the documents, made a considerable mark on the settlement pattern both in regions of dispersal and nucleation. They might take over all of their neighbours' land in a small hamlet, or just a group of holdings in a nucleated village. They were often simply making productive use of vacant land, but we must be suspicious that their anti-social behaviour played some part in driving neighbours away, and that they could have had an active role in encouraging the further shrinkage or even total desertion of their villages. The impact that they made on fields is less easily observed, though they are known to have played their part in piecemeal consolidation and enclosure, and they have doubtless left their mark on the field boundaries of those numerous villages subject to 'enclosure by agreement'. Here the pattern of ridge and furrow has dictated the line of modern hedges, because the new enclosure boundaries followed the lines of strips and headlands of the original open fields, as groups of 'lands' or even whole furlongs were detached from common control and fenced.[31]

The other significant figures of the 'transition' period were the farmers. Particularly in the period 1380–1420 the larger estates of lowland England took the difficult decision to abandon direct management of agriculture, which was being made increasingly unprofitable by rising wages and falling prices, and to lease their demesnes. The lessees were called farmers because they paid a fixed rent, a farm, but the word came to mean an agricultural entrepreneur. Farmers had to manage large units of production (demesnes varied in size between 100 and 500 acres), invest in buildings, livestock and equipment, employ wage labour, and respond to the market, if they were to fulfill their aims of paying their rent and making a living for themselves. The rise of the farmers involved a social upheaval, as the lords transferred the management of great quantities of productive land into the hands of people well below the ranks of the magnates. Some were gentry, merchants and clergy, but the majority had previously been peasants.[32] All of this coincided with profound changes in lord-tenant relations, as labour services were finally ended, rents and other dues reduced, serfdom withered away, and in the agricultural economy arable gave way to a higher proportion of pasture.[33]

These changes are imprinted on the minds of those using documents because the leasing of demesnes removes the records of agricultural production from the manorial accounts. The material evidence may not show any change at all, because the farmer would take over the demesne as a working agricultural unit and continue to use its buildings and fields. Many manorial barns, built by lords in the 13th and 14th centuries, have survived until the present day because they were maintained by the farmers, though sometimes either by the terms of the contract or by negotiation, the lord would pay at least part of the cost. So the barn which still stands at Bredon (Worcs.), originally built for the lord of the manor, the bishop of Worcester, in the 1340s, was repaired in 1457 at the expense of the lord for the use of the farmer. If buildings were to be replaced the cost usually fell on the lessee, and indeed this expenditure must have represented the main investment made by these early capitalists. Occasionally the lord paid, and an impressive T-shaped house still standing at Overton in Hampshire, together with a barn originally of nine bays, is recorded as costing the bishop of Winchester's estate more than £80 in the years between 1497 and 1507.[34]

Recent work on sheepcotes, long narrow buildings which were used primarily to house flocks in the winter, and to store fodder, suggests some of the continuities and new developments that could result from the advent of the farmers. Lords built sheepcotes in the 13th and 14th centuries, and sometimes kept them and the associated pastures under direct management after the less profitable arable demesnes had been leased. When the pastures were eventually granted out to farmers, they were managed often as separate units of production, not as part of an integrated combination of arable and pastoral farming, and the functions of the buildings changed. New pasture farms were being developed in the 15th and 16th centuries, such as those occupying the

Fig. 5.4 Aerial photograph of the deserted village of Hillborough (in Temple Grafton, Warwicks.), from the south-east. The village street runs southwards from the manor house (with a circular dovecot). The village was deserted by c.1500. In the parched conditions of 1976, when this photograph was taken, the foundations of a number of large buildings are visible on both sides of the south end of the village street. Their large scale suggests that they may have belonged to an engrosser or farmer and were occupied at a late stage of the village's decline. Between these buildings and the dovecot, on the east side of the field near the prominent road, the distinctive stone foundations of a sheepcote can be seen, a narrow building c.40m long, on an alignment different from that of the village, and evidently built after desertion to house a flock of sheep grazing the former fields (Cambridge Committee for Aerial Photography, BTO 088).

former arable fields of deserted villages, and the farmers themselves built new sheepcotes, on or near the sites of the villages, of which the traces of a building at Hillborough (Warwicks.) provide a striking example (Fig. 5.4).[35]

Many demesnes were not leased as a block to a single farmer, but were split up into more manageable units, presumably as a result of negotiations between lords and potential lessees. This could have significant effects on settlements and the organisation of the landscape. For example, at Hanbury (Worcs.)

the manor house and associated agricultural buildings were perched on a hill on the northern edge of the estate, and the fields of the demesne lay partly nearby, and partly scattered over the rest of the large parish, even to a distance of 4 km. The first farmer at the end of the 14th century took on the whole demesne, but by about 1410 it was subdivided and let in parcels. The manorial *curia* was abandoned, and new farms were eventually built on the various parts, including one on the demesne field called Morecroft, which was occupied according to pottery

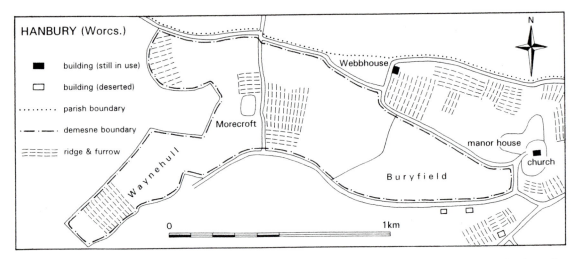

Fig. 5.5 *Map of part of the demesne of Hanbury (Worcs.), showing the site of the manor house, redundant after the demesne was leased in parcels, and of Morecroft, one of the new farm houses. The tenant of Webbhouse also became a demesne farmer, but his land was at the other end of the parish (for sources see note 36).*

finds and documentary evidence from the end of the 15th century until recent times (Fig. 5.5).[36]

The tendency for larger medieval demesnes to be split up when they were leased is best documented in the case of monastic granges. When the Cistercians and other orders created these compact blocks of land in the 12th and 13th centuries they could exceed 400 acres. As the farmers after 1400 preferred smaller units, the granges were commonly leased in two or more parcels. The grange at Holeway (now known as Hollowfields) (Worcs.) was leased in the 15th century by the monks of Bordesley Abbey to two farmers, by which time the site of the original grange buildings had been abandoned. At first the farmers seem to have shared the land without making a strict territorial division, but in the late 15th century they decided to draw a boundary by planting a new hedge through the fields of the grange. When evidence was collected in a tithe dispute in about 1530, witnesses referred to 'William Hunte's new house', showing that the division of the land resulted in a new settlement, and presumably two of the three farms now standing on the former territory of the grange were founded in the 15th or 16th centuries.[37] The same phenomenon of granges divided between lessees has been observed on the Yorkshire estates of Fountains Abbey, and at Cayton as at Holeway

the medieval grange buildings were abandoned and a new farm built out in the fields.[38] These changes in boundaries and settlements were often accompanied by shifts in land use, like the conversion of much of Holeway to pasture by the 1530s.

New settlements in a period of shrinking population and village desertion seems a paradox, yet they were by no means confined to farms on outlying demesnes and the sites of monastic granges. The labour requirements of the farmers would be one of the reasons for the building of cottages. These are conventionally thought to have resulted from squatters establishing themselves on roadsides or on the edges of commons in the late 16th century and later, but there is much documentary evidence especially from woodland districts of new cottages, purprestures (enclosures from the waste) and even assarts (woodland clearances, a term most common in the 12th and 13th centuries) from the mid 15th century.[39] When such new houses have subsequently been abandoned, they can be located by field-work – there are examples in Loddon (Norfolk), on the edge of the common at Hanbury (Worcs.) and at Burton Dassett (Warwicks.).[40] A proliferation of new houses and cottages was associated with the increase in employment opportunities arising from the growth of industries, such as tin mining and cloth making.

Some farms on Dartmoor may have been founded in the late 15th century when tinning expanded, and Castle Combe (Wilts.), a clothing village, grew in size, was largely rebuilt, and acquired more cottages after c.1430, in contrast with the decay in most settlements.[41] The congregation of cloth workers must have encouraged the renewal of the fabric of many villages and hamlets in which numerous late medieval and early modern buildings are still visible on the Suffolk/Essex border, or in the weald of Kent.

A related development recently highlighted in documentary studies of rentals and surveys of the 15th century has been the accumulation of a number of cottage holdings by wealthy tenants who had also gathered substantial quantities of land. The most likely explanation lies in the need for hired workers, and that these were 'tied cottages' sublet to labourers who would be expected to work on the yeoman's land.[42] If, as is often the case, the cottages had originated in the 13th century or earlier as separate tenements located in hamlets and along village streets, their tenurial connection with one of the tenants of a larger holding would not be apparent in the material evidence. Well-preserved village sites, however, like Croxby or Firsby in Lincolnshire include tofts with a number of buildings visible as grassed over foundations, some of which might have included cottages for workers built on their employers' holdings.[43]

The landscape was sometimes reordered in the 15th and 16th centuries by the enclosure of large areas of formerly open pastures and wastes. This has been noted in local studies in many parts of the country, from Cornwall to Cumbria, and can sometimes be linked with new forms of settlement, such as the 'ring fence farms' on the Cornish moors.[44] Unlike the encroachments on the wastes for cultivation in the 13th century, the main purpose was to increase the area of pasture held in 'severalty', and the effects of this can be noted in descriptions of land use in the midlands and the south-west which show dramatic increases in the areas of privately owned pasture.[45] But the trend, which judging from the documents was especially marked from the 1440s, deserves systematic investigation by landscape historians. More attention has been given to the creation and enlargement of parks, a movement which had been at its peak in earlier centuries. In our period more of these pleasure grounds and status symbols, which often had an economic function as grazing for cattle and sheep, were introduced into champion landscapes.[46]

Finally, the desertion or severe shrinkage of villages needs to be considered as a transition in the landscape. Most work on desertion tends understandably to concentrate on the end of the peasant community rather than the subsequent use of the site. The process of abandonment as we have seen from both excavated and documentary evidence could have been a gradual one, even if at a final stage the remaining peasants were removed on a specific day, as recorded in a number of cases by the Commissions investigating the 'throwing down' of houses and conversion of arable to pasture in 1517. A demesne farmer could use his resources and influence to hasten the departure of his unwelcome peasant neighbours who retained common rights and continued to work a truncated field system. This seems to have been the situation at Burton Dassett (Warwicks.) where Roger Heritage farmed the demesne in the 1480s and 1490s, using it as pasture as much as possible, but under his son John, when a new acquisitive lord came into his inheritance, the final enclosure took place in 1497 and the land was converted entirely into a large specialist pasture.[47]

After desertion the manor house was often the only inhabited building, but when there was no resident lord a single house in the village might have been retained or rebuilt for the use of the farmer, or a shepherd, and sometimes a modern farm house which is aligned on the village street appears to be standing on the site of this last survivor of the settlement. Such a building, now called Aston Farm, can be identified at Little Aston (Glos.).[48] The enclosures that were used to divide up the village and its fields usually have a distinctive character. Around Wormleighton (Warwicks.), which was finally depopulated and enclosed in 1499, double hedges with ditches were set out, and John Spencer later defended the planting of the hedges by claiming that the wood that they provided was a useful addition to the sources of fuel in a landscape without many trees (Fig. 5.6). At Wormleighton and other midland village sites, such as Lark Stoke (Warwicks.)

Fig. 5.6 *Aerial photograph of the site of the village and fields of Wormleighton (Warwicks.). The modern pattern of enclosure originated with the hedges planted soon after 1499 when the arable fields were converted to pasture (author's photograph).*

(abandoned in the 15th century), the post-desertion enclosures have an irregular form, and often failed to observe the former boundaries of the furlongs (Fig. 5.7). In contrast the new enclosures at Burton Dassett (Warwicks.) and East Layton (co. Durham) seem to have followed the boundaries of the old fields of the village.[49] The size of the new closes was presumably related to calculations of the anticipated needs of flocks and herds that would henceforth graze the site, but the layout of these early enclosures deserves further systematic research.

The conclusion can be drawn that the English countryside in the period of 'transition' saw some major shifts both in social and economic life and in the landscape. Quantification of such a period is always dangerous, but it is worth suggesting that about 2,000 villages were deserted between 1400 and 1600, and that at least twice as many became

severely shrunken. In the areas of dispersed settlement 20,000 or more hamlets were either totally abandoned or were reduced to a few farms or even a single holding. This was mostly in the period 1380–1520, and it was at the same time that at least a million acres of arable land were converted to grazing – with changes in demand after 1540 the ploughed area in some regions began to grow once more. A recent estimate that by 1600 47 per cent of all land was enclosed includes the very extensive crofts and closes dating back to the early Middle Ages, in woodland regions where open fields had never existed. But an important contribution to the figure came from the 10 per cent or more of the former common arable which was enclosed by agreement, and the sites of abandoned villages, together with sections of former commons and wastes 'privatised' by conversion into 'several'

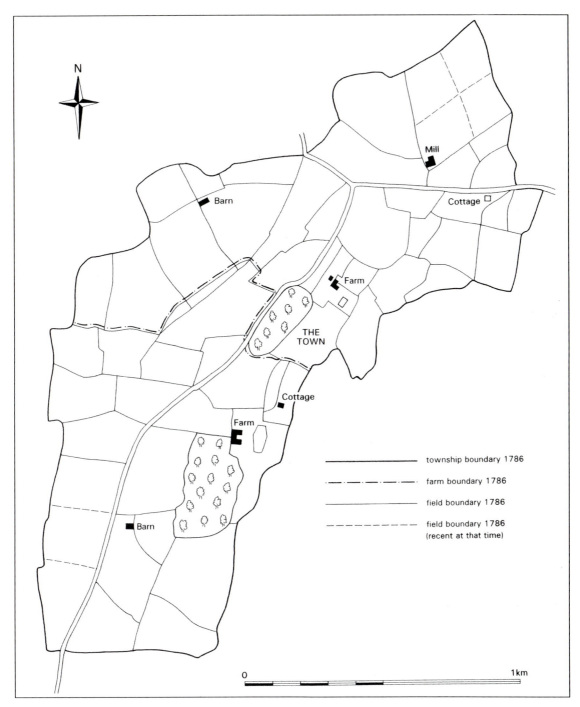

Fig. 5.7 *Map of the township of Lark Stoke in Admington (Warwicks.) in 1786. The village was deserted slowly in the 15th century, and stood in the field called The Town. The hedges reflect the division of the village fields into irregularly shaped pasture closes after desertion; some of the straighter hedges (shown as dotted lines) were probably late modifications. By 1786 two farms, Lower and Upper Lark Stoke, occupied land once cultivated by a dozen peasant families. At some time after desertion two cottages were built, presumably for workers on the farms (the estate map on which this is based is in private hands).*

pastures in the period 1400–1600.[50] Among the villagers, those with more than 50 acres were quite rare before the Black Death, certainly below 5 per cent of tenants, but by the 16th century they represented perhaps one in eight of the rural land holders, amounting to about 50,000 households in the middle of the century.[51] Large scale farmers of demesnes must have numbered at least 5,000. This minority was very influential and accounted for much of the change in settlement and landscapes through their amalgamation of holdings, adaptations in the use and management of land, and building of new farmhouses.

Having made the case for the transitional period being one of radical and widespread change, the qualification must be made that, as always, there was much continuity. Many landlords in 1600 lived on their rents in a traditional way, and peasants with holdings little larger than their high medieval predecessors continued with familiar farming practices, requiring no great changes in the landscape. In dispersed settlement areas of mixed farming the combination of arable and pasture was quietly adjusted in line with shifts in labour supply and demand for produce. Even in the open-field villages modifications to rotations and the use of land could be negotiated to enable them to keep up with new techniques.

The village communities achieved much more than just survival in this period. Their cohesion and continued energy is portrayed for us in the material evidence of the churches in many regions, which were rebuilt, improved and decorated as never before, not generally through the patronage of wealthy lords, or the gifts of wool merchants or clothiers, but mainly as a result of collective fund raising among the whole body of parishioners by the church wardens. As well as the church itself, the communal building programme extended in the late 15th and early 16th centuries to church houses and guild halls to accommodate ales, feasts and other collective celebrations.[52] When the village community was supposed to be threatened by the widening gap between rich and poor, it seems to have been stronger than ever. Perhaps the village elite, later to be known as the 'middling sort', always important but now enjoying more wealth and power, promoted this surge in community life. A typical

move was to make more formal provision for the village poor, including the building of poor houses and almshouses. Whatever the explanation, elements of the social and material world of the Middle Ages were still alive and flourishing on the eve of the Reformation.

The early stages of capitalism involved material changes, and have left indelible marks on the fabric of the English countryside. The investments and innovations of 1400–1600 may not have matched the scale of those of the 18th and 19th centuries, but they have a special importance because they represent formative stages and a break in continuity. The houses surrounded by the earthworks of deserted villages and hamlets, the gaps along village streets left by engrossing, the piecemeal abandonment of houses as the settlement pattern contracted, the new farm houses and cottages, the hedges, ditches or walls cutting through former common fields and pastures, the marks made by rural industry, all provide impressive testimony to the strength of the innovative forces. The new structures were not always imposed from outside, as the story of engrossing and piecemeal enclosure by acquisitive peasants shows. Nor did the pursuit of improvement by individuals necessarily erode the village community.

Notes

1. Aston & Philpin 1985, 48–9, 58–9, 294–7.
2. Razi 1993; Barry & Brooks 1994; Campbell & Overton 1991; Shammas 1990.
3. Allen 1992.
4. Holton 1985.
5. Overton 1996, 8–11.
6. Dyer 1995a, 172–9; Britnell 1993, 102.
7. Mayhew 1995, 62–5.
8. Britnell 1993, 119–23.
9. Langdon 1987; Bennett 1996; Birrell 1969.
10. Hilton & Rahtz 1966, 111–34; Rahtz 1969, 103–23.
11. *Vernacular Architecture* 1981, 12, 39; 1983, 14, 62; 1990, 21, 47; 1992, 23, 58.
12. Britnell 1993, 81–90; Dyer 1996.
13. Smith 1988, 189–96.
14. Fox 1989, 49–55.
15. Johnson & Rose 1994, 93–8, 107–9.
16. Dyer 1994, 63, 65; *Medieval Village Research Group Annual Rep 1981,* 13.

17. Davison 1990, 33–5, 68.
18. Ivens, Busby & Shepherd 1995, 85–103.
19. Harvey 1984, 349–53.
20. Hilton 1975, 166.
21. Holden 1963, 80–1.
22. Dyer 1994, 138–49.
23. Evans, Jarrett & Wrathmell 1988, 140–9; Beresford 1975, 53–4; Mynard & Zeepvat 1992, 51–91.
24. Titow 1994.
25. Harvey 1984, 244–51.
26. Hurst & Hurst 1964, 94–114.
27. Hayfield 1988, 26–32, 84–90.
28. Aldred & Dyer 1991, 156–7; Everson 1994, 25–6.
29. *Medieval Village Research Group Annual Rep* 1974, 22–3.
30. Aldred & Dyer 1991, 148.
31. Taylor 1975, 113–14, 120–3.
32. Hare 1981, 1–15.
33. Miller 1991, 1–33.
34. Charles 1997, 28; Roberts 1995.
35. Dyer 1995b, 157–8.
36. Dyer 1991, 32, 42, 55–7.
37. Platt 1969, 104–7; Dyer 1991, 56.
38. Michelmore 1981, xlii–xliii.
39. Miller 1991, 84–5, 113, 117.
40. Davison *op. cit.*, 36, 69; Dyer, 1991, 57; *Medieval Settlement Research Group Annual Rep 1988*, 24–5.
41. Newman 1994; Beresford & St Joseph 1979, 268–9.
42. Fox 1995.
43. Everson, Taylor & Dunn 1991, 198, 212.
44. Winchester 1987, 52–4; Austin, Gerrard & Greeves 1989, 224–34.
45. Miller 1991, 77–80, 152–4.
46. Beresford 1984, 205–15.
47. Dyer 1994, 315–21.
48. Dyer 1985, 167, 175.
49. Thorpe 1962, 50–63; Alcock 1981, 27–32; Beresford 1967, 257–60; see also Taylor 1975, 115–17.
50. Wordie 1983, 502.
51. Tawney 1912, 63–72 is the basis of the estimate.
52. Hutton 1994, 49–68; Kumin 1996; Williams 1992.

Bibliography

Alcock, N.W. 1981, *Warwickshire Grazier and London Skinner 1532–1555* British Academy Records of Social and Economic History, new ser 4, Oxford

Aldred, D. & Dyer, C. 1991, 'A Medieval Cotswold Village: Roel, Gloucestershire', *Trans Bristol and Glos Archaeol Soc* 109, 139–70

Allen, R.C. 1992, *Enclosure and the Yeoman. The Agricultural Development of the South Midlands 1450–1850*, Oxford

Astill, G.G. & Grant, A. (eds) 1988, *The Countryside of Medieval England*, Oxford

Aston, T.H. (ed.) 1987, *Landlords, Peasants and Politics in Medieval England*, Cambridge

Aston, T.H. & Philpin, C.H.E. (eds) 1985, *The Brenner Debate. Agrarian Class Structure and Economic Development in Pre-Industrial Europe*, Cambridge

Austin, D., Gerrard, G.A.M. & Greeves, T.A.P. 1989, 'Tin and Agriculture in the Middle Ages and beyond: Landscape Archaeology in St Neot Parish, Cornwall', *Cornish Archaeol* 28, 5–251

Barry, J. & Brooks, C. (eds) 1994, *The Middling Sort of People. Culture, Society and Politics in England, 1550–1800*, Basingstoke

Bennett, J. 1996, *Ale, Beer, and Brewsters in England. Women's Work in a Changing World, 1300–1600*, New York and Oxford

Beresford, G. 1975, *The Medieval Clay-Land Village: Excavations at Goltho and Barton Blount*, Soc for Medieval Archaeol Monograph Ser, 6

Beresford, M.W. 1967, 'East Layton Co Durham in 1608', *Medieval Archaeol* 11, 257–60

Beresford, M.W. 1984, *History on the Ground*, 2nd edn, Gloucester

Beresford, M.W. & St Joseph, J.K. 1979, *Medieval England: an Aerial Survey,* 2nd edn, Cambridge

Birrell, J.R. 1969, 'Peasant Craftsmen in the Medieval Forest', *Agric Hist Rev* 17, 91–107

Britnell, R.H. 1993, *The Commercialisation of English Society 1000–1500*, Cambridge

Britnell, R.H. & Campbell, B.M.S. 1995, *A Commercialising Economy. England 1086 – c.1300*, Manchester

Campbell, B.M.S. & Overton, M. 1991, *Land, Labour and Livestock. Historical Studies in European Agricultural Productivity*, Manchester

Charles, F.W.B. 1997, *The Great Barn of Bredon*, Oxford

Davison, A. 1990, *The Evolution of Settlement in Three Parishes in South-East Norfolk*, East Anglian Archaeol, 49

Duvosquel, J.-M. & Thoen, E. (eds) 1995, *Peasants and Townsmen in Medieval Europe. Studia in Honorem Adriaan Verhulst*, Ghent

Dyer, C. 1987, 'The Rise and Fall of a Medieval Village: Little Aston (in Aston Blank), Gloucestershire', *Trans Bristol and Glos Archaeol Soc* 105, 165–81

Dyer, C. 1991, *Hanbury: Settlement and Society in a Woodland Landscape*, Univ of Leicester Dept of English Local Hist Occasional Paper, 4th ser, 4

Dyer, C. 1994, *Everyday Life in Medieval England*

Dyer, C. 1995a, 'How Urbanized was Medieval England?', in Duvosquel and Thoen 1995, 169–83

Dyer, C. 1995b, 'Sheepcotes: Evidence for Medieval Sheepfarming', *Medieval Archaeology* 39, 136–64

Dyer, C. 1996, 'Market Towns and the Countryside in Late Medieval England', *Canadian J of Hist* 31, 17–35

Evans, D.H., Jarrett, M. & Wrathmell, S. 1988, 'The Deserted Medieval Village of West Whelpington, Northumberland: Third Report, part two', *Archaeologia Aeliana* 5th ser, 16, 139–92

Everson, P.L., Taylor, C.C. & Dunn, C.J. 1991, *Change and Continuity: Rural Settlement in North-West Lincolnshire*

Everson, P. 1994, 'The Deserted Village Remains of North Marefield, Leicestershire', *Medieval Settlement Research Group Annual Rep* 9, 22–7

Fox, H.S.A. 1989, 'Peasant Farmers, Patterns of Settlement and Pays: Transformations in the Landscapes of Devon and Cornwall during the Later Middle Ages', in Higham 1989, 41–73

Fox, H.S.A. 1995, 'Servants, Cottagers and Tied Cottages during the Later Middle Ages', *Rural Hist* 6, 125–54

Hare, J.N. 1981, 'The Demesne Lessees of Fifteenth-Century Wiltshire', *Agric Hist Rev* 29, 1–15

Harvey, P.D.A. 1984, *The Peasant Land Market in Medieval England*, Oxford

Hayfield, C. 1988, 'Cowlam Deserted Village: a Case Study of Post–Medieval Village Desertion', *Post-Medieval Archaeology* 22, 21–109

Higham, R. 1989, *Landscape and Townscape in the South West*, Exeter

Hilton, R.H. 1975, *The English Peasantry in the Later Middle Ages*, Oxford

Hilton, R.H. & Rahtz, P. A. 1966, 'Upton, Gloucestershire, 1959–1964', *Trans Bristol and Glos Archaeol Soc* 85, 70–146

Holden, E.W. 1963, 'Excavations at the Deserted Medieval Village of Hangleton, part I', *Sussex Archaeol Coll* 101, 54–181

Holton, R.J. 1985, *The Transition from Feudalism to Capitalism*, Basingstoke and London

Hurst, J.G. & Hurst, D.G. 1964, 'Excavations at the Deserted Medieval Village of Hangleton part II', *Sussex Archaeol Coll* 102, 94–142

Hutton, R. 1994, *The Rise and Fall of Merry England*, Oxford

Ivens, R., Busby, P. & Shepherd, N. 1995, *Tattenhoe and Westbury*, Bucks Archaeol Soc Monographs, 8

Johnson, N. & Rose, P. 1994, *Bodmin Moor. An Archaeological Survey. Vol 1: The Human Landscape to c.1800*

Kumin, B. 1996, *The Shaping of a Community. The Rise and Reformation of the English Parish c.1400–1560*, Aldershot

Langdon, J. 1987, 'Horse Hauling : a Revolution in Vehicle Transport in Twelfth- and Thirteenth-Century England', in Aston 1987, 33–64

Mayhew, N. 1995, 'Modelling Medieval Monetization', in Britnell and Campbell 1995, 55–77

Michelmore, D.J.H. (ed.) 1981, *The Fountains Abbey Lease Book,* Yorkshire Archaeol Soc Rec Ser, 140

Miller, E. (ed.) 1991, *The Agrarian History of England and Wales, iii, 1348–1500*, Cambridge

Mynard, D.C. and Zeepvat, R.J. 1992, *Great Linford*, Bucks Archaeol Soc Monographs Ser, 3

Newman, P. 1994, 'Tinners and Tenants in Southwest Dartmoor: a Case Study in Landscape History', *Devonshire Assoc Rep and Trans*, 126, 199–238

Overton, M. 1996, 'Re-establishing the English Agricultural Revolution', *Agric Hist Rev* 44, 1–20

Rahtz, P.A. 1969, 'Upton, Gloucestershire, 1964–1968. Second Report', *Trans Bristol and Glos Archaeol Soc* 88, 74–126

Razi, Z. 1993, 'The Myth of the Immutable English Family', *Past and Present* 140, 3–44

Roberts, E. 1995, 'Overton Court Farm and the Late-Medieval Farmhouses of Demesne Lessees in Hampshire', *Proc Hants Field Club* 51, 89–106

Shammas, C. 1990, *The Pre-Industrial Consumer in England and America*, Oxford

Smith, R. M. 1988, 'Human Resources', in Astill & Grant 1988, 188–212

Tawney, R.H. 1916, *The Agrarian Problem in the Sixteenth Century*

Taylor, C.C. 1975, *Fields in the English Landscape*

Thorpe, H. 1962, 'The Lord and the Landscape, Illustrated through the Changing Fortunes of a Warwickshire Parish, Wormleighton', *Trans Birmingham Archaeol Soc* 80, 38–77

Titow, J 1994, 'Lost Rents, Vacant Holdings and the Continuation of Peasant Cultivation after the Black Death', *Agric Hist Rev* 42, 97–114

Williams, E.H.D. 1992, 'Church Houses in Somerset', *Vernacular Architecture* 23, 15–23

Winchester, A. 1987, *Landscape and Society in Medieval Cumbria*, Edinburgh

Wordie, J.R. 1983, 'The Chronology of English Enclosure, 1500–1914', *Econ Hist Rev* 2nd ser 36, 483–505

6   Innovations, Tradition and Disruption in Tomb-Sculpture

Phillip Lindley

The remarkable stylistic revolution visible in sculpture executed in England in the first half of the 16th century has justifiably excited a good deal of attention from art-historians and archaeologists.[1] Of all the media influenced by the Renaissance in the first half of the century, sculpture has attracted so much scholarly scrutiny because it was the only one to be entirely dominated by Italian practitioners, if by domination one means the virtual monopoly of the most significant royal or 'court' patronage.[2] Accordingly, the first purpose of this paper will be to summarise the key phases in the arrival of Italian sculptors and Renaissance styles in sculpture in England. The internationality of the Renaissance, however, as Peter Burke justly argued, does not mean that it was an homogeneous movement:[3] the pace and process of cultural penetration in England varied from that in other nations or regions and different media were also differently affected. Scholarly focus on the arrival of Italian artists and the production of Renaissance sculpture in England can overshadow other issues, such as the 'reception' of Renaissance art in England and the question of how, or even whether, the stylistic innovations introduced by the Florentine sculptor Pietro Torrigiano and his successors were assimilated by indigenous sculptors. Until recently, the role of other European sculptors in importing Renaissance and 'antique' forms into England has also generally been underestimated, yet it is clear that other artists, particularly French-trained sculptors, played a vital role in the dissemination of the Renaissance in England.[4]

The primary focus in this paper will be on tomb-sculpture, the genre to which much of Pietro Torrigiano's most important surviving work in England belongs. The issue of *survival* is an important one: because Reformation iconoclasm obliterated most of the sculpture executed in England in the first half of the 16th century, tomb-sculpture is the sole category of three-dimensional imagery to have survived in any considerable quantity.[5] Tomb monuments also, of course, continued to be commissioned during and after the Reformation. Indeed, because they provided virtually the only consistently important field for sculptural endeavour in post-Reformation England, they provide a gauge with which we can measure continuity and change throughout the 16th century. Yet monuments must be assessed with care and a due regard for the sort of evidence they provide. The second purpose of this paper will consequently be to provide a sketch, albeit a cursory one based on selected case studies, of the effects of the Reformation on the style and subject matter of tomb monuments. Finally, I want briefly to consider the functional changes caused by the Reformation, changes which have not hitherto received enough attention. I shall suggest that if tomb-monuments are analysed with a degree of sophistication, they may provide important material evidence for attitudes towards mid-century religious changes.

Periodisation, stylistic change and the Renaissance

The *Oxford History of English Art* series employed the convenient, but often artistically meaningless, background of political history to define the scope of individual volumes.[6] Unfortunately, the book covering the years 1461–1553, assigned to David Piper, never appeared, leaving a crucial lacuna between Joan Evans's 1307–1461 volume and that written by Eric Mercer extending from 1553 to 1625.[7] In the absence of this general survey, it is hard to know whether any real rationale could have been provided for its terminal dates. For art and architectural historians, the arrival of the Renaissance is often employed as a convenient means of demarcating the end of one 'period' and the beginning of another. It is for this reason that Lawrence Stone's monograph, *Sculpture in Britain: the Middle Ages*, excludes consideration of Torrigiano's sculpture in England, though Stone, paradoxically perhaps, considers later sculpture executed in a Gothic style.[8] There can be no doubt that a concentration on the stylistic and iconographic changes which England witnessed with the arrival of the Renaissance is of remarkable importance, but it should not exclude consideration of even more fundamental changes which can be revealed with particular clarity in the field of tomb-monuments before, during and after the Reformation.

The Italian Renaissance came late to England even in the field of sculpture. Yet there is, surprisingly perhaps, some evidence of a knowledge of Italian art in English sculpture of the first half of the 14th century (and perhaps of a direct experience rather than a second-hand one, mediated through manuscripts or panel paintings). Xenia Muratova has highlighted features of the sculpture from the west front of Exeter Cathedral, such as the demi-figures, the mourning angels' gestures of despair and the relief spandrels of the western door – all of which ante-date the Black Death – as showing a knowledge of Italian forms.[9] This meditation on Italian models is a further testimony to Bishop Grandisson's well-documented interest in Italian and Italianate art, a taste in which, of course, he was far from alone in the period.[10] It is also arguable that some 14th-century

Fig. 6.1 *Duke Humphrey of Gloucester's chantry chapel, St Alban's Abbey: detail showing his badge (Copyright author).*

tombs evince an indirect knowledge of Italian and even of classical models.[11]

There is, though, a profound conceptual difference between an acceptance of Italian innovations in the 14th century, and the assimilation of 15th-century Italy's reawakened interest in classical forms, an architectural language of which there were, of course, almost no extant examples in England. The earliest English sculpture which can be argued to show any direct decorative indebtedness to Renaissance prototypes appears to be the mid 15th-century chantry chapel of Humphrey Duke of Gloucester at St Alban's, where Duke Humphrey's badge, representing the Gardens of Adonis, is depicted (Fig. 6.1). The Gardens of Adonis were small pottery vases filled with earth in which quick-growing plants were sown as part of the Adonis ceremonies. After they flourished they were thrown away with the images of the dead god into the sea or springs. Their primary proverbial sense in the 15th century was as a symbol of transience and it is as a memento mori that they seem to have been rediscovered early during the Renaissance. Perhaps, it has been suggested, Duke Humphrey learnt of the motif from the Italian humanists with whom he associated, such as Piero Del Monte, papal collector in England between 1435 and 1440, or Tito Livio Frulovisi, the Duke's secretary, or from his friend Abbot John of Whetehamstede, the author of indexes to classical life and himself an interesting example of a late-medieval polymath directly in contact with the new generations of Italian humanism.[12]

The English sculptors of Duke Humphrey's chapel had evidently been provided with a two-dimensional model which they copied and the motif is featured as a humanist badge on a structure which is unaffected in any other way by Renaissance ideas. It is not until the reign of Henry VII, when Italian humanism was widely valued in administrative and academic circles, particularly for its stylistic superiority in modern Latinity, that there is evidence for the penetration of Renaissance forms into sculpture executed in England. It is perhaps partly as a result of this new recognition of the stylistic superiority of Italian humanists and scholarly interest in classical antiquity that Italian Renaissance art was increasingly valued and Italian artists came to England, though the appearance of Italian artists and Renaissance forms in the Netherlands and France was to be even more significant in determining the new fashion in England.[13]

The first documentary references to an Italian sculptor in this country date from around 1506 when Guido Mazzoni was working on designs for a tomb-project for King Henry VII and Queen Elizabeth of York.[14] We can judge from Mazzoni's preceding work, the tomb of Charles VIII of France in St Denis, and from the detailed estimates for Henry's monument how revolutionary a work it would have been in the English context.[15] Since Mazzoni supplied a detailed pattern for the architectural mouldings, it is quite clear that it would have featured classicising Renaissance forms for the first time in English sculpture.[16] For a variety of reasons, Mazzoni's project ultimately came to nothing but, if the bust in the Royal Collection is correctly identified as a portrait by him of the future Henry VIII, Mazzoni may already have paid a visit to England c.1498–1500, and the first terracotta portrait bust here by an Italian sculptor may just precede the turn of the century.[17]

Whatever the case, the first tomb monuments actually to be constructed in an Italian Renaissance style are those of Margaret Beaufort, and of Henry VII and Queen Elizabeth of York, in Henry VII's chapel, Westminster Abbey (Fig. 6.2). When the Florentine sculptor Pietro Torrigiano signed the

Fig. 6.2 King Henry VII's and Queen Elizabeth's tomb, Westminster Abbey, by Pietro Torrigiano: detail showing architectural detail and putto with royal arms (Copyright author).

contract for the Beaufort tomb on 23 November 1511, he was constrained to follow the two-dimensional designs by a painter, probably of Netherlandish origins, Maynard Vewick, for the effigy, beast and tabernacle.[18] This appears to have been a traditional way of proceeding in English contracts; indeed the effigy and metalwork were generally assigned to a separate workshop from that responsible for the stonework.[19] Where Torrigiano was not similarly constrained, in the tomb-chest itself, he produced what must have seemed a startlingly novel design with roundels of laurel-leaf enclosing coats of arms and a classical architectural repertoire.[20] The whole working procedure foisted on him must have been profoundly irritating to Torrigiano, whose technical skills meant he was perfectly capable of both designing and executing the whole work and whose self-image as a creative artist had been fostered in Renaissance Florence.

In the later monument for Henry VII and Queen Elizabeth of York, for which Torrigiano signed the contract in October 1512, he was not obliged to follow another artist's designs.[21] Our knowledge of the contract reveals that he was able to bring a radically new way of working to bear on these prestigious projects. The Italianate conception of the artist as a profoundly important creative individual was a novelty in 16th-century England, where sculpture was purchased by the foot.[22] Torrigiano was able to combine the role of the master-mason as designer and executant of the tomb-chest with an ability to design and execute (with appropriate technical support) the metalwork components. It is one consequence of Torrigiano's increased freedom that the tomb-monument for Henry VII and Queen Elizabeth exhibits purer Italianate forms than its predecessor. In 1516 Torrigiano produced the monument to Dr Yonge, now in the Public Record Office, a monument revolutionary in a number of ways: for instance for its Florentine-type sarco-phagus, for its use of terracotta for the effigy, for the employment of a death mask for the head (and with its eyes closed, extremely unusual in the English tradition), and for the terracotta seraphs which flank the great head of Christ dominating the lunette above the effigy.[23] On 11 March 1517 he contracted for the High Altar of Henry VII's chapel and in January 1519 a draft contract was drawn up for the tomb monument of Henry VIII and Katharine of Aragon.[24] The high altar was only set up after Torrigiano's departure from England to Spain, and nothing came of the draft indenture for Henry VIII's tomb, but the Florentine Renaissance bridgehead which Torrigiano had established was consolidated when Benedetto da Rovezzano began work on Cardinal Wolsey's tomb, by June 1524 at the latest.[25] This monument was explicitly intended – so the sculptor relates – to match, at least, the tomb of Henry VII and Queen Elizabeth of York, and from the detailed inventory drawn up by the sculptor after Wolsey's fall we can attempt a reconstruction which

shows that it was of a remarkable, indeed unprecedented, size and scale, and that it more than rivalled any previous English royal monument. After Wolsey's fall, those of its materials which could be reused were appropriated by King Henry VIII, who put Benedetto to work alongside another Florentine sculptor, Giovanni da Maiano, on an even more grandiose tomb.[26] Henry VIII's monument was never finished though it was worked on by Nicholas Bellin da Modena and its incomplete materials were moved to Windsor in 1565. It was never, therefore, able to exert a direct impact on English canons of taste.[27]

By the third decade of the 16th century, then, all the most recent royal monuments, and some other key works, such as Dr Yonge's tomb, the high altar of Henry VII's chapel and the roundel for Sir Thomas Lovell were in the hands of Torrigiano; the employment of other Florentine sculptors such as Giovanni da Maiano and Benedetto da Rovezzano provides clear evidence that the greatest patrons, the King and his advisers (in particular Cardinal Wolsey) recognised that Italian sculptors were the best available. It is well known, though, that Italian Renaissance forms were disseminated in England by a wide variety of different media: manuscripts, woodcuts, printed books and paintings for instance.[28] What the patrons frequently sought was the fashionable decorative repertoire of the antique rather than a purely Florentine Renaissance style such as hardly any of them would anyway ever have seen. Wolsey, for instance, never visited Italy. The most up-to-date patrons would therefore have been quite as likely to look to France and the Low Countries, or to seek 'Antique' forms in the work of artists such as Holbein, as they would have been to think of Florentine artists as the arbiters of taste. They were also perfectly capable of adding fashionable antique elements to late gothic structures, such as we find in Bishop Fox's c.1513–18 chantry chapel at Winchester where little classical volutes appear to have been applied to a structure which otherwise shows no influence whatsoever of Renaissance forms.[29] A different and later example is provided by Abbot Islip's chapel at Westminster, which incorporated a marble bust of Christ by Torrigiano, now in the Wallace Collection, into a late Gothic structure, rather as Wolsey's Hampton Court featured roundels by Giovanni da Maiano.[30] There is no evidence that most contemporary English patrons were perturbed by such combinations of what now appear dramatically incongruous styles.

From very early in the 16th century, Italianate forms came to England via France. What has been termed the 'Château Gaillon' style is exhibited in works such as the Winchester Cathedral presbytery screens of 1525. After Nicholas Bellin da Modena fled to England in 1537 the Franco-Italian Mannerist style of Fontainebleau was imported into England, its most notable appearance being, of course, at Nonsuch.[31] One very interesting example of the style is found at Winchester in Bishop Gardiner's chantry chapel (Fig. 6.3). Gardiner was an ardent Catholic imprisoned for his beliefs in 1551–3 but reinstated under Queen Mary. He was (re)buried at Winchester

Fig. 6.3 Bishop Gardiner's chantry chapel, Winchester Cathedral (Copyright author).

in 1556 and what must be the last chantry chapel in England was subsequently constructed for him. Gardiner had left £400 'for the erection of a chantry that I may be praied for' and £300 for a tomb.[32] The chantry chapel seems to have been erected under his successor, Bishop John White, one of Gardiner's executors who, after preaching at Mary's funeral in December 1558, was put under house arrest. Gardiner's chantry chapel can therefore be precisely dated between 1556 and 1558. In basic form it is close in many particulars, even to the cadaver effigy, to Bishop Fox's on the other side of the presbytery, but of course it differs sharply in its Fontainebleau-derived style from Fox's chapel, executed forty years before.[33]

Not all mid-century sculpture in England is of the elevated quality of Gardiner's chantry chapel. Margaret Whinney's damning indictment of English sculpture in the 16th century as 'a sorry tale' and her comment that 'though the quantity produced was great, its quality is at once mediocre and monotonous' appears to be born out by two case studies.[34] In the case of John Parker, a tomb-sculptor first documented in Burton-upon-Trent in 1532, it is possible to trace his career from c.1530 to 1570, right through the critical years of the Reformation.[35] The first reference to Parker as a tomb-maker occurs in 1534 when William Blount made a will in which he stated that he had 'devysed' a tomb with Parker and a mason called John Smith, of Derby. If Parker should die 'afore the saide tombe be made and leve not a sufficiente man to fynyshe and parforme the saide tombe, then I will and desire myn executors to see it made according to the plot which I devised'.[36] This tomb does not survive, but one for which Parker was paid £20 in 1544, for Thomas Manners, the first Earl of Rutland, at Bottesford (Leics.), does (Figs 6.4 & 6.5), and forms the basis for the attribution of other tombs to him.[37] On Parker's death in 1570, his workshop included six alabaster stones some of which would doubtless have been employed for a tomb for Richard Harford of Bosbury, Herefordshire, from whom Parker had already received £4 down-payment. (When the tomb was finally completed in 1573, it was made by John Gildon of Hereford.[38]) The changes between Parker's early tombs and those of the 1550s and later are fairly

Fig. 6.4 *First Earl of Rutland's tomb, Bottesford (Copyright author).*

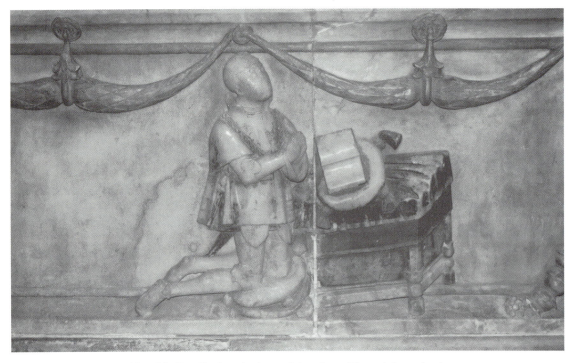

Fig. 6.5 *Detail of tomb-chest of the above (Copyright author).*

minor: religious imagery disappears (an Annunciation at Eye (Herefs.) closely resembling one from c.1530 at Ross-on-Wye (also Herefs.), probably dates from as late as the 1540s, just before the end of Henry VIII's reign), but then again the very plain Bottesford tomb-chest has no religious imagery, though the inscription contains an invocation to Christ, and there is a kneeling figure of the earl's son at a prayer desk at the west end (Fig. 6.5). Kneeling groups of figures gradually disappear from the tomb-chests – the Andrew tomb at Charwelton (Northants.), is apparently the last – in favour of individual figures displaying heraldry as on the Sacheverell tomb at Ratcliffe-on-Soar (Notts.). The later tombs are also marked by an increasingly standardised design. Parker's workshop employed Renaissance vase patterns in low relief on corner pilasters, whose meaninglessness to the workshop is illustrated by the fact that in one late example the pattern is actually carved upside down.[39]

The effects of the Dissolution on tomb-sculpture have never been systematically examined and it is clear that the whole subject demands serious attention. Jon Bayliss has claimed that John Parker's career was adversely affected by the religious and political changes of the Reformation and the same factors seem to have affected the Richard and Gabriel Royley workshop, which similarly operated out of Burton.[40] Bayliss documents instances – such as the tomb of Sir Richard Knightley at Upton, Northamptonshire – where earlier effigies, made available by the Dissolution, were partially recut and reused.[41] An instance of this practice occurs in the Royley shop's output, at Monks Kirby in Warwickshire, where Sir William Fielding's (d.1547) effigy is apparently, an earlier product, appropriated and recarved.[42] The palimpsesting of brasses has, of course, a long precedent, but the Dissolution evidently made numbers of sculpted effigies available for those who were not too proud to be commemorated by second-hand figures.

The Royley workshop's tomb-chests display individual family members holding shields, or simply large heraldic shields by themselves, with square-sectioned pilasters reflecting Renaissance models at some considerable distance. On the tomb of Sir John Salusbury (d.1578) at Whitchurch (Denbyshire), and on the Fermor tomb at Somerton (Oxon.), there is apparently a reminiscence of Torrigiano's putti on Henry VII's tomb, though here they have been transformed into 'grotesquely deformed [figures], with enormous bloated bodies and tiny legs'.[43] Katharine Esdaile describes the later works of this shop as 'lamentable shadows of works by the earlier Burton generation, degenerate both in their human types and in their would-be Italian decoration'.[44]

If the preceding assessment of the Parker and Royley workshops suggests that, in purely stylistic terms, the standards of indigenous sculpture were often lamentably low, the puzzling group of tombs at Framlingham in Suffolk demonstrates that there were top-quality sculptors, probably of French origin, active in East Anglia at the same time other French workshops were at Winchester. Consideration of the tombs also suggests that stylistic analysis can open up other avenues of enquiry for the historian, and provide evidence which can be of use in the long-running debates about the popularity of, and attitudes towards, the Reformation.

The Cluniac Priory of Thetford had been the mausoleum of the Mowbray Dukes of Norfolk and by adopting it as their own burial place, the Howard Dukes of Norfolk stressed their continuity with their predecessors (just as the Despensers, for example, had with the Clares at Tewkesbury Abbey).[45] John Howard, the first Howard duke, was buried at Thetford in 1485 and was followed in 1524 by his son Thomas. The third duke intended to be buried there too and work had already begun, before the Dissolution, on a tomb for himself and one for his son-in-law, Henry Fitzroy, Henry VIII's bastard son (d.1536). We know this because the third duke petitioned the king to save the priory in 1539:

> thentent of the saide Duke is...to make a parisshe Churche of the same, wher nowe doth lye buryed the bodie of the late Duke of Richemond the kings naturall sonn...and also doth entende to lye their hymself, havyng alrady made twoo Tombes, one for the saide Duke of Richmond and an other for hymself, which have alredy and woll cost hym, or they can be fully set uppe & fynisshed, iiij^c li. at the least.[46]

However, in spite of the third duke's efforts, the priory was dissolved in February 1540 (though the duke was able to buy the site and estates). Exactly

Fig. 6.6 *Tomb of the fourth duke's wives, Framlingham (Copyright author).*

Fig. 6.7 *Tomb of the third duke and his wife, Framlingham (Copyright author).*

what the duke's plans now were is unclear, but it seems that he decided in the 1540s that the parish church of Framlingham, close to his great castle, would be a safer location for his mausoleum. By 11 November 1547 a certificate of the churchwardens of Framlingham stated that the duke had 'plucked down' the old chancel of the church intending to rebuild it on a larger scale, work which had ceased abruptly when the duke was imprisoned in 1546; indeed, the third duke was only saved from the executioner (his son was not so fortunate) by the fact that Henry VIII died on the day destined for his execution.[47] The rebuilding plans were certainly connected with the duke's decision to move the two incomplete tombs and establish a new mausoleum in a new chancel at Framlingham: in the meantime the Howards had maintained intact the church of the dissolved priory at Thetford, as a royal inventory of the disgraced duke's property reveals.[48] The third duke remained in prison until Mary's reign and work at Framlingham cannot therefore have resumed before 1553 (he died the next year): in 1554, the duke left it to his executors to decide where he should be buried and as late as 1557 work on the church was still not finished.[49]

Four tombs relevant to this paper survive at Framlingham. Two of them – that for two of the fourth duke's wives (Fig. 6.6; there is a space for his effigy which was never put in place), and the tomb of Elizabeth Howard – date from 1558–67, close in date to the stylistically analogous Hoby brothers tombs at Bisham Abbey of c.1566.[50] These two tombs can be used to help date the monuments of the third duke and his wife (Fig. 6.7), and of Henry Fitzroy (Fig. 6.8): the effigies of the two wives of the fourth duke are stylistically so close to the effigies of the third duke and his wife that they must all be by the same workshop. The tomb-chest of the Fitzroy monument (which has no effigies) is stylistically close to the Elizabeth Howard tomb-chest. Such comparisons could suggest that all four monuments belong to the late 1550s or 1560s. However, fragments discovered at Thetford Priory are nearly identical to the tomb-chest of the third duke's tomb and the Old Testament reliefs of the Fitzroy tomb. These fragments, Richard Marks has argued, must be from the two tombs which were underway in

Fig. 6.8 Detail of Henry Fitzroy tomb, Framlingham (showing Expulsion relief) (Copyright author).

1539.[51] It seems that the tomb-chest of the third duke's monument, which may have been near completion in 1539, was moved after 1553 to Framlingham from Thetford and completed by the addition of effigies of the duke and one of his wives.[52] A scratched date, 1559, on the tomb, seems to bear out this theory. The monument is therefore essentially a work of c.1539, moved, reassembled and completed after 1553. The tomb of Henry Fitzroy, however, may have been further from completion in 1539 (it is unclear whether work continued on the monuments into the 1540s). Perhaps only the Old Testament reliefs could be moved to Framlingham, where they were incorporated into a new tomb-chest, which has a date 1555 scratched on it.[53] No effigies were ever supplied. In Marks's view, both tombs are therefore composites: the tomb-chest of the third duke's monument is a work of c.1539, with effigies of two decades later added to it; the Fitzroy tomb-chest incorporates reliefs from c.1539, but is largely a work of c.1553–5. He backs up his views by citing French stylistic precedents.[54] The high cost of the two monuments – at £400 the pair – claimed in 1539, may have been an exaggeration, but could be explained by the complex and luxurious treatment intended for the tomb-chests and by the fact that no fewer than five effigies were originally to have been carved. The large investment in the monuments by the third duke helps explain why the unfinished works were moved from Thetford.

These two great monuments must have been moved and reconstructed in Mary's reign: in that of her predecessor, to move a tomb-chest covered with relief statues of saints would hardly have been conceivable, even on the monument of so staunch a defender of traditional religion: the fact that the third duke was in prison throughout Edward's reign effectively rules out such a possibility. The scratched date 1559 on the third duke's tomb suggests that it was actually finished at the beginning of Elizabeth's reign. The moving of the two monuments, their completion and siting in a parish church chancel, rather than the monastic church for which they had been intended, all this provides a remarkable insight into religious disruptions and continuities under Henry VIII, Edward VI and Mary I. The tombs had been conceived in years when the Dissolution seemed far from inevitable, even to a close councillor of the King. Whilst the third duke languished in prison, the fate of the unfinished monuments hung in the balance, and the rebuilding scheme at Framling-ham was left incomplete. The equivocal phrasing of his will suggests that in 1554 the third duke may even have been hoping for a restoration of Thetford Priory. Finally, they were completed by his grandson, and set up at Framlingham. Equally revealing is the fact that the two later monuments, those of the fourth duke's two wives and of Elizabeth Howard – construction of which must have immediately followed completion of the first two – feature no religious imagery whatsoever, and are entirely dominated by heraldry. The fourth duke completed his grandfather's work, but on the new monuments opted instead for coats of arms as the decoration of

the tomb-chests. By the time that these later tombs were erected it must have been clear that any hope of a return to traditional Catholicism under Elizabeth was a pipe-dream. The Royal proclamation of 1560 designed to save the monuments of the nobility from iconoclastic attack, strongly suggests that images such as were found on the two early monuments were being attacked by radical Protestants, just as they must have been ten years earlier when an Edwardian act ordered all religious images to be destroyed:

> Provided always that this act or any thing therein conteyned shall not estend to any Image or Picture sett or graven upon any tomb in any Church – only for a Monument of any King, Prince or Nobleman or other dead person which hath not been commonly reputed and taken for a Saint.[55]

Commissioning of new religious imagery under Elizabeth would merely have invited trouble. Just as the two composite monuments of the third duke and of Henry Fitzroy provide evidence for religious attitudes under Queen Mary, so do the two later tombs reveal something about the Elizabethan settlement.

A very similar point can be made about Bishop Gardiner's chapel at Winchester (Fig. 6.9). Potentially more significant than its stylistic difference from Bishop Fox's tomb is the total absence of religious imagery from the exterior of Gardiner's chapel, imagery with which the chapels of Fox, Waynflete and Beaufort had bristled. The interior of the chapel contains only two images, above the altar – *Synagogue* and *Ecclesia* – symbolic imagery, not statues of saints: the difference of tone from the Eucharistic emphases in Fox's chapel is remarkable. The explanation for these differences between Gardiner's chapel and its predecessors lies in the Chantries Act of 1547. Unlike the Henrician Act of 1545, this Act attacked the whole theological foundations of the chantries, the 'phantasising vain opinions of purgatory and masses satisfactory, to be done for them which be departed'.[56] The measure eradicated at a stroke the religious underpinning of intercession for the dead. The desire for prayers on behalf of the deceased, and a profound belief in their efficacy, lay at the root of the rituals thus effaced: 'I knowe well', declared John Clopton in his will of

Fig. 6.9 Figure of Synagogue, from reredos of Bishop Gradiner's chantry chapel (Copyright author).

chantry chapel brings before us issues which a purely stylistic analysis of tomb-monuments is not equipped to detect. What disappeared with the Edwardian Reformation (and one should not underestimate the resistance to this state-sponsored destruction of religious imagery and of the doctrine of Purgatory) was what one might term the 'para-tomb,' meaning not just the physical structures associated with chantries (chantry altars and screens, for example) but the ritual ones, the whole structures of provision for mortuary masses, ceremonies, candles and alms, designed to ensure the hastening of the souls of the commemorated through the pains of Purgatory.[60] The other episcopal chantry chapels' statuary were probably destroyed at Winchester after Bishop Gardiner's attempted defence of the use of imagery and his subsequent imprisonment in 1548. Even if these images had survived, the wholesale attack on such statues elsewhere from 1548 to 1553 onwards must explain the cautious, discrete and private use of sculpture in Gardiner's chapel after 1556, for both the cult of saints and the belief in purgatory were 'abiding casualties of the preceding Reformations'.[61]

The abolition of chantries and the related attack on all religious imagery in 1548 had profound repercussions. The vast majority of *all* sculpture before the Reformation was religious imagery. Of course, tomb monuments continued to be built after the Reformation even if they were no longer housed in chantry chapels crowded with imagery – such as those of Bishops Fox of Winchester, or West of Ely, completed in 1534 – or studded with invocations for intercession. The omission of saints and intercessory phrases from tomb-chests may not be very important from the stylistic point of view. However, the fact that tomb-chests and effigies continue to be carved and that there is no great *stylistic* caesura between those before and after Edward VI's reign tends to mask the profound *functional* change in tomb monuments which now concentrate predominantly on their memorial role and issues of power, status and allegiance (this is not to say, as has been recently claimed, that post-Reformation tomb monuments did not even address issues of aesthetics).[62] The stylistic changes of early 16th-century sculpture have masked the fact that the tombs had effectively the same functions whether they are what we term late Gothic

1494, 'that prayers is a singuler remedie for the deliverance of soules in purcatory and specially the offering of the Blessed Sacrement of Our Lorde's body', and his will accordingly makes lavish provision for intercession on his soul's behalf, through masses and alms.[57] Clopton's chantry chapel at Long Melford (Suffolk) is full of the penitential poetry of Lydgate, and his tomb stands in the location where the Easter Sepulchre would be placed during the easter ceremonies.[58] Under Edward VI, the wholesale destruction of religious images and the abolition of the doctrine of Purgatory forced fundamental ruptures with the past, ruptures which were, finally, never to be repaired.[59] The whole panoply of intercession, concentrated on chantries and obits and given enduring visual form in chantry chapels, was abolished. There is, then, a sense in which Gardiner's or Renaissance in style. The significant break is not stylistic but functional and occurs with the Reformation. That a concentration on style may blind one to functional disjunctions can be illustrated by comparing two examples of royal funeral ritual approximately a century apart.

Funeral effigies were used in royal exequies as a substitute for the encoffined corpse of the deceased, which, prior to the introduction of an effigy at the funeral of Edward II, had itself been displayed.[63] The use of temporary effigies representing the deceased was an admirable solution to the obvious problems of exhibiting rotting corpses. Queen Elizabeth of York's effigy dating from 1503 is well documented and is the first for which an official account of the funeral survives.[64] In addition, a hitherto unpublished early 16th-century drawing in a Wriothesley manuscript in the British Library (Fig. 6.10) records the appearance of the funeral car and of the banners of Our Lady which accompanied it (showing the Annunciation, Visitation, Nativity and Madonna and Child). This is the first 'antiquarian' representation of a specific royal funeral procession to survive from England.

The effigy of Queen Elizabeth played a central role in the funeral procession from the Tower to Westminster Abbey, lying above the coffin containing the dead monarch's corpse. The effigy was censed on removal from the funeral chariot and again stood above the coffin in the hearse, a focal point for the funeral services: ladies watched over it all night and after matins, 'the prior of that place with the Convent full devoutly came from the quire and stood about the Corps saying divers psalmes Deus misereatur nostri Deprofundis...'; later, palls were laid over the effigy, ladies kissing the feet of the figure as they made their offerings. It was only separated from the coffin just before the latter was interred.[65]

Modern commentators have almost entirely neglected the role of the effigy in the religious ceremonial of the funeral. Yet no one who reads an account of pre-Reformation services in which funeral effigies were used can fail to notice that they were the visual foci for the singing of requiem masses and prayers for intercession. Paradoxically it is the continued use after the Reformation of royal funeral effigies which has tended to obscure the fact that there was a profound mutation of function when the English church abolished the doctrine of purgatory. At Henry VIII's funeral, the use of the funeral image

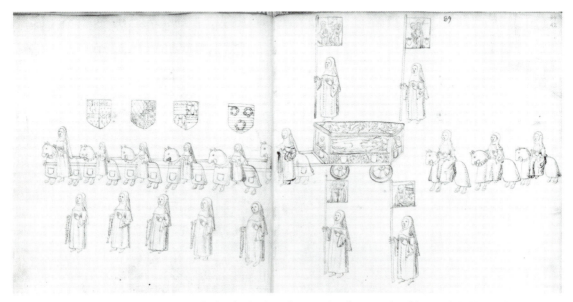

Fig. 6.10 *Funeral Procession of Elizabeth of York, British Library MS Additional 45131 ff. 41ᵛ–42 (Copyright Trustees of the British Library).*

was accompanied by thousands of masses. These were omitted under Edward VI but reintegrated again under Mary. At her funeral, the religious banners – the Trinity, the Virgin Mary, St George and Mary Magdalene – were used for the last time. For her brother, the funeral effigy had been surrounded by heraldic banners instead (in this case the Order of the Garter, Red Cross, the arms of Edward's mother and of the Queen Dowager) and these were to be used thereafter.[66] This is symbolic, for as the intercessory element collapsed, it was succeeded by a dramatic increase in the role and power of the heralds.[67] Now the funeral image's function was largely confined to the evocation of pity and sadness at the loss of the deceased. Henry Petowe, a spectator at Elizabeth I's funeral writes:

Oh, yee spectators, which did view that sight!
Say, if you truelie say, could you refraine,
To shed a sea of teares in deathes despight,
That rest her hence, whome Art brought backe againe?
He that knew her, and had Eliza seen,
Would sweare that figure were faire England's Queene.[68]

The emphasis on accurate portraiture, which had been present from the first use of royal effigies in the funeral rituals, had now superseded any other function for the funeral effigy. It had lost one of its chief functions in a service where its role as a focus for intercessory prayers and services had hitherto been so important: now it was a cue for sorrowful memory not for prayer. The reformed dead, as Eamon Duffy has indeed shown, had been carried beyond the influence of the living.

Acknowledgements

Dr S.F. Baylis and Dr T. Hartley provided valuable assistance with this paper. Dr G. Walker and Dr D. Chaproniere also made useful suggestions.

Notes

1. Higgins 1894; Whinney 1964, chapters 1–2; Darr 1979, 1982; Galvin & Lindley 1988; Lindley 1995.
2. Lindley 1995, 47–72
3. Burke 1992, 6
4. Among the more important contributions are Whinney 1964, 5–9, relying heavily on work later published by Blunt (1969); Biddle 1993. Yet the important paper by Baggs (1968) has still not been adequately followed up.
5. Whinney 1964, xxi and l.
6. This is made explicit on the dustwrappers where it is stated that they 'will consider the subject chronologically, treating all branches of the visual arts as part of the general history of England. The series aims at ... providing an account of the arts as seen against the background of history.'
7. The scope (and author) of the missing sixth volume is listed on the dustwrapper of the 1968 corrected impression of Boase 1953.
8. Stone 1972, 230–3.
9. Muratova 1989. See also Allan & Blaylock 1991.
10. Rose-Troup 1928; Randall 1974.
11. Martindale 1989.
12. Kendrick 1946.
13. See above n. 4 and Kipling 1977. See, for another medium, Marks 1993, chapter 10.
14. Lindley 1995, 54–7.
15. British Library, MS. Harley 297, ff. 28–30; Verdon 1978, 119–34; Lugli 1990, 331.
16. Verdon 1990, 282–3.
17. Larson 1989; Lugli 1990, 331–2.
18. Scott 1915.
19. Lindley 1995, 47–72.
20. Higgins (1894, 132) who was unaware of the documentation for Margaret Beaufort's tomb, already realized that it predated Henry VII and Queen Elizabeth's monument
21. The lost indentures are rehearsed in the later draft for Henry VIII's tomb: see Illingworth 1812 (now Public Record Office SP1/18, pp. 2–5).
22. Stone 1972, 4.
23. See the results of the conservation analysis by Carol Galvin in Lindley 1995, 188–206.
24. Westminster Abbey Muniments 6638*; Britton 1809, III, 23–5; Public Record Office SP1/18, pp. 2–5; Illingworth 1812.
25. Bodleian Library, Masters manuscript, Jesus College MS. 74, ff. 189–90; Higgins 1894, appendix II.
26. Lindley 1991.
27. Biddle 1966; Colvin *et al.* 1975, 321.
28. Thurley 1993, chapter 6.
29. Lindley 1993, 115.
30. Darr 1982.
31. Biddle 1984.
32. See the magisterial account by Biddle (1993); Nichols & Bruce (eds) 1863, p.43.

33. Biddle 1993, 282.
34. Whinney 1964, 1.
35. Bayliss 1990.
36. *Ibid.* 39.
37. *Ibid.* 41.
38. *Ibid.* 41.
39. *Ibid.* 48: the tomb is that of Andrew Nowell at Old Dalby, Leics.
40. *Ibid.* 51. See, however, Bayliss's comments on the Blount tomb at Kinlet (Shrops.), where it is suggested that the tomb was made following the transfer of the body from the London Greyfriars'. Such instances may have provided extra work for sculptors. For the other Burton shop see Bayliss 1991.
41. Bayliss 1990, 51.
42. Bayliss 1991, 39.
43. Whinney 1964, 7 and pl. 2b.
44. Esdaile 1946, 48.
45. Stone & Colvin 1965.
46. Marks 1984, 260–1.
47. Stone & Colvin 1965, 161. See also *ibid.* n. 12 for a survey of the church.
48. Robinson 1982, 37–8.
49. Stone & Colvin 1965, 161, 166.
50. Marks 1984, 259 for a characteristically acute examination of stylistic parallels. The absence from the tomb of the fourth duke's first two wives of his own effigy is accounted for by the fact that he was convicted of treason and executed in 1572.
51. *Ibid.* 261–2.
52. No explanation has yet been advanced for the carving of the faces of the duke and his wife as separate mask-like pieces.
53. The dates were first noted by Stone & Colvin 1965, 166.
54. Marks 1984, 262–3.
55. Phillips 1973, 97. See also Bishop Gardiner's defence of imagery (*ibid.* 90–3) and, for attacks on tomb-monuments, 117–18; Hughes & Larkin 1969, 146–8.
56. Duffy 1992, 454. *Statutes of the Realm, IV,* 1819, 24; Kreider 1979, chapter 8.
57. Howard (ed.) 1866, 34.
58. Dymond & Paine 1992, 4.
59. Wood-Legh 1965.
60. See Duffy 1992, chapter 10.
61. Hutton 1987, 131. The fact that these two images were left in place emphasizes that even Bishop Horne (1561–79) did not find them offensive. A good deal more work needs to take place on tomb-monuments commissioned during Mary's reign; it is too often

assumed that tombs with religious imagery ante-date Henry VIII's death. Biddle (1993, 282) is wrong in his claim that chantries were still 'technically illegal'. See also Whiting 1983.
62. In a stimulating essay Llewellyn (1990, b) argues that 'Post-Reformation English tombs were not erected to show off their patrons' tastes ... the kinds of issues which the monuments address were those of status, power and allegiance, not of aesthetics'. See *idem* 1990 (a), 220.
63. Lindley 1995, 97–112.
64. Harvey & Mortimer 1994, 44–9.
65. Grose & Astle (eds.) 1784, 241–50.
66. Anglo 1992, 103. See also Fritz 1981 and the important work by Gittings (1984, 216–34); Llewllyn 1990 (a). I intend to deal with the issue of Tudor royal funerals in a forthcoming essay.
67. Gittings 1984, 224.
68. Anglo 1992, 104.

Bibliography

Allan, J.P. & Blaylock, S. 1991, 'The West Front I: The Structural History of the West Front', in *Medieval Art and Architecture at Exeter Cathedral*, Leeds, 94–115

Anglo, S. 1992, *Images of Tudor Kingship*, Guildford

Baggs, A.P. 1968, 'Sixteenth-Century Terracotta Tombs in East Anglia', *Archaeological Journal* 125, 295–301

Bayliss, J. 1990, 'Richard Parker "The Alablasterman"', *Church Monuments*, 5, 39–56

Bayliss, J, 1991, 'Richard and Gabriel Royley of Burton-upon-Trent Tombmakers', *Church Monuments*, 6, 21–41

Biddle, M. 1966, 'Nicholas Bellin of Modena: an Italian artificer at the courts of Francis I and Henry VIII', *Journal of the British Archaeological Association* 29, 106–121

Biddle, M. 1984, 'The stuccoes of Nonsuch', *Burlington Magazine* 126, 411–16

Biddle, M. 1993, 'Early Renaissance at Winchester', in J. Crook (ed.), *Winchester Cathedral*, Chichester, 257–304

Blunt, A. 1969, 'L'influence française sur l'architecture et la sculpture décorative en Angleterre pendant la première moitié du xvie siècle', *Revue de l'Art*, 4, 17–29

Boase, T.S.R. 1953, *English Art 1100–1216*, Oxford

Britton, J. 1809, *The Architectural Antiquities of Great Britain*, London, vol. II

Burke, P. 1992, 'The Uses of Italy', in R. Porter & M.

Teich (eds), *The Renaissance in National Context*, Cambridge, 6–20

Colvin, H.M., Ransome, D.R. & Summerson, J. 1975, *History of the King's Works*, III

Darr, A.P. 1979, 'The Sculptures of Torrigiano: the Westminster Abbey Tombs', *Connoisseur* 200, pp. 177–84

Darr, A.P. 1982, 'From Westminster Abbey to the Wallace Collection: Torrigiano's Head of Christ', *Apollo* (November 1982), 292–8

Duffy, E. 1992, *The Stripping of the Altars: Traditional Religion in England 1400–1580*, New Haven

Dymond, D. & Paine, C. 1992, *The Spoil of Melford Church: the Reformation in a Suffolk Parish*, Ipswich

Esdaile, K.A. 1946, *English Church Monuments 1510–1840*

Fritz, P.S. 1981, 'From 'Public' to 'Private': the Royal Funerals in England, 1500–1830', in J. Waley (ed.), *Mirrors of Mortality*, London, 61–79

Galvin, C. & Lindley, P.G. 1988, 'Pietro Torrigiano's Portrait Bust of King Henry VII', *Burlington Magazine* 130, 892–902

Gent, L. & Llewellyn, N. (eds) 1990, *Renaissance Bodies*

Gittings, C. 1984, *Death, Burial and the Individual in Early Modern England*

Grose, F. & Astle, T. (eds) 1784, *The Antiquarian Repertory* 4, 241–50

Harvey, A. & Mortimer, R. 1994, *The Funeral Effigies of Westminster Abbey*, Woodbridge

Higgins, A. 1894, 'On the Work of Florentine Sculptors in England in the Early Part of the Sixteenth Century; with Special Reference to the Tombs of Cardinal Wolsey and King Henry VIII', *Archaeological Journal* 51, 129–220.

Howard, J.J. (ed.) 1866, *The Visitation of Suffolke, made by William Hervey*

Hutton, P.L. & Larkin, J.F. (eds) 1969, *Tudor Royal Proclamations*, II

Hutton, R.H. 1987, 'The Local Impact of the Tudor Reformations', in C. Haigh (ed.) *The English Reformation Revised*, Cambridge, 1987, 114–138

Illingworth, W. 1812, 'Transcript of a Draft of an Indenture of Covenants for the erecting of a Tomb to the Memory of King Henry the Eighth, and Queen Katherine his Wife...' *Archaeologia*, 16, 84–8

Kendrick, T.D. 1946, 'Humphrey, Duke of Gloucester, and the Gardens of Adonis', *Antiquaries Journal* 206, 118–122

Kreider, A. 1979, *English Chantries: The Road to Dissolution*, Cambridge Mass.

Kipling, G. 1977, *The Triumph of Honour: Burgundian*

Origins of the Elizabethan Renaissance, Leiden

Larson, J. 1989, 'A polychrome terracotta bust of a laughing child at Windsor Castle', *Burlington Magazine*, 131, 618–624

Lindley, P.G., 1991, 'Playing check-mate with royal majesty? Wolsey's patronage of Italian Renaissance sculpture', in S.J. Gunn and P.G. Lindley (eds), *Cardinal Wolsey: Church, state and art*, Cambridge, 261–85

Lindley, P.G. 1993, 'The medieval sculpture of Winchester Cathedral' in J. Crook (ed.), *Winchester Cathedral: nine hundred years*, Chichester 1993, 97–122

Lindley, P.G. 1995, *Gothic to Renaissance*, Stamford

Llewellyn, N. 1990a, 'The Royal Body. Monuments to the Dead, for the Living', in Gent & Llewellyn (eds) 1990, 218–40

Llewellyn, N. 1990b, 'Accident or Design? John Gildon's Funeral Monuments and Italianate taste in Elizabethan England', in E. Chaney and P. Mack (eds), *England and the Continental Renaissance: Essays in Honour of J.B. Trapp*, Woodbridge, 143–51

Lugli, A. 1990, *Guido Mazzoni e la rinascita della terracotta nel quattrocento*, Allemandi

Marks, R. 1984, 'The Howard Tombs at Thetford and Framlingham: new discoveries', *Archaeological Journal* 141, 252–68

Marks, R. 1993, *Stained Glass in England during the Middle Ages*

Martindale, A. 1989, 'The knights and the bed of stones: a learned confusion of the fourteenth century', *Journal of the British Archaeological Association* 142, 66–74

Muratova, X. 1989, 'Exeter and Italy: Assimilation and Adaptation of a Style; the Question of Italian Trecento Sources in the Sulptured Front of Exeter Cathedral (Fourteenth Century)', in I. Lavin (ed.), *World Art: Themes of Unity in Diversity*, Pennsylvania, 117–24

Nichols, J.G. & Bruce, J. (eds) 1863, *Wills from Doctors' Commons: a selection from the wills of eminent persons proved in the prerogative court of Canterbury 1495–1695*, Camden Society

Phillips, J. 1973, *The Reformation of Images: Destruction of Art in England, 1535–1660*, Berkeley

Randall jr, R.H. 1974, 'A fourteenth-century altar-frontal', *Apollo*, November 1974, 368–71

Robinson, J.M. 1982, *The Dukes of Norfolk. A quincentennial history*, Oxford

Rose-Troup, F. 1928, 'Bishop Grandisson: student and art-lover', *Reports and Transactions of the Devonshire Association* 60, 239–75

Scott, R.F. 1915, 'On the contracts for the tomb of the

Lady Margaret Beaufort, Countess of Richmond and Derby, mother of King Henry VII, and foundress of the colleges of Christ and St John in Cambridge; with some illustrative documents', *Archaeologia* 66, 365–76

Stone, L. & Colvin, H. 1965, 'The Howard Tombs at Framlingham, Suffolk', *Archaeological Journal* 122, 159–171

Stone, L. 1972, *Sculpture in Britain: the Middle Ages*, Harmondsworth

Thurley, S. 1993, *The Royal Palaces of Tudor England*

Verdon, T. 1978, *The Art of Guido Mazzoni*, New York

Whinney, M. 1964, *Sculpture in Britain 1530–1830*, Harmondsworth

Whiting, R. 1983, 'For the Health of My Soul: Prayers for the Dead in the Tudor South West', *Southern History* 5, 68–94

Wood-Legh, K. L. 1965, *Perpetual Chantries in Britain*, Cambridge

7 Whitehall Palace and Westminster 1400–1600: a royal seat in transition

Simon Thurley

In Shakespeare's *Henry VIII*, a gentleman at Anne Boleyn's coronation, remarks:

> You must no more call it York Place; that's past
> For, since the cardinal fell, that title's lost:
> 'Tis now the king's, and call'd Whitehall.
> *Act IV Scene I.*

This remark neatly summarizes the transition from archiepiscopal inn to royal palace which is a familiar part of the story of Henry VIII's Whitehall Palace. Yet for Henry VIII and his subjects a far more vivid comparison for the new royal residence was not the old archbishop's house but the former Westminster Palace, the ancient and principal seat of English kings. This paper explores the metamorphosis of the palace of Westminster between 1512 and 1547. It examines the characteristics of the medieval palace of Westminster and compares them with Henry VIII's new palace of Whitehall a few hundred yards to its north. It concludes that, although the geographical transition was only a short one, and the period of evolution equally brief, the form, function and context of the new palace was radically different from the old. The nature of that difference is highly informative about the attitudes and architecture of the English Crown in the late Plantagenet and early Tudor periods.

The *Oxford English Dictionary* defines the word *palace* as the 'official residence of an emperor, king, pope, or other sovereign ruler'.[1] The term derived from the Palatine Hill in Rome, the residence favoured by Hadrian (117–138) and other Emperors,

and by the 12th century it had become used throughout Europe to describe the principal residences of kings and bishops. In the British Isles the term was being used by King David of Scotland by the 1130s as well as by the English episcopate,[2] but the earliest written evidence of the use of the term in connection with the king's house at Westminster dates from 1236 when Matthew Paris describes Henry III leaving the Tower of London and making for his 'palatium'.[3] Chronologically the next English use of the term I can identify is in the last quarter of the 12th century when in William Fitzstephen's *Life of Archbishop Becket* Westminster is described as 'palatium regium' and the Tower of London 'arcem palatinam'. Yet despite these isolated uses, in official (i.e. state) papers, Westminster continued to be called 'the king's house (*domus*)', 'the king's *curia*' or the 'king's manor' for another half century.[4] It was only in 1265 that the term 'palace' was used in an official communication, on the occasion of Henry III's grant of the keepership of the palace of Westminster to John de Sumerset. The term, once adopted, has remained in use for Westminster to this day.[5] Other than for Westminster, the use of the term palace in England was very sparing down to the early 17th century and even then it was confined to three Crown properties, Westminster, the Tower of London and Guildford. Of the three, Westminster was the only one to be consistently called a palace, being as it was, by the early 13th century, the Crown's governmental, legal, ceremonial, sacerdotal and residential base - literally the *palatium* of realm. The use of the word in connection with the Tower of London was more specialised and literary. Fitzstephen's use of 'arcem palatinam' should be seen in the context of his History in which London is compared with ancient Rome and its female inhabitants with the Sabines. Whilst Fitzstephen uniquely saw the Tower of London as an imperial citadel,[6] Westminster was identified in a much more exacting manner as 'the palace'.[7] The description of Guildford Castle as a palace was restricted to the reign of Edward I: it almost certainly reflected the occupation of the castle by the king's mother, Eleanor of Provence in her widowhood, and then by his second wife, Margaret of France – evidently Guildford was their *palatium*, their principal residence.

Clearly the use of the term palace was restricted to a small number of specific buildings, but particularly to Westminster. It is tempting to suggest that the adoption of the term at Westminster in 1265 was an overdue recognition of Westminster's ousting of Winchester in the bid to become the Crown's permanent base. But there is no evidence to corroborate this. More certainly its adoption reflects the determination of Henry III to elevate the Crown in all its elements and institutions. The elevation of the vill of Westminster was part of this, achieved by rebuilding both the early medieval king's house there and the Anglo-Saxon abbey.[8]

With the construction of Westminster Hall by William II the king's house at Westminster became the ceremonial heart of the kingdom. Yet it was only in the reign of Henry II that the Exchequer was moved there, was housed in a purpose built structure, and set a pattern for other royal offices. In the 13th century the Court of Common Pleas was accommodated in part of Westminster Hall, and a hundred years later the Court of the King's Bench was quartered in the same building nearby. The arrival of these two courts made Westminster not only the principal administrative centre of the realm but also the headquarters of English justice. The trend to consolidate power at Westminster was continued by Edward III, who erected the building which became known as Star Chamber for meetings of his council, and during his reign the members of the baronage and religious leaders summoned to attend Parliament met increasingly regularly in the White or Parliament Chamber.[9]

Hand in hand with these legal and administrative developments at Westminster extensive building works by successive Plantagenet kings ensured a standard of magnificence and luxury worthy of their royal status and Westminster became the most frequently visited house for the majority of medieval monarchs. By the reign of Edward II it is possible to discern a distinction in the functional distribution of the buildings on the site which held true until 1512. First there was the Great Hall with adjoining public buildings: then there was the more private and residential area, called appropriately the privy palace, set slightly apart, and thirdly accommodation for the heir apparent called the 'prince's palace', in another geographically distinct area (Fig. 7.1).

In 1512, three years after Henry VIII's accession, there was a serious fire. The antiquarian John Stow wrote 'a great part of this palace at Westminster was once againe burnt...since which time it hath not beene reedified; only the great Hall, with the offices neare adionyning, are kept in good reparations, and serve as before for feasts at Coronations, Arraignments of great persons charges with treasons, keeping of the courts of justice &c'[10] The fire, which involved the destruction of the privy palace, left the king without a residence in Westminster where, as Stow noted, the law courts sat and the king's council and parliament continued to meet. In the years immediately following 1512 Henry VIII used Archbishop Warham of Canterbury's house at Lambeth just across the river from Westminster whenever necessary and began work on a new house called Bridewell adjoining the Fleet in London. Lambeth had two advantages over York Place, in Westminster, the residence of the Archbishop of York: it had been recently modernised, and archbishop Warham was Chancellor, and in all but name the King's chief minister. York Place, originally built in close proximity to Westminster palace by Hubert de Burgh, Chief Justiciar at the beginning of Henry III reign, was used by him and successive owners, all high in royal service, as a base for their rule. For ten years until his fall in 1232, de Burgh used the property to direct his policy of strong centralised royal administration.[11] It was de Burgh who transferred the property to the see of York, and as the residence of the archbishop York Place continued to

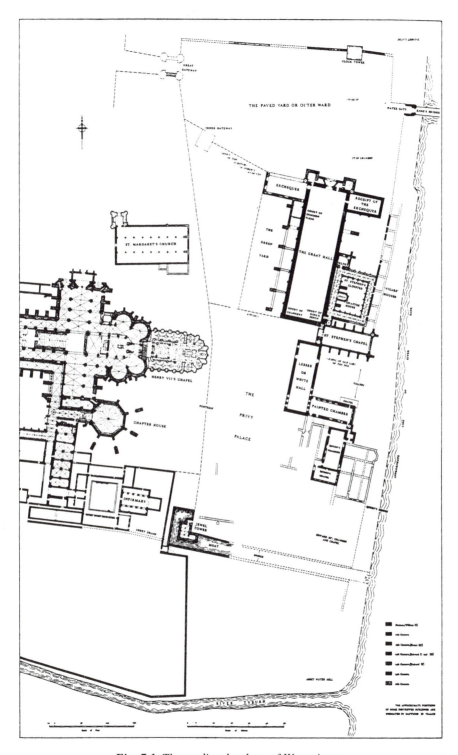

Fig. 7.1 *The medieval palace of Westminster.*

provide an ideal political location for successive archbishops. As Caesarean clergy no less than four of York Place's occupants were, *inter alia,* chancellors: John Kempe (1426–52), George Neville (1465–76), Thomas Rotherham (1480-1500) and Thomas Wolsey (1515–29). For each of these men their occupation of York Place was both a geographical convenience and, through the magnificence of their residence, a representation of their secular and temporal power.

The House that Wolsey acquired in 1514 on his appointment as archbishop was the mansion largely rebuilt by George Neville in the 15th century. It was a large brick and stone inn, typical of many contemporary episcopal houses of its age, such as Croydon, Fulham or Southwell. However, it was not large or modern enough for Wolsey who proceeded to extend it as a backdrop to the theatre of his power. William Cavendish, his Gentleman Usher and biographer, describes his lavish, stage-managed, daily procession from York Place to Westminster Hall during the sixteen weeks of the Law term.[12] By 1529 York Place, although much smaller than Wolsey's other houses, Hampton Court and The More, was yet an up-to-date, commodious and impressive residence befitting the home of the King's chief minister. The desirability of York Place did not escape Henry VIII whose deteriorating personal relations with Warham made their joint use of Lambeth difficult, and who never warmed to the attractions of Bridewell. The fall of Wolsey in 1529 enabled the King to appropriate York Place to his own use and immediately set out to convert it into his principal residence with characteristic energy and speed.

There were a number of phases of building work at York Place between 1529 and the King's death in 1547, and even then the palace was barely completed. Figure 7.2 shows the royal apartments in 1547; they were divided into two parts, a king's side and a queen's side. The king's side was divided into three areas: the public rooms, called the outward chambers; the main residential rooms of the palace, called the privy lodgings; and the king's own private rooms called the secret lodgings. Within the privy lodgings were all the spaces needed for ruling the kingdom, a council chamber, a treasury and space for the clerks and records.[13]

This tripartite distinction in the royal apartments was an entirely revolutionary novelty in royal architecture. Medieval royal residences had provided private residential areas for the monarch in physically separate locations. At Woodstock in Oxfordshire Henry II and Henry III had built a separate complex called 'Everswell' or 'Rosamunds' some two hundred yards from the main house. This was a self-contained retreat for the royal family with its own kitchen, chapel and residential accommodation set in water gardens. At Windsor Castle the same function was served by Windsor Manor, much embellished by Edward I; here he could relax away from the large, formal and crowded castle. Richard II built a substantial retreat alled 'La Naught' on an island in the River Thames at Sheen. At Kenilworth Castle Henry V built a retreat called the Pleasaunce sited on the other side of a pool before the castle. There lay a moated pleasure house with a hall and other chambers all set in gardens. Like these retreats the privy palace at Westminster was a separate, more private, domestic quarter of an otherwise very public residence.[14]

What was significantly new about Whitehall was that the king's privy accommodation was a fully integrated part of the palace, contained within one building under one roof. The barriers, which gave the king privacy, were not topographical, but organisational. The creation of the household sub-department, the Privy Chamber, by Henry VII had been a device to exclude those courtiers who were not part of the king's closest entourage. Exclusion was achieved by etiquette and enforced by a number of strategically placed locked doors with master keys. Whitehall was the first English royal residence to combine public and private accommodation in this way.[15]

The redevelopment of York Place as Whitehall ended the ancient, traditional, proximity of the royal apartments with the financial and legal machinery of the Crown. In other words the executive became separated from the administrative when it moved into a new building two hundred yards to the north. The space previously occupied by the monarch at Westminster thus became free for further administrative development, and between 1536 and 1542 alongside the law courts, Exchequer, Parliament

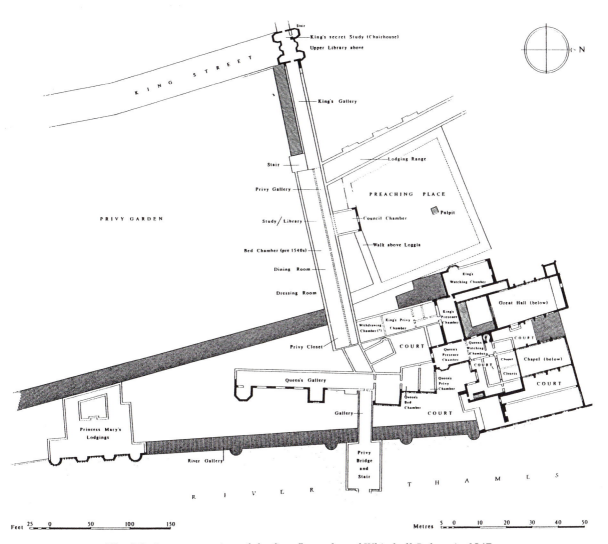

Fig. 7.2 *A reconstruction of the first floor plan of Whitehall Palace in 1547.*

Chamber and Star Chamber Henry VIII established the Courts of Augmentations, of First Fruits and Tenths, of Wards and Liveries, and of Surveyors. In 1548 after the dissolution of the collegiate churches, Edward VI provided the House of Commons with a permanent meeting place in St Stephen's Chapel. During the Elizabethan period several of these courts and offices were rebuilt and extended, reinforcing Westminster as the legal, financial and parliamentary centre of the kingdom.[16]

The transition of the king's physical presence had an important effect on the machinery of government, the precise significance of which is the subject of fierce historical debate. This centres on the precise nature of the changes in monarchical rule, dubbed by Sir Geoffrey Elton as 'a revolution in government', which occurred in the latter part of the reign of Henry VIII. Under Henry VII the king's council had a permanent home, the Star Chamber, a building situated immediately east of the north-east corner of Westminster Hall. But it also moved with the king from place to place combining both legal and administrative tasks. Early in Henry VIII's reign the council met almost daily in term time, under Wolsey's chairmanship, in Star Chamber at Westminster. What concerned contemporaries was that Star Chamber combined judicial and executive functions, and to circumvent this the two functions were split by 1540. While Star Chamber retained its legal role, the executive role of the council, as the king's own private or 'privy' council, moved with the king to Whitehall. What this did was to bring the king's council right into the heart of the residential part of the palace, indeed into the king's innermost sanctum, his Privy Chamber.[17]

The establishment of the Privy Council in the privy lodgings at Whitehall characterizes not only the nature of Henry VIII's palace but also the nature of his rule. Not only did Whitehall combine under one roof the private and public parts of the king's residence, it also provided the locus for the king's executive council. In other words the king could rule through his council from his own inner apartments. This was household government *par excellence*. Like his predecessors, Henry VIII ruled from his entourage, and created an appropriate setting to do so. Whitehall was therefore both retrospective and innovative in its function. While in one sense it was profoundly 'medieval', retaining its role as the seat of the executive, it was also the first modern royal palace combining public and private functions in a single building.

Yet there was another sense in which Whitehall was profoundly different to its ancient predecessor. Until the Dissolution Westminster was a manorial vill dependant on the Benedictine abbey of Westminster, and for ten years from 1540 a city under the Bishop of Westminster. Its position remained anomalous after the ejection of the Marian monks under Elizabeth I, a period during which the dean of Westminster was effectively in charge. Westminster's government was only finally resolved by Parliament in 1585 when the inhabitants were given a say in its running.[18] From at least the 11th century the abbey's manorial authority had been augmented beyond received rights by a series of royal grants. These had considerably extended the abbey's jurisdiction allowing, for instance, the detention of offenders in the abbey's own prison, trying them and

hanging them within sight of the king's own courts at Westminster.[19] This extraordinary authority did not extend to the precincts of the royal palace, which was an enclave wholly outside ecclesiastical jurisdiction. The abbey's supremacy in Westminster was also tempered while the king was in residence when the Court of the Verge could overrule abbatial jurisdiction within the manor on certain offenses.[20] Therefore, throughout the Middle Ages the King's Palace of Westminster was an island of royal authority within a sea of abbatial power and privilege.

The fall of Wolsey and sequestration of his property gave Henry VIII an opportunity to create a new palace unfettered by its proximity to administrative offices and law courts. In grasping this opportunity he was determined not to be constrained by local rights or abbatial lordship. His intention was to create a palace combining traditional residential and executive functions with a sport and recreation centre, a park for hunting, and accommodation for the Office of Works and for transport facilities, by land (horses, coaches and carts) and by river (barges and yachts) (Fig. 7.4). All this was to be set within a legal and jurisdictional framework which provided absolute royal authority and freedom of movement over a carefully defined geographical zone around the palace.

To achieve his aim Henry VIII embarked upon one of the most complex series of land transactions ever undertaken by an English king, acquiring vast tracts of largely church property. In this the King was following the example of Wolsey, who had begun to enlarge York Place by buying land on its north side called 'Scotland', from the Crown, and other property from Westminster Abbey. As with the king's other territorial purchases these sales and exchanges were forced and reluctant, yet the evidence shows that a fair price was paid. Nor can it be argued that with the Dissolution (which could not have been foreseen in 1530) he could have reduced his outlay as the Court of Augmentations would have expected a realistic figure for any ex-monastic property acquired for his personal use.

First, he secured York Place from the archdiocese of York on 12 February 1530. Concurrently he entered into negotiations with the leaseholders of the properties lining King Street, the majority of

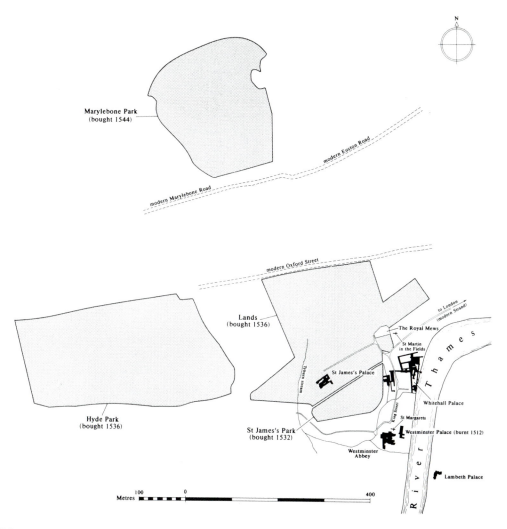

Fig. 7.3 *Westminster in 1547 illustrating the extent of lands purchased by Henry VIII and their relation to the old and new palaces of Westminster.*

whom he bought out in 1531.[21] An Act of Parliament early in 1532 confirmed an exchange made the previous autumn between the king and Westminster Abbey whereby he obtained the freehold of the King Street properties with 100 acres of pasture (soon to be transformed into St James's Park) for an ex-monastic house at Paughley, in Berkshire.[22] At the same time Eton College made over the house and lands of St James's Hospital, to the north of the park.[23] Negotiations followed for a large part of the manor of Westminster – from Abingdon Abbey (60

acres), Burton Lazar Hospital (another 60 acres) and the Mercers Company (94 acres). He also acquired land in Covent Garden, the vast manor and park of Hyde (620 acres) and the substantial manors of Neate and Ebury to the west from Westminster Abbey.[24]

By 1536 Henry VIII had acquired almost all the land which today covers the area from Ebury Bridge in the west, to Oxford Street in the north and to St Martins Lane in the east (Fig. 7.3). But the core of this vast tract of land was the new palace precinct itself which in the parliament of that year was defined

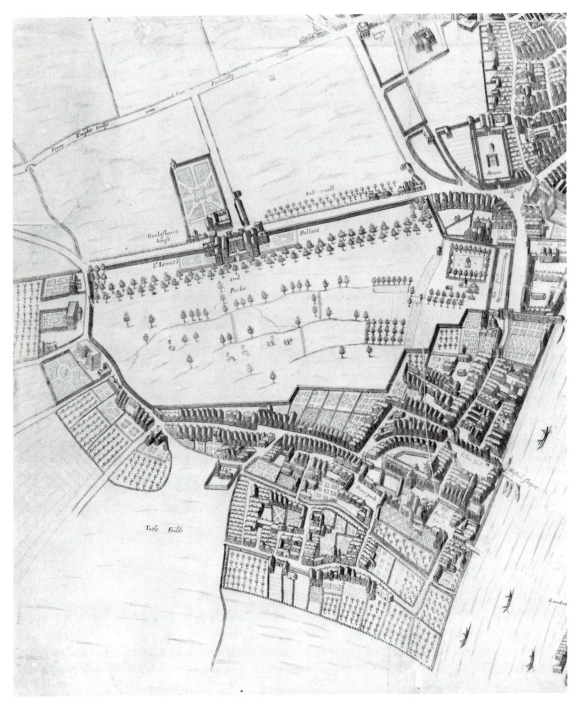

Fig. 7.4 *Faithorne and Newcourt's 'Exact Delineation' of the cities of London and Westminster done in 1658 clearly shows the nucleus of the royal estate. Whitehall Palace sits on the right hand margin of the map with St James's Park stretching out to the left. Above and below Whitehall can be seen the Royal Mews and old Westminster Palace.*

by Act..... 'Forasmuch as the King's Palace at Westminster, builded and edified there before time of mind... is and of a long time hath been in utter Ruin and Decay and that our most dread Sovereign Lord King *Henry* the Eighth...hath lately obtained and purchased one great mansion place and house, sometime parcel of the...Archbishopric of York...and the King's Highness now of late upon the soil of the said mansion Place and House and on the ground thereunto adjoining most sumptuously and curiously hath builded and edified many and distinct beautiful costly and pleasant Lodgings buildings and mansions... and thereto adjoining hath made a park, walled and environed with brick and stone...Be it therefore enacted...that all the said ground soil mansion and buildings...shall be from henceforth the King's whole Palace at Westminster...'. The extent of the palace was then defined as being all the land along King Street from Charing Cross to the door of Westminster Hall from the Thames in the east to the park wall on the west. To the new palace was transferred... 'All such and like prerogatives Liberties Pre-eminences Jurisdictions and Privileges, as to the King's ancient Palace within this realm have at any time heretofore belonged...And that the same old and ancient Palace of *Westminster* from henceforth be reputed deemed and taken only as a member and parcel of the said new palace...'[25]

The Act's careful delineation and definition of royal land and jurisdiction was undoubtably the work of the king's secretary, Thomas Cromwell, an expert drafter and promoter of legislation whose career had started as a land agent acting for Cardinal Wolsey in the 1520s. Cromwell's skills in efficiently expediting land transactions underpinned the rapid development of Whitehall, and in a list of his achievements in the service of the king, probably dating from 1536, he proudly cites the acquisition of land in Westminster as his work. Presumably he also exploited his stewardship of Westminster Abbey's estates to the advantage of his royal master.[26] Simultaneously with his work at Whitehall, Cromwell, who was Master of the King's Jewels, undertook major overhaul of both the defences and royal accommodation at the Tower of London which culminated in 1536 with a precise statement of the extent of the Tower's liberties (Fig. 7.5). This defined royal rights and privileges in a

geographically distinct region around the Tower, in a similar manner to Cromwell's work at Westminster.[27] There is no evidence that this was part of a more general definition of urban royal prerogatives, but the fact that simultaneously at both Whitehall and the Tower royal liberties were defined suggests a particular concentration on the issue in the mind of the King at this time.

Conceived by Henry VIII and realised by Cromwell, Whitehall had, within six years, become the focus of a considerable series of land holdings. But more was to come, for after the Dissolution, in 1544, the king acquired substantial new lands to the north including Marylebone (later Regent's) Park. These acquisitions resulted in further legislation in 1545 erecting an honour 'within his Grace's Citie of Westminster' thus formally recognising the king as the seignior of all the manors and lands acquired since 1536.[28] A proclamation made in July 1545 designed to protect hunting rights within the honour defined its extent. In a great circle encompassing much of Middlesex it extended from 'his said palace of Westminster to St Giles-in-the-Fields, and from thence to Islington to our Lady of the Oak [today Gospel Oak], to Higate, to Hornsey Park, to Hampstead Heath, and from thence to Shootup Hill, to Willesden, to Acton in Chiswick, to Cheese heath, and from there to his said palace.' (Fig. 7.3). [29]

The new palace was therefore conceptually and legally a different entity to its predecessor. Henry VIII had succeeded in placing his new principal residence at the hub of an estate of which he was undoubted master. Not only did he enjoy property rights, rights of passage, the control of hunting and an unimpeded access to water supply, he replaced the abbot of Westminster at the abbey's dissolution in 1540 as the principal landowner in the area, a situation not reversed when in the mid 1550s Mary I temporarily re-established the abbey. Thus Whitehall also epitomises, in a strikingly unique way, the change in landowning that occurred during the English Reformation and, more importantly, the complete secularisation of the setting of the new palace in contrast with its predecessor to the south.

The medieval Palace of Westminster had been conceived together with its *Eigenkloster*, a great monastery founded to pray for the royal family and

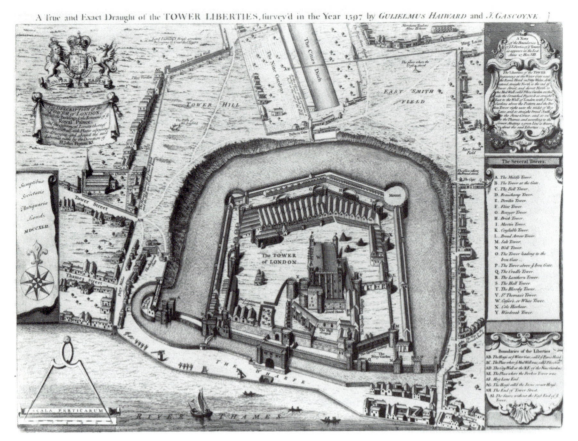

Fig. 7.5 *A map of the Tower Liberties drawn in 1597 but illustrating the Liberties as developed under Henry VIII by Thomas Cromwell.*

to be its mausoleum and place of coronation (Fig. 7.1).[30] Westminster was not alone and the linkage of great churches with royal palaces endured down to the reign of Henry VIII. Henry V founded a monastery for Carthusian monks at Sheen, Edward IV, rebuilt St George's chapel at Windsor, and endowed a Fransciscan Observant friary at Greenwich and Henry VII established another Fransiscan Observant house at Richmond and built a new tombhouse for the Tudor dynasty at Westminster, which was completed by his son Henry VIII.[31] Henry VIII was to break with this tradition within twenty-five years of his accession, and his appointment of the master of the Chapel Royal at Whitehall, Thomas Thirlby, as bishop of Westminster in 1540, was symptomatic of this break as well as an assertion of the State's primacy over the Church. With the king's property transfers and Thirlby's appointment the stranglehold over all Westminster hitherto enjoyed by the abbey came to a complete and definitive end.

Henry VIII's construction of Whitehall can tell us much about the nature of his rule, his court, his use of public and private space, his attitudes to ecclesiastical power and the geographical definition of royal authority. The 1536 Act which confirmed the creation of a new royal residence of unprecedented magnitude since late antiquity, covering some 200 acres stretching westwards from the Royal Mews at Charing Cross to St James's park and palace and southwards to the administrative and legal headquarters at the old palace. This was the epicentre of a vast honour of several thousand acres of which the king was undoubted master. Unlike Henry VII, the king was lord of all he surveyed, and his principal residence, his *palatium,* was closer to the domicile of the Roman Emperors on the Palatine Hill than the house of his predecessors which had nestled in the shadow of the great abbey at Westminster. With his classical education and erudition the King was doubtless aware of the comparison. Thus the building of Whitehall can be seen as another expression of Henry VIII's imperial aspirations, and Whitehall as the palace of 'the empire of our realm of England'.

Notes

1. The use of the word 'palace' has not received much scholarly attention. There are brief discussions in Colvin 1963–82, I, 120 and Dawson 1976, 188–9. I am also grateful to Dr Edward Impey, Dr David Carpenter, Stephen Priestly, Sir Howard Colvin and Jeremy Ashbee for discussing this with me.
2. Ritchie 1954, 250; It is interesting to note that a Winchester annal describes Henry of Blois' palace at Wolvesey as 'domus quasi palatium', which might suggest that in this case 'palatium' was seen as the seat of temporal authority and the allusion may have been to Westminster (Luard 1865, 2, 51).
3. Luard 1876, 2, 363.
4. Colvin 1963-82, I, 120; Robertson and Sheppard 1875, 3, 3.
5. Clay 1944, 1–6; *Cal. Pat. Rolls 1258-66,* 448.
6. In the chronicle of Richard of Devizes (1171) the Tower is 'arx Londoni' (Howlett 1886, 3, 414, 418), and in Gesta Stephani it is 'turrim regis' (Potter 1976). I am grateful to Stephen Priestley for these references. For the Tower's role more generally in this period see Carpenter 1995 and Thurley 1995.
7. There is also another sense in which the Tower can be seen as an Imperial fortress. Henry II was the most powerful king in Europe in the 1170s and presided over a substantial continental empire. Fitzstephen was perhaps also making the point that the Tower of London, seated in a city which he compared with ancient Rome, was an imperial headquarters.
8. Rosser 1989, 16–17; for the religious aspect Binski 1995, 3–9 and *passim.*
9. Colvin 1963–1982, I, 491–552.

10. Kingsford 1908, vol. 2, p. 117.
11. Rosser 1984, 24.
12. Thurley 1991, 76–102; Thurley forthcoming; Sylvester 1962, 24–5.
13. Thurley forthcoming. Also see the summary in Thurley 1993, 136–8.
14. Thurley 1993, 8–9.
15. Thurley 1993, 51–6.
16. Colvin 1963–1982, 4, 288–90, 293–8.
17. The argument over the changes which took place in the Privy Council are summarized in Elton 1988, 433 and Starkey 1988, 922–7. Also see Guy 1986, 59–85 and for Starkey's most polished exposition of his view Starkey 1991, 175–203.
18. Bindoff 1982, 1, 144; Hasler 1981, 1, 202–3; *Acts of The Realm,* 27 Elizabeth Cap. 31.
19. The definitive treatment of this subject is in Rosser 1989, 226–48. Also see Tout 192–13, 487–502.
20. For the exemption of the Palace see Brayley and Britton 1836, 86–7. For the Court of the Verge, Jones 1970, 1–29 and Given-Wilson 1986, 48–53.
21. The full details of this can be found in Rosser and Thurley 1990, 57–77.
22. *Acts of the Realm,* 23 Henry VIII Cap. 21.
23. *Letters and Papers Henry VIII,* 5, no. 406.
24. These transactions are explained and identified in Kingsford 1926, *passim;* Larwood 1873, 4–8; Ashton 1896, 1–8; *V.C.H. Middlesex,* II, 1911, 231–2.
25. *Statutes of the Realm,* 28 Henry VIII Cap. XII.
26. I am grateful to Philip Ward for discussing his important work on Cromwell's early career with me; *Letters and Papers Henry VIII,* 10, no. 1231; Westminster Abbey Register 2, ff. 288, 298 (ex inf. Alasdair Hawkyard).
27. For Cromwell's Work at the Tower see Colvin 1963–1982, III, 264–70. The boundaries agreed in 1536 are shown on a plan of 1597 by Haiward and Gascoyne (Fig. 7.5) and the Henrician rights and liberties were reiterated in letters patent of 1687: Bayley 1821, plate II and cxiv–cxxi. I am grateful to Stephen Priestley who alerted me to the definition of the liberties in 1536.
28. 36 Henry VIII Cap. xviii (*Letters and Papers Henry VIII,* 20, no. 850 (24)).
29. *Letters and Papers Henry VIII,* 20 (i), no. 1129; Hughes & Larkin 1964, 356.
30. Binski 1995, 4-6.
31. Thurley 1993, 200.

Bibliography

Ashton, J. 1896, *Hyde Park from Doomsday Book to Date*

Bayley, J. 1821, *The History and Antiquities of the Tower of London*

Biddle, M. 1986, *Wolvesey. The Old Bishop's Palace*

Bindoff, S.T. (ed.) 1982, *The History of Parliament: The House of Commons 1509–1558*

Binski, P. 1995, *Westminster Abbey and the Plantagenets*

Brayley, E.W. & Britton, J. 1836, *The History of the Ancient Palace and Late Houses of Parliament at Westminster*

Carpenter, D.A. 1995, 'King Henry III and the Tower of London', *London Journal* 19 (2), 95–107

Clay, C.T. 1944, 'The Keepership of the Old Palace of Westminster', *English Historical Review* 59, 1–6

Colvin, H.M. (ed.), 1963–1982, *The History of the King's Works*

Dawson, G.J. 1976, *The Black Prince's Palace at Kennington, Surrey*, British Archaeological Reports, 26

Elton, G.R. 1988, 'Tudor Government', *The Historical Journal* 31, (2), 425–34

Given-Wilson, C. 1986, *The Royal Household and the King's Affinity*

Guy, J.A. 1986, 'The Privy Council Revolution or Evolution', in Coleman, C. & Starkey, D. (eds), *Revolution Reassessed*, Oxford, 59–85

Hasler, P. W. (ed.) 1981 *The History of Parliament: The House of Commons 1558–1603*

Howlett R.S. (ed.) 1884–9, *Chronicles of the Reign of Stephen and Henry II and Edward I*, Rolls Series

Hughes, P.L. & Larkin, J.F. 1964, *Tudor Royal Proclamations 1485–1553*, New Haven & London

Jones, W.R. 1970, 'The Court of the Verge', *Journal of British Studies* 10, 1–29

Kingsford, C.L. (ed.) 1908, Stow, J. *Survey of London*

Kingsford, C.L. 1926, *The Early History of Piccadilly Leicester Square Soho and Their Neighbourhood*, Cambridge

Larwood, J. 1873, *The Story of the London Parks*

Luard, H.R. (ed.) 1865, *Annales Monastici*, Rolls Series

Luard, H. R. (ed.) 1876, *Matthew Paris, Chronica Majora*, Rolls Series

Potter, K.R. (ed. and trans. revised, Davis R.H.C.) 1976, *Gesta Stephani*, Oxford

Ritchie, R.L.G. 1954, *The Normans in Scotland*, Edinburgh

Robertson, J.C. & Sheppard, J.B. (eds) 1875, *Materials for the History of Thomas Becket*, Rolls Series

Rosser, G. 1989, *Medieval Westminster 1200–1540*, Oxford

Rosser, G. & Thurley, S. 1990, 'Whitehall Palace and King Street Westminster: The Urban Cost of Princely Magnificence', *The London Topographical Society* 26, 57–77

Rosser, G. 1984, 'Medieval Westminster: The Vill and the Urban Community, 1200–1540', PhD Thesis, University of London

Starkey, D. 1988, 'The Tudor Government: The Facts', *The Historical Journal* 31, (4), 922–102

Starkey, D. 1991, 'Court, Council and Nobility in Tudor England', in Asch, R. G. & Birke, A.M. (eds), *Princes, Patronage and the Nobility*, Oxford, 175–203

Sylvester, R.S. 1962, *Two Early Tudor Lives*, London & New Haven

Thurley, S. 1995, 'Royal Lodgings at the Tower of London 1216–1327, *Architectural History* 38, 36–57

Thurley, S. 1991, 'The Domestic Building Works of Cardinal Wolsey', in Gunn, S. & Lindley, P. (eds), *Cardinal Wolsey, Church, State and Art*, Cambridge, 76–102

Thurley, S. forthcoming, *Whitehall Palace: An Architectural History*

Thurley, S. 1993, *The Royal Palaces of Tudor England*, London & New Haven

Tout, T.F. 1921–3, 'The beginnings of a modern capital: London and Westminster in the fourteenth century', *Proceedings of the British Academy* 10, 487–502

8 Civic Buildings and Courtier Houses: new techniques and materials for architectural ornament

Maurice Howard

In a collection of papers dedicated to evaluating the contribution of archaeology to questions of continuity and change, any consideration of architectural ornament has to begin with an acknowledgement of the great upturn there has been in quite recent times in the investigation of standing secular buildings of the 15th and 16th centuries. Pioneering studies of the close examination of the structure and high standards of the recording of great country houses were set by the key articles of Paul Drury on Audley End and Hill Hall (both in Essex).[1] Following these a large number of investigations of large domestic buildings of the Tudor period has been undertaken, though there is at the time of writing very little of any extensive nature in print. Conferences, such as that held on the Tudor and Jacobean Great House at Oxford in 1994, have resulted in the circulation of papers which have released a certain amount of information but certain key buildings, such as exciting new work on Sutton Place, Surrey and East Barsham, Norfolk, await their more sustained elucidation.[2] Some houses, such as Westhorpe (Suffolk) and Laughton Place (East Sussex), both partially excavated and recorded, have been well served, with new documentation coming to light alongside excavated materials and a firmer sense of the original plan.[3] Other much longer reports have, or will emerge in the near future on houses such as Ightham Mote (Kent), Sutton House at Hackney (London) and Acton Court (Glos.).[4] A group of monastic foundations, adapted into country houses in the 1530s and 1540s, have been re-examined and

their immediate, post-Dissolution history is now clearer than before: the Augustinian houses of Mottisfont (Hants.) and the nunneries of Lacock and Wilton (both in Wilts.), and the Cistercian house of Netley (Hants.).[5] Francis Kelly's rethinking of the building sequence at Berry Pomeroy (Devon) has corrected previous assumptions and an archaeological report on Wollaton Hall (Notts.), commissioned by the Nottingham Civic Society, has revealed much not only about the original plan and foundations but also seems to have verified the largely original quality of the exterior stonework, previously only guessed at.[6]

It is principally with the surface character of buildings that this brief paper is indeed concerned and it seeks to summarise what recent work appears to be telling us. The surface of the building is by its very nature vulnerable to change and modification, by refacing, changes to doors and windows, the removal of heraldic and other signs as function changes, or simply by the effects of the weather. It is only as the careful of investigation of standing buildings has taken place that the quality of original surfaces has come more into focus by the careful cleaning and recording of what survives on the outside or the discovery within buildings of walls originally external, concealed at a time when their original surface remained.[7] Sometimes these processes have revealed a more intricate pattern of stone-facing than was previously understood and thereby elucidated a more complex building history; this was the result, for example, of a recent investigation of the lower storeys of the west front of West-minster Abbey.[8] In other cases rare examples of an original surface patina have come to light, as in the case of the painted brickwork on the original external east wall of the chapel at Hampton Court Palace.[9]

A key issue that seems to have emerged concerns the notion of permanence in the appearance of buildings: how far did owners seek it and how far was this subsumed in a constant programme of repair and re-presentation? Scholars, both archaeologists and architectural historians, who have worked on this period, have noted the need we have of a sense of 'sliding scale' in evaluating whether this or that building was made to last, or given the appearance of a building made to last. There are two related aspects to this question. First, the period is one where the pressure to build ostentatiously had markedly increased, particularly among the courtier group, and this often resulted in building operations being carried out to a tight schedule such that a surface glamour of appearance had to be effected by mimicking materials that would have taken longer to manufacture and complete the final dress, the clothing of the structure. The very speed of so many of the monastic adaptations appear to show the readiness of building contractors to simulate some-thing more carefully considered.[10] Second, one offshoot of buildings as manifestations of power was the need to entertain one's peer group to lavish standards of hospitality, creating the need for temporary ranges of lodgings built to order for special occasions and redundant thereafter. If the 'sliding scale' of both the reality and the appearance of great country houses changes as the 16th century progres-ses then it is the sense that part of the move away from rambling courtyard structures towards the more integrated plans of the Elizabethan and Jacobean age marks a shift towards houses that are better built and better serviced. The value and meaning of appear-ances, of making things seem what they are not, are obviously caught up with the changing economy of great house building and with the wider cultural context of the period, neither of which can be explored here, but are of profound importance.[11]

To open the record that we now have of the ornament and decoration of buildings we must turn to those structures hitherto unmentioned but whose

investigation has proved the key, namely the royal palaces. They are the key because, unlike most great secular buildings even of the courtier class, the archaeology of recent times is attended by a wealth of documentation not available for other buildings. Of course we may lament essential gaps, but the survival of at least part of the building and running repair accounts for the palaces among the state papers means that our sense of the surface appearance of these structures is sharper and better attested. The Tudor royal palaces were archaeologically investig-ated in a series of campaigns during the 1950s, '60s and '70s; without the results of these the great and indispensable volume in the History of the King's Works covering the palaces from 1485 to 1660 could not have been written so persuasively.[12] Speed of construction is in itself often highly revealing, but it is also in the accounts of running repair that much is unveiled about an attitude to the use and appearance of the building that is especially vivid for these vehicles of royal display and ceremonial. The royal palaces were left with skeleton staff during the absence of the monarch, often in the hands of stewards (usually leading courtiers) who might use the building themselves on occasion, and in anticipa-tion of the next royal visit, usually a frantic campaign of consolidating doors, windows, roofs, and so on was necessary.[13] The temporary palace constructed for the Field of Cloth of Gold in 1520, preserved for us visually in the famous painting in the Royal Collection and verbally by some accounts of con-struction in the state papers and the chronicle of Edward Hall, may have been one of the most elaborate temporary structures of its time but its making was only relatively more elaborate and carried out at somewhat greater speed, than the usual work the Royal Works were familiar with.[14]

Mention has already been made of the painting of the east wall of the chapel at Hampton Court. This is a rare survival of the common practice of the painting of brickwork, usually in a presumably protective medium which re-inforced the red colour of the brick, but sometimes other colours were used, as at Dartford (Kent), the former Augustinian priory converted for Henry VIII's use, where red, black and ochre were all recorded as employed in 1542–3.[15] Not all brickwork would necessarily be painted, however,

Fig. 8.1 *The Bishop of London's palace at Fulham, c.1510–20.*

or rather it often carried with its own range of possible distinguishing features which enabled it to be used for significative purposes. The use of burnt headers in patterns to form heraldic motives has long been recognised; it is notable, for example, on the surviving ranges of the Archbishop of Canterbury's Palace at Croydon. Patterned brickwork also appears on Fulham palace, London, built for the Bishop of London c.1510–20 (Fig. 8.1). Diapered brickwork could also simply signify the more prestigious parts of the house; it has been noted recently, for example, that brick diapering at Sutton House, Hackney, seems to have been used to designate the more important upper floor, where rooms of state and entertainment were placed.[16]

The royal accounts also provide the most extensive record of the ubiquitous painting of 'anticke' work both internally and externally. This form of decoration included acanthus, forms of candelabra, playful chrubs or *putti* and various grotesque, half-

human, half-animal forms based loosely on ornament copied from surviving remains, found chiefly in Italy, from the ancient. In the early 16th century it is likely that, given the plethora of newly-engraved ornament prints of the time, there was a sense of a changing fashion for this mode of decoration but as the century wore on the motives became more standardised and a standard pattern of 'anticke' more recognisable. It is this well-established fashion that Peacham describes in his famous passage on the anticke in 1611.[17] At this date, it was still being used extensively over wide areas of the royal palaces, as for instance on gable ends at Whitehall in that year,[18] but it was a mode that was, in court circles anyway, about to lose its pre-eminence as new ideas of classical ornament emanated from the works of Inigo Jones and his contemporaries.

Two of the aspects of royal building discussed above, namely the sense of building for occasion and the changing fashions in classical ornament, are equally relevant if we turn for a moment to another kind of building, one of whose most notable examples has recently been extensively examined and recorded, namely civic architecture. The rebuilding of the great street frontage to Exeter Guildhall (Devon) in the 1590s is a prime example of the need to understand the reasons behind quite deliberate and ostentatious splendour[19] (Fig. 8.2). Recent work on such civic structures has suggested that far from being simply the result of a surplus of money in the civic coffers, sums were often expended when trade was unpredictable and the identity of the town uncertain.[20] Overtly classical motives were used not for any belief in the value of classicism *per se* but because they provided a new and convincing framework for traditional civic heraldry.[21] The recent survey of Exeter has shown that the now bland, off-white aspect

Fig. 8.2 *The new front to Exeter Guildhall, 1590s.*

to the great frontispiece (originally also a storey higher) was continually repainted during the years after its construction and a great range of colours used; at one time green on the modillions of the cornice, blue on the frieze and yellow on the billet of the window frames. But it was the columns themselves that carried the chief message, that of the city's colours of red and black. An oil-rich medium allowed for the effect of veining to simulate marble, grey on the black, vermilion on the red. For a sense of the original colour scheme of a building such as this we can turn to contemporary tomb structures, now often heavily restored in such a way that can make their historians suspicious of the exact authenticity, but nevertheless carrying conviction as far as the overall power of colour re-inforcing design. The cheek-by-jowl Elizabethan and Jacobean tombs at the near-by Devon church of Colyton, for example, provide a close parallel of coloured columns and architectural detail as supporters not only of the representation of the dead but of their family heraldry that ensures the survival of their personal reputation[22] (Fig. 8.3).

It has long been recognised that the early Tudor period used the medium of decorative terracotta to impart a surface richness to brick building via the fashionable mode of antique ornament. Terracotta decoration could suggest similarities to another building employing this material that the patron wished to emulate (indeed there is some evidence of moulds passing from place to place) but it invariably supplied a distinctive quality through personalised heraldry and insignia.[23] Recent archaeological work on buildings showing terracotta ornament has if anything challenged any assumptions we might have had about a necessary order or programme to its use; indeed in the spectacular example of Sutton Place, Surrey, it has been shown that the supposed order is a creation, using some original and some copied material, from a time some two centuries after the house's initial construction.[24] Excavations at Hampton Court, Laughton Place (East Sussex) and Westhorpe (Suffolk), have however revealed more about terracotta as a facing material, used on plinths and on the flat surfaces of gatehouses perhaps, as opposed to its more familiar and recognised use as a surround for windows and specially commissioned, heraldic pieces.[25]

Fig. 8.3 Colyton, Devon, 17th-century tomb to the Holt family.

At Laughton, alongside the well-known terracotta decoration of the tower, the one fragment of the medieval and early Tudor house that survives, excavation revealed further terracottas from the moat which, together with footings of an entrance wall of brick to the site with non-functioning (i.e. as staircases, window projections or garderobes) projecting turrets, must have made for a splendid facade to an essentially casually planned site, without any axiality of building ranges. This quality of early Tudor building whereby facades are approached, understood (in term of function as entrance ranges with perhaps a gatehouse, then a hall range within the court with a specified entrance to the hall of the house) in a sequential way separates these buildings from the more regularly planned, often symmetrical, and in the most advanced examples such as Wollaton

or Hardwick (Derbys.), comparatively equal in aspect back and front, of the Elizabethan period. The concern for the individual facade in the early 16th century is most apparent at somewhere like the monastic conversion of Titchfield Abbey (Hants.), where the grand new entrance front made out of the south side of the abbey church using imported Caen stone for a new gatehouse, was quite at odds with the back of the building (as recorded in Grose's view in the 18th century) and probably from the hall facade within the court as well, both of which retained much of the medieval characteristics of the building.[26] Recent work at Ightham Mote (Kent), has shown that the western entrance front of Kentish ragstone was never matched by any covering of stone on the south side of the central tower; the brick that we see there is the way it was left, making the stone facade merely the skin-deep appearance of the house[27] (Fig. 8.4).

Fig. 8.4 Ightham Mote, Kent, the western entrance front, 15th and 16th centuries.

Elsewhere we do know that the surface was disguised to give the appearance of another, costlier material. At Hill Hall, the north and west courtyard elevations of brick were originally covered by a thin layer of plaster and probably limewash.[28] It has also been suggested however that we should not perhaps always characterise such covering as simply a cheaper way of finishing the building. Sometimes the covering of brick in a similar colour to adjacent stone on dressings such as copings or window and door surrounds was carried out to present a subtlety of surface that the building would not otherwise have enjoyed. Very little survives in the direct form of building accounts to suggest the nature of these kinds of decisions but we should perhaps never deny 16th-century builders the choice of preferring the rough and the ambiguous finish which lent an interest to the surface of their buildings. Even as wonderful a survival as Hardwick Hall may today have looked somewhat different if the coarser surface of the stone still found in places on the turrets at roof level had been allowed to survive restorations which have, over the rest of the house, replaced this surface with the smoothness of finely dressed material, albeit one which is true to local sources, thus keeping a colour match and grain close to the original (Fig. 8.5).

One of the things that recent work has also revealed is the significance of local materials and building traditions as the means of explaining certain decisions about the finish of buildings. Such explanations are a useful counter, through a stress on

Fig. 8.5 Hardwick Hall, Derbyshire, 1590s, surface of one of the roof turrets.

traditional appearances, to the usual tendency to look automatically to the Royal Works, the leading centre of imported skills and craftsmen, as a necessary source of innovation. In the 1538 survey of Westhorpe there is mention of the brickwork being covered with 'plaster checker with white and blak', a reference to the East Anglian fashion for chequer work on the surface of buildings.[29] Westhorpe is not the only example of the power of this local tradition. About 1550, Lord Darcy of Chiche converted the former monastery of St. Osyth's (Essex) into a country house. In respect to the 15th-century gatehouse patterned with alternating squares of flint and stone, he covered the towers of his new house with a similar mixing of materials (Figs 8.6, 8.7). Given the fact that many appeals to the Crown for the preferential sale of former monastic sites stressed the prospective owner's respect for the local respons-ibilities that the former monasteries carried (indeed Lord Audley, an earlier petitioner for St. Osyth's, had offered to continue using the house as a place of accommodation for travellers in this area) Lord Darcy may here have been seeking an instant local credibility on his new estates.[30] Sometimes the evidence of local expertise can answer the problem of dating a building in a way that other visual evidence and documentation cannot. The use of local materials, and especially the plasterwork, at Berry Pomeroy (Devon) on the north range with its loggia, echoes that on other work on buildings in this area of about 1600, helping to underline the suggested dating for the completion of this range to the end of the century in a way otherwise unproven.[31]

We cannot know how far contemporaries were willingly deceived by surface appearances; it is likely surely that the practice of simulation in particular was so widespread that it was an accepted part of any great building's final presentation. When the most privileged guests to Hardwick Hall visited the owner's banqueting houses on the roof and trod the leads they would have seen the backs of the Countess of Shrewsbury's coats of arms with their supporters (which seem from the ground as if to grow from parapet level) as the propped-up, one-dimensional (for of course they are not carved at the back) achievements that they really are (Fig. 8.8). But their manufacture in stone and their survival to this day

Fig. 8.6 *St Osyth's, Essex, 15th-century gatehouse.*

Fig. 8.7 *St Osyth's, Essex, ruins of the c.1550 range.*

Fig. 8.8 *Hardwick Hall, Derbyshire, 1590s, back of the arms of Bess of Hardwick at roof level.*

(however much restored) are witness to the ways in which patrons made the surface message of their buildings more permanent as the 16th century went by, and explored the widest possible range of material to do so.

Notes

1. Drury 1980, 1983.
2. Airs (ed.) 1994.
3. Gunn and Lindley 1988; Farrant *et al.* 1991.
4. The most accessible summary of Ightham is Pearson *et al.*, 1994, 74–7; work on Acton Court is summarised in Starkey, (ed.) 1991 and by Bell & Rodwell 1994.
5. Wilton is summarised in Bold & Reeves 1988, 31–3; Netley in Hare 1993.
6. Kelly 1994; Marshall 1994.
7. See Drury 1980 and 1983.
8. Tatton-Brown 1991.
9. Curnow 1984, 2.
10. See Howard 1987, chapter 7.
11. On the economy of building Airs 1995 and Howard 1994. On wider issues see Thomson 1993 and Evett 1991.

12. On the history of the King's Works, see Colvin *et al.* 1982, with reference to earlier excavation at Nonsuch, Bridewell, Greenwich, Eltham, Enfield and Richmond. Subsequently, on the royal palaces, see Thurley 1993.
13. Howard 1987, 29–30.
14. On the painting, Anglo 1996.
15. Colvin *et al.* 1982, 72.
16. From the forthcoming report by Victor Belcher, *pers comm.*
17. See Croft-Murray 1962, 26–7.
18. Mercer 1954, 159–60.
19. Blaylock 1990.
20. Tittler 1991, 71–2; Howard 1995.
21. Christy Anderson 1995, 239–86; Vaughan Hart 1993.
22. Cherry and Pevsner 1989, 280.
23. Howard 1987, 131–5.
24. Nicholas Cooper 1994, 33–54.
25. On Hampton Court, see Thurley 1993; on Laughton, Farrant *et al.* 1991; on Westhorpe, Gunn & Lindley 1988.
26. Howard 1987, 149, 153. The rear view of the hall range is published in the *V.C.H. Hampshire*, III, 1908.
27. In an unpublished report on Ightham Mote, by Sarah Pearson.
28. Drury 1983, 108.
29. Gunn & Lindley, 1988.
30. See *Royal Commission Historical Monuments. NE Essex*, 1922, 198–204.
31. Kelly 1994.

Bibliography

Airs, M. (ed.) 1994, *The Tudor and Jacobean Great House*, Oxford

Airs, M. 1995, *The Tudor and Jacobean Great House. A Building History*, Stroud

Anderson, Christy 1995, 'Learning to Read Architecture in the English Renaissance', in Gent (ed.) 1995, 239–86

Anglo, S. 1966, 'The Hampton Court Painting of the Field of Cloth of Gold considered as an historical document', *Antiquaries Journal* 46, 287–307

Bell, R. & Rodwell, K. 1994, 'Acton Court, Avon: an early Tudor Courtier house', in Airs (ed.) 1994, 55–60

Blaylock, D. 1990, 'Exeter Guildhall', *Proceedings of the Devon Archaeological Society* 48, 123–78

Bold, J. & Reeves, J. 1988, *Wilton House and English Palladianism. Some Wiltshire Houses*

Bold, J. 1991, *Recording Historic Buildings*

Cherry, B. & Pevsner, N. 1989, *The Buildings of England, Devon*, 2nd edn. Harmondsworth

Colvin, H.M. *et al* 1982, *The History of the King's Works, vol. IV 1485–1600, part II*

Cooper, Nicholas 1994, 'Sutton Place, East Barsham and some related houses', in Airs (ed.) 1994, 33–54

Croft-Murray, E. 1962, *Decorative Painting in England* vol. I, *Early Tudor to Sir James Thornhill*

Drury, P. 1980, 'No other palace in the kingdom will compare with it: the evolution of Audley End 1605–1745', *Architectural History* 23, 1–39

Drury, P. 1983, '"A Fayre House Buylt by Sir Thomas Smith": The Development of Hill Hall, Essex 1557–81', *Journal of the British Archaeological Association* 136, 98–123

Evett, D. 1991, *Literature and the Visual Arts in Renaissance England*, Athens, Georgia

Gent, L. (ed.), 1995, *Albion's Classicism*, New Haven and London

Gunn, S. & Lindley, P. 1988, 'Charles Brandon's Westhorpe; an Early Tudor Courtyard House in Suffolk', *Archaeological Journal* 145, 272–189

Hare, J. 1993, 'Netley Abbey: Monastery, Mansion and Ruin', *Proceedings of the Hampshire Field Club & Archaeological Society* 49, 207–27

Hart, Vaughan 1993, 'A peece rather of good Heraldry, than of Architecture. Heraldry and the Orders as joint emblems of chivalry', *Res: a journal of anthropology and aesthetics* 23, 52–66

Howard, M. 1987, *The Early Tudor Country House. Architecture and Politics 1490–1550*

Howard, M. 1994 '"His Lordshp was the chiefest architect" Patrons and Builders in 16th-Century England', in Worsley (ed.) 1994, 7–13

Howard, M. 1995, 'Classicism and Civic Architecture in Renaissance England', in Gent (ed.) 1995, 29–49

Kelly, Francis 1994, 'Berry Pomeroy Castle: an interim review of its 16th century development', in Aris (ed.) 1994, 73–90

Mercer, E. 1954, 'The Decoration of the Royal Palaces 1553–1625', *Archaeological Journal* 110, 150–63

Pearson, S., Barnwell, P.S. & Adams, A.T. 1994, *A Gazetteer of Medieval Houses in Kent*

Starkey, D. (ed.) 1991, *Henry VIII. A European Court in England*

Tatton-Brown, Tim 1991, 'The Recent Recording of the Western Towers of Westminster Abbey', in Bold (ed.) 1991, 41–44

Thomson, D. 1993, *Renaissance Architecture, Critics, Patrons, Luxury*, Manchester

Thurley, S. 1993, *The Royal Palaces of Tudor England*, New Haven and London

Tittler, R. 1991, *Architecture and Power. The Town Hall and the English Urban Community 1500–1640*, Oxford

Worsley, G. (ed.) 1994, *The Role of the Amateur Architect*

9 The Gentry House in the Age of Transition

Nicholas Cooper

Early in 1997 the Minister of State for the Environment, John Gummer, called for the building of a new generation of aristocratic houses to ornament what little is left of the English countryside. It remains to be seen whether his vision will be fulfilled, or whether the rich will continue to prefer the seclusion they have increasingly sought for their houses since the First World War. However, before the present century there have been three critical periods in the development of the larger English house. The first of these was the amalgamation of discrete functional elements – of hall, chambers, chapel and other accommodation – to form a single if still heterogeneous body of building. There is still much that is uncertain about this process, but it had clearly taken place before the 13th century. The third is the advent of picturesque planning and of architectural historicism at the end of the 18th century. Between these two, in the course of the 16th century, the house evolved from a structure whose form was actively expressive of the social hierarchy of its uses, to one that expressed externally nothing of its internal functions but in which the whole building reflected the standing of its owner. Inside the house there is a simultaneous multiplication of rooms and a development of new rooms for unprecedented uses, providing for new standards of privacy and of physical comfort and for changing relationships between the owner of the house and the community of household, neighbourhood and peers.

Of these three stages of development, the first was initially determined by convenience and elaborated in the later Middle Ages into a display of hierarchy, the third by considerations that were primarily visual and associative. The second, 16th-century phase is that in which formal factors begin to succede to functional as determinants of the house's overall design and layout, and in which the amenities of genteel existence first supplement and then to a degree supplant the display of status. It is this development in the way in which the house is conceived and regarded that makes the transition between the late medieval and early modern periods perhaps the most crucial in any century since the initial, medieval formation of the unified dwelling.

Earlier writers on the history of the upper-class house have established definitively the broad chronology of their styles and forms, so that with a few noteworthy exceptions there has been little new to say in the last thirty years about the dating of particular buildings or of major physical innovations.[1] But only recently have some more fundamental questions been asked. In spite of the work of Mark Girouard, in particular on Robert Smythson, and Malcolm Airs's researches into the organisation of building works, not enough is yet known about the actual conceptual processes that lay behind late medieval and Tudor house building or about the relative inputs of clients and masons. These, however, are also questions about ideology and meaning and about the way in which the house was perceived as the appropriate expression of its owner's standing. For this reason any account of the development of the houses of the governing classes in this period has to recognise the enormous amount of work that has been done over the last generation on the class's culture, numbers, wealth and powers.

In the late medieval house, the distinction of its parts corresponds to the distinctions of rank that were necessary to a society where order was seen as depending upon hierarchy. The opposition of high and low ends is both hierarchic and functional, with the hall mediating between the two and also between the house's owner and the outside world. The architectural prominence of the hall, both inside and outside, announced its owner's standing and the importance of his house in the community. In the absence of strong, centralised government the hall retained a powerful symbolic function as the seat of

justice, as the focus of hospitality and as a public display of its owner's wealth. Similarly, the house's principal chambers were graded both visually and by location to the ranks of their occupants. When ties of honour and personal duty were at least as important as those which bound the *nobilitas* to the Crown, the accommodation both of the house's owner and of his guests in accordance with their rank was of paramount importance.

These functional distinctions were elaborated in display that reached its height in the later 15th century and which corresponded closely to the social and political structures of the time. The prominence of the castellated gate tower in such houses as Oxburgh (Norfolk) or Coughton (Warwicks.) is the

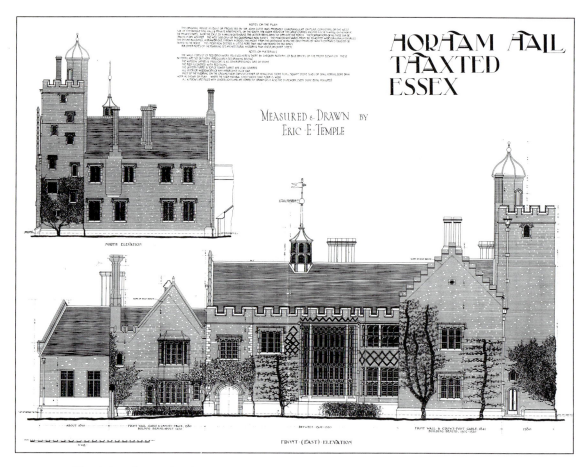

Fig. 9.1 *A hierarchical house: Horham Hall, Essex, c.1480–1580. Principal elevations*
(Eric Temple, The Building News, *1909).*

Fig. 9.2 *A symmetrical house: Shaw House, Newbury, Berkshire, c.1577–82. Reconstruction drawing of the principal front (RCHME 1995).*

visual equivalent of the troops of liveried retainers that maintained their masters' honour; the lodging towers of Raglan, Gainsborough (Lincs.) and South Wingfield (Derbys.) – whether for owners or guests – are proportioned to the standing of their occupants. At a lower social level, gentry houses distinguish between high and low ends by the size and ornament of gables and windows; if timber framed, with decorative framing and a jetty.

At the same time, the houses that incorporate this display face not outward but inward. In those houses that are built around a courtyard, outer faces are generally inexpressive of internal arrangements and the sole architectural display towards the outside world may be a gatehouse range in which subordinate structures are disposed symmetrically either side of the gatehouse itself. These generally have some service function that calls for no visual discrimination. An exception may sometimes be the chapel, as at Hengrave (Suffolk) or Compton Winyates (Warwicks.) – a part of the house that was commonly used by a wider range of people than any other except the hall. Even in those houses that do not surround a courtyard there was generally an enclosed forecourt, and not only are gatehouses frequently unaligned on the hall porch but are sometimes placed at right angles to it. Thus it is not until one has passed

through the gatehouse that one is aware in any detail of the range of accommodation that the house provides. This outward inexpressiveness and the concentration of the principal display towards the courtyard has its origin in security, but by 1500 defence is no longer the sole (or even a primary) consideration. What is expressed besides its hierarchies, however, is the continuing self-containment of the household.

Figure 9.3 shows the outer face of the high-end range of Little Moreton (Cheshire) with its irregular line of garderobe projections and chimneys that correspond to, but do not advertise, the internal arrangements. Only the chapel is housed in a rather more prominent projection. Little Moreton Hall is very different from Eastbury (Greater London) (Fig. 9.4) which is still less expressive of its internal plan but is wholly regular and outward-facing. The late medieval house contained in microcosm the perception of society at large.

Within the late medieval house, however, the accommodation is simple and room uses tend to be generalised. Although ground floor parlours are normal in upper-class houses by 1500, they still commonly contain beds and seem to be for the entertainment both by day and by night of guests of equivalent rank to the owner. Hence, like chambers,

Fig. 9.3 *An inward-looking house: Little Moreton Hall, Cheshire, c.1420–1560 (RCHME 1995).*

they quite often appear in contemporary surveys to have been provided with privies. Chambers themselves are few in number, and serve also as dayrooms for their occupants. The hall acts as a common room for servants as the place where they take their meals. Personal servants may sleep in their master's chamber; other servants above secondary and service rooms that generally no longer exist. Circulation too is simple: stairs at high and low ends of the hall are purely functional, without any decorative or architectural enhancement; a lack of passages is simply the consequence of a small number of rooms.

The transformation of the gentry house was the result of the class's growing numbers, wealth, education, and political and administrative power. A free land market and numerous new opportunities for making money were making possible a wide redistribution of property, while land itself was available from aristocratic owners and from dissolved monasteries. Together, these factors caused the amount of land owned by the gentry as a class to rise from around 25 per cent to 50 per cent between 1500 and the early 17th century. While the average size of gentry holdings fell slightly, this was more than compensated for by the huge increase in their numbers and consequently in their social and political prominence. Whereas there was perhaps a resident lord of the manor in one in ten English villages in 1500, there was something like a squire to every three villages 120 years later. Their houses,

Fig. 9.4 *An outward-looking house: Eastbury Manor, Barking, London, 1570–75 (RCHME 1996).*

by their affinities with one another and by their distinction from the houses of lesser men, announce the standing of each owner and the dominance of the class to which he belonged.

The political powers of the class would grow hugely as an increasingly powerful and centralised state sought to replace the old, territorial aristocracy as a means of of governing the provinces, and thus gave ever more administrative and judicial duties to the gentry – a class already broadly based throughout the country but which lacked the aristocracy's power to to provide an alternative power base to central government. Among the gentry, loyalty to the Crown as the source of honour and authority would increasingly supplant loyalty to an intermediate feudal overlord. To the long-standing manorial lordships enjoyed by many of the gentry there would be added an ever growing range of statutory powers and duties vested in the gentry by virtue of their nomination to the magistracy: duties and appointments that tended to be resisted in the 15th century but which were increasingly accepted as of right in the 16th in recognition of the standing of a class whose self-awareness was growing is step with its wealth and authority. Such powers deriving from central government and imposed by statute would increasingly supplant the local and traditional customs of the manor court.

The role of a broadening upper class as the agent of central government reinforced its sense of exclusivity. Decline in the autonomous exercise of power paralleled a deeper cultural shift towards a new concern for privacy and personal distinction which has also been seen as a product of the changing role of the state. In the late Middle Ages government was weak and decentralised, and the individual was left by default to establish his own position and to maintain his own security by means of a personal affinity of retainers and a public display of strength. From the late 15th century onwards, however, not only in England but in much of Europe, states that were rapidly growing in authority were increasingly able to circumscribe the powers of the individual and at the same time better able to guarantee his freedom within strictly defined boundaries. No longer needing – or even permitted - to secure power by his own efforts, the individual is left to make good his claims to status and authority not only through the exercise of powers bestowed on him by the state but by the cultivation of more personal distinctions.

Whereas once, courtesy – courtly behaviour – was a sign that one was qualified to mingle with other courtiers, a cultivation of the self that went deeper than the acquisition of social skills was now leading to a recognition that manners are a sign of character as much as of social acceptability. In the cultivation of civility – the favourite word of 16th-century writers – the gentleman displayed behaviour that marked him off from from the lower orders, but the purpose of civility is no longer merely social distinction on its own account so much as participation in a communion of like-minded, civilised individuals. In the course of the century, numerous books – home-grown like Sir Thomas Elyot's *The Governor* and translations such as Sir Thomas Hoby's of Castiglione's *The Courtier* – discussed the appropriate behaviour of the cultivated man. Civility was a sign of inward morality, a message that was preached by Erasmus and in due course could easily be translated into religious terms by preachers who taught that a man's outward behaviour indicated the state of his soul. But though the purpose of civility in forwarding human relationships was rather different from the purpose of courtesy in the Middle Ages, it tended to be no less exclusive in its application: the cultivated (or the saved) showed the

fact in their daily lives, while those who were uncivilised remained outside the pale.

It is this notion of exclusivity that connects the cultivation of the individual with the development of privacy. In the Middle Ages, the important person's every action was valueless unless it was performed in public, with suitable marks of status. But once the individual had come to place a value on his own actions, regardless of their public acclaim, it became not merely irrelevant that they should be done publicly but it might positively devalue them. How a private man lived was ceasing to be public business. Beyond his private beliefs he might be justified by his work for the public good and his standing displayed by proper ceremonial on public occasions, but the lines between public and private were increasingly tightly drawn. At the same time, the increasing power of the state and the decline in the role of the local community in determining the person's place within it, increased the scope for the individual to choose his own company and to find congenial companions among those of a similar education and class. In the cultivation of friends a man excluded others whose claims to companionship were based solely on community or household. Such a change led to a new importance of the family as an emotional centre and as a sanction for behaviour; the decline of the extended household of retainer-companions that had been brought about by the growing role of the state, coincided with a decline in the felt need for such comradeship. In 1623 Sir Henry Wotton saw the place of the house in the self-fulfilment of the individual as

> Everyman's proper Mansion House and Home, being the Theatre of his Hospitality, the Seat of his Self-fruition, the Comfortablest part of his own Life, the Noblest of his Sonne's Inheritance, a kinde of private Providence; Nay, to the Possessors thereof, an Epitome of the whole World.[2]

Such a domestic picture could not have been painted a century before.

However, the scope for display was not diminished: rather was there a change in what was displayed. In a time of rapid social change, both old gentry and new sought confirmation of their own status and reassurance about their neighbours', and showed a keen interest in anything that proclaimed their standing. The most obvious of such statements are made in costume and dress, and in the 16th century the authorities attempted by laws and proclamations to prescribe the clothing costume that might be worn by the different orders of society. The only architectural equivalent of these sumptuary laws was a statute of 1522 that prohibited men below a certain rank from employing foreign craftsmen, the masters of up-to-date decoration and ornament at the highest end of the trade, but though the ostensible purpose was the protection of English-born artisans the effect was to recognise the appropriateness of such furnishings in the houses of the elite.

But the principles of display had in any case been stated explicitly. Vitruvius, with the authority of the ancient world and accessible through several printed editions by 1560, told readers that 'for persons of high rank who hold office and magistrates and whose duty it is to serve the state, we must provide princely vestibules, lofty halls and very spacious peristyles'.[3] Such recommendation was readily accepted by the class of the expanding English magistracy. Contemporary aesthetic judgements are more about what Vitruvius called *decor* – fitness for purpose – than any abstract notion of beauty. Equally potent, broader in appeal and of longer standing was the Aristotelian sanction for display. The word generally translated as 'magnificence' in Aristotle has now no direct English equivalent: 'greatness of mind' is included, but lacks the element of appropriate public behaviour inherent in Aristotle's description of the magnificent man. The essential point for Aristotle is a moral one: that appropriate display by the man whose wealth and standing merit it, is a virtue and even a public duty. Aristotelian thought remained pervasive in the 16th century, but the late medieval condemnation of governors (such as Henry VI) whose behaviour was inappropriate to their standing had also conformed directly with Aristotle's ethics. Visible distinction was an important rhetorical element in the moral society.

For as long as external distinctions were marked, a house's internal hierarchies could be read from the outside. If such a display of functions precluded symmetry, this was irrelevant. Medieval builders were of course perfectly well acquainted with the notion of symmetry and where appropriate applied it rigorously, but the dwellings of the great had other meanings that required expression. Symmetry and the suppression of hierarchic distinction both increase in the course of the 16th century, and the first wholly symmetrical houses would be built in the late 1570's.

It has been customary to ascribe this change to the influence of the Renaissance, but the direct influence of France and Italy on English building actually declines after the 1550s and only revives again with Inigo Jones. This decline of direct continental influence is only partly compensated for by the growing availability of architectural pattern-books: those of Hans Blume, Serlio, Shute, Vignola and various editors of Vitruvius who by illustrating details and the classical orders did little to advance a view of the house's overall form. More relevant is a more abstract derivation of classicism, a humanist recognition that building involves more than a mere collage of decorative devices and embraces a platonic ideal of order whose realisation is among the duties of the public man. The incorporation of such an ideal in the overall appearance of the house makes a statement about its owner that is very different from that made through the hierarchic expression of its parts. The popint has already been made with the contrast of Little Moreton and Eastbury. One can similarly contrast Horham Hall in Essex (Fig. 9.1), whose different elements are clearly distinguished, with a house such as Shaw outside Newbury (Berks.) (Fig. 9.2). Shaw, probably begun around 1577, is the home of a man who does not require the onlooker to know which is his bedroom, which his kitchen and even which is his hall, because these are his own business. But at the same time, the forecourt was broad, deep and enclosed by no more than a wall of modest height, and being built on a hillside the house in any case shows well above it. At Shaw, the display is towards the outside world. Similarly at Wilderhope (Shrops.) (Fig. 9.5) the high and low ends are differentiated; at Ludstone in the same county built some 25 years later (Fig. 9.6) even the principal entrance is concealed in the interests of symmetry. It is only when the visitor is within the house that he may see as much or as little of the arrangements as the owner cares to show him. What Shaw's and

Fig. 9.5 *A hierarchical house: Wilderhope Manor, Shropshire, c.1580 (Author, 1994).*

Ludstone's builders advertise is that they are men of culture and learning, whose public duty is as much to civilise their neighbours as to entertain them.

A related but still more abstract reason for the increasing imposition of order on the external appearance of the house may perhaps be in the mental climate of the age. The Tudors above all dreaded disorder. The chaos of the 15th century was something that neither Tudor monarchs nor their subjects wished to repeat. To explain architectural changes simply as aspects of contemporary mentality is to beg too many question, yet one can see this increasing regularity of the exterior of houses in such a light, and perhaps, conversely, this growing regularity itself illuminates the attitudes of the age. We now see such castellated, Elizabethan houses as Bar-

lborough (Derbys.) and Lulworth (Dorset) as architectural manifestations of wider aspects of late Elizabethan culture, and link them to a fashion for chivalrous romance. One may see the increasing regularity of houses as an aspect of similar but deeper concerns, in which order no longer subsists in the hierarchies of the local community but rather in the standing of the man of wealth, education and authority among his peers and in the government of the well-ordered nation.

The change from the legible to the illegible house, so to speak – from the house whose plan could be read from the outside to the house with the uniform and symmetrical exterior – took place alongside a steady rise in standards of living and taste that derived from superior education and from the

Fig. 9.6 *An inexpressive house: Ludstone, Shropshire, c.1605 (Author, 1994).*

increased wealth that had led to the proliferation of such houses in the first place. One aspect of rising living standards is the multiplication and increasing specialisation of rooms – of parlours, formal sequences of state rooms, chambers designated by the name of an occupant or of a decorative element, closets appropriated to chambers, withdrawing rooms, galleries, dining parlours for grand occasions and for daily use, studies for the exclusive use of the head of the house, and rooms permanently distinguished by from each other by fixed architectural decoration and by distinctive colour schemes. Such innovations demanded flexibility and innovation in planning.

Once it became unnecessary to mark externally the location of principal rooms, they could be relocated. There is a general tendency in the course of the 16th century to move the owner's own chamber from the high end of the house to the low end. This is largely in order to increase the space available for entertainment at the high end – a further indication of the growing importance of the peer group. The need for more upper-floor accommodation is also among the reasons for the loss of the tall, two-storeyed hall – although its decling usefulness made owners increasingly willing to sacrifice its symbolic importance and made easier a uniform treatment of the outside of the house. In only one other way does such internal sophistication show itself externally, and that is in the increase in the number of windows. Although facilitated by the readier availability of window glass, the great expanse of glass of late

Elizabethan houses was not wholly new: what has changed is not the maximum size of windows but their number and their uniformity, as houses come to accommodate the behaviour that wealth and education made possible and as the outside of the house ceases to express anything but its owner's cultivation.

Norbert Elias, Phillipe Aries and others have shown how the 16th century saw fundamental behavioural changes in the development of new taboos and in a new awareness of the self by which, in place of the individual's realising himself by reference to his companions, he might do so in a variety of more private ways, ways that might be described as mental rather than social. The vast increase in the quality and in the quantity of the furnishings of rooms similarly indicates a concern to define oneself by behaviour that is sophisticated and exclusive, and in the houses of the great, fashion and conspicuous consumption take the place of an army of retainers as a form of self-advertisement. There is a difference between privacy and exclusivity, and one cannot understand notions of privacy unless one understands household relations in regard to class, sex and generation, spouses, servants, children, siblings, friends and acquaintances which are all different and all of which vary over time. What is difficult to know is how often rooms were shared and with whom: inventories tell about the presence and numbers of beds, but not how many people may have slept in them, and household sizes and composition are notoriously difficult to calculate. But the multiplication of rooms for special purposes is evidence of changes in manners and in behaviour, and such an increase is clearly evident both from documents and from houses themselvees.

The hierarchical plan had been essentially a linear one: the best rooms at one end and the services at the other. The great planning innovation of the years around 1600 was what was later described as the double pile – the house of two ranges deep with a rectagular plan that at once seems to be of the modern era. With a few isolated exceptions the double pile plan first appears in suburban houses and lodges, houses built for the higher ranks of society but which are unrelated to territorial functions or to the local community. This cannot be a coincidence. The double pile need not have its hall at the centre: in fact in a four-square house it cannot do so. The double pile house need not have its principal stair opening off the superior end of the hall, and it may be actually rather inconvenient if it does so, but it only becomes acceptable to place the stair at the low end when the hall's hierarchical role is all but abandoned. The form lends itself particularly well to a compact, upright treatment: a silhouette that was increasingly popular from the late 16th century and was clearly adopted as a way of making the house as visually prominent as possible: here was the house of someone who is setting himself apart from his neighbours at the same time as announcing prominently his importance in his neighbourhood. When in the 17th century architectural writers begin to discuss specific house plans and the relative advantages of different arrangements, the double pile is commended for economy, for warmth and for ease of circulation. But these innovations were only possible once hierarchical arrangements were superseded by other factors in settling the form of the house.

The multiplication and increasing diversity of rooms combined with the transformation of the outside of the house to prompt a new approach towards its overall design: an approach in which scholarship and connoisseurship would take the place of the appropriate discrimination of its parts. Even though symmetry was not immediately the result of the spread of classicism, connoisseurship was reflected in the spread of classical ornament that derived from models that were as readily available to the educated man as to the artisan who was building his house. The change is directly reflected in the fast growing esteem, from the late 16th century, for educated craftsmen: for the architect who not only possessed the technical skill to supervise the work of building, but also the connoisseurship to be able to discuss its form and decoration with an educated patron – or who had enough knowledge to be able to put up a house that would impress those of his patron's friends who had such taste themselves. It is reflected too in the increasing number of educated men who are known to have involved themselves actively in the detailed design of their own houses.

If a single picture expresses the tensions and possibilities of the age, it is perhaps that of the courtyard of Little Moreton Hall (Fig. 9.7). The house

Fig. 9.7 *The courtyard front of Little Moreton Hall, c.1420, c.1480 and 1555 (RCHME 1995).*

still displays its distinct elements towards the courtyard, with a prominent porch to invite visitors to enter. Hall and parlour ranges are much grander than is the kitchen range to the left. These great windows are themselves additions to an older fabric. They provide for a new chamber inserted above the hall and, carved with the name of the builder, they are identified expressly with his standing. But though they are windows for display, this is still merely towards those who have already passed the gatehouse and as yet they do not look out over, or can be seen from, the wider world. Little Moreton looks both forward and backward, the perfect expression of the gentry house in the age of transition.

Notes

1. Two such are Sutton Place in Surrey, which had been regarded as a piece of precocious symmetry of 1525 but which is now known to have reached its present form in 1720, and Barrington Court, Somerset, re-dated by A.P. Baggs to the 1550s from 1514. Both of these new dates fit far better with the established sequence of development for such houses. For Barrington, see *V.C.H. Somerset*, 4, 1978, 112–14; for Sutton Place, Cooper 1994.
2. Prideaux 1903, 65.
3. Myers 1914, 182.

Bibliography

Airs, M. (ed.) 1994, *The Tudor and Jacobean Great House*, Oxford

Cooper, N. 1994, 'Sutton Place, East Barsham and some problems arising' in M. Airs (ed.) 1994, 33–54

Myers, M.H. (trans.) 1914, Vitruvius, *The Ten Books of Architecture* (repr. New York 1960)

Prideaux, S.T. (ed.) 1903, Sir Henry Wotton, *The Ten Books of Architecture*

10   Urban Housing in England, 1400–1600

John Schofield

The study of English housing in the medieval and Tudor periods has been biased in favour of the rural. Peter Smith, President of the Vernacular Architecture Group in 1984–5, considering the contrasts between vernacular buildings in England and those on the Continent, has said 'for most of us [the] medieval hall-house, whether farmhouse or manor house, is the starting point of our studies of vernacular architecture'.[1] This paper seeks to show that there were other forms of buildings in towns, and even to suggest that the rural models which have indeed been the point of departure of thinking in vernacular architecture studies may be inappropriate, at least for some of the larger towns in the 15th and 16th centuries. I shall deal briefly with the variety of plan forms; significant developments in rooms and spaces, in structural features, and materials; and the conclusions to be drawn from these developments.

The range of plan forms

For a partial typology of English house-plans around 1500 we can turn to two articles by W.A. Pantin in 1962–3; but he left out both the grandest mansions and the smallest houses. I have also sought to establish a simple classification of house-plans for London in 1600, based on the surveys of Ralph Treswell.[2] But typologies can have a deceptive and ultimately meaningless rigour, and many houses do not fall into the ideal types. It is the same in Scottish towns, where, for the period 1560 to 1700, there is a variety of house-types that defy attempts at neat

architectural classification.[3] It may therefore be that we should use classification of house-plans as only a general indication of preferred arrangements of buildings on the urban plot. Further, as noticed in Hertfordshire as a whole, houses of one build conforming to a type seem to be comparatively rare. Rather, the notion of types arising mainly through alteration is closer to reality and a larger sample might produce a typology of transformation of one house type into another.[4]

Houses can, however, be usefully divided into large, medium-sized and small. The largest houses in towns were usually built around a courtyard; this had been the case since the 12th century, and possibly before. Small town examples include Hampton Court, King's Lynn and The Hermitage, now part of the George Hotel, Stamford, both courtyard houses in stone of the 14th and 15th centuries respectively.[5] It often took generations for a family to acquire all the land to lay out a courtyard house; or, as in the case of the Pastons' house at Elm Hill in Norwich after the fire of 1507, a disaster made land available for the whole complex at once.

The courtyard houses were also under pressure. During the 15th century, two processes affected the larger residences in the City of London (many of which were originally noble or religious town-houses of 13th- or 14th-century date): some became halls for the craft guilds (there were about sixty of these by 1600), and others were turned wholly or partially into taverns. The latter was particularly true of the town houses belonging to religious institutions from outside town, which were not otherwise part of the urban property market.

Among the houses of the most affluent London citizens were some new constructions with palatial overtones. At the highest level was Crosby Place in Bishopsgate (1466–75), the hall of which has survived though now transposed to Chelsea. The hall and parlour block of this mansion were of ashlar-fronted brick on brick undercrofts; a semi-octagonal oriel window at the dais end of the hall incorporated Crosby's crest in its stone vault. The hall resembles that of Eltham Palace (Kent) of 1479 and may have been built, like Eltham, by the king's mason, Thomas Jurdan. During the first four decades of the 16th century some of the houses of the monarch or the royal circle were built in London itself, such as Baynard's Castle, Bridewell Palace and Suffolk House in Southwark, but these new palatial residences do not seem to have influenced the houses of the well-off citizens of London to any degree. After 1535, however, the proliferation of grand town-houses on the sites of the dissolved monasteries, in London and in many other English towns, must have provided new opportunities for the well-placed courtier and speculator (often a merchant or other urban professional with spare cash) to be more up-to-date.

A number of elite urban residences were constructed within religious precincts (of which London had more than twenty), adapting the monastic buildings and clothing them in timberwork and glazing and inserting fashionable interiors.[6] The constraints of developing a restricted urban site, already fairly full of substantial stone buildings, must however have hampered any attempt to indulge in large-scale planning of suites as might be possible in contemporary rural grand houses. It is difficult to identify suites of rooms – the great chamber, withdrawing chamber, bedchamber and closet, and long gallery – which are a feature of large houses of this period elsewhere. As an example we can cite the mansion of Thomas Audley at Holy Trinity Priory, Aldgate (after Audley's death in 1544, one of the London town-houses of the Duke of Norfolk), since plans of about 1586 survive. The domestic ranges of the prior's lodging were kept as the core of the house, though the facade to the outer court was refenestrated

and heightened; from the first-floor hall a gallery led along the former north aisle of the priory church, the nave of which was now a roofless garden with the stubs of piers, to a banqueting house called the Ivy Chamber which lay in the upper part of the 12th-century crossing. This had large windows to the nave on one side and to the also roofless Romanesque choir on the other. One feature of these extraordinary mansions, in London as in rural examples such as Acton Court near Bath, was the use of glass in large flat windows, forty years before the better-known Hardwick Hall (Derbys.). In both large and small towns, the grand houses carved out of monastic precincts in the 1540s and 1550s are a largely forgotten and poorly known generation of innovative urban residences.

The rest of this paper will be concerned with houses outside the sphere of the privileged or extraordinarily rich. Merchants occupied courtyard houses, large rambling properties (Fig. 10.1) which included halls sometimes partly of stone or brick, by 1550 being floored over, and working yards surrounded by warehouses (of which more below). They had counterparts in many European towns, and in such dwellings it is easy to set Thomas Mann's *Brothers Buddenbrook*. Such a house, occupied by an extended family and servants, must have been a

---

Fig 10.1 (opposite) Houses in Abchurch Lane (left) and St Nicholas Lane (right), including Foxe's Court, London; from a survey by Ralph Treswell for the Cloth-workers' Company, 1612. In this and Figures 10.2–4, the numbers on the plan refer to individual tenancies; rooms and external spaces (as described in 1610–12) are as follows:

B	Buttery	P	Parlour
C	Cellar	Sd	Shed
Ch	Chamber	Sh	Shop
E	Entry	St	Study
G	Garden	W	Warehouse
H	Hall	Wa	Waterhouse
K	Kitchen	Y	Yard

The houses are mostly timber-framed; brick walls are shown by hatching, and stone walls in Fig. 10.4 by irregular outlines.

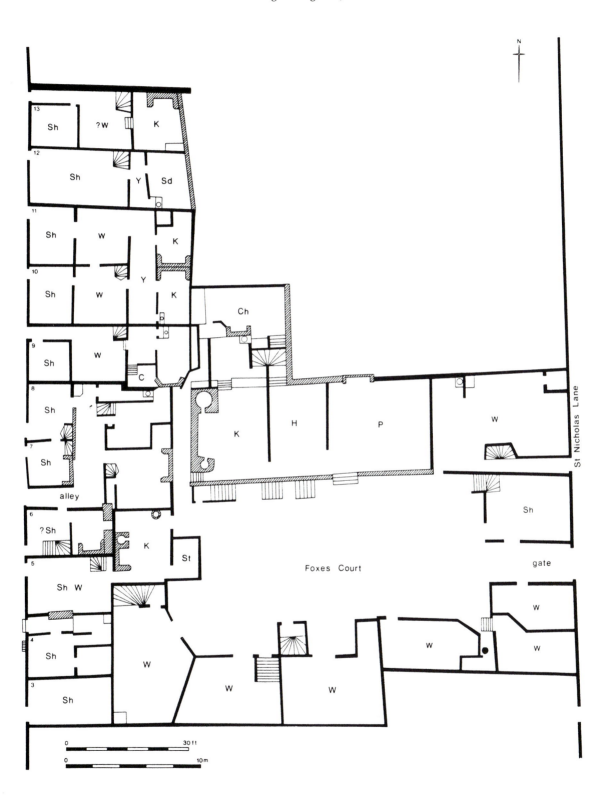

John Schofield

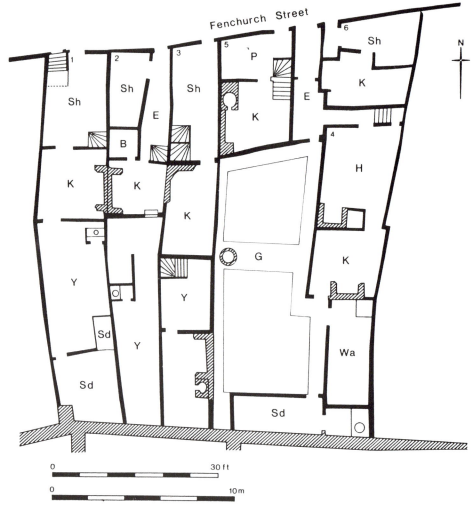

Fig 10.2 *Houses on the south side of Fenchurch Street, London, surveyed by Ralph Treswell for the Clothworkers' Company in 1612. A 'medium-sized' house is shown on the right, though by 1612 it was divided into four tenancies. The hall in tenancy 4 had by then been floored over.*

miniature community with its own rules and customs like the larger territorial units of parish and town. They were the urban equivalent of farms in that they were working complexes or compounds of buildings.

Below the level of the courtyard mansion, there was a variety of ground-floor plans according to the size of the ground available. Some had a hall on the ground floor, comparatively lofty and open to the roof, and others had no open hall but a chamber called a hall which was ceiled over like the other

chambers. This could be on the ground floor, but in many town centres was on the first floor. The omission of the open hall is one of the most significant urban characteristics of houses of this period.

The medium-sized house (Fig. 10.2), of three to six rooms in the ground-floor plan of its main range (i.e. not counting separate buildings such as kitchens) did not have a true courtyard, though it might have a yard with buildings along one side, or an alley running the length of a long, narrow property. Some properties were broader, or several narrow properties had been acquired by one owner and made into a single site. By 1450 in Salisbury, better houses included a compact form two bays wide and two or three bays deep, and a narrow passage leading from the street to the backyard: examples in the town include 3 Minster Street, 13 and 56 High Street, and 8 Queen Street.[7]

Properties of this size, midway between the courtyard mansion and the smaller row along the street, could often include an open hall. In the 15th century, in medium-sized towns such as King's Lynn, a normal property would have an open hall behind a street range.[8] Buildings with open halls could also be ranged with their long side along the street when the property was wide or there was no pressure on space. An open hall along the street with a simple cross-passage was common in Stamford around 1500.[9] A variant was the Wealden house, always timber-framed, normally comprising an open hall with two-storeyed jettied wings at each end, all under one roof; the eaves of the roof were carried over the recess in the middle on prominent arch braces. The Wealden house is found in largest numbers in Kent and Sussex, though the type is known in all the south-eastern counties, as well as in Bedfordshire, Cambridgeshire and Norfolk, and in towns such as Coventry, Newark and York. The form dates from the late 14th century to perhaps the 1530s, and a London origin for the design has been suggested by several commentators, though it might also have originated more generally from the cross-wing house in the countryside.[10] It was clearly common in smaller towns, or in the backstreets of larger towns: there are still nine examples standing in Rye, and others in Canterbury, Saffron Walden, Hitchin, Hemel Hempstead and Winchester.[11]

The next size of house down, smaller and more uniform in its characteristics, was a compact house with two rooms on three or more floors, such as those surveyed by Treswell in 1612 in Abchurch Lane in London (Fig. 10.1). This type is known from documentary and archaeological evidence in the City from the early 14th century; five in Abchurch Lane may have been those built on the site shortly before 1390.[12] It was particularly common in situations where no adjacent private open space was available,

especially forming the street frontages of larger houses which lay in their own grounds behind. In the Abchurch Lane examples, the kitchen was a separate building reached across a small yard, but in the majority of the type as surveyed by Treswell the kitchen occupied a back room on the first floor. The ground floor was usually a shop and warehouse, sometimes with the two rooms thrown together to form one, or perhaps a tavern, which required very little change in structure or furnishings.

This type of house is also found in other towns from the middle of the 14th century. Three out of an original block of five built in 1385–6 still survive in the Cornmarket, Oxford, in the Middle Ages comprising a frontage to an inn; 52–54 High Street Salisbury, erected by 1341, has two bays on the ground floor and three bays in the storey above.[13] A row of three houses excavated at Pottergate, Norwich, destroyed in a fire of 1507, were also of this type.[14] With a shop on the ground floor, the two-room unit of two or three floors was used to colonise market areas and make up Middle Rows, as at 30 Middle Row, Dunstable.[15]

The types of medium-sized house just described were arranged, in the main, with their gables to the street, even when they were several bays wide. On frontages with less pressure of space, such as in the backstreets of towns and sometimes along major streets in small towns, there was more variety and less observance of these compact forms. Even when the house presented its eaves to the street, however, it could have a first-floor hall, as at the New Inn, New Street, Salisbury, where the arrangement of the roof trusses suggests that two bays of the first floor were the hall.[16]

In medieval towns there must have been many houses which were only one room in plan, and often only of a single storey; but the latter were disappearing from towns in the 16th century.[17] A 'classic small house of the late Elizabethan East Anglian town' noted in King's Lynn and Norwich comprised a single room on two or more floors, the ground floor entered by opposed doors at the lower, non-chimney end.[18] In London, many one-room plan houses with only one entrance (because they had no back yards) are shown by Treswell in the surveys of 1607–14, with examples probably dating from before

1528; but by 1600 they were of three or more storeys (Fig. 10.3). Houses with only one room on each floor, sometimes incorporating an entry or passage to the stair on the ground floor, were to be found both on principal streets, where they formed a screen for the larger houses behind, or in courts (dead-end alleys or the slightly larger spaces at the ends of them) where they could assume awkward, angular shapes to take up the available space. They were also used when whole new streets were being laid out; of about 175 new houses built over the old fair ground at St Bartholomew Smithfield, London, between 1598 and 1612, about 140 were of a uniform one-room deep plan. Each consisted of a shop on the ground floor, a cellar below, and two chambers and a garret on the floors above.[19]

Small dwellings were also known as 'rents', where an alley or a garden was crammed with new, poor housing; in London, this was happening in Southwark (in some respects, an unregulated suburb) in the 1520s and 1530s.[20] The Treswell surveys furnish several examples of London alleys where housing was concentrated, for instance off Fleet Lane, part of the estate of the Clothworkers' Company.[21] At the side of a large house was Blacksmith's Court: here a widow lived in a single ground-floor chamber 12 feet square, and another house across the court consisted of two superimposed chambers, the lower 11 feet by 10 feet and the upper only slightly larger. More such cramped accommodation, including tenancies of only one room each, could be found across the City next to another prominent merchant's courtyard house (Fig. 10.4).

Almshouses provided generally better-built and better-maintained variations on the theme of the house of one-room plan. The first almshouses in towns, or indeed in the countryside, date from the opening decades of the 15th century. The earliest recorded in London were founded by the Merchant Taylors (1414), followed by the Cutlers (1420–40), Brewers (1423) and Salters (1454). The foundation of almshouses was particularly a feature of the immediately post-Dissolution years, and two sets with different plans were surveyed by Treswell. One, the result of a bequest by the Countess of Kent to the Clothworkers' Company in 1540, lay south of Fleet Street, and comprised a single timber range with ten

individual chambers, five on each of two floors. The other, belonging to Christ's Hospital and built in the period 1581–1610, comprised a court of six brick houses (or at least, brick on the ground floor), where each occupant had two superimposed chambers and a garret.[22]

When houses of the 15th and 16th centuries, or their remains in the ground, are investigated, these neat typologies, however, are seen to be only a rough mapping out of the perceptible major forms. Due to widespread destruction of deposits of this period in the larger towns and in London, remains of buildings are often fragmentary and survive only where deposits are deeper such as along the banks of rivers (Fig. 10.5). Urban excavations commonly produce sequences of buildings, which show change and adaptation according to specific circumstances. At Alms Lane, Norwich, for instance, the period 1450–1600 was covered by three periods of building.[23] In Period 6 (1450–1500) three small rectangular buildings, each of two unequal rooms in plan, were constructed with eaves to the street. There were no signs of any permanent fireplaces and no stairs, but one house possibly had a loft, presumably reached by a ladder. In Period 7 (1500–75), all were rebuilt, with axial fireplaces now dividing the rooms. These buildings were certainly of two storeys, with stairs. And in Period 8 (1575–1600), the houses were rebuilt and extended, possibly higher since in one case a stair turret from the courtyard was added. Presumably this sequence illustrates houses growing upwards from simple one-storey beginnings.

Many town houses below the level of the courtyard house included shops on the street; but distinct blocks of shops with houses behind and above were erected in many English towns from the 14th century. From the time of the Lady Row, Goodramgate, in York of 1314, institutions (in that case, a parish church) were selling or leasing their street frontages in more or less unitary blocks often called Rows. There are examples of the 15th and early 16th century at King's Lynn[24] and Tewkesbury. These blocks were often constructed by religious houses to be a source of revenue. Butcher Row, Shrewsbury, of three storeys c.1500, was possibly an urban investment of Lilleshall Abbey; 85–89 Micklegate, York, also of c.1500 and comprising three storeys, was apparently

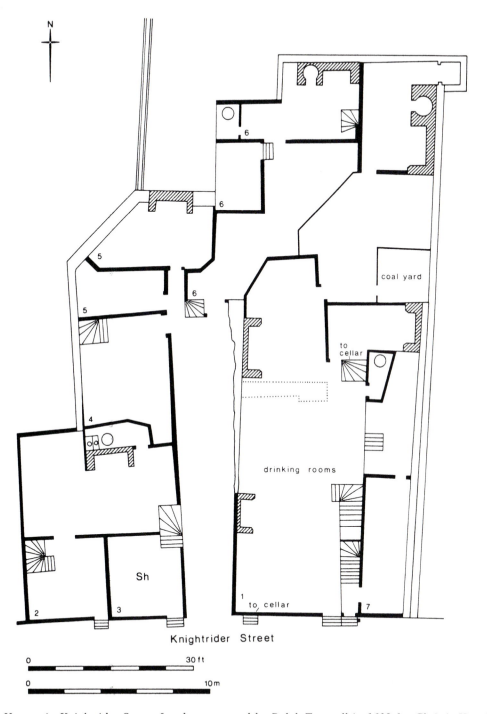

Fig. 10.3 *Houses in Knightrider Street, London, surveyed by Ralph Treswell in 1610 for Christ's Hospital. Tenancy 1 was a tavern, the White Hart, which still had some walls of stone. Tenancy 3 only had one room on the ground floor, but it spread out in the upper storeys.*

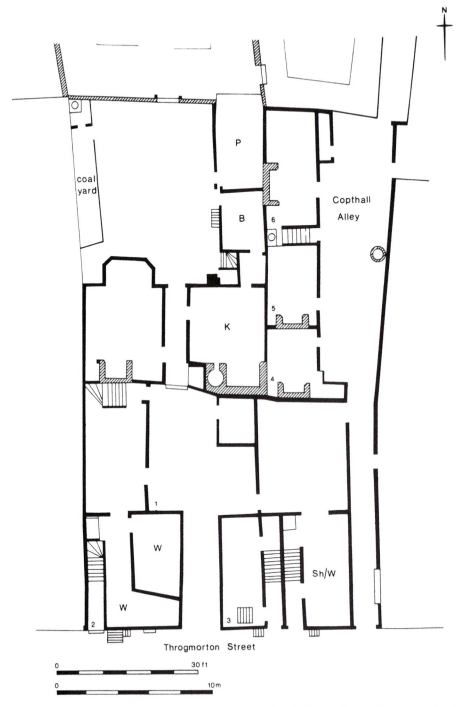

Fig. 10.4 *Houses in Throgmorton Street, London, surveyed by Ralph Treswell in 1612 for the Clothworkers' Company. A large house with a long garden (off the plan to the top) had a bay window on the private side. Next to this house, in Copthall Alley, were smaller units; tenants 5 and 6 had only one room each, tenant 4 had a room above, but without internal access; and there were two further tenancies on the first floor of one room each and a garret, reached by the stair in the middle of the range. The Alley had its own well.*

Fig. 10.5 *New Fresh Wharf, London, excavated 1974: the cellar down the alley of a long waterfront tenement, built in the 16th century and destroyed in the Great Fire of London in 1666 (Museum of London Archaeology Service).*

a speculation along the street frontage of Holy Trinity Priory.[25] By the late 14th century, prominent citizens were also constructing rows of shops, sometimes with domestic accommodation above, as investments; and towards the end of the 15th century, the block might be given by bequest to a craft organisation. An imposing range of this kind was Goldsmiths' Row in Cheapside, London, built by Thomas Wood in 1491 and managed by the Goldsmiths' Company. This comprised at least seven houses with shops, four further lock-up shops and a tavern, in a block of three storeys and garrets.[26]

Development of rooms and spaces

Over the two centuries surveyed here, the internal arrangement and organisation of the urban house underwent changes. Some of these were shared with contemporary houses in the countryside, but others may have been necessary only in towns, either by reason of the pressure on space, or because conscious and unconscious fashions tended to start in towns.

One urban characteristic being shown by London houses already in the 14th century, and by 1400 well established, was the practice of having the hall on the first floor: such an arrangement was specified in three contracts of 1310, 1383 and 1410 for houses with shops in the central area (Cheapside, Addle Lane and Friday Street respectively). Domestic first-floor halls are common in the Treswell surveys of 1607–14, in houses of one-room and two-room plan form; in the two-room plan the hall always occupied the front room over the street when the position is specified. The first-floor hall is found in houses in other towns such as Bristol (a contract for a house in the High Street in 1472), Exeter, Rye (Sussex) and Watford (Herts.) from about 1450, and was clearly a form necessitated by the use of the whole ground floor area for commercial purposes.

In smaller towns the hall open to the roof persisted, even as late as the late 15th century;[27] but at Bury St Edmunds halls open to the roof were out of fashion before 1500, and there is no evidence from the surviving houses in Stamford for open halls being built after about 1500. In King's Lynn, there is one case of a hall being floored over in the 15th century (12–20 Priory Lane), but this may be a very early example. During the 16th and 17th centuries most of the existing open halls in Stamford were floored over; in London, halls were subdivided to form two chambers as well.[28]

The room which developed as the hall declined in status was the parlour. During the late 14th and 15th centuries several company halls in London were provided with a parlour, either when being rebuilt or as a specific addition. The position of the parlour in the house or the company hall was significant; not only was it deep within the property in terms of access, and was most often on the ground floor, but it usually overlooked, and occasionally had access into, the garden (Fig. 10.4). This proximity was often emphasised by the parlour having a prominent window on the garden side; in certain houses, a quasi-octagonal window took up much of the gable end of the room, and the parlour (often a rectangular rather than square room) may have been deliberately placed to exploit a view into the garden from its narrower end. The association of parlours with gardens was taken up by taverns and inns: the Green Dragon in Southwark, in 1544, had at least four parlours, three of them set together beside the garden , and another example of a 16th-century inn with a range of several parlours on the garden side has been recorded at Rye.[29]

During the 15th and especially 16th centuries, certain other new functions and new rooms can be seen developing in town houses: the warehouse, the Great Chamber, galleries, and stairs.

In the most prestigious medieval houses, a vaulted undercroft formed a large, perhaps the main storage room. The term *warehouse* was used by the 16th

century to signify something different from an ordinary storehouse. It may have been especially a room required by drapers and other people of the cloth trade, literally to house their wares. On waterfront properties in London, warehouses of imposing dimensions could be found on both first and second floors of tightly-packed buildings. On properties away from the river, warehouses were to be found across small yards or, in the largest houses, around a courtyard (Figs 10.1 and 10.4). On inland sites, warehouses were always on the ground floor, and where space allowed could be independent structures of one or two storeys; but they were usually built into the congested building complex as one of many rooms. In all situations they tended to have a single entrance and no internal stairs; they were still thought of as undercroft-sized spaces. Perhaps some of them had been adapted from previous lives as industrial buildings, such as dye-houses. By 1600, much of the waterfront zone comprised alleys full of merchandise in utilitarian storage buildings up to four storeys high;[30] perhaps these were specially-designed warehouses similar (at least in plan, though not in materials) to those being erected at this time in Amsterdam and Bruges. Brick warehouses are also found in King's Lynn from the 15th century.

Developments were also taking place on the first and higher floors of the house. In the urban residences with noble overtones there would be a Great Chamber on the first floor, as at Crosby Place by 1466. Nor was this an emphasis only in the superior sort of urban houses; it has also been noticed that throughout the 15th century the best room in superior houses in rural Kent was on the first floor, and was often called a chamber.[31] When houses of the 16th century had halls which were floored over, the chamber above the new ground-floor hall, being the largest on the first floor, naturally became the Great Chamber. This is found in both rural and urban examples (e.g. Sutton House, Hackney, 1533–4; Eastbury Manor, Barking c.1570; at Nantwich (Cheshire) in the houses built after a town fire of 1583).[32] By 1620 the Great Chamber was usually called the Dining Chamber in polite houses.

The term *gallery* covers several different types of construction; a passage or corridor, a lobby or vestibule, or a long room intended primarily for exercise and recreation. First-floor galleries between buildings, often between the main house and a rear block, are known in London from the early 15th century and in post-medieval Exeter and Chester.[33] In early 14th- and 15th-century houses in Southampton, and in 15th-century Winchester, the gallery was used to communicate between two blocks of two-storeyed buildings by running through the upper part of the open hall which lay between them.[34] Galleries of this type were made necessary by restricted sites: in comparison, galleries are generally absent in King's Lynn, where houses were mainly side-on to the street or with an alley down the property when end-on to the street.[35]

Garden galleries were a feature of noble town-houses in London and Paris in the 1530s.[36] These were timber structures of one or two storeys which went round one or more sides of a garden; they incorporated many glazed windows and sometimes had fireplaces. They must have functioned in part like modern conservatories. There were also galleries which were incorporated into the structure of the house itself, on the first or higher floors, which were similarly intended to be more than mere passages. The 'long gallery' of the principal tenant at the Clothworkers' Throgmorton Street estate in the City (Fig. 10.4) was of this larger kind, 11 feet wide and 30 feet long 'beside the window', which implies that the window was positioned at one end. Presumably this was the garden end, since the plan suggests the gallery lay over the buttery and parlour on the east side of the back yard of the house and terminated overlooking the large garden. An even larger 'long gallery' could be found at another great house in Fenchurch Street, which had served as Fullers' Hall in 1520–8. Here on the second floor of the range along one side of the garden was a gallery 68 × 15½ feet; it occupied the entire top floor of the range.

Presumably these true long galleries (having a width greater than six feet and so probably being intended for something more than communication between chambers) had the recreational functions attributed to them in royal palaces and noble houses. The most famous in London, because of its collection of painting and sculptures, was that at Arundel House in the Strand. A gallery is shown leading from the main range to the river on the 'Agas' panorama which

is based on the copperplate map of c.1560; it must have been rebuilt by Thomas Howard by 1629, and possibly by 1618.[37] Howard's gallery, though it had some classical ornament, was essentially a traditional form of building; it led, like others, alongside the garden to a square block with large windows overlooking the river.

During the 13th and 14th centuries the urban house had grown upwards, and stairs were developed to articulate this vertical growth. Sometimes the stair used the chimney stack for support as it reached first-floor level; it has been noted in Chester that stairs developed in concert with chimney stacks.[38] By the late 16th century there was a variety of forms of stair inside smaller buildings: straight stairs, newel stairs, and others which were a little more self-contained as partitioned spaces. It may be significant that from about 1590 in southern England, stairs in houses both in small towns and in the countryside have distinctive newels and handrails.[39] This would indicate that they were being taken more seriously as pieces of interior architecture, both in use and as part of the embellishment of the house.

One development of the late 15th and especially 16th centuries was the appearance of the staircase which formed a stately route from the ground floor to a Great Chamber. This occurred in houses which were large enough to have an open hall and a parlour block in a separate wing; but also in medium-sized houses, where the largest chamber was on the first floor over the hall, either from the beginning or through rebuilding. The framed staircase with an open stairwell, being expensive in oak, is found throughout England in the 16th century (as at the Charterhouse, London, by 1571)[40] and in Wales in the 17th; but not in Scotland, which may have had less oak, and where the French fashion of a similar stair around a stone pillar was preferred.[41] By 1600, many polite houses in town and country had two stairs, one for the servants; there are examples in the contemporary collection of house designs, some of which were executed, by John Thorpe (mostly of 1597–1603). Some Tudor mansions such as Sutton House of 1534 and Eastbury Manor of c.1570 show the evolution of this idea, though whether backstairs appeared first in town houses or in rural mansions is not yet evident. There are no two-stair houses in the

DRAWN AND ETCHED BY J.T.SMITH.   DOMESTIC ARCHITECTURE.   DRAWN IN JULY 1791

SOUTH EAST VIEW OF THE OLD HOUSE LATELY STANDING IN SWEEDON'S PASSAGE, GRUB STREET.

EXTERNAL SPECIMEN OF THE   THE ABOVE, IS A SINGULARLY CURIOUS SPECIMEN, (IN LONDON) OF AN EXTERNAL WINDING STAIR CASE.   THIS HOUSE WAS TAKEN DOWN
HEAVY TIMBER STYLE.   IN MARCH 1805.

LONDON PUBLISHED AS THE ACT DIRECTS JAN.Y 29 1811, BY JOHN THOMAS SMITH N.º 18, GREAT MAY'S BUILDINGS ST MARTINS LANE.

Fig. 10.6 *An external stair on a 16th-century house in Sweeden's Passage, Grub Street, London,*
drawn by J.T. Smith in 1791.

Treswell surveys of London houses in 1600, but they were perhaps not grand enough.

A second 16th-century development, and one which was probably quickly taken up, if indeed it was not invented, in towns, was the placing of all the vertical communication routes together in one stair which led to all floors from the ground, and sometimes with a door to the outside yard at its base (Fig. 10.6). By the middle of the 17th century, perhaps following patterns already present in French townhouses, the stair to all floors could be combined with horizontal galleries, so that the main stair and gallery (or superimposed galleries) formed a block between the main house and a rear building, as at the Hoop and Grapes, Aldgate, London.

The development of this form of stair, whether it leads to galleries or to plain landings, is particularly noteworthy because its presence sometimes at the house entrance would suggest to the visitor that upstairs is an *alternative* to the ground floor, not a secluded section of the house to be reached *through* the ground-floor reception rooms; and such a stair would have encouraged the division of a multi-storeyed building into horizontal flats, as was the case in 16th-century Edinburgh houses or in Dundee, where Gardyne's House remains as a five-storeyed stone tower-block of about 1600.[42] By the 16th century the main English universities, and by the 17th century (if not before) the Inns of Court, had series of chambers (i.e. suites of rooms for individuals) off staircases; but this was otherwise not done in England. The Scots way of living, both in towns and in the countryside, was still novel to Daniel Defoe when he saw and described it in the first quarter of the 18th century.

Around 1600, the traditional and still usual configuration of a tenancy, whatever its compact or rambling nature, was to have at least one room, and not only an entry, on the ground floor. In London, from the 15th century, and possibly before, there were however two more ways of dividing the house into tenancies. Firstly, individual chambers were let out in specialised circumstances: for widows, either individually or sometimes living in a house as a group; and to foreign merchants, for instance merchants of Venice who leased a large house in Botolph Lane, using ten of its rooms as individual

bedrooms (none containing more than one bed), two as offices and two as parlours; no hall is mentioned for this businessmen's lodging.[43] Secondly, by 1600 as shown in Throgmorton Street (Fig. 10.4, the entry to tenancy 2), a new kind of tenancy could be totally on the first floor or higher, with only stairs down to the street. This was presumably a suite of rooms for a professional person or for rural gentry, neither of whom would need or want chambers on the ground floor next to the street.

The 16th-century London house also had other fashionable and rather special rooms: the closet, the study, and sometimes a banqueting house in the garden. Nor was the capital unique in having houses with these refinements. In Bristol both the Red Lodge and the White Lodge were houses built as 'lodges' in the last decade of the 16th century. By the early 17th century they had become residences in their own right.[44]

Development of structural features and materials

The changes described so far were largely concerned with the plan of the building, but there were also some urban developments in building technology, material and architectural style. The roof spaces of urban buildings were being exploited by the introduction of clasped purlin roofs from the late 14th century, as in 1386 at Zacharias's, Cornmarket, Oxford.[45] The wider use of purlins is generally placed in the first half of the 15th century; in some roofs they were combined with the older crown-post and collar purlin form.[46] Some small towns even in south-east England, from surviving examples, however, did not have many side-purlin roofs until c.1500 (for example, at Watford),[47] and in York attics were not developed until the late 16th century.

Houses with back-to-back chimneys were common in London houses by 1500, and were becoming so in Norwich. With the new emphasis on constructing chimney stacks within the main building of the house, the separate kitchen went out of favour in some towns in the 16th century. In contrast, detached kitchens continued to be the norm for better houses in 17th-century towns in south-west England, such as Bristol, Exeter, Totnes and Plymouth.

There are still many 16th-century houses in English towns (though usually only one or two in each) which feature prominent timber bracing, particularly for the street elevation. It is clear that the larger town-houses of the richer members of the civic community shared an urban style which combined local materials and fashionable bravado. For some towns, this meant prefering timber over local supplies of stone. In a small town such as Burford (Oxon.), which had only 800 inhabitants in 1545, the medieval houses had been largely if not completely of stone, and timber framing particularly of the front of the house was a short-lived feature of the 16th century.[48] The chief change in timber-framing during the two centuries surveyed here, however, was that jettying was going out of fashion (and was being banned) in the larger towns by 1600, though still employed in other places such as Salisbury (91 Crane Street, rebuilt about the same time with a rubble ground floor and a jetty for two floors above).[49] Timber frames were generally rendered over after 1650, as known from surviving buildings at Ipswich and Stamford; but motifs in external plasterwork date from the 1580s. Perhaps the contemporary fashion for pargetting was influencing the change of taste away from leaving the timbers exposed; another possible cause is that timbers were becoming thinner, more spindly and less appealing to look at.   Houses completely of brick, apart from almshouses, are rare in towns in the 15th and 16th centuries, even in London. In some towns, the first notable buildings entirely in brick are of the early 17th century: c.1600 in Micklegate, York, c.1616–18 at Rowley's Mansion in Shrewsbury, 1621 in Nantwich;[50] but even later in Exeter.

Areas of the house: commercial, domestic and service

The idea of separating trade and domestic areas in the house was widespread from earliest times, and had consequences for both the architecture and the decoration of the building. From a study of thirty standing structures which incorporate medieval shops in the south-east counties, Stenning has suggested that shops with an adjacent small open hall, usually in the bay immediately behind the shop

which fronted the street, were an early form which went out of currency by 1500. Thereafter access to the shop from the domestic accommodation was most often via a cross passage.[51] Thus a basic separation between trade and domestic areas was common in buildings in small towns by the early 16th century.

In one example of a large merchant's house in London, surveyed in 1610, the ground floor was further separated into areas concerned with domestic or family life, storage, commercial and service functions.[52] At a pivotal point in the ground-floor plan, having passed the trade rooms which lay near the street, the visitor could go one of three ways, which led to clearly-defined domestic, storage or service areas of the complex. In this case 'service' means the kitchen, buttery and similar chambers. Accommodation for servants can rarely be distinguished in the archaeological or documentary record. By 1540, in a substantial London house, there were separate sleeping chambers for men and women servants, and in another reported in 1543, separate privies for the male and female servants.[53] But generally servants, children and the elderly are shadowy figures at best and the provisions for them are almost completely unknown.

In medium-sized and smaller houses, when shops occupied all the ground floor, it was natural that the domestic accommodation started on the first floor. This evidently led to the embellishment of the first floor where the hall or main domestic room lay. In Elizabethan and Jacobean houses of this type in many towns, the front room on the first floor would be the one most likely to have a plastered ceiling, the largest (and architecturally most significant) fireplace, and panelling.

The separation of the context of production of material goods and services from the physical and social context of household relations is held to be congruent with the rise of capitalism. Johnson,[54] analysing rural evidence, places the divergence between the worlds of work and home 'by the later 17th century'; this includes the development of separate kitchens (and decline in the practice of preparing food and eating it in the hall), a marginalization of women's household activities, and a general segregation of the household space. While this may be true of houses in the countryside, it was so different in towns that Johnson's thesis is not acceptable. The worlds of work and home were being separated in urban domestic territorial units during the 15th and especially 16th centuries. In the larger towns, parts of the household space were being allocated specific functions when houses rose in height from the 13th century. On the other hand, even the most developed Tudor town-house did not have all or even most of its internal spaces assigned 'male' or 'female'. There was, rather, a series of distinctions which operated within the territorial unit: front and back, public (the street) and private (the parlour and garden), and the designation of spaces for waste and ablutions. Where archaeological work on houses of this period has taken place, for instance in Norwich, it is suggested that the later 16th century saw a greater frequency of cesspits for each house and more provision of cellars, along with an increase in material culture.[55] Above all, there was by 1550 a new feeling that business affairs should be settled by businessmen working in their own space, in sharp opposition to particularly the religious traditions of previous generations; prudence and piety could be combined if each was kept in its own place. The post-Reformation shopkeeper and trader, having replaced religious imagery on the front of his house with grotesques and moderately classical motifs recalling a more ancient and noble civilisation, could expand the commercial part of his property without guilt and with enthusiasm.[56]

Late medieval decline and houses in towns

After the Black Death, because there were considerably fewer people in towns, several processes took place. Shops disappeared from central streets; some houses became larger, while the unwanted margins of settlement crumbled, decayed and were covered with their own version of dark earth, the deposit normally associated with the Saxon centuries. Some of these processes, for instance the amalgamation of properties into larger units, can be seen in other European cities and towns. The protests and whingeing of medieval corporations are well documented and generally believed by modern historians. Many towns were decaying, though some, such as ports, survived by attracting new business.

Any evidence of the late medieval decay of towns will therefore be found more easily among its smaller structures and at the edge of the settlements.

The houses of towns at this period give confusing signals. In King's Lynn, although there are signs of an early halt to the expansion of the built-up area of the town, there is no evidence of depopulation of streets and buildings. The town remained at a steady level of prosperity from the 15th to the 17th century.[57] The same can be argued for Saffron Walden, with its notable number of standing buildings. So one model for some towns must be that by 1600, and in some cases by 1500, they had reached their fullest extent for two or three centuries. Other towns, like Winchester and York, may have suffered particularly in the first half of the 15th century when there were widespread difficulties for towns: at York, for instance, very few houses dating from the first half of the 15th century have been found, and none in the area of the ancient suburb of Micklegate south-west of the river.[58] On the other hand, Mercer has argued that the belief that periods of prosperity and of architectural splendour go hand in hand is a myth.[59] He suggests, in the case of Shrewsbury, that buildings erected during a period of depression in the late 15th century were rarely equalled by those of the later more prosperous age.

In general, except perhaps for a class of house which is the subject of a suggestion to be made at the end of this paper, houses were modernised but not rebuilt to new plans. Radical changes to life in urban houses, and to building forms, came later, in the 17th and 18th centuries. A similar pattern can be seen in continental cities such as Lübeck, where many houses were refurbished and sometimes rebuilt in the 16th century; but the changes were in style, particularly in decoration, and not in plan form.

Conclusions

This brief survey has pointed to a number of developments of 1400–1600 in urban housing in England.

Firstly, people below the level of gentry may have been influential in demanding or building new forms of houses. Previous work has highlighted the grander end of the range of urban houses, and we must correct

Fig 10.7 17 Broad Street, Bristol, probably built in 1622 (Bristol City Museum, M2435; cf. Leech, in prep.). Both external and, as far as is known, internal details in such houses proclaimed the urban bourgeois Renaissance style.

And thirdly, there was much rebuilding and adaptation of houses during these centuries, but few if any new forms of buildings; therefore, perhaps, there were no violent changes in culture or thought as far as houses were concerned. The main exception to this, I suggest, is the creation of a new building-form towards the end of the 16th century in some of the larger and even middle-sized towns: the large house in timber, often called for convenience a merchant's house. As suggested by Mercer in the case of Shrewsbury, an urban oligarchy dominated by a few great men, and in alliance with their like in the countryside, achieved homogeneity and a sense of corporate, urban independence from previous forms of higher authority. These changes were reflected in the cessation of the building of large stone houses based on rural models, and in the building instead of large timber properties both for themselves and as speculation.[61] These houses, in Bristol (Fig. 10.7), Canterbury, Chester, Exeter, London and many other larger towns used the new fashionable Renaisssance style in woodwork as a mark of self-assertion; in some houses, such as in two at Nantwich, the woodwork included carved portraits of the house owner and, in one case, his wife.[62] The county town of the 17th century was emerging, and its prominent citizens had houses to suit.

this bias by more study of the middling and poorer structures, right down to the house with one chamber on each floor. In doing this we discover that there were preferred or widespread building forms for ordinary people, such as the house of two rooms on several floors, with the hall on the first floor near the street. A similar new group of medieval users has been identified recently in a rural setting, Kent, where Pearson argues that the new house type with two jettied storeys throughout, and no open hall, which became common in the county after 1500, is to be associated with wealthy yeomen, not gentry; the former had no need of such halls.[60]

Secondly, there are some elements and probably developments we can call peculiarly urban, in both plan form and structural features. The first-floor hall, galleries, exploitation of the roof space and development of stairs are some of them.

Acknowledgements

The Treswell plans used in this paper were redrawn by Alison Hawkins. I am grateful to Roger Leech for the Bristol illustration, and to him and to Brian Ayers, Richard Bond, Jane Grenville, Jeremy Lake, Julian Munby and Paul Stamper for comments and parallels.

Notes

1. Smith 1985, 18. For reviews of late medieval urban housing which are not otherwise cited here see Wadham 1972; Taylor 1974; Priestley & Corfield 1982; Smith 1983; for continental parallels, Büttner & Meissner 1983, Chastel & Guillaume 1983.
2. Pantin 1962–3, and 1963; Schofield 1987; 1995.
3. Stell 1980, 7.

4. Smith 1992, 97.
5. Parker 1971, 40–1, 196; RCHM 1977, 102–3.
6. Schofield 1993; 1995, 41–3.
7. RCHM 1980, xlvi.
8. Parker 1971, 58.
9. RCHM 1977, liv.
10. Rigold 1963, 353; Airs 1983; Barley 1986, 153–4; Pearson 1994, 80–1.
11. Martin & Martin 1986, 64; Smith 1992, 158; Lewis *et al.* 1988, 61.
12. Schofield 1995, 205–6.
13. Munby 1992; RCHM 1980, 68–9; for other examples in Oxford, Pantin 1947.
14. Evans & Carter 1985, 70–1.
15. Bailey 1979, 23.
16. RCHM 1980, 78–9.
17. E.g. Dyer 1981, 213.
18. Parker 1971, Fig. 25; O'Neil 1953, Figs 7–10; Carter in Evans & Carter 1985, 70.
19. Leech 1997.
20. Carlin 1996, 58–9.
21. Schofield 1987, 79–82; 1995, Fig. 49.
22. Schofield 1995, 208, 226.
23. Atkin 1985, 247–8.
24. Parker 1971, 66.
25. RCHM 1972, 82–3.
26. Schofield 1995, 173.
27. RCHM 1977, 67; Hewett 1980, 206–7.
28. RCHM 1977, liv; Schofield 1995, 66.
29. Carlin 1996, 198; information on Rye houses from D. Martin and B. J. Martin.
30. Schofield 1995, 216–7.
31. Pearson 1994, 100.
32. Lake 1983.
33. Pantin 1963, 460–5; Portman 1966, 34.
34. Platt & Coleman-Smith 1975, i, 94–6; Lewis *et al.* 1988, 65–6.
35. Parker 1971, 88.
36. Babelon 1977, 197–8.
37. Rosalys Coope, pers. comm.
38. Brown *et al.* 1987.
39. Martin & Martin 1980.
40. Schofield 1995, 82–3.
41. Barley 1986, 219.
42. Stell 1980, 12–14.
43. Thrupp 1948, 135.
44. Schofield 1995, 81–9; Leech in prep.
45. Munby 1992.
46. Hewett 1980, 196, 203; Lake 1983, 42.
47. Castle 1977, 31.
48. Laithwaite 1973, 67.
49. RCHM 1980, 7–8.
50. RCHM 1972, lxvi; Morriss & Stamper 1995; Lake 1983.
51. Stenning 1985.
52. Schofield 1995, 91.
53. *Ibid.* 87.
54. Johnson 1993; 1996, 8, 176–7.
55. Atkin & Margeson 1985, 15 (a considered summary of work reported in detail in Atkin 1985).
56. Tawney 1926 (repr 1990), 236–7, 243.
57. Parker 1971, 4.
58. RCHM 1972, lxii. This may require revision: work currently in progress by Jane Grenville and Sarah Rees-Jones suggests that the Micklegate suburb contained several mayoral residences of the first half of the 15th century, but they have not survived or been recorded.
59. Mercer 1989, 160.
60. Pearson 1994, 134.
61. Mercer 1989, 166–7.
62. Lake 1983, 106, 110.

Bibliography

Airs, M. 1983, 'Timber-framed Buildings', in Cherry & Pevsner 1983, 104–12

Atkin, M. 1985, 'Excavations on Alms Lane', in Atkin *et al.* 1985, 144–260

Atkin, M., Carter, A. & Evans, D. (eds) 1985, *Excavations in Norwich 1971–78 Part II*, East Anglian Archaeol 26

Atkin, M., & Margeson, S. 1988, *Life on a Medieval Street*, Norwich Survey

Babelon, J.-P. 1977, *Demeures Parisiennes sous Henri IV et Louis XIII*, Paris

Bailey, J. 1979, *Timber-framed buildings: a study of medieval timber buildings in Bedfordshire and adjoining counties*, Dunstable

Barley, M.W. 1986, *Houses and History*

Büttner, H. & Meissner, G. 1983, *Town Houses of Europe*, Leipzig (trans P. and B. Ross)

Carlin, M. 1996, *Medieval Southwark*

Chastel, A. & Guillaume, J. (eds) 1983, *La Maison de Ville à la Renaissance*, Paris

Brown, A.N., Grenville, J. and Turner, R.C. 1987, *Watergate Street: Third Interim Report of The Rows Research Project*, Chester City Council and Chester County Council

Castle, S.A. 1977, *Timber-framed Buildings in Watford*, Chichester

Cherry, B. & Pevsner, N. (eds) 1983, *London 2: South*, Buildings of England Series, Harmondsworth

Foster, I. & Alcock, L. (eds) 1963, *Culture and Environment: Essays in Honour of Sir Cyril Fox*

Dyer, A. 1981, 'Urban Housing: a Documentary Study of four Midlands Towns 1530–1700', *Post-Medieval Archaeology* 15, 207–18

Evans, D. & Carter, A. 1985, 'Excavations on 31–51 Pottergate', in Atkins, Carter & Evans 1985, 9–86

Everitt, A. (ed.) 1973, *Perspectives in English Urban History*, London

Ford, B. (ed.) 1989, *Renaissance and Reformation*, The Cambridge Guide to the Arts in Britain vol 3, Cambridge

Gilchrist, R. & Mytum H. (eds) 1993, *Advances in Monastic Archaeology*, British Archaeol Reports 227

Hewett, C. 1980, *English Historic Carpentry*, Chichester

Johnson, M.H. 1993, *Housing Culture: Traditional Architecture in an English Landscape*, London

Johnson, M.H. 1996, *An Archaeology of Capitalism*, Oxford

Laithwaite, M. 1973, 'The Buildings of Burford: A Cotswold Town in the Fourteenth to Nineteenth Centuries', in Everitt 1973, 60–90

Lake, J. 1983, *The Great Fire of Nantwich*, Nantwich

Leech, R.H. 1997, 'The Prospect from Rugman's Row: the Row House in the late 16th and early 17th Century London', *Archaeological J* 153 [in press]

Leech, R.H. in prep, *A study of the City House and Tenement in Bristol*

Lewis, E., Roberts, E. & Roberts, K. 1988, *Medieval Hall Houses of the Winchester Area*, Winchester City Museum

Martin, D. & Martin, B.J. 1980, 'Timber Staircases', *Historic Buildings in Eastern Sussex* (Rape of Hastings Architectural Survey) vol. 1 no. 6, 137–59

Martin, D. & Martin, B.J. 1986, 'Rye', *Historic Buildings in Eastern Sussex* (Rape of Hastings Architectural Survey) vol. 2, no. 3

Mercer, E. 1989, 'The Town of Shrewsbury', in Ford 1989, 158–67

Morriss, R.K. & Stamper, P.A. 1995, *A Structural Survey and Documentary History of Rowley's House and Mansion, Shrewsbury*, Shropshire Archaeol Service Report 69

Munby, J. 1992, 'Zacharias's: a Medieval Oxford Inn at 26–29 Cornmarket', *Oxoniensia* 57, 245–309

O'Neil, B.H.StJ. 1953, 'Some Seventeenth-century Houses in Great Yarmouth', *Archaeologia* 95, 141–80

Parker, V. 1971, *The Making of King's Lynn*, Chichester

Pantin, W.A. 1947, 'The Development of Domestic Architecture in Oxford', *Antiquaries Jnl* 27, 120–50

Pantin, W.A. 1962–3, 'Medieval English Town-house Plans', *Medieval Archaeology* 6–7, 202–39

Pantin, W.A. 1963, 'Some Medieval English Town Houses: A Study in Adaptation, in Foster & Alcock 1963, 445–78

Pearson, S. 1994, *The Medieval Houses of Kent: An Historical Analysis*, RCHM

Platt, C. & Coleman-Smith, R. 1975, *Excavations in Medieval Southampton, 1953–69*, Leicester

Portman, D. 1966, *Exeter Houses 1400–1700*, Chichester

Priestley, U. & Corfield, P.J. 1982, 'Rooms and room use in Norwich housing 1580–1730', *Post-Medieval Archaeology* 16, 93–124

RCHM: Royal Commission on Historical Monuments (England)

RCHM 1972, City of York: vol. iii, *South-West of the Ouse*

RCHM 1977, *The Town of Stamford*

RCHM 1980, *City of Salisbury*, vol. i

Rigold, S. 1963, 'The Distribution of the Wealden House', in Foster & Alcock 1963, 351–4

Schofield, J. 1987, *The London Surveys of Ralph Treswell*, London Topographical Society Publication 135

Schofield, J. 1993, 'Building in Religious Precincts in London at the Dissolution and Later', in Gilchrist & Mytum 1993, 29–42

Schofield, J. 1995, *Medieval London Houses*, New Haven and London

Simpson, A.T. & Stevenson, S. (eds) 1980, *Town Houses and Structures in Medieval Scotland: A Seminar*, Scottish Burgh Survey, Glasgow

Smith, J.T. 1983, '[The] English town house in the XVth and XVIth centuries', in Chastel & Guillaume 1983, 89–98

Smith, J.T. 1992, *English Houses 1200–1800: the Hertfordshire Evidence*

Smith, P. 1985, 'The Winter Conference 1984: some thoughts on Anglo-Continental contrasts', *Vernacular Architecture* 16, 18–19

Stell, G. 1980, 'Scottish Burgh Houses 1560–1707', in Simpson & Stevenson 1980, 1–31

Stenning, D.F. 1985, 'Timber-framed shops 1300–1600; comparative plans', *Vernacular Architecture* 16, 35–9

Tawney, R.H. 1925, *Religion and the Rise of Capitalism*

Taylor, R. 1974, 'Town houses in Taunton, 1500–1700', *Post-Medieval Archaeology* 8, 63–79

Thrupp, S. 1948 (repr 1977), *The Merchant Class of Medieval London*, University of Michigan

Wadham, M.C. 1972, 'The development of buildings in Witham from 1500 to c.1800', *Post-Medieval Archaeology* 6, 1–41

11   Rethinking Houses, Rethinking Transitions: of vernacular architecture, ordinary people and everyday culture

Matthew H. Johnson

I am writing this opening paragraph at home, with the list of contributors to the Transitions volume and the titles of their papers in front of me. It has taken several hours sitting in front of the computer to get going. The prospect of having a paper on vernacular architecture included in such a collection is daunting. By the time the reader encounters this paper he or she will have read of so many exciting things: the glories of Whitehall, courtier houses, town houses, churches and tombs.

What on earth can vernacular houses, by definition 'ordinary, common, regional and small' and occupied by households below the level of the elite, have to offer after this? Aren't vemacular builders traditional, conservative creatures with a limited, local view of the world? Doesn't change in vernacular architecture just drift along in the wake of much larger and more exciting developments? If Whitehall Palace is 'in the vanguard of change',[1] isn't peasant architecture to be found lurking somewhere in the baggage train? What possible relevance have raised upper crucks, hearth-passage plans, longhouse distribution and tie-beam lap-dovetail joints to the big cultural and social questions of the 15th and 16th centuries?

My trepidation is compounded by the present state of vernacular architectural studies. After the publication of Eric Mercer's *English Vernacular Houses* in 1975, large syntheses that present a model of development in vernacular architecture that can be matched to wider social and cultural developments have been few. There has been a plethora of fine regional studies, most notably in the last few years the Royal Commission's outstanding volumes on medieval houses in Kent. It is telling, however, that even in the 1990s many historians, when speaking of change in rural dwellings, refer only to Hoskins's 1953 article on the Great Rebuilding; very little else has had the scope in its scholarship and boldness in its interpretation necessary to impinge on the wider historical consciousness.[2]

Currently, archaeologists working in this period seem to have made a fine art out of saying more and more about less and less, to the extent that one prominent scholar recently concluded in a review article that any kind of national synthesis is now a 'will o' the wisp'. The prehistorian Richard Bradley has spoken recently of archaeology's 'loss of nerve' as a discipline, its recent reluctance to take on big questions of human development; as one branch of historical archaeology, the study of vemacular buildings has suffered particularly from this loss.[3]

Now this loss of nerve is certainly not due to lack of evidence. We have many thousands of vernacular houses surviving in the English countryside for the 15th and 16th centuries. Much hard work since 1945 has gone into researching basic questions of the distribution, forms, social groups and economic impetus behind the building of these houses. Houses before 1550 built for socially middling groups, that is houses below the manorial or gentry level, survive in their thousands in many areas of the Home Counties, Essex, Suffolk, Kent and Sussex. Elsewhere, some hundreds of structures of a similar social level can be found in other areas of England. Now heavily modified, such houses nevertheless are far better preserved than the bread-and-butter of the medieval settlement archaeologist, excavated dwellings.

One aspect of our loss of nerve has been a tendency to stress the limitations and possible biases in this body of evidence. The work of Chris Currie in modelling attrition rates on houses has spearheaded a rethinking of an automatic link between numbers of houses surviving today and social and cultural forces in the past.[4] The result of all this uncertainty is that the linkage of present patterns to past changes such as the so-called rise of the middling sort or between house building rates and the economic prosperity of a given region is open to doubt.

But these problems can be stressed too much. With the qualifications raised above in mind, we still find that time and again detailed regional studies have linked waves of rebuilding of vernacular houses with the middling sort. The best recent example is the work of the Royal Commission in Kent, headed by Sarah Pearson. In Kent, the middling sort were building substantial houses that survive as dwellings to this day from the later 14th century onwards. 'They are as large and as fine as the best timber framed houses erected fifty or a hundred years later, and they must have been built by ... wealthy peasants or yeoman farmers'. Huge numbers of Kentish houses built before 1500 have now been identified (the Royal Commission found 695 in 60 parishes alone). Numbers of very large houses from the Weald contrast with smaller houses with end jetties in central Kent (Figs 11.1 & 11.2).[5]

Such houses rarely have the necessary documentation to be sure about the social status of their late medieval builders and owners, though Pearson concludes that they are 'true peasant dwellings' above the poorer sort. As happens very often in such studies, we cannot say with absolute certainty that this or that house was built for a person with this or that specific status, but we can view the wave of rebuilding as a whole as eloquent testimony to the rise of an emergent class of households headed by those classified in the later 16th and 17th centuries as 'the middling sort': prosperous husbandmen, yeomen, and the lesser gentry.

My own work in western Suffolk found a steady rate of rebuilding of socially middling houses between 1460 and 1560. This was founded on a combination of arable and dairy farming, favourable conditions of tenure (again), and the benefits of the cloth industry; after 1560 the cloth industry declined in importance although continued agricultural prosperity was linked to continued rebuilding at the socially middling level.[6]

So what does the form of these houses tell us about their inhabitants? I want to summarise here arguments put forward previously,[7] but I shall continue by looking at their broader implications. In particular, I want to argue for a view of vernacular architecture that stresses the context of these houses – relating the study of vernacular building outwards, to the vernacular/polite divide, to social and cultural history, and to the understanding of the transformation of the landscape as a whole.

Though the regional style, decoration and specific form of these houses varies from area to area, almost without exception they share a central open hall. The form of such halls is well known, precisely because its meanings are so familiar from other contexts, in particular larger versions of such arrangements from upper social levels. The hall is divided into upper and lower ends, each with solar and service respectively beyond (Fig. 11.3).

The point I want to stress here is the deliberate ambiguity and multiple meanings of this architectural space. The hall is in one sense open to all, but in another sense a rigidly divided space. It asserts commensality and implies some form of community, most obviously at mealtimes, but does so in the act of enshrining inequality. Note that those features that stress unequal relations between upper and lower ends – bench fixed against the dais end, wider upper bay, window, positioning of opposed doors at the lower end – are precisely those that are fixed. In houses lacking open halls from the later 16th century onwards, marking of status becomes mobile, through movable goods such as chairs, other furniture and decorative items, and mobile both physically and mentally.[8]

Notice also that though the hall is loquacious about formal relations of status and the host/guest relationship, it is remarkably silent about relations

Fig. 11.1 *Waternill House, Beneden, Kent: a late medieval Wealden house.*

Fig. 11.2 *Spoute House, Plaxtol, Kent: a 15th-century end-jetty house of two phases.*

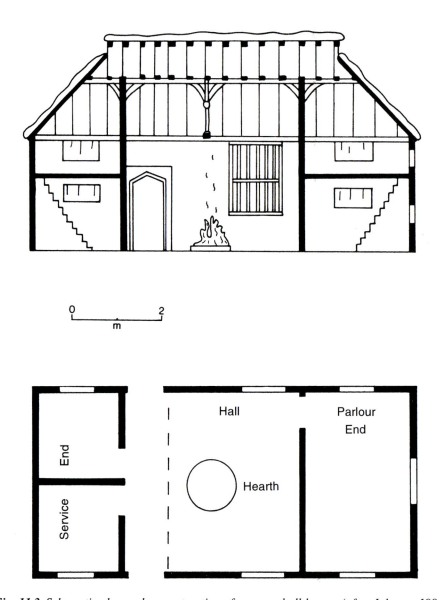

Fig. 11.3 *Schematic plan and reconstruction of an open hall house (after Johnson 1989).*

of gender, between master and wife – in fact, we could suggest that it deliberately fails to acknowledge this aspect of social relations. In some sense, though, the house as a whole can be seen as gendered as feminine, as the woman's sphere of legitimate activities as opposed to the fields and the wider community of 'men', as it was to be seen explicitly by the earlier 17th century.[9]

Is this interpretation fanciful, tendentious? Am I reading 'too much' into domestic space? If I had presented a similar analysis of the symbolism of a piece of polite culture, for example a portrait of Queen Elizabeth or of the arrangement of rooms at Burghley House, there would be very little exceptional or avant-garde in such an analysis. Indeed, such analyses are the very core of the techniques and methods of the New Historicism, a school of thought that has done so much to transform our understanding of Renaissance culture (Veeser 1989). There is less written evidence for the interpretation of vernacular space offered here because the participants were largely illiterate, but also and more fundamentally because the patterns of meaning I discuss here were played out not in terms of a written code, but in terms of everyday activity.

Let me clarify this idea of the everyday, and in particular the relationships between everyday actions, cultural meanings, and the structure of the house. Where husbandmen sat at mealtimes, the way women and men moved around the houses and fields in their community, the ways in which their attitudes, mannerisms, facial expressions expressed (or failed to express) deference; all these actions were full of meaning to observers. Of course, like most 'every-day' activity, this was rarely expressed or overtly commented upon, but it was full of significance nevertheless. In short, we cannot expect human beings in the past to have less complex or meaningful lives simply because they were illiterate or of a lower social order. As M.T. Clanchy has remarked in a rebuttal of traditional historical attitudes, 'where only a minority of a population are literate, those who are illiterate do not necessarily pass their lives in 'mental confinement'. It may be some modern academics, rather than peasants, who risk mental confinement within the 'small circumscribed world' of their field of specialisation.[10]

There are two striking points of uniformity in these halls, between region and between social status. To a great extent building materials, framing techniques and decorative styles vary from area to area, but the fundamental principles underlying the form of the hall remains the same. In parallel, though houses of different social levels vary widely in terms of size and ostentation, the form of the open hall remains strikingly similar. Both these observations strengthen my suggestion that the meanings of the open hall gain resonance through repeated activity – they form a common visual code through which one knows how to behave because it has happened so many times before.

This uniformity between social levels raises a second problem: that such an analysis in fact merely goes over familiar ground. We 'know' from a variety of literary and other documentary sources about many of the meanings that high status open halls had, and I have argued that these meanings pertained to halls in the houses of the middling sort also. It might also be questioned how much we really do 'know' from written sources – a text can always be read in a variety of ways, given a multiplicity of overt and hidden readings. In any case the rarity of written comments like that of Piers Plowman is shown by the way in which writers on the open hall are forced to resort to quoting them over and over again.[11] The point I want to make here, however, is that they largely relate to upper social levels, and it is interesting to find them repeated at a lower level. In short, the hall is also a statement of affiliation to certain social and cultural values that run up and down the social scale. In the rest of this paper, I suggest that the closeness of this affiliation between upper and lower social levels breaks down in the later 16th century, and that the divergence of vernacular and polite building into two much more distinct traditions is one symptom of this breakdown.

Elements of Change

How did vernacular architecture change in the middle to later 16th century? In many areas, particularly southern and eastern England, the open hall was lost, and replaced by a room that was smaller, no longer open to the roof, less central. As a result of this and other changes the house became more private in terms of circulation pattern, more 'comfortable'. In terms of Colin Platt's recent arguments, we are on the way to the 'neat compact boxes' of the later 17th century,[12] though unlike Platt I do not see this transition either as an inevitable process or as primarily the result of foreign influence.

We are obviously dealing here with a much longer-term process than that envisaged by W.G. Hoskins when he spoke of a Great Rebuilding between 1560 and 1640, and much longer-term even than the period 1400 to 1600. Much of the thrust of Chris Dyer's work has been to suggest that 13th- and 14th-century houses were in many respects not dissimilar to their later counterparts.[13] I do not accept these arguments fully, but if we are looking for a

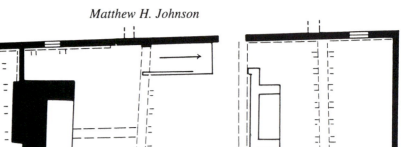

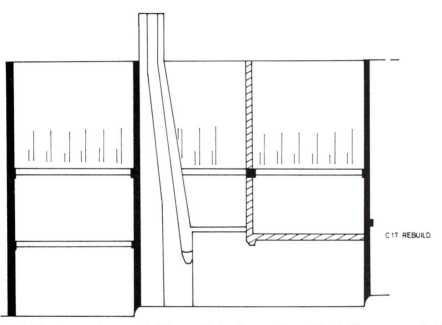

Fig. 11.4 *The closure of an open hall house: Tudor Cottage, Brent Eleigh. Here, an open hall has been enclosed in stages, first with partial ceiling and 'smoke bay', then with a timber chimney-stack, later replaced in brick. In the process the hall has become smaller, visually less impressive, and has lost its centrality to the house as a whole.*

definition of a transition with a capital T in housing standards, its chronology does need to be substantially lengthened. It definition also needs to be more firmly theorised.

The changes of the 16th century are much more than simply those of layout and plan form. They are also to do with a series of other issues. The first of these is the relationship beween vernacular and polite. As we have already seen, we can understand some of the meanings of the vernacular open hall by looking at larger versions of the same structure; status was articulated in terms of repeated architectural terms of reference. Now the period 1400–1600 sees a profound change in this relationship, though this is a change that accelerates and, I think, changes qualitatively in the 17th century. A yeoman farmer would understand the basic arrangement of John of Gaunt's hall range at Kenilworth, for all its scale and splendour. By c.1600, larger and smaller houses are qualitatively different houses; a yeoman farmer would find much that was alien if he were allowed to wander through the corridors of Hardwick Hall. We also see the emergence of supra-vernacular houses between elite and middling levels: I would interpret the changes Nick Cooper has delineated again as active statements about the changing affiliations of gentry.[14] Just as the social lives of the gentry reflected tensions in juggling relationships of patronage and deference above and below them, so the architecture of their houses reflects similar tensions.

We also need to theorise the so-called 'rise of material comfort' seen in the Great Rebuilding. I see this stress as a characteristically middle-class sentiment, and note that the middling sort is a currently fashionable topic in social history. For Jonathan Barry, 'our understanding of early modern English society will be incomplete without a self-conscious consideration of where to place the middling sort and how to assess the significance of those groups occupying the social space between the landed elite, on the one hand, and the poor, on the other'. Barry identifies four themes in the definition of the middling sort. First, the absence of legal and social definitions; second, the complicating factors of life-cycle and gender; third, the interplay of economic, cultural and political criteria; and fourth, the opposing forces of community and class.[15]

I have suggested elsewhere that the rise and fall of the Great Rebuilding thesis mirrors closely the rise and fall of an interpretation of early modern England centred on the rise of the middling classes. Two points are relevant here. First, Hoskins's thesis needs to be much more severely qualified with respect to regional variation. Second, the rebuilding and attendant rise in domestic living standards was almost certainly not exclusive to the middling sort of people. According to Stuart Wrathmell, a large class of semi-permanent structures in northern England have almost entirely disappeared. The clear distinction, therefore, that many have seen between perman-

Fig. 11.5 A late medieval house with 16th-century wing at Alpheton, Suffolk.

ent and impermanent structures is an illusion created by differential survival in the present. His conclusion is that no hard and fast divide can be drawn between the standard of habitation of different social groups.[16]

The first need is to theorise the ethic of improvement that lies behind these houses. Material improvement is not a normal and natural thing common to all societies, particularly in peasant communities; indeed, Barry and Brooks identified it as a characteristically middle-class sentiment. So a rise in quality and permanence of building in any given area reflects several different characteristically middling social attitudes or sentiments.

The first of these sentiments is security. Many writers, as we have seen, have related propensity to housebuilding to security of tenure. Willingness to invest in housebuilding also betrays a commitment not just to a higher valuation of material affluence, but more broadly to the house as a commodity and a greater desire to invest on a long-term basis. As Bob Machin has pointed out, expenditure on housing is one form of long-term investment, and as such it is investment in something that may be bought and sold. The higher the investment, the greater the quality and permanence of the house.

Quality and permanence of housing is also bound up in the relationship of the middling sort to the community at large. With his parlour now heated and its windows glazed, and with more items of comfortable furniture within it, the yeoman's parlour was an ever more attractive temptation away from the outdoor culture of the village as a whole. Where a yeoman may previously have spent his time in the alehouse or playing stoolball on the village green with other elements of the community, his later counterpart may have been more tempted to invite friends of his own 'sort' to his home for more private, cultured entertainment. Such a community was, of course, homosocial; such a shift holds implications for the structuring of gender relations also.

The changing technology of the house – the way it was built and maintained – also reflected this withdrawal from community. Impermanent architecture often requires regular upkeep, what Robert Blair St George has termed 'maintenance relationships'. Let me clarify this with one very small example. A thatched roof needs regular repair by a fellow villager; a tiled roof needs a larger initial outlay, but the owner was henceforth freed from one part of the community of credit that was the early modern village.

The point that emerges out of the case studies above is the need to theorise the development of specifically vernacular architecture as the architecture of the middling sort. The values of material comfort, long-term investment, and privacy are not self-evident; they are, rather, distinctively middle-class (as such, they often appear self-evident to many academics). But at the same time such houses display regional as well as class affiliations. Such houses were well built, but in vernacular style.

These arguments have the capacity to be extended outwards: to look at the ethic of improvement as it affected enclosure and agricultural change, and in particular as it affected literacy. As students of material culture, trying to understand what things meant to their makers and users, possibly the most significant change between 1400 and 1600 that we have to grapple with is the rise and changing nature of literacy. Literacy does more than just condition what evidence we have; as anthropologists, most notably Jack Goody, have pointed out, literacy brings with it a very different way of relating to the physical and cultural environment in the home and the landscape as a whole.[17]

I have argued[18] that all these changes can be grouped under the umbrella term of 'closure'. Closure involves not just different forms of houses and fields but a different way of relating to the landscape as a whole. It involves a move away from the values of the medieval village community towards the more abstracted technologies of class relations. It leaves different artefacts in its wake, ranging from different arrangements of rooms to different kinds of religious belief such as Protestantism and Puritanism.

It is worth repeating that such an argument does not suggest that Puritanism was directly responsible for change in houses or that they can be matched up in any kind of simplistic cause-and-effect way. To repeat, 'enclosure of houses and of fields was not caused by Puritanism: both are manifestations of a deeper social and cultural shift, ripples betraying stronger and more complex economic, social and cultural currents beneath the surface of history.[19]

What I do want to argue for is a fourfold inversion that, I suggest, is central to new ways of looking at vernacular architecture.

First, we should draw attention to cultural and mental elements of a transformation that is usually portrayed in primarily economic terms.

Second, we should locate in the countryside a sentiment that is more usually located in the towns, most famously with Max Weber's 'Protestant Ethic' thesis of links between Protestantism and nascent capitalism in the great Northern European cities.

Third, we should look to the small-scale and the local for the origins of a much larger change.

Fourth, we should look at archaeology for changes that are usually grappled with through the documentary evidence.

One of the things that is striking about socially middling households is the way that their attitudes only emerge in the documentary record in the 17th century, and then only darkly and via the subtlety of historical interpretation. But many of the attitudes generally characterised as those of the middling sort can be located in the 16th century, using the archaeological evidence of architectural, settlement and housing forms, as well as the changing quantities and forms of artefacts.[20] This should not surprise us. Ethnoarchaeologists have often shown that new attitudes, new ways of life, new mentalities are often hammered out in practice before they are given conscious articulation. Patterns of everyday life and the material framing of those patterns, therefore, show definite evidence of emergent individualism and new trends before these emerge in the documentary record. I therefore oppose the widely held view, usually based on documentary evidence alone, that continuity rather than change is the rule in the English countryside before 1600.

Conclusion

In conclusion, I wish to set the evidence of vernacular architecture in the context of the archaeology and cultural history of the period as a whole.

First, I am uncertain about the proposition that public and private is a valid distinction for the period before 1600. My lack of certainty increases the further back one goes. Cultures can only draw a sharp divide between the public and the private if they have a strong sense of the individual in the first place. Such a strong sense did not necessarily exist during the period 1400–1600. Further, if such a sense is part of 'Renaissance culture' and specifically linked to literacy, then there is every reason to question its existence as part of the medieval or pre-Renaissance mentality. Many of the papers in this volume assume a clear public/private distinction throughout this period; I feel that we need to think more carefully and critically before such a divide can be assumed.

Many of the artefacts that are commonly interpeted in terms of 'the private' actually have quite other meanings. The classic recent example is the redefinition of the word closet as it is applied to polite architecture. The closet is generally seen as a 'private' room, but Stewart's masterly reanalysis of the term concludes that 'the male closet is not designed to function as a place of individual withdrawal, but as a secret nonpublic transactive space between two men behind a locked door', most notable for its inaccessibility to women.[21] In other words, what we see as a natural desire for privacy is actually all about the location of power within the house and the exclusion of women from that power. I would argue in parallel that our designation of particular areas of 15th- and 16th-century life as 'private' need similar rethinking.

If public and private needs rethinking, so do perceptions of rural life and vernacular tradition as unchanging and inherently conservative. Such an assumption is present in much of the literature dealing with the period, though it is rarely stated overtly. It is seen lurking behind the assumption that when change does arrive in the countryside it does so through social diffusion, the desire to copy urban or elite patterns of living, rather than through internal dynamics of change.

One of the most all-pervading and pernicious features of 'early modern' cultural history is the way that a model of competitive emulation suitable for the later 18th century, and well explored in that context,[22] has been uncritically pushed back into the 17th, 16th and even 15th centuries. This is often done implicitly and without further theorisation, which compounds the problem. I think that there may be an earlier period and context, specifically urban bourgeois society in the early to mid 16th century, where models of emulation are appropriate;[23] but this, again, needs arguing through with reference to the specific features of that period and social class.

Part of the problem here is that assumptions that I am challenging – those of competitive emulation, of the household as a domestic retreat, of notions of privacy – are assumptions that underpin not just our own way of life but also ways of life for much of the modern period. The temptation is therefore to regard them as normal and natural to the human condition, or at the very least to argue that they were present from the Renaissance onwards. It is, however, ultimately misguided; New Historicist critics would rightly term it 'essentialist'. If we are serious about adopting 1400–1600 as a meaningful unit, then we can and should highlight just how limited in use these concepts are in 'our' period, particularly for social levels below that of the elite.

I started this paper with some trepidation. How could vernacular architecture possibly be of interest within a volume full of the riches of polite culture? What I have tried to show is that the implicit theoretical ideas and classifications that underpin the way we look at the period lead us to regard vernacular architecture as inherently undynamic, less meaningful and more conservative than polite culture. If we agree that such a perception is limited, it follows that the underlying ideas and classifications therefore need to be questioned. They may be valid in some contexts; but this needs arguing through, qualifying, critical analysis, definition of terms. In short, such concepts need to be put within a sophisticated and rigorous theoretical framework. This will be a difficult and intellectually demanding task, but I suspect that there is something wrong with our disciplinary practices if we expect the study of the past to be easy.

If we do this, then some exciting possibilities open up. To look at vernacular buildings as cultural statements in their own right; to examine social and cultural life at the level of the rural, the unspoken, the small scale, the taken-for-granted; these are the real prizes at stake here. It is on this terrain, I suggest, that the future lies not just for the future of the study of vernacular architecture, but the future of late medieval and early modern archaeology as a whole.

Notes

1. Thurley, this volume.
2. Pearson 1994; Hoskins 1953.
3. Quiney 1994, 238; Bradley 1993, 131.
4. Currie 1988.
5. Pearson 1994.
6. Johnson 1993a, 87–8.
7. *Ibid.*
8. Johnson 1996, 171
9. Amussen 1988.
10. Clanchy 1993, 9.
11. For example Thompson 1994.
12. Platt 1994.
13. Dyer 1985.
14. Cooper, this volume.
15. Barry 1994.
16. Johnson 1993a; Wrathmell 1984.
17. Goody 1986.
18. *Ibid.*
19. *Ibid.* 176.
20. Brooks and Barry 1994; Gaimster 1994 and this volume.
21. Stewart 1995.
22. McKendrick *et al.* 1982.
23. For example Gaimster, this volume.

Bibliography

Amussen, S.D. 1988, *An Ordered Society: Gender and Class in Early Modern England*, Oxford

Barry, J. 1994, 'Introduction', in Barry and Brooks (eds) 1994, 1–32

Barry, J. Brooks, C. (eds) 1994, *The Middling Sort of People: Culture, Society and Politics in England, 1550–1800*, Basingstoke

Bradley, R. 1993, 'Archaeology: the loss of nerve', in Yoffee and Sherratt (eds) 1993, 131–3

Clanchy, M.T. 1993, *From Memory to Written Record: England 1066–1307*, 2nd edition, Oxford

Currie, C. 1988, 'Time and chance: modelling the attrition of old houses', *Vernacular Architecture* 19, 1–9

Dyer, C.C. 1986, 'English peasant buildings in the later middle ages (1200–1500)', *Medieval Archaeology* 30, 18–45

Gaimster, D. 1994, 'The archaeology of post-medieval society, c.1450–1750: material culture studies since the war', in Vyner (ed.) 1994, 293–312

Goody, J. 1986, *The Logic of Writing and the Organisation of Society*, Cambridge

Harris, R. 1989, 'The grammar of carpentry', *Vernacular Architecture* 20, 1–8

Hoskins, W.G. 1953, 'The rebuilding of rural England, 1560–1640', *Past and Present* 4, 44–59

Johnson, M.H. 1993a, *Housing Culture: Traditional Architecture in an English Landscape*

Johnson, M.H. 1993b, 'Rethinking the Great Rebuilding', *Oxford Journal of Archaeology* 12:1, 117–24

McKendrick, N., Brewer, J. and Plumb, J.H. 1982, *The Birth of a Consumer Society*

Pearson, S. 1994, *The Medieval Houses of Kent: An Historical Analysis*

Platt, C. 1994, *The Great Rebuildings of Tudor and Stuart England*

Quiney, A. 1994, 'Medieval and post-medieval vernacular architecture', in Vyner (ed.) 1994, 228–43

Stewart, A. 1995, 'The early modern closet discovered', *Representations* 50, 76–100

Thompson, M.H. 1995, *The Medieval Hall: The Basis of Secular Domestic Life, 600–1600 AD*, Aldershot

Veeser, H.A. (ed.) 1989, *The New Historicism*

Vyner, B. (ed.) 1994, *Building on the Past: Papers Celebrating 150 Years of the Royal Archaeological Institute*

Wrathmell, S. 1984, 'The vernacular threshold of Northern peasant houses', *Vernacular Architecture* 15, 29–33

Yoffee, N. and Sherratt, A. (eds) 1993, *Archaeological Theory: Who Sets the Agenda?* Cambridge

12 Defending the Realm: the changing technology of warfare

Jonathan Coad

Although practically any period can be turned into an Age of Transition, the two centuries begining in 1400 were witness to revolutionary changes in the technology of warfare. These changes were to remain largely unchallenged in their scope until the mid 19th-century development of shell-firing guns and steam-driven armoured warships. To use modern defence jargon, this paper is divided into two main parts: a consideration of the new weapons and a look at the weapons' platforms, or, in plain English, the fortifications and warships and their attendant support services.

Compared to earlier centuries, contemporary documentation is relatively plentiful, notably for royal fortress building. Advances in knowledge over the last thirty years have been the result of historians and archaeologists working either independently of each other, or, more fruitfully, together. Gaps in knowledge have been highlit and research sometimes directed accordingly. As John Guilmartin noted in a paper in 1988, up to 1977 students of naval ordnance had available for study only a single early modern gundeck, that of the *Vasa*, 'plus a handful of scattered artifacts, notably the Anholt guns and the Deane brothers' 19th-century recoveries from the *Mary Rose*'.[1] Less than twenty years on, the picture is very different, but with so much going on a paper now can only be the briefest and most cursory of surveys.

Historians are fond of debating the causal changes in history, but in the context of this paper the single most important development in warfare between 1400 and 1600 was the introduction of gunpowder and effective heavy ordnance. This was no sudden event, but was spread out over a considerable period. This is not the occasion to rehearse in detail the history of early ordnance – that is a well-worn but not always clear path – but it is worth identifying a few key dates and developments. In this context, it is worth noting that archaeology *per se* so far has had little to contribute to knowledge of the *early* evolution of ordnance. Most new information has come from documentary research and the study of surviving structures and weapons. Guns and gun-powder first made their appearance in the 13th century, but in embryonic form the new weapons posed more a psychological than a real threat. Early handguns were cumbersome, none too accurate, were slow to load and had limited range. The long-bow and the cross-bow for long remained more effective weapons.

Heavy ordnance was similarly cumbersome, but it was growing in power. At the battle of Crecy in 1346 guns were apparently used by the English, but at best they may have frightened the French cavalry, while at the subsequent siege of Calais the weapons were too weak to have any effect on the town walls. A century later, when the Sultan Mahomet II laid siege to Constantinople in 1453, careful preparations by his gunfounders enabled him to bring with him 56 small guns and 13 heavy cannon. The largest of these, a monster siege weapon constructed by a Hungarian engineer, Urban, needed a team of 60 oxen.[2] It could be said that the fall of Constantinople owed more to what might be termed traditional siegecraft –

overwhelming numbers of attackers and a lack of relief supplies for the besieged – than to the impact of the new weapons.

But even before the siege of Constantinople, events with a greater impact on ordnance development were taking place in France. Here, Charles VII was actively encouraging innovation and reform of the royal artillery. Under the Bureau brothers, cast iron shot was substituted for stone, enabling mass-production of shot and the reduction in calibre and hence in the overall size of the guns themselves. Lighter guns made for more mobile artillery as was shown in 1449 during the reconquest of Normandy when the French gunners apparently were involved to a greater or lesser degree in 60 sieges in one year.[3] The effect of carefully-sited massed artillery in a defensive field-work was amply demonstrated in 1453 when Jean Bureau's serpentines and culverines cut down the Anglo-Gascon troops under John Talbot, Earl of Shrewsbury, ending for ever English hopes of regaining Gascony.[4]

Iron gunshot and lighter guns increasingly made 15th-century artillery a force to be reckoned with, but one of the key developments which perhaps has not had the attention it deserves, is the so-far undated invention of the trunnion. Incorporated into the barrel, trunnions made it easy to elevate or depress the gun in contrast to bed-mounted artillery. As important, they enabled guns to travel on their firing carriages and, by substituting horse power for oxen, to keep up with field armies.

It may be said that field artillery came of age in 1494 when Charles VIII invaded Italy with 18,000 troops and a train of at least 40 really mobile siege guns of a power which medieval fortifications in their path were unable to withstand.[5]

In England, guns had long been found in a number of royal castles, but their limited power meant that they remained an 'add-on' weapon within the general armoury of weapons then available and it was not until the 16th century that they started to determine the actual design of the fortifications themselves. Until then, it was considered sufficent to add gun-ports to what were essentially medieval defences, as happened at Canterbury (Kent), Quarr Abbey (Isle of Wight), Southampton city walls or Bodiam Castle (Sussex), to name only a few examples.[6]

Parallel to improvements in the guns themselves were developments in the composition and hence the explosive force of gunpowder. Early gunpowder was of varying quality and power. Its very fineness made it slow burning; its effect heavily dependent on the skill of the gunner ramming it into the barrel. It suffered from the further serious disadvantage that its constituent parts tended to separate when it was subject to vibration, as inevitably happened when it was transported. This latter failing was partly overcome in the 15th century by the invention of corned powder where the powder cake was broken down to grain-sized granules instead of fine powder. This development is first mentioned in 1429, but the new corned powder produced so much power that it could not be used in the wrought-iron guns of the time and its use had to be restricted to hand-guns until bronze and iron gun-founding technology could catch up.[7] This in itself took some time – it is notable that a 1548 inventory of ordnance in the King's fleet shows that the majority of iron ordnance was still 'made up' using wrought iron strips, and it was apparently as late as c.1580 before the Royal Navy was issued with corned powder.[8]

While cast bronze guns had superior strength to the 'made up' wrought iron guns, the cost of their metal militated against mass-production. It was this which probably lay behind the famous instruction in December 1496 to Henry Fyner, goldsmith of Southwark, to establish a works on the Ashdown Forest to produce iron for the king's artillery on its Scottish campaign. There is little doubt that the site at Newbridge (Sussex) saw the first blast furnace to be constructed in England. Early production included iron shot and the metal parts of gun carriages.[9] Accounts for 1509 show that by then the works at Newbridge were producing, perhaps only experimentally, two-part cast cannon. Little is known of these, or of their production process, and the site remains tantalising uninvestigated. By 1520, the Weald had only two furnaces, both, as Crossley has suggested, heavily dependent on military orders from the Crown. The French and Scottish campaigns of Henry VIII, together with the great fortification programme along the south coast, gave a further tremendous impetus, so that by 1548 it was claimed that there were 53 furnaces and iron mills in Sussex alone.[10] Among these was Buxted Furnace (Sussex) where what was probably the first one-piece iron cannon was cast in 1543. This in a sense marked the real begining of the Weald as the centre for iron ordnance and production expanded rapidly from that date.

In the last thirty years, the Weald iron industry has been the subject of considerable documentary research, backed by field investigation, excavation and publication, largely under the auspices of the Wealden Iron Research Group. Six blast furnaces have been dug and at four of these – Batsford (Sussex), Pippingford (Sussex), Cowden (Kent) and Maynards Gate (Sussex) – gun-casting pits have been found. These excavations have supplemented the documentary research giving us a much more detailed knowledge of the technical processes which lay behind the rise of English cast-iron ordnance production and of the ability of Wealden gun-founders to supply the Crown and, sometimes less legally, other markets.[11]

In a brief yet broad survey such as this, generalisations, despite their risks, have to be used as a kind of literary short-cut. From faltering beginings in the 14th century, ordnance by the begining of the 16th century was poised to attain a dominant role in warfare. Once production was mastered, cast-iron guns were durable and comparatively cheap compared to bronze weapons. In all essentials, the cast iron gun as developed by the mid 16th century had all the features which its successors were to retain until the development of rifled ordnance in the 1850s.

The rest of this paper will examine how research over the last thirty years has increased our understanding of the impact of artillery. Guns made their impact in three distinct spheres: with field armies, on the design of land fortifications and at sea. This paper will consider the effect on the last two.

Sophisticated field artillery sounded the death knell of most medieval fortifications. Reducing the height of defences, to make them less of a target, was one obvious effect of the new weapons. Employing massive earth banks, either on their own or to revet masonry walls, to give extra strength and to absorb the impact of gunfire, was another. But in actual plan the new artillery fortifications differed radically from their medieval predecessors. As J.R. Hale wrote over

thirty years ago, 'The most significant of all architectural forms evolved during the Renaissance was the angle bastion. ...its speedy adoption by state after state during the 16th century dramatically altered the appearance of cities throughout Europe – and further afield. ... The international style *par excellence* of the Renaissance was that of military architecture, and its module was the angle bastion'.[12]

For any student of British fortifications, one of the most significant advances in the last thirty years has to be that magisterial series *The History of the King's Works*. Here, for the first time, we have laid before us the documentary building history and architectural development of the royal fortresses from the time of the Conquest to the 17th century. With a few comparatively insignificant exceptions, artillery defences within England were built only by the Crown; hence their early evolution within this country can be traced within this series. It is difficult to overestimate the value to scholarship of the research here, and we should be thankful that it was instigated and firmly established at a time when government was prepared to underwrite such apparent overtly academic projects. The *King's Works* has not been alone in the field. O'Neil (1960), Quentin Hughes (1991), Andrew Saunders (1989) and J.R. Hale (1983), amongst others, have all made important contributions based on documentary accounts and the study of standing structures. Archaeological research, however, has been more limited.

There is no need to repeat in detail already-published information. Volume IV of the *King's Works* fully describes Henry VIII's remarkable fortification programme of the late 1530s and goes far to explain why it was that England initially opted for a design of artillery fort in which the angle bastion played no part.[13] The squat, rounded outlines of Henry VIII's coastal fortresses are familiar to us, their uniform design reflecting the centralised, royal control of the building works; their apparent cohesive appearance strongly suggesting that they sprang fully-developed from the royal drawing office.

That this was not so was first suggested by an analysis of their building accounts. While most were broadly comparable, Camber Castle, guarding the Camber or sheltered anchorage in eastern Sussex

Fig. 12.1 *Camber Castle from the north-west showing the central gun-tower, the lower part of which dates from 1512–14. Between this and the semi-circular bastions completed in 1543 can be seen the work of 1539–40. A 1986 air photo (Copyright, English Heritage).*

formed by the merging of the rivers Brede and Rother before they entered the English Channel, at nearly £16,000 cost around three times that of similar forts. In 1965 selective excavations were begun; these were continued intermittently until 1982 and the final excavation report is currently being written-up by the Oxford Archaeological Unit.

A changing coastline had made Camber obsolete by the early 17th century and it had been abandoned in 1638. As a result, it never underwent the modernisations which occurred at the majority of the other Henrician fortresses. Aside from the quantity of artefacts illustrating garrison life, the excavations

revealed a series of remarkable changes of plan compressed into the construction period 1539–1543. The core of Camber is the circular gun-tower built to protect the mouth of the Camber between 1512–1514. Around this was added in 1539 an octagonal curtain with a rectangular gatehouse on the western side. On the compass points beyond this octagonal curtain were sited four low-level, semi-circular, bastions backed by rectangular vaulted chambers which appear to have served as flankers. Behind these were stirrup-shaped towers linked to the octagonal curtain and to a ring-passage around the base of the original central tower. Both the bastions

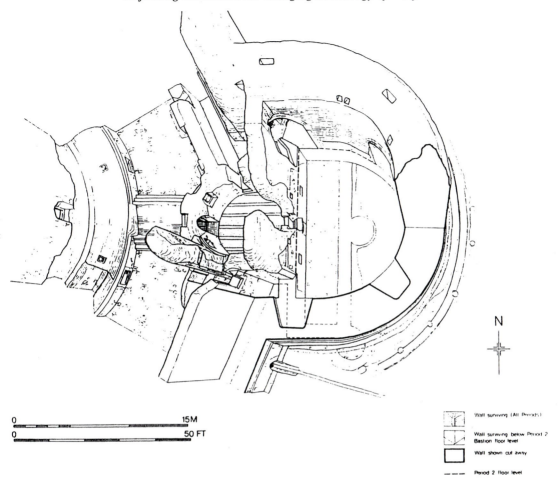

0   15 M
0   50 FT

Wall surviving (All Periods)

Wall surviving below Period 2
Bastion floor level

Wall shown cut away

– – – Period 2 floor level

Fig. 12.2 *Camber Castle. A cut-away axonometric view of the east bastion showing the 1543 bastion above the remains of the 1539–40 rectangular vaulted chamber which backed the first low-level bastion. From a preliminary reconstruction drawing by Richard Warmington.*

and the curtain were apparently protected by a shingle glacis. This work of 1539–40 was hardly completed before the bastions were reduced to foundation level and replaced by four massive semicircular bastions, linked by their own eight-sided curtain built onto the front of the existing wall. Coeval with this work went alterations to the central keep. This final remodelling brought Camber into design line with the other major Henrician castles such as Hurst (Hants) or Walmer (Kent).[14]

So effective was the final remodelling that it was only careful archaeological work which revealed clues to the design of the first set of bastions. This

1539/40 work can be firmly attributed to Stephen von Haschenperg. We must await the final excavation report for the full story, but already suffcent has been discovered for the authors of the *King's Works* to be able to write of this 1539 phase 'For all its faults... it represents an early attempt to build in England an artillery fortress of ultimately Italian inspiration: the flankers and surrounding earthworks are suffcent evidence of this, but it seems clear that Haschenperg had never seen, or at least appreciated, the vital significance of the angle bastion'.[15]

Stephen von Haschenperg retreated to the Continent in 1543; the final phase at Camber, described in the *King's Works* as looking 'only backwards' was firmly under the control of Henry's own works organisation.[16] By chance, Sandgate Castle (Kent), Haschenperg's only other surviving fortification in England, was the subject of extensive excavations between 1976 and 1979. As the *King's Works* noted, Camber and Sandgate 'share certain features which are not found elsewhere'[17] but Sandgate was so thoroughly reformed between 1805 and 1808 that the excavations were not able to add significantly to knowledge about the Haschenperg period.[18]

Poor old Henry and his 'in-house' design team have had rather a bad press from architectural historians. 'How typical of the English to adopt an obsolete form of fortification' has been something of an implicit theme of much writing on the subject. Yet at the time when Henry was faced with the need to protect likely landing places and harbours, it was by no means certain that the angle bastion system of defence was the best for the task. What was needed was the ability to prevent a hostile fleet from landing an army. This meant an ability to concentrate fire-power. Before the 19th-century introduction of explosive shells, it was almost unheard of for a warship to emerge the victor in a ship-shore duel. If we leap ahead two and a half centuries to 1794, a round gun tower with three guns on a headland on Corsica repulsed two Royal Navy ships with a total armament of 106 guns and formed the model for the subsequent Martello chain of gun towers on England's south-east coast.

The Mortella Point tower mounted only three guns; Sandgate, by contrast had over 60 gun ports or embrasures at four different levels for heavy guns.[19] Here, and in all the other Henrician castles, the designers were alive to the need for efficent smoke dispersal and for the need for adequately splayed embrasures. Round gun towers, such as at the mouths of Portsmouth Harbour and at Camber, already existed; Henry's engineers extended and improved the basic design, dramatically increasing the firepower.

The one possible threat to Henry's castles would have come from a siege train, but not until 1588 did the Spanish Armada become the first major invasion fleet to carry a proper siege train of heavy artillery. Even had this been landed, quick success was by no means assured. In 1648, the Kentish castles at

Sandown, Deal and Walmer sided with the Kentish rebels. Walmer surrendered after three weeks, probably because of lack of provisions, as the parliamentary forces besieging the castles lacked any heavy artillery. When this artillery arrived and was deployed against Deal Castle, it took a further three weeks before the garrison finally capitulated.[20]

While there is no disputing Hale's thesis of the dominance of the angle bastion throughout Europe and almost wherever Europeans settled and colonised, other simpler forms of artillery fort also did stoic if less-fashionable service. I would further venture to suggest that Henry VIII's engineers well knew what they were doing with their fortresses with their tiers of guns. They were compact and, compared to bastionned forts with their elaborate traces and outworks, were economical of manpower. Multiplicity of angle bastions essentially aided the defensive rather than the offensive capabilities of a fort, while Henry's tubby bastions, although offering a bigger target to a besieger, provided more space to manoeuvre guns.

Where of course the angle bastion system of defence was most effective was in protecting large areas such as towns, and it is significant that it was at Portsmouth in the mid 1540s that proposals were first drawn up for such a defence system.[21] With the notable later exception of Berwick-upon-Tweed and a number of civil-war works, nearly all of England's investment in major angle bastion defences was concentrated on protecting the new dockyard towns, for reasons discussed in the last part of this paper.

In the context of the conference theme, archaeological excavation as such so far has made little contribution to the study of the defences of this period, as a glance at Kenyon's invaluable bibliographies will show.[22] Aside from Camber and Sandgate, virtually the only other archaeological excavations have been those undertaken by Victor Smith on two of the Thames blockhouses.[23] More recently, opportunity has been siezed at Plymouth to learn more about the important Elizabethan fort lying under the Royal Citadel; trial trenches have shown that substantial remains of this irregular bastionned fort built in the early 1590s remain under the later works of 1665–72.[24]

Part of the explanation for the lack of much

archaeological work lies in the continuing military occupation and military redevelopment of many such sites. However, by the end of this period, early settlers overseas were starting to provide themselves with defences and it is here that future archaeological research may yield dividends. This has already started to happen. Bermuda was formally colonised on 11 July 1612. Between then and 1622, eleven forts were built to protect the settlers. One of these was destroyed in 1619, but more than half of the rest remain in various stages of preservation, largely undisturbed by later military occupation or alterations. This is an important group for they were built at a time when labour and money were scarce, so they are very much functional, utilitarian structures, designed principally for shore to ship combat.

Excavations were begun at the King's Castle, one of this surviving group, by Edward Harris in 1993. King's Castle guards one side of the approach passage to Castle Harbour at the eastern end of Bermuda. In essence it consists of irregular rectangular upper and lower gun platforms, with a captain's house and cookhouse tacked onto the rear. The Captain's House was added in 1621; as such, it can lay claim to being the oldest standing English domestic building in the New World.[25] In actual design, however, the fort itself is little more than a simple masonry artillery platform, designed to bring the maximum number of guns to bear in one direction. As such, it is similar to dozens of other later fortifications scattered particularly among the islands of the Caribbean, while its basic design, while much simpler in execution, harks back to the gun platform of Henry VIII's Yarmouth Castle (Isle of Wight) of 1546.[26]

As already mentioned, English artillery forts initially were concentrated to deter possible seaborne invasion, then to guard the expanding dockyard towns and associated defence installations. It is now time to consider briefly the third thread of this paper – sea-borne warfare, for it was surely here that the most revolutionary changes took place during the period under discussion, and it is here that archaeology has made some of the most spectacular recent strides.

In the English context, medieval sea warfare was essentially local – in the 13th and 14th centuries, nearly every naval engagement was fought in the vicinity of the coast of south-east England and off Flanders.[27] Ships were manoeuvred alongside each other so that archers and soldiers could board and victories were determined by the number of enemy killed and ships captured rather than sunk. In such warfare, merchant ships were interchangeable with royal ships and indeed formed the majority of vessels in such engagements. The Cinque Ports were still expected to provide up to 57 ships for a maximum of fifteen days when necessary, but by the 15th century these ports were already in decline from silting.[28] Although successive monarchs did have their own royal ships, these were seen very much as their personal property. Henry V built up a fleet of 36 vessels, but on his death the bulk of these were sold.[29] The accounts for the early years of Henry IV's reign mention six royal ships; shore facilities for these were minimal.[30] A royal navy was not seen as an essential priority by most medieval monarchs.

But the 15th century saw the decline of the oared fighting ship – the ballinger, a cross between the Viking long ships and the Mediterranean galley – and its replacement by the 'full-rigged ship- one of the greatest technological inventions of medieval Europe'.[31] These vessels, with their vastly better sailing qualities, rugged construction and large cargo capacity, were key to the voyages of discovery, colonisation and trade. Their robust qualities, and not least their comparatively high sides, also made them ideal fighting platforms. Technical details for these ships are scarce – there are no English shipwrights' manuals for the 15th century and we are largely dependent on the illustrations on seals and occasional church carvings, none of which are necessarily accurate. These ships, however, were the carracks of Henry V's royal fleet. Most were captured vessels, but Henry also commissioned four larger ones which became known as the 'King's Great Ships'. The largest of these, and the only one with three masts, was the *Gracedieu*, 'probably the largest clinker-built ship ever made'.[32] By an extraordinary quirk of fate, she was laid-up in the River Hamble in Hampshire and in 1439 was burnt to the waterline after being struck by lightning. Her remains still lie there, a designated site under the Protection of Wrecks Act. These have been investigated in a limited way on a number of occasions, most recently in the 1980s by the National Maritime Museum. The chief interest here is how the shipwrights scaled-up a clinker hull to resist hogging and how they retained the hull shape while building it shell-first. The unique triple-thickness planking has been subject of debate, most recently by Gillian Hutchinson.[33]

Although Henry V's fleet carried heavy ordnance, its use was extremely limited. Only fifteen ships carried a total of 42 guns. We have no idea how these were disposed around the particular vessels, but the evidence does point to the majority being breech-loading guns – an important factor in the necessarily confined spaces on board a ship.[34] Such small numbers though indicate that these weapons were little more than tokens – the nautical equivalent of adding a couple of gunports to a medieval gatehouse. Heavy guns could only become primary weapons once they were of sufficent power to become effective chase guns and were carried in sufficent numbers to form a broadside. This meant the introduction of hinged gunports as the weight of such weapons meant that they had to be carried on a ship's lower decks. Hinged gunports appear to have been a technical impossibility in a clinker-hulled vessel, thus forcing the change to the framed carvel hull. With the introduction of the gunport we start to see the begining of specialisation in ship construction, the divergence between the purely trading vessel and the man-of-war, the growth of European navies and their associated specialist shore facilities.

Hinged gunports are known from the 1470s, but it is only after 1500 that northern European powers begin to construct 'great ships' – warships displacing about 1,500 tons and well armed with heavy weapons. When Henry VIII died in 1547, he left a fleet of 53 vessels with a total displacement of some 15,000 tons. Between them, these carried almost 200 heavy guns of nine-pounder calibre and above. Fifteen of these vessels were 'great ships' which carried the bulk of the heavy armament. Forty years later, in 1595, Elizabeth's fleet totalled 38 fighting ships but their combined displacement now approached 20,000 tons. Even more significantly, the total of heavy guns exceeded 600. Twenty-three of Elizabeth's capital ships were the new 'race built' ships introduced by the Queen's shipwrights from 1573

onwards – the lead vessel, like a similar revolutionary warship just over three centuries later, named the *Dreadnought*. These were distinguished from their predecessors by their sleeker lines, longer gun decks and the reduction in size of the fore and aft castles. The significance of these 'race built' ships lay in their superior sailing qualities, better manoeuvrability, larger 'weapons' platforms' and in the reduction of the towering castles, the latter the last vestiges of the medieval approach to sea warfare with its emphasis on close combat with hand weapons.[35] Their armament benefitted from the reforms and standardisation of naval ordnance introduced in 1569 by Sir William Wynter, Master of the Ordnance of the Navy.[36]

The capabilities of such ships widened men's horizons. Henry VIII's navy was still seen essentially as a coastal defence force, like its medieval predecessors, but by the 1580s, with experience gained from expeditions such as that of Sir John Hawkins, it was considered perfectly possible to wage war on Spain in the New World. By the 1590s we see the start of the emergence of a 'blue water' strategy which was to dominate England's strategic thinking for the next 300 years and the permanent establishment of the navy as 'an autonomous and fully formulated military arm'.[37]

Behind all this of course lay other no less significant developments. Financially, in 1557 the Royal Navy was put on a more secure footing compared to its medieval predecessors when the Privy Council secured it a peacetime budget, or ordinary, of £14,000 per annum. This was overdue recognition that warships were expensive and with their shore facilities needed to be maintained on a permanent footing.[38]

We know little of the detail of early shore establishments. Henry IV kept the royal ships either alongside the Tower of London or downriver at Greenwich where there were apparently some form of repair facilities. Later, Southampton was favoured and in 1420 nearly £200 was spent constructing a forge and storehouse, but these were sold along with many of the royal ships on Henry V's death two years later.[39] It is only with the construction of what was probably the world's first dry-dock at Portsmouth, Hampshire, in 1495 that the Crown begins to establish permanent bases.[40] Portsmouth was to be followed by yards in Kent at Erith, Deptford, Woolwich and Chatham.

Only at Woolwich have there been archaeological excavations on any scale when in 1972 and 1973 Terry Courtney excavated part of the central area. Much of what he excavated dated from the 17th century or later, but a sloping 'trough' was tentatively identified as a 16th-century building slip.[41] Woolwich, unfortunately, is less well documented than other royal dockyards; that and the limited nature of the excavation means that the identification is not absolutely assured.

Apart from the dockyards, a burgeoning navy also needed other supplies. Weapons came from the Tower; victuals were more of a problem. Contractors played a key role, but around 1560 Elizabeth established the first naval victualling yard in the former Cistercian Abbey of St Mary Graces hard by

the Tower of London. This was extensively excavated in the mid 1980s and revealed evidence for 16th-century baking, barrel manufacture and storage.[42] Given the fairly comprehensive documentation associated with the Victualling Board, the final report on these excavations with luck will shed important light on this aspect of naval operations.

If the archaeology of naval shore establishments has perhaps not made the headlines, the same cannot be said of the archaeology of early warships. The excavation and subsequent recovery of the *Mary Rose* in 1982 has given us for close study one of Henry VIII's 'Great Ships' fully provisioned for war. Quite properly, efforts have been concentrated on the conservation of the wreck and its artefacts; the definitive report on the ship has yet to be completed, leaving us for the present with Margaret Rule's popular account and with tantalising glimpses of shipboard life.[43] This, however, makes abundantly

Fig. 12.3 The Mary Rose *in the 18th-century No 3 Dock at Portsmouth Dockyard. This view from the stern clearly shows her construction and the gun ports (Copyright,* Mary Rose *Trust).*

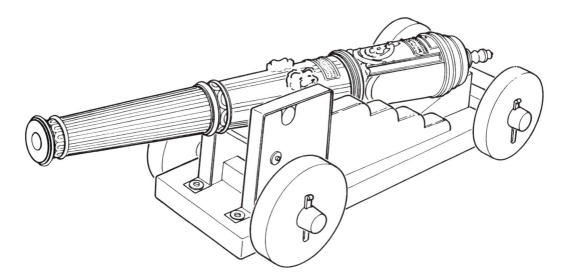

Fig. 12.4 *A reconstruction drawing of one of the truck carriages with its ordnance recovered from the* Mary
Rose. *Henry VIII's warships may have been among the earliest to use truck carriages which would have been
much easier to manoeuvre in the confined spaces on board than guns on trail carriages*
(Copyright, Mary Rose *Trust).*

clear the riches which await detailed study and
dissemination. Here we have a multi-decked, three
masted, carvel-built warship with a heavy armament
arranged on a main gun-deck and firing through gunports – all the developments which set these ships
apart from their medieval predecessors.

The armament itself reflect the new thinking as
well as the old concept of close-combat using hand
weapons. Two thousand arrows and nearly 150
longbows attest to a reliance on traditional methods
of waging war at sea.[44] Wrought-iron and bronze
guns and cast-iron hailshot pieces are some of the
most spectacular artefacts recovered. But no less
interesting are the gun carriages. The ship mounted
its armament both on two-wheeled trail carriages,
more appropriate to field artillery than to the confines
of a gundeck, and on four wheel truck carriages,
ancestors of those still to be seen on the decks of
HMS *Victory*.[45] These truck carriages must have been
demonstrably superior in action, yet nearly fifty years
later, as Colin Martin has shown, the Spanish Armada
was still heavily reliant on the cumbersome trail-
mounted artillery.[46]

Yet it is as well to remind ourselves that the

archaeological discoveries of the *Mary Rose* and of
Armada ships can only show us the material remains
and, with luck, hint at their use. The mix of armament
on the *Mary Rose*, for example, is indicative of a
transitional period: the old weapons for waging sea
battles were still held to be important, perhaps more
so than the heavy ordnance. Here, the final excavation report and documentary sources should shed
further light. One example concerns the use of heavy
ordnance. It is apparent that English ships in the 16th
century were manning their guns with fewer than a
quarter of the men considered necessary in the 18th
century. As Nicholas Rodger has pointed out, the
inescapable conclusion has to be that teams of men
moved from gun to gun. Hence the English tactic of
bearing down on the enemy, discharging the guns
and then withdrawing out of range for a lengthy
period of reloading. This too probably accounts for
the practice of each gun firing on a fixed bearing, to
be aimed by the ship. Hence too, the calculation that
during the week's chase of the Armada up the
Channel in 1588, 'expenditure... cannot on average
have much exceeded five rounds per gun per day'.[47]
Even post-Armada, tactics could still be rooted in

Fig. 12.5 *The Elizabethan demi-culverin on display at Pevensey Castle in Sussex. This gun is known to have been here since the 16th century and is a good example of a locally-produced weapon from a Wealden ironworks. The carriage is a replica, constructed in 1965; although relatively manoeuvrable on land, the difficulties of working such a carriage in the confined space on board ship are readily apparent (Photo: J.G. Coad).*

Fig. 12.6 *Bermuda. An aerial view of the King's Castle. Prominent in the centre are the Captain's House and the Cookhouse (Photo: Bermuda Maritime Museum).*

the earlier world of closing an enemy and fighting by hand. In the great fight of the *Revenge* under Sir Richard Grenville, he was for long pictured holding the Spanish fleet off with the ship's great guns. More recent research has suggested that in fact these were fired only briefly before the *Revenge* closed the nearest ship for fifteen hours of hand-to-hand fighting.[48] Was this just conservatism, or was it an inability to reload the guns swiftly for whatever reason ?

One definition of an Age of Transition is of a period of fairly rapid evolution which leads to a different order. In the context of the technology of warfare, there is little doubt of the momentous alterations during this period and of what one might call the period of comparative stablity which followed. Had the Elizabethan Sir William Monson been spirited forward 200 years to HMS *Victory*, there would have been little that would have been unfamiliar to him. The warship would have been larger and would have had sailing qualities and endurance superior to the ships which he knew, but not radically so. The same could not be said if he had been spirited back to a ship of the time of Edward II. A similar time-travel by Elizabeth I's military engineer Sir Richard Lee would have produced the same sense of recognition had he been spirited from his work at Berwick-upon-Tweed to look over the shoulder of Lieutenant-Colonel John Evelegh, busy rebuilding Fort Cumberland in the 1790s. The bastions, ramparts and general layout would have been instantly recognisable. Similarly, both Monson and Lee would have felt at home with the heavy armament on board *Victory* and at Fort Cumberland. These are perhaps obvious examples, but they are aposite in the context of the evolution of the period covered by this conference.

Acknowledgements

I am very grateful to the *Mary Rose* Trust for providing illustrations of the warship and its artifacts. I am particularly grateful to Richard Warmington for providing the cut-away illustration of Camber Castle in advance of the final publication of the main excavation report. Edward Harris, as always, has been very generous in his provision of information on his work in Bermuda, which it is a pleasure to acknowledge. In the space allowed, attempting such a wide-ranging survey as this inevitably means that I have had to be very selective within my chosen topics; I hope that those whose work I have failed to mention will not be offended.

Notes

1. Guilmartin 1988, 35.
2. Reid 1976, 55.
3. Hughes 1991, 62.
4. Wade Labarge 1980, 225.
5. Parker 1988, 9.
6. Kenyon 1981, 208–9.
7. Marshall 1915, 18; Hogg 1974, 26.
8. Kenyon 1983, 63–65; Trollope 1994, 25.
9. Cleere & Crossley 1985, 112.
10. *Ibid.* 117.
11. Bedwin 1980, 105.
12. Hale 1983, 1.
13. Colvin 1982, 380–1.
14. *Ibid.* 419–447.
15. *Ibid.* 443.
16. *Ibid.* 443.
17. *Ibid.* 378.
18. Harris 1980, 81.
19. Colvin 1982, 585; Sutcliffe 1972, 20.
20. Coad & Hughes 1992, 11.
21. Colvin 1982, 504–507.
22. Kenyon 1978, 1983 and 1990.
23. Smith 1979 and 1982.
24. Pye 1996, 125–6.
25. Barka & Harris 1993, 31.
26. Colvin 1982, 565–9; Rigold 1978, 4.
27. Friel 1995, 139.
28. Hattendorf 1993, 34; Rose 1982, 28.
29. Rose 1982, 5.
30. *Ibid.* 31.
31. Parker 1996, 270; Rose 1982, 46.
32. Rose 1982, 45.
33. Hutchinson 1995, 23.
34. Friel 1995, 15.
35. Parker 1996, 270–1.
36. Trollope 1994, 24.
37. Hattendorf *et al.* 1993, 60.
38. *Ibid.* 70–1.
39. Rose 1982, 31, 39, 53.
40. Coad 1989, 90.
41. Courtney 1974, 10–11.

42. *Post-Medieval Archaeology* 21, 1987, 268.
43. Watt 1983, 3.
44. Rule 1982, 17.
45. *Ibid.* 156, 159–6.
46. Martin 1988, 70–1.
47. Rodger 1996, 313.
48. *Ibid.* 308.

Bibliography

Barka, N. & Harris, E. 1994, 'The 1993 Archaeological Investigations at Castle Island, Bermuda, *Bermuda Journal of Archaeology and Maritime History* 6, 1–80

Bedwin, O. 1980, 'The Excavation of a late-sixteenth century Blast Furnace at Batsford, Herstmonceaux, East Sussex 1978', *Post-Medieval Archaeology*, 14, 89–112

Blackmore, H.L. 1976, *The Armouries of the Tower of London. I. Ordnance*

Bound, M. (ed.) 1995, *The Archaeology of Ships of War*, Oswestry

Cleere, H. & Crossley D. 1985, *The Iron Industry of the Weald*, Leicester

Coad, J.G. 1989, *The Royal Dockyards 1690–1850.* Aldershot

Coad, J.G. & Hughes, G.E. 1992, *Walmer Castle and Gardens*

Colvin, H.M. (ed.) 1982, *The History of the King's Works, Volume IV 1485–1660 [part II]*

Courtney, T.W. 1974, 'Excavations at the Royal Dockyard, Woolwich 1972–1973, Part One: The Building Slips' *Post-Medieval Archaeology* 8, 1–28

Friel, I. 1995, *The Good Ship. Ships, Shipbuilding and Technology in England 1200–1520*

Guilmartin, J.F. Jr. 1988, 'Early modern naval ordnance and European penetration of the Caribbean: the operational dimension', *The International Journal of Nautical Archaeology and Underwater Exploration* 17.1, 38–53

Hale, J.R. 1983, *Renaissance War Studies*

Harris, E. 1980, 'Archaeological Investigations at Sandgate Castle, Kent, 1976–9', *Post-Medieval Archaeology* 14, 53–88

Hattendorf, J.B., Knight, R.J.B., Pearsall, A.W.H., Rodger, N.A.M. & Till, G. 1993, *British Naval Documents 1204–1960*, Aldershot

Hogg, I.V. 1974, *A History of Artillery*

Hughes, Q. 1991, *Military Architecture*, Liphook

Hunter Blair, C.H. & Honeyman, H.L. 1954, *Warkworth Castle*

Hutchinson, G. 1995, 'Henry V's warship *Grace Dieu*', in Bound (ed.) 1995, 22–25

Kenyon, J. 1978, 1983, 1990, *Castle, town defences, and artillery fortifications: a bibliography*

Kenyon, J. 1981, 'Early Artillery Fortifications in England and Wales', *Archaeological Journal* 138, 205–40

Kenyon, J. 1983, 'Ordnance and the King's Fleet' *International Journal of Nautical Archaeology*, 12.1, 63–65

Marshall, A. 1915, *Explosives. Their Manufacture, Properties, Tests and History*

Martin, C.J.M. 1988, 'A 16th century siege train: the battery ordnance of the 1588 Spanish Armada', *The International Journal of Nautical Archaeology and Underwater Exploration* 17.1, 57–73

O'Neil, B.H.St J. 1960, *Castles and Cannon: A Study of Early Artillery Fortifications in England*, Oxford

Parker, G. 1988, *The Military Revolution*, Cambridge

Parker, G. 1996 'The Dreadnought Revolution of Tudor England' *The Mariner's Mirror* 82.3, 269–300

Pye, A.R. 1995, 'Elizabethan Fort, Royal Citadel' in 'Post Medieval Britain in 1994', *Post-Medieval Archaeology*, 29, 125–6

Reid, W. 1976, *The Lore of Arms*, Gothenburg

Rigold, S.E.R. 1978, *Yarmouth Castle*

Rodger, N.A.M. 1996, 'The Development of Broadside Gunnery 1450–1650', *The Mariner's Mirror* 82.3, 301–324

Rose, S. 1982, *The Navy of the Lancastrian Kings*

Rule, M. 1982, *The Mary Rose*

Runciman, S. 1969, *The Fall of Constantinople 1453*, Cambridge

Saunders, A.D. 1989, *Fortress Britain*, Liphook

Smith, V.T.C. 1979, 'New Tavern Fort Restored', *Coast and Country*, 8.4, 47–52.

Smith, V.T.C. 1982, 'Excavations on the site of Milton Blockhouse, Gravesend', *Fort* 10, 127–9.

Sutcliffe, S. 1972, *Martello Towers*, Newton Abbot

Trollope, C. 1994, 'The Guns of the Queen's Ships during the Armada Campaign, 1588', *Journal of the Ordnance Society*, 6, 22–38

Wade Labarge, M. 1980, *Gascony. England's First Colony 1204–1253*

Watt, J, 1983, 'Surgeons of the *Mary Rose*: The Practice of Surgery in Tudor England', *Mariner's Mirror*, 69.1, 3–20

13   English Households in Transition c.1450–1550: the ceramic evidence

David Gaimster and Beverley Nenk

Introduction

A truly comprehensive survey of material change and innovation in the households of late medieval to early modern England would draw on a range of archaeological, architectural and curated evidence, including furniture, wallpainting, wall hangings, window glass, floor tiles and other domestic fittings along with treen, ceramics, glass and metal utensils. However, due to the nature of the archaeological record and bias in the curatorial tradition, this survey would be patchy at best, and inadequate for systematic comparison between social units. Yet one medium stands out as it is represented archaeologically at all levels of English society during the period in question. By virtue of its ubiquity in the ground and its relatively short lifespan, ceramics have proved to be one of the most sensitive indicators of social and economic behaviour. The widespread distribution of ceramics offers the opportunity for comparative analysis on an inter-site basis, the results of which provide both a quantitative and qualitative index of change across individual communities.[1] The growth of rescue archaeology over the past 30 years, particularly in towns, has generated a material corpus which can now begin to be examined with some precision in order to identify both general trends in domestic consumption along with individual episodes of innovation, emulation, adoption and adaption.

This paper aims to review the contribution of archaeological ceramics to the question of transition in the late medieval and early modern English household – in units ranging from the royal palace and aristocratic residence to the monastery and urban tenement.[2] The period c.1450–1550 witnessed a dramatic increase in the number and variety of bodies, forms and products deriving from regional and long-distance sources on the English domestic pottery market.[3] Traditionally these changes in the ceramic profile of the late medieval to early modern period have represented the division between the respective disciplines of medieval and post-medieval archaeology in this country.[4]

Refinement in technology and ornamental repertoire, the multiplication of form linked to functional specialisation and an enhancement of status characterise the transformation of domestic ceramics of north-west Europe during the late medieval to early modern period. This role-change can be linked to a series of broad economic and cultural trends. These include closer commercial and cultural links across international boundaries,[5] the increasing purchasing power of the urban mercantile and artisan classes,[6] refinements in dining habits and a greater emphasis on individual (as opposed to communal) utensils,[7] changes in the food supply and dietary habit (see Chapter 14) and changes in housing arrangements which, with the formal separation of working and living spaces, meant greater personal comfort and privacy.[8] Thus, as on the Continent of Europe, the expanding role for ceramics in English homes cannot be explained by permissive factors alone, such as advances in manufacturing techniques or modes of production. Rather, a full understanding of the transformation of the English ceramic market after c.1450 must also be sought in the changing social pressures and motivations of the period.[9]

This review of the English 'post-medieval ceramic revolution'[10] comprises a series of case-studies – ranging from imported finewares and native imitations to ceramic fittings such as tile-stoves and floor tiles – which made such a profound impact on the native ceramic market. In each case it is hoped to examine the nature and timing of individual innovations, along with their technological and social effect.[11]

Cross-Channel trade: an ethnic dimension?

The expansion in cross-Channel trade during the 15th century is a well-charted phenomenon in European economic history,[12] but little attention has been paid thus far to the cultural impact of commercial contact which meant dramatic changes and innovations in the English household. The impact can be measured by the arrival of new commodities along with the establishmment of communities of immigrant merchants and artisans in the ports and manufacturing towns of south-east England. The 'Strangers' imported not only domestic products which were familiar to them, but also new lifestyles in which these products were used. One effect was the emergence of an urban middle class of merchants and artisans which became increasingly cosmopolitan – indeed Continental or 'Hanseatic' – in its taste, purchasing habits, religious beliefs and lifestyle.[13] It is no accident that excavations in towns with significant alien populations, including Norwich and Colchester which were not sea ports, have produced some of the most substantial assemblages of imported ceramics and other Continental-style goods.[14]

Urban centres, such as the East Anglian cloth-manufacturing towns of Norwich and Colchester, and the City of London and its suburb of Southwark, supported substantial communities of 'Dutch' and German traders and craftsmen between the 15th and mid 16th centuries. Exchequer records of taxes levied on aliens reveal that most Dutchmen came from the towns of Utrecht, Haarlem and Middelburg, that Bruges supplied the majority of Flemings, and that the Cologne/Aachen region was the principal source of German immigrants.[15] At the beginning of

the 1441 tax year around 1,500 alien names were reported in the City of London.[16] Between 1440 and 1540 the Southwark parish of St Olaves supported around 350 *Doche* immigrants alone.[17] The most prominent of the northern aliens were merchants of the Hanseatic League who by the final decades of the 15th century had established a trading position even more priveleged than denizen traders. During the 1490s as many as 80 Hanseatic merchants were quartered in the League's permanent trading post and residence of the Steelyard which was centrally placed on the City waterfront.[18] In contrast the generally more wealthy Italians accounted for only 20 City householders and the same number of non-householders in 1441. For 1464 there are 57 names.[19] Despite periodic tensions these communities assimilated into English life over the course of the next hundred years, so much so that the first churches for Protestant Strangers were founded in 1550.[20] By 1541 it is estimated that there were over 2,500 Strangers living in the City of London alone, with Dutchmen, Germans, Flemings and Walloons forming the principal ethnic groups.[21] However, scaled calibration of the figures indicate that between five and six thousand aliens were resident in the City by the end of Henry VIII's reign, which equates to between five and eight per cent of the total metropolitan population.[22] In Norwich the Stranger community numbered some 6,000 out of a total population of 16,000 at the beginning of the 16th century.[23]

However impressive, demographic statistics mask something of the transitory character of England's foreign community during the 15th and 16th centuries. Merchants came and went across the Channel in the course of business and not all craftsmen settled permanently; many returned to their homelands for short periods to visit their families or to buy materials for their trades.[24] The constant interchange would have maintained the immediacy of Continental culture and ideology in England. Indeed, much of the dissemination of Protestant ideas in London during the early 16th century can be attributed to the alien community.[25] The archaeological evidence, and particularly the ceramic record, suggests that Stranger influence on the English consumer was equally profound.

The English pottery market in the late Middle Ages

The highly decorated pottery of the 13th and early 14th centuries, with its repertoire of applied, slipped, modelled, stamped and polychrome ornament, gave way during the mid 14th century to a less varied and much plainer range of kitchenware comprising large pitchers or jugs, cisterns, cooking pots, cauldrons, drinking jugs, and large bowls and dishes. Decorative techniques were confined to simple incised lines, occasional painted slip, and the sparse use of lead glaze. The emphasis was on producing functional vessels, rather than elaborately decorated objects for display. Pottery is an elastic commodity, and at this time treen and other organic materials such as leather probably formed a more economic alternative to ceramic tableware.[26] These trends are reflected in the range of vessels produced by the potters of the Surrey Whiteware industries from the mid 14th century.[27] The Cheam potters supplied London with fine, undecorated jugs and drinking vessels, notably biconical jugs, while Coarse Border Ware, produced at kilns on the Surrey-Hampshire border, accounted for larger cooking and storage forms, such as jars, cisterns and cooking pots.[28] On consumer sites of the period, such as Kennington Palace, London, the pottery dating to the mid 14th to mid 15th century phase is limited in variation to these standard plain jugs and cooking pots.[29] The gradual contraction of the native ceramic industries with their concentration on a narrow range of standardised utilitarian products tends to reflect the general economic and demographic decline of 14th- to mid 15th-century England.[30] Where high-quality tablewares exist in the excavated record, they are represented in the main by Continental imports such as Rhenish stonewares, French earthenwares and Iberian lustrewares.[31] However, the social distribution of imported ceramics at this stage was still narrow and numbers remained relatively low.

The next hundred years show a substantial rise in the quantities and variety of imported ceramics throughout southern Britain. The transformation in demand reflects the improving purchasing power and changing social motivations of an increasingly broad spectrum of society. The impact of Continental goods and customs was to have a profound effect on native industries.

Imported finewares

Stoneware

From the mid 14th century stonewares from the Rhineland formed a regular and increasingly significant component of Continental ceramic products traded across the Channel to English ports. Their technical superiority over rival wares was ensured by their robust and impervious body, a lustrous ash and salt glaze, a stain-resistant and odour-free surface, and a varied typology which suited the multifarious demands of drinking, decanting and the transporting of beverages along with storage and sanitary needs. Such was the success of the product that Rhenish stoneware remained the largest single category of ceramics to be traded to Britain until the mid 18th century. Mass-production on an industrial scale for both home and international markets resulted in a relatively low cost to the consumer and an ability to reach a broad spectrum of the population.[32]

The increase in the size, frequency and nominal value of shipments of stoneware to England over the mid 15th to mid 16th centuries can be seen in the customs accounts and port book of major English ports such as London, Southampton and Exeter.[33] London customs accounts for the period 1380–1480 show a steady rise in the numbers of ceramic imports of north-west European origin which averaged between 127 and 1,159 vessels per month over this period.[34] By the early 16th century, one single customs account of imports by aliens into London between April and June 1509 lists consignments of 3,000, 2,000, 1,500 and 800 *cruses* (a common contemporary reference to stoneware vessels) and three dozen 'covered' (mounted) *cruses,* the practice of applying pewter lids being exclusive to the Netherlands at this time.[35] Outside London, annual Exchequer accounts for Exeter in 1509–10 record 1,700 stonewares being landed that year.[36] During the reign of Elizabeth I (1558–1603) it is estimated that around 3,500 vessels were landed in Exeter every year with the numbers rising to 4–5,000 in some years.[37]

The documentary record corresponds closely to the excavated evidence for the period which indicates a rise in the frequency of ceramic imports across the social scale. Numbers of Rhenish stoneware (primarily from Siegburg and Langerwehe) rose steadily in the City of London from c.1350 and with increasing typological diversity from c.1400.[38] The most dramatic increase in the frequency of stoneware imports to England can be dated to the final quarter of the 15th century. At Southampton around 20 per cent of all imported ceramics (by weight) found in late 15th-century contexts came from the Rhineland.[39] The increase coincided with the conversion at Raeren to mass-production for international export. Raeren stonewares dominate imported pottery assemblages of the early 16th century in London and across the south-east, both on sites of upper and middle-class status. For instance, this centre supplied all the stoneware found in pits sealed by the construction of Whitehall Palace in 1532, and almost a third of vessels, and almost all mugs, cups and decanting vessels found in the Norwich Pottergate fire horizon groups of 1507.[40] London sites such as the Tower of London Postern Gate are dominated by Rhenish stonewares where they account for over 12 per cent (estimated vessel equivalents) of all ceramics found and over 50 per cent of all Continental imports in the early to mid 16th century phases.[41] Sites such as Norwich Pottergate and Toppings and Sun Wharves, adjacent to London Bridge, Southwark, which both produced large assemblages of Raeren stoneware for the table together with Dutch-style redware for the kitchen, suggest that a good proportion of the trade in these wares may have been ethnically motivated.[42] The widespread social distribution of stoneware in early 16th-century England is emphasised by the Raeren vessels excavated at the village of Wharram Percy in North Yorkshire and the poorer quarters of Exeter.[43]

A multiplication in the range of vessels designed for table use characterises production in the Rhineland from the end of the 14th century and dominates it after c.1450. Refinements in dining habits over the course of the 15th century, particularly among the town-based mercantile and artisan classes, are probably responsible for an increasing variety of stoneware cups, mugs, beakers and drinking jugs – some suitable only for wine drinking, others for beer[44] – along with jugs of various sizes designed for decanting liquids into individual drinking vessels. Stoneware captured a niche in the popular tableware market of north-west Europe, enabling the socially aspirant mercantile and artisan classes to imitate aristocratic rituals in a less expensive medium, substituting precious and base-metalware and imported coloured drinking glasses with a range of fine-bodied ceramics which imitated their role.[45]

Netherlandish panel-paintings of the late 15th to early 16th century authentically illustrate the use of individual stoneware mugs and bowls alongside glass and base-metals in urban homes of the period.[46] Such scenes would not have been out of place in London, Norwich or Southampton. The depiction of stoneware in early 16th-century representations of *The Marriage of Cana* emphasises how the utilitarian superiority of this ceramic body enabled it to penetrate into the households of the patrician classes[47] (see cover illus). Such a scenario might explain the relatively high numbers of Raeren pitchers excavated from early 16th-century contexts at the Tower of London Postern Gate and Broad Arrow Tower sites, the Tower being a royal residence.[48] Netherlandish and North German panel-painting of the period also includes a number of Annunciation scenes which depict Rhenish stonewares in an explicitly devotional or sacral role. Rather like contemporary tin-glazed earthenwares (see below) they are often depicted as vases holding the sacred flowers of the Virgin and symbolic of her purity.[49]

The introduction of applied surface ornament based on contemporary printed sources at the beginning of the 16th century marked a further shift in the social value of Rhenish stoneware in north-west European dining culture. The new development, initiated in Cologne by c.1500–10 and followed in Siegburg and Raeren by 1550, gave stoneware a radically new dimension: the relief decoration enabled it to compete in terms of looks as well as function at the dining table with the more ornate metal and glassware and the polychrome-painted tin-glazed ceramics of Italy, Spain and the Low Coun-

Fig. 13.1 Salt-glazed stoneware mug applied with trailing acorn and oak-leaves, the neck with portrait medallions. Made at Cologne, c.1525–50. Excavated in London (Courtesy of the Museum of London MoL A25211).

tries (see below). The innovation transformed Rhenish stoneware from an essentially utilitarian commodity into a fashion item (Fig. 13.1).[50] By the end of the first quarter of the 16th century highly decorated imported stoneware had reached the dining tables of monasteries, the aristocracy and of the court.[51] Excavations at the Tudor courtier house of Acton Court, Avon, produced an entire group of Cologne-type stoneware containing mugs and jugs with applied botanical relief, the single largest group of stoneware represented among the debris associated with the royal visitation of August 1535. Rhenish stoneware accounted for between around 23 and 45 per cent of all imported pottery dating to the period c.1500–1535/50.[52] At the same time demand for decorated stoneware rapidly migrated to urban communities. Cologne mugs with characteristic botanical relief have been found in contexts of c.1500–30 at the merchant's house identified on the site of Guy's Hospital, Southwark.[53]

Tin-glazed earthenwares

The last decade of the 15th century saw a significant rise in the numbers and range of Continental painted tin-glazed earthenwares imported alongside the Rhenish stonewares through English ports. Spanish lustrewares, Italian polychrome-painted maiolicas and their Netherlandish imitations form the three principal categories of these 'luxury' wares.[54] Characteristic north Italian and South Netherlandish products, such as the 'flower-' or 'altar-vase', have been found on over a hundred sites in Britain alone, ranging in status from royal and episcopal residences, country manor-houses, to merchant houses in London, Southampton, Norwich and elsewhere. These products are depicted in contemporary Flemish panel paintings of the period c.1490–1510, particularly in still lifes and Annunciation scenes by Hans Memling and his contemporaries.[55] The designs on the vases (most frequently the The Holy Monogram), combined with the religious character of the paintings, in which they invariably hold the Flowers of the Virgin, suggest that these wares were designed specifically for display or even devotional purposes. In comparison to even relief-decorated stoneware, the production of Italian and Netherlandish maiolica was a much longer and more expensive process requiring a biscuit firing prior to painting and glazing (in the case of Spanish lustreware, an additional third firing was required to bond the silver or copper lustre). Tin-glazed earthenware was ideally suited to the role as a status possession as the repertoire of painted decoration could be rapidly adapted to new styles without the need for technical change or additional investment in production.[56] In this new medium, therefore, the response to fashion was immediate.

The social premium attached to imported tin-glazed earthenwares of the early 16th century can be observed in microcosm among the waste assemblages, including those associated with the royal visit of 1535, at the gentry house of Acton Court, Avon. Here 'Italian' wares accounted for between 1 and 19 per cent of imported ceramics by sherd count, South Netherlandish wares between around 2 and 11 per cent, and various Iberian lustrewares made up between 2 and 38 per cent of the Continental totals found in the layers dating to c.1500–1535/50.[57] Further evidence of the status accorded to imported

Fig. 13.2 *Maiolica vases painted with the royal arms of England, c.1500.*
Left: excavated from the moat of the Tower of London in 1938; right: a comparable example from the City
of London, now in the Victoria and Albert Museum. Chemical analysis of the earthenware body by the BM
Department of Scientific Research indicates the vessels were made in northern Italy for export abroad
(Photograph courtesy of the Trustees of the British Museum).

Italian and South Netherlandish maiolicas can be observed in the pits sealed by the construction of Whitehall Palace in 1532; at the Old Manor, Askett, Buckinghamshire; and at the Tower of London which has produced a pair of vases painted with the royal arms of England (Fig. 13.2).[58] As with relief-decorated stoneware, the demand for polychrome maiolica and lustreware spread early on to mercantile and artisanal consumers, and a number of urban excavations have produced assemblages of around 1500. The cosmopolitan nature of the Guy's Hospital site, Southwark, and the Southampton Simnel Street tenement provide an opportunity to examine the social emulation process in microcosm.[59]

Native ceramic industries

It is no coincidence that there was a radical diversification and refinement in the output of the English lead-glazed earthenware industries during the course of the 16th century. In the redware industries based along the Thames Valley in London and Surrey, and in Essex, there was a proliferation of new forms, many in a greater range of sizes than previously: from large pitchers, cauldrons, pipkins, frying pans and dripping dishes, to chafing dishes, condiment dishes, dishes, bowls, basins, goblets, beakers, cups, culinary stamps, water-sprinklers, distilling aparatus, bird-pots, and fuming pots (Fig. 13.3).[60] Influenced by developments on the Continent and by contemporary imports, slip and incised ornament was re-introduced in order to improve the retail potential of even the most utilitarian of redware products. The widespread social distribution of slipped and incised redware pottery, and new emphasis on tableware and specialised forms for the kitchen, are characteristic of this period.[61] Chemical analysis has confirmed that highly decorated specialised products such as basins with modelled anthropomorphic lug-handles, which parallel prototypes of early 16th-century date

found in the Low Countries and northern France, were made by the London-area redware industry.[62] Probably used in conjunction with ceramic ewers and lavabos, the basins were designed to meet a specific functional and social role at a significantly lower cost to the consumer than contemporary metal vessels. However, their distinctive plastic ornament represented a more exclusive product than the more common and rudimentary wooden counterparts of the same form.

The transformation of the English pottery market with its new emphasis on the manufacture of fine-bodied, untempered drinking wares in the Contiental style can be most clearly observed in the development of two regional lead-glazed earthenware industries: one operating on the Surrey-Hampshire border producing green- and yellow-glazed whitewares (so-called 'Tudor Green'), the other in Yorkshire and the north Midlands producing redwares with dark iron-rich glazes and applied white clay decoration (so-called 'Cistercian Ware'). From the end of the 15th century much of the repertoire of Tudor Green whiteware made in the Surrey-Hampshire border district was based directly on imported wares, particularly Rhenish stonewares (Fig. 13.4).[63]

Fig. 13.3 *Slip-decorated London redware vessels, c.1500–1600.*
Left to right: fuming pot with pierced decoration (BM MLA 1899,5–8,15); anthropomorphic basin handle (BM MLA 1856,7–1,1573); goblet (BM MLA 1915,12–8,197); fuming pot or chafing dish with pierced decoration (BM MLA 1856,7–1,1582)(Courtesy of the Trustees of the British Museum).

Within the London area there was a wide distribution of these imitations on royal and aristocratic sites, such as Whitehall Palace and Baynards Castle in the City[64] and Arundel House on the Strand, in west London,[65] and in mercantile and artisanal areas as illustrated by the vessels recovered from the late 15th- to early 16th-century levels at Guy's Hospital, Southwark.[66] The largest group comes from excavations at the Inns of Court, London, where accounts survive for bulk orders of 'white cups' from Farnham in 1482–3.[67] Although outnumbered by Continental imports and locally-produced wares, the discovery of Tudor Green drinking vessels in Southampton on the south coast and at Sandal Castle in West Yorkshire reflects the emergence of a national distribution network for native ceramics during the final decades of the 15th century.[68] This development is paralleled in the north of England and Wales by the distribution of Cistercian ware at castles, towns and in the pre-Dissolution phases of monastic houses.[69] The growth of both industries during the late 15th to early 16th centuries illustrates the extent to which the English pottery market had been transformed by the influx of imported finewares.

Fig. 13.4 *Lead-glazed whiteware drinking cup made on the Surrey-Hampshire border (left) in imitation of imported Siegburg stoneware (right). BM MLA B.211 (found in the City of London); and BM MLA 1855,7–25,4 (Courtesy of the Trustees of the British Museum).*

Further research is required to establish the extent to which immigrant potters were directly responsible for this innovation in the native industries.[70] Whatever the case, there is clear archaeological evidence for an increase in demand for high-quality (thin-walled, untempered and chromatic) tablewares which could satisfy the changing social aspirations of the time.[71]

Ceramic stoves

A dramatic introduction into the domestic interior of late 15th- to 16th-century England was the smokeless ceramic tile-stove. Besides a radical innovation in domestic heating technology and a solution to the desire to physically separate cooking and living spaces, ceramic stoves also injected a new visual dimension into the contemporary interior. The lead-glazed, often polychrome-painted surfaces, plastic relief and ornamental forms of the tiles echo the increasing emphasis on material comfort, colour and ornament in the domestic furnishings and fittings of 15th-century transalpine Europe.[72] This innovation belongs to the fashion for 'Continental'-style furnishings in late medieval England, others being wainscot panelling, cupboards, stools, chests and painted wall hangings.[73]

Archaeological evidence has demonstrated that the fashion for Continental-style ceramic stoves spread across the Channel during the late 15th- to early 16th-century period.[74] According to the chemical analysis of excavated finds, most stove-tiles of the period were imported, the Rhineland being the most common source followed by northern Germany and the Low Countries.[75] Finds of late Gothic and early Renaissance-style stove-tiles from Fountains Abbey in North Yorkshire and the Abbey of St Mary Graces, London (Fig. 13.6), are representative of the social *locus* of the majority of tiles imported into England prior to the Dissolution.[76] Armorial niche-tiles found at the Broad Arrow Tower, Tower of London,[77] and on the site of York Place, Westminster, the London residence of the Archbishops of York and Cardinal Wolsey's principal home after 1529 (Fig. 13.5),[78] provide the few contemporary secular contexts for this luxury practice in the London area. Imported tiles of similar

late Gothic style and construction excavated on the site of the Earls of Shrewsbury's hunting lodge at Sheffield Manor, South Yorkshire, suggest that the fashion spread rapidly among court circles during this period.[79]

There appears to have been little delay in the adoption of these smokeless ceramic heating systems by urban middle class consumers. The late Gothic niche-tile fragments from the Norwich Pottergate

Fig. 13.5 *Gothic-style heraldic stove-tile in green-glazed red earthenware. Made in north Germany for export. Composite reconstruction based on fragments excavated beneath the Banqueting House, Whitehall, London (formerly the site of York Place, the London residence of Cardinal Wolsey, Archbishop of York) and from various sites in the City of London and Southwark (for precise findspots and Museum of London registration numbers see note 81). Probably c.1475–1525 (Drawing by J.C. Thorn, BM).*

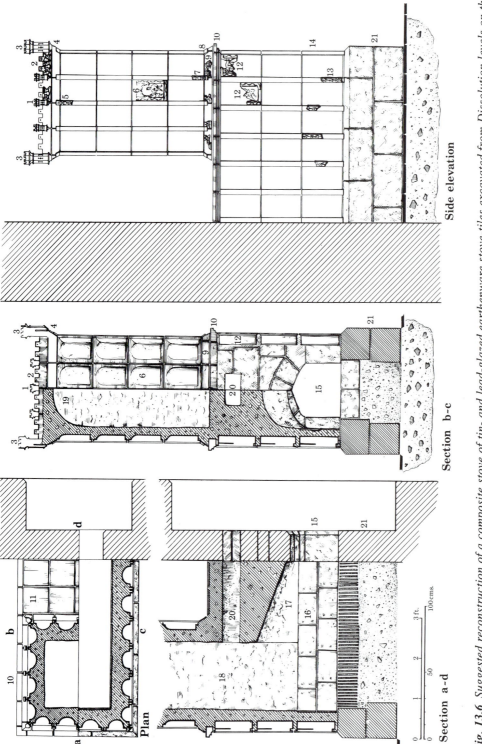

Fig. 13.6 *Suggested reconstruction of a composite stove of tin- and lead-glazed earthenware stove-tiles excavated from Dissolution levels on the site of the Abbey of St Mary Graces, London. Probably made in the South Netherlands and northern Germany c.1475–1525. Reproduced from Gaimster et al. 1990, fig. 7 (Drawing by J.C. Thorn, BM).*

fire deposit of 1507 represent the earliest archaeologically reliable evidence for the use of such stoves in a modest artisan's town house of the period.[80] Fragments of armorial niche-tiles of a similar mould-type to that found on the site of York Place, Westminster (see above), have been recovered on a number of sites in the City of London and Southwark, suggesting that cost of ceramic stoves was within the grasp of some of the wealthier members of London's mercantile community by c.1500.[81] Further finds of imported late Gothic-style stove-tiles have also come to light in Cardiff and Oxford.[82] This trend in southern Britain is comparable with that in the Low Countries and the Lower Rhineland, where ornate late 15th-century niche-tiles have been found on residential tenements in Amsterdam, s'Hertogenbosch, Deventer and Duisburg.[83] Contemporary woodcut engravings record the presence of tiled-stoves in the German urban interior from the 1480s onwards.[84]

A growing corpus of finds from gentry residences across southern Britain offers further evidence for the spread of imported ceramic stoves over the course of the 16th century. Findspots include castles and former monastic sites which had been converted into country houses by the newly-emergent landed middle classes.[85] One of the largest groups found in the country to date is the assemblage recovered from the North Bastion and courtyard of the Henrician coastal fort of Camber Castle, Sussex. Although part of the late 16th-century demolition debris, these figure-, portrait-, frieze- and crest-tiles correspond on a chrono-stylistic basis to the period immediately following the early 1540s refurbishment of the Castle.[86] The tiles emphasise the high degree of material comfort enjoyed by (some) members of the garrison of an early modern artillery fortress.

The post-Dissolution period also saw more stoves in urban households, including those of merchants and the professional classes. The London distribution of imported Renaissance-style panel-tiles with figurative designs can be linked to a number of wealthy residential households and districts on the edge of the City such as Fleet Street, Duke's Place, Aldgate, and the site of Norfolk House, Lambeth, where the structural foundations of the stove survived *in situ*.[87] The figurative separator-tile from Gun Wharf,

Wapping, comes from an entirely mercantile milieu.[88]

Contemporary documentary sources also help to reveal the impact of Continental stove technology on English society during this period. William Harrison, writing in his *Description of England* published in 1587, was impressed enough to comment,

> As for stoves, we have not hitherto used them greatly, yet do they now begin to be made in diverse houses of the gentry and wealthy citizens, who build them not to work and feed in as in Germany and elsewhere, but now and then to sweat in, as occasion and need require it.[89]

The success of the ceramic stove trade stimulated the potters of the earthenware industry sited on the Surrey-Hampshire border to enter into competition and produce their own tiles for the English market. Surviving products of this industry are mainly of rectangular panel form, the exterior surface moulded in relief with versions of the arms and monograms of Tudor and Stuart monarchs, ranging from Henry VII (1485–1509) and Henry VIII to Edward VI, Elizabeth I and James I (d.1625). The same moulds were also used to produce additional household products such as cisterns and candle-sconces.[90] This distinctive group of armorial tiles has been the subject of detailed study, including chemical analysis to confirm the source of manufacture.[91] The archaeological distribution of 16th-century armorial stove-tiles, which is concentrated within London and its immediate hinterland, ranges from royal palaces, manors and aristocratic residences to town houses which significantly form the majority of findspots in the City of London, Southwark, Colchester and Southampton.[92]

The largest single group of native armorial stove-tiles, along with other previously unrecorded stove elements such as pediments, cornices and corner-tiles, was excavated in 1939 just outside the *bayne* on the ground floor of King Henry VIII's lodgings on the east side of Whitehall Palace.[93] This chamber was first cited in an account of 1531. The ornamental repertoire and heraldic detail of the relief-moulded tiles suggests a manufacturing date during the late 1530s to late 1540s (Fig. 13.7). The close archaeological association of stove-tiles and lined sunken bath of the bathroom at Whitehall provides crucial

Fig. 13.7 *Green-glazed earthenware stove-tile moulded with the arms of Henry VIII for c.1540. Found in the vicinity of the King's bathroom or* bayne *on the ground-floor of the Privy Gallery at Whitehall Palace in 1939. Made in the Surrey-Hampshire border region. From Gaimster forthcoming (e), type 5. Drawing by J. Farrant and J.C. Thorn, BM (Courtesy of the Historic Royal Palaces Agency).*

evidence of the original function of the stove. According to the documentary and pictorial record, closed ceramic stoves were frequently built in Continental bathrooms during the 16th and 17th centuries. Francesco Salviati's representation of *Psyche at her Bath* of c.1530 and depictions of ceramic stoves in public bath houses in Germany by Hans Sebald Beham of the 1540s correspond closely with William Harrison's 1570s description of the English fashion for using ceramic stoves to create a steam-bath atmosphere (see above).[94] A precedent for this practice in royal houses may have been set

earlier at Greenwich where excavations produced green-glazed armorial stove-tiles in the vicinity of the bathroom of the royal manor house which was cleared in 1499 in readiness for Henry VII's new Palace.[95]

The antique ornament of the Whitehall stove closely echoes the detail of Hans Holbein's design for a fireplace of 1540 which may have been intended for Henry's London palace of Bridewell.[96] This migration of printed design into the architectural medium is not without precedent in early Renaissance England, as manufacturers of architectural terracotta were already exploiting designs by the late 1530s. Winged cherub-heads and foliate candelabra strips are a feature of the reliefs surviving on the vertical window mouldings of Sir William Pelham's house at Laughton Place, Sussex, completed before his death in 1538.[97] The ornament of Whitehall stove-tiles underlines the profound impact of Continental fashion and court style on native craft industries of the early Tudor period.

Ceramic hearth bricks

The adoption of Continental fashion and Renaissance ornament in the English domestic interior is also illustrated in the archaeological record by finds of Flemish hearth bricks (Fig. 13.8). Dating from the 16th century, these decorative bricks were used to face the rear of wall fireplaces, and the area surrounding the fireplace.[98] Made in a fine red, unglazed fabric, the bricks are moulded on the front with a series of Renaissance designs, depicting Biblical subjects and secular images, including heraldic devices and portrait heads. Produced in Antwerp and Liège, they were exported abroad, notably to Britain, where they have been found on sites along the east coast from Kent to Scotland, principally in London and various sites in East Anglia and Durham.[99] The distribution of these objects suggests they were adopted by a mercantile population, and the concentration of finds in eastern England emphasises the close cultural links of the immigrant communities in those regions with the Low Countries.

Floor tiles

Imported maiolica tiles

The earliest manifestation of the Renaissance on decorated tile floors in England is found on the imported polychrome maiolica pavements of the first half of the 16th century. Maiolica floor tiles are known from a range of sites in England. The most notable example is that now laid in the chapel at The Vyne (Hants.), and identified as the products of the Antwerp tile industry (Fig. 13.10).[100] The Vyne was built between 1500 and 1520 by William Sandys,

Fig. 13.8 Flemish hearth bricks, c.1500–1600. Moulded in relief with profile heads between foliate scrolls terminating in dolphin-heads. Found near London Bridge. (BM MLA 1839,10–29,64–65) (Courtesy of the Trustees of the British Museum).

employed as Treasurer of Calais by Henry VIII, and the tiles are traditionally dated to c.1520.[101] The tiles, which are both hexagonal and square in shape, are painted with a range of subjects, including male and female portraits in both classical and contemporary dress, animals, birds, fruit, flowers and wreaths.[102] The tiles correspond to the maiolica pavement at Herckenrode Abbey, Flanders, also thought to be a product of the Antwerp industry, and which is dated to the early 1530s.[103] Early maiolica tiles of this type have been recorded from a number of high status sites in England, many associated with royalty and the nobility, and date to the period between the 1520s and 1540s. Notable findspots include the royal palaces of Whitehall[104] and the Tower of London

Fig. 13.9 Late medieval slip-decorated earthenware floor tiles. A sixteen-tile design from the pavement found at Canynges House, Redcliffe Street, Bristol, c.1480–1515. Products of the Bristol tilers (Eames 1992, fig. 75).

Fig. 13.10 Polychrome maiolica floor tiles from The Vyne, Hampshire, c.1520. Probably made in Antwerp, South Netherlands. Decorated in blue, green, yellow and orange (After Rackham 1926, pl. 12).

(Fig. 13.11),[105] the Manor of the More, Herts[106] and Titchfield Abbey, Hampshire.[107] Fragments have also been found on sites in London, including a tile from the site of Guy's Hospital, Southwark.[108] The remains of a polychrome maiolica pavement found during excavations on the site of the manor house at Place Farm, Bletchingly, Surrey (Fig. 13.12), probably date to the period c.1520–1550.[109]

The influence of early maiolica floor tiles is apparent in a group of tiles produced at Brémontier-Massy, near Neufchâtel-en-Bray (Seine-Maritime), in northern France (Fig. 13.13), a small number of which have been found in England.[110] Decorated with a series of Renaissance designs, the tiles were produced in hexagonal, square and rhomboid shapes, and in two distinct fabrics, a light grey, near-stoneware body and a red earthenware. Many of the light grey hexagonal tiles are covered with a distinctive blue glaze, which, although not a tin-glaze, seems to have been an attempt to produce tiles resembling the shape, colour and decoration of maiolica tiles. The tiles made in red earthenware, and covered with a white slip and lead glaze in the medieval tradition, were decorated with the same stamps as the hexagonal tiles, and are thus thought to be contemporary. Tiles of this group have been found at several places in Sussex, and at a small number of sites elsewhere in England. Although most are stray finds lacking dating or contextual evidence, an indication of date and social status is suggested by a group of tiles, now in the Musée de Dieppe, from the site of a town house in Dieppe known to have been built in 1525 by Jean Ango.[111] Further work on the chronology of this group of tiles may reveal whether they were seen as cheaper substitutes for maiolica tiles, or whether they were intended to form pavements of comparable prestige in the period before maiolica tiles became widely available.

English floor tiles: the late medieval tradition

The production of decorated floor tiles in the 14th century was dominated in many areas by large commercial tileries making vast numbers of slip-decorated tiles. Mass-production resulted in a widespread distribution of decorated pavements, from royal palaces, monasteries and churches, to

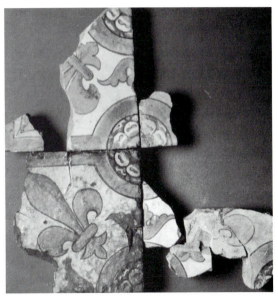

Fig. 13.12 *Polychrome maiolica floor tiles. Larger fragment (lower left) unprovenanced (BM MLA OA 4386); remaining fragments from the site of Place Farm, Bletchingly, Surrey. Decorated in blue, green, yellow and orange, c.1520–50 (Photograph courtesy of the Trustees of the British Museum).*

Fig. 13.11 *Two painted maiolica tiles excavated from the lower fills of the Broad Arrow Tower, Tower of London. Painted in the style of tiles made in Antwerp in the South Netherlands c.1520–40 by potters of north Italian descent.*

Top: *a square tile painted in shades of dark blue with a roundel containing an allegorical representation of* Luna *ruling over the zodiacal sign of Cancer in the Planet Gods series taken from contemporary printed sources (length/estim. width 120mm).*

Bottom: *a hexagonal tile painted in dark blue, yellow and orange with a central quatrefoil flower of formalised petals and leaves (length 220mm).*

(Photographs courtesy of the British Museum)

merchants' houses and urban sites.[112] Tiles of varying quality continued to be made during the 15th and early 16th centuries: the mid 15th-century revival of well-made, specially commissioned tiles, using medieval techniques and designs, which were produced initially for the church, originated in Great Malvern and subsequently influenced production over a wider area. These industries produced tiles decorated with the heraldry and rhebuses of individual patrons, indicating a revival of interest in decorated floors, and their distribution subsequently widened. For example, tiles with designs made especially for two of the abbots of St Augustine's Abbey, Bristol, between c.1480 and 1515 continued to be made after the original commission was completed, and were used to pave the floors of merchant houses and rural manor houses in the surrounding area. The pavement from Canynges House, Bristol (Fig. 13.9), a product of the Bristol tilers, includes a number of tiles originally designed for St Augustine's, while some of the designs found in the Canynges pavement have been identified at the manor house at Acton Court, Avon.[113]

Slip decorated tiles: the 16th century

The influence of maiolica pavements, and of the Renaissance motifs with which they were decorated, can be seen on a small number of earthenware tiles decorated in the two-colour, technique. One group of tiles produced in the Low Countries during the 1550s is decorated with designs reflecting those found on maiolica tiles of the early to mid 16th century.[114] The tiles are square, but were intended to imitate the hexagonal shapes of many maiolica tiles by incorporating the outlines of similar patterns into the designs (Fig. 13.15, bottom). Significantly, the industry which produced these tiles also made tiles decorated in the late medieval style, including several with a series of mottos designed in late Gothic script (Fig. 13.15, top), demonstrating the use of both styles in a single industry at this period. Examples of these tiles have been found distributed through southern England. They occur at the royal palaces of Nonsuch and Eltham, and at monastic sites which, during the 1550s, were undergoing conversion into private residences.[115] They have also been found at several

Fig. 13.13 *Floor tiles decorated with Renaissance motifs and profile heads, made at Brémontier-Massy, near Neufchâtel-en-Bray (Seine-Maritime), c.1525–50.* **Top:** *square red earthenware tile (Eames 1980, design 159). Examples have been found at Keymer Park and at Hurstpierpoint, Sussex.* **Bottom:** *hexagonal light grey near-stoneware tile, with blue glaze, found at Tuxford, Nottinghamshire (BM MLA 1905,10–8,4) (Drawing by J. C. Thorn, BM).*

Fig. 13.14 *Two slip-decorated earthenware tiles, probably from Lacock Abbey, Wiltshire. Made for William Sharington, owner of Lacock Abbey, and decorated with Renaissance motifs, his badge, a scorpion, his initials, and those of his wife, Grace, c.1550–3. Eames 1980, designs 1413 and 1458 (BM MLA 1969,2–1,1–2).*

Fig. 13.15 *Two slip-decorated earthenware floor tiles, Flemish, c.1550–60.* **Top**: *motto tile with Gothic lettering, from Halnaker House, Chichester, West Sussex. Eames 1980, design 1431 (BM MLA 1947,5–5,1360).* **Bottom**: *tile incorporating double-outlined hexagonal design and stylised foliate decoration, from London. Eames 1980, design 2732. (BM MLA 1947,5–5,2212).*

manor houses being built at this period, notably in Kent and Sussex, as well as at urban sites in London, Exeter and Southampton. Their distribution and context are thus largely secular, and correspond to those of the early maiolica tiles, but perhaps representing a less expensive version of the poly-chrome tiles. Their occurence, however, clearly signifies an awareness on the part of the consumer of the latest Continental fashion in tiled floors.

A small number of tiles decorated with Renaissance designs were produced in England during the mid 16th century, such as those from Lacock Abbey

(Wilts.). Made for William Sharington, the first lay owner of Lacock Abbey after the Dissolution, they were laid in a pavement which also included designs derived from those of the Lower Severn series of floor tiles, but two of the designs were made specifically for Sharington (Fig. 13.14).[116] They incorporate Renaissance motifs and lettering, Sharrington's badge, a scorpion, and the initials of William and his third wife, Grace, and are closely dated to the period 1550–1553. These are the latest inlaid tiles to which a firm date can be given. Decorated with secular designs, they demonstrate a contemporary awareness of, and demand for, pavements decorated in the Renaissance style. Although relief-decorated earthenware tiles continued to be produced during the post-medieval period,[117] by the later 16th and early 17th century tin-glazed floor tiles were being produced in London,[118] and the fashion for maiolica pavements had superceded that of the inlaid earthenware tiled floor.

Concluding remarks

Traditionally historians have tended to view the 15th century in north-west Europe as a continuation of the period of general economic and demographic decline which divides the High Middle Ages from the Renaissance.[119] The archaeological record, however, confirms more recently generated documentary evidence for increasing purchasing power, social mobility and material comfort and sophistication – particularly for those communities living in towns and ports with access to national and international markets.[120] The ceramic evidence suggests that a climate receptive to new goods, culture and lifestyle was in place by the late 15th century.

In England, the impact of increased commercial and cultural contact with the Continent can be seen directly in the ceramic sphere with the rise in demand for imported wares and introduction of a more diverse range of products in the native industries. Gradually it is possible to observe a revolution of the ceramic medium in the English household over this period, whereby it was transformed from an essen-

tially utilitarian product in the early 15th century into a medium with dual domestic and social functions by c.1550. In terms of its changing status, we see the migration of ceramics from the kitchen and the cellar to a central position on the table and, as stoves or floors, into the very centre of the private sphere, competing and even substituting for other media. Ceramics were being used by the court, country gentry, merchants and artisans alike in the social emulation process. In relation to the previous phase of ceramic innovation in the cross-Channel zone during the 12th to 13th centuries (described by Verhaeghe in Chapter 3), the changes of the mid 15th to mid 16th centuries can be characterised by an increasing multiplicity of ceramic products on the market (ranging from domestic utensils to interior fixtures and fittings) and a distinctive multidimensionality (in fabric, form, surface treatment and ornament). By 1550 these developments ensured that ceramics performed a much greater range of domestic functions than before and enabled a wider community of consumers to participate in the latest material fashions. In the case of interior fittings such as tiled floors and tile-stoves, those not part of the patrician classes could at least emulate them as the ornamental repertoire of the Continental Renaissance found in royal palace and country house architecture was translated via the ceramic medium into the urban interior. Indeed it appears that pottery was in the vanguard of the migration of cosmopolitan Renaissance culture into southern Britain. As such, archaeological finds in this medium can be studied as an index of the European acculturisation process in late medieval and early modern England.

However, if we are to be absolutely confident about when and at what scale or tempo changes in the domestic ceramic inventory took place in this period, then these interpretations urgently require more testing on the microscale. So many excavated assemblages critical to this study (ranging from royal palaces to urban sites, especially in London) remain unpublished and inacessible for study. Many have the advantage of a documented function or social status.[121]

Notes

1. Gaimster 1994, 286–7.
2. This paper develops a number of issues concerning the 'post-medieval ceramic revolution' discussed in previous publications by Gaimster (1993a, 1994).
3. Gaimster 1994, 287–94.
4. See Editorial in *Post-Medieval Archaeology*, vol. 1 (1967).
5. For the increasing cross-Channel trade see various papers in Power & Postan (eds) 1953; Pollard and Crossley 1968, 114–118.
6. Dyer 1982, 33; and 1990, 24–5, 204–5, 210, for rise in urban consumption in late 15th-century England; Hasse 1979 for survey of late medieval urban material culture in northern Germany.
7. Hundsbichler 1986b, 210–14.
8. For sub-division of English urban housing see Schofield 1995, 92–3; Dyer 1990, 204. Cf. Mohrmann 1985 for increasing compartmentalisation of the North German town house during the 15th to 16th centuries.
9. Cf. Goldthwaite 1989 for a discussion of the socio-economic role of ceramics in Renaissance Italy. See also Orton 1985; and Hundsbichler 1986a, for the question of innovation through social as well as technological pressure. See Blake 1980 for the archaeological study of ceramic supply and demand.
10. Dawson 1979; Barton 1992; Gaimster 1994, 287.
11. Hundsbichler 1986a, 70–4.
12. Power & Postan (eds) 1953; Carus-Wilson 1967.
13. Gaimster 1993a on the emegence of a 'Hanseatic' material culture in late medieval England; Petegree 1986 on influence of protestant immigrants on London's religious culture during the early 16th century.
14. For ethnically motivated commodities trade at this time see Gaimster 1993b; Margeson 1993, 235–7; Evans 1987.
15. Thrupp 1969, 259; Hirschfelder 1996, 25; and Cotter 1997, 31, for importance of Colchester and Norwich to Cologne and Netherlandish cloth merchants.
16. Thrupp 1969, 258 (see Appendix for alien lay subsidy records for the London area 1440–1484).
17. Edwards 1974b.
18. Carus-Wilson 1973; Dollinger 1989, 319–23; Petegree 1986, 10.
19. Thrupp 1969, 260–1; Petegree 1986, 9–10.
20. Pettegree 1986, 9.
21. Ramsey 1975, 33; Petegree 1986, 11–16.
22. Petegree 1986, 17.
23. Margeson 1993, 235.
24. Petegree 1986, 18.
25. *Ibid.* 19.
26. Blake 1980 on the economic sensitivity of ceramic production.
27. Orton 1982 for products of the Cheam industry; Pearce 1992, 88–9.
28. Vince 1985, fig. 21, for London sequence.
29. Dawson 1976.
30. Dyer 1982; and 1990, 5, 188–9. Orton 1985 for effect of economic crisis on production; Braudel 1984, 77–8 for general economic downswing in western Europe during 14th to 15th centuries.
31. Vince 1985; Blackmore 1994.
32. Gaimster 1997a, Chapter 3, for a full survey of the medieval to later international stoneware trade. See Gaimster forthcoming (d) for survey of the global maritime evidence.
33. Gaimster 1997a, Chapter 3.4, for survey of documentary evidence.
34. Le Patourel 1983, Tables 3.2–3.4.
35. Gras 1918; Kashden 1988 for pewter lids attached to stoneware jugs found in the Thames.
36. Allan 1984, 117.
37. *Ibid.* 118.
38. Gaimster 1987; 1997a, Chapter 3.4; Vince 1988; Blackmore 1994, 37.
39. Brown 1993, fig.1.
40. Gaimster 1997a, Chapter 3.4; Huggins forthcoming for Whitehall; Evans 1985 for Norwich Pottergate.
41. Lynn Blackmore & Roy Stephenson (MOLAS) pers. comm.
42. For Norwich Pottergate see Evans 1985; for Toppings and Sun Wharves, Southwark, see Orton *et al.* 1974.
43. Hurst 1979, nos. 85–6 for Wharram Percy; and Allan 1984, 113–19, 158–9 for Exeter.
44. Clevis 1992.
45. Hundsbichler 1986b, 210–14 for changes in table habits during the 15th century; Gaimster 1997a, Chapter 4.4 for discussion of custom change on ceramics.
46. Gaimster 1997a, Chapter 4.4; and forthcoming (b) for survey and discussion.
47. Gaimster 1997a, Chapter 4.4, for discussion.
48. Blackmore forthcoming for Tower of London Postern Gate; Nelson forthcoming for the Broad Arrow Tower.
49. Behling 1957, 66–67; Gaimster 1997a, Chapter 4.5; and forthcoming (b) for examples and discussion.
50. Gaimster 1997a, Chapter 4.4, for discussion. See also individual catalogue introductions on Cologne,

Siegburg and Raeren for the development of applied relief ornament based on printed sources.

51. Gaimster 1987; 1994, 293–4; and 1997a, Chapter 3.4 for surveys of distribution of Cologne stoneware in England.

52. Vince & Bell 1992, tables 4 and 8 (Raeren and Cologne stonewares only); see Gaimster 1997a, Chapter 3.4, for further finds of Cologne stoneware in other early 16th-century English contexts.

53. Dawson 1979, fig. 11, nos. 176–7.

54. Gaimster 1994, 291, for commentary on this phenomenon. See Hughes forthcoming for a chemical separation study of the respective production sources of Netherlandish and Italian maiolicas of the late 15th to early 16th centuries.

55. Gaimster forthcoming (b) for full survey and discussion.

56. Orton 1985 for discussion.

57. Vince & Bell 1992, tables, 3, 5, 6.

58. Huggins forthcoming for Tudor-period ceramics from Whitehall; Hurst 1971 for vessels found in a mid 16th-century context at the Old Manor Askett, Buckinghamshire; Rackham 1939b for the Tower of London finds.

59. Dawson 1979, fig. 11, nos. 182–92 for Iberian finewares and nos.197–204 for Netherlandish maiolica in levels of c.1480–1530 at the Guy's Hospital site, Southwark; and Southampton 1976 for Italian and 'Netherlandish' maiolicas from Simnel Street, Southampton.

60. See Moorhouse 1972; Edwards 1974a, 4–7; Pryor & Blockley 1978; Cunningham & Drury 1985; Stephenson 1991; Nenk 1992; Gaimster & Verhaeghe 1992; Nenk forthcoming (a).

61. See Orton 1982, 79–84. For examples of London assemblages, see Sheldon 1974; Dawson 1979, 34–48; and Huggins forthcoming.

62. Gaimster & Verhaeghe 1992.

63. Matthews & Green 1969, 8–9; Holling 1977, nos. 2, 7 and 14, for Border Ware drinking vessels based directly on Siegburg and Raeren stoneware prototypes. See also Moorhouse 1979; Pearce 1992, Chapter 7, fig. 56; and Gaimster 1997a, Chapter 3.4 for full discussion.

64. Huggins forthcoming for Whitehall Palace; Pearce 1992, 90–91, for Baynards Castle, London.

65. Haslam 1975, fig. 7, no. 11 for rare pedestal cup base probably imitating the raised frilled bases of contemporary Rhenish stoneware.

66. Dawson 1979, fig. 4, no. 18 for Border Ware jug with raised frilled base in a context of c.1480–1520.

67. Matthews & Green 1969, nos. 25–6 and 36–8.

68. Brown 1993, 79, for Southampton finds; Moorhouse 1983 for 11 examples found at Sandal Castle, West Yorkshire; Dyer 1982, 40; and Moorhouse 1979 for general discussion.

69. Moorhouse 1984; and Barker 1986 for full discussion of Cistercian Ware industry and its market.

70. Pearce 1982, 89–91.

71. Moorhouse 1979; and 1984.

72. Mohrmann 1985; Hundsbichler 1986b, 263–8; and Felgenhauer-Schmiedt 1995, 125–6, for discussions of increasing material comfort of the late medieval urban household in northern and central Europe. See Appuhn and Wittstock 1982 for the ornamental influence of furniture during the 15th century.

73. Schofield 1995, 118–26 for a discussion of internal decoration and fittings in the late medieval London house.

74. Gaimster 1988a; 1994, 292; and Gaimster *et al.* 1990 for syntheses of the evidence.

75. Cowell 1990.

76. Gaimster 1988a for the Fountains Abbey tiles; Gaimster *et al.* 1990 for the St Mary Graces finds. See also Cotter 1993, fig. 1, for a late Gothic niche-tile from the Dissolution levels at St Augustine's Abbey, Canterbury.

77. Gaimster forthcoming (a) for single armorial niche-tile from this site.

78. Gaimster forthcoming (e) for niche-tile fragments excavated beneath the Banqueting House, Whitehall, the former site of the episcopal palace of York Place.

79. Excavations by the City Museum and Mappin Art Gallery, Sheffield. Report on the tiles in preparation by D. Gaimster.

80. Gaimster 1993b.

81. Findspots include Cloak Lane, City (Museum of London A3909), Butlers Wharf, City (MoL 87/84/1–3), and 129 Lambeth Road, Southwark (Orton 1988, no. 1563 misidentified). These were residential and mercantile districts during the 15th to 16th centuries (pers. comm. Derek Keene, Institute of Historical Research, London).

82. For Cologne-type niche-tile fragment found in Cardiff see National Museum of Wales (NMW inv. 64.51); for Cologne tile of the same type found at the Hall's Brewery site, Oxford, see Mellor forthcoming.

83. Dubbe 1980; and 1987 for Dutch finds; Gaimster forthcoming (c) for Duisburg tiles.

84. Strauss 1968, figs 8 and 9.

85. For imported Renaissance stove-tiles associated with houses built in former monasteries see figurative

panel-tile of c.1572 from St Gregory's Priory, Canterbury (Cotter 1993, fig. 1, no. 2); and panel-tile of c.1575 moulded with the 60 Year Old in the Ages of Man series found in the ruins of St Rade-gund's Abbey, near Dover, Kent, and possibly associated with Simon Edolph's house built on the site in 1590 (Gaimster 1989). Additional finds include various green-glazed and polychrome frieze-tiles of mid to late 16th-century date found at Tattershall Castle, Lincolnshire, which are now part of the National Trust display at the site.

86. Report in preparation by Gaimster for the Oxford Archaeological Unit; see interim excavation report in *Sussex Archaeological Newsletter* 39 (1983), 316.

87. Gaimster 1988a, cat. ii. for Fleet Street; cat.v and vi for Duke's Place. Webber 1991, fig. 3, for Cologne-type panel-tile with the figure of Musica, c.1561, from Lambeth.

88. Gaimster 1988a, cat. iv.

89. William Harrison, *The Description of England* (ed. G. Edelen), New York (1968, reprinted 1994), p. 197. Further evidence of the spread of the fashion for closed ceramic stoves is provided by Pierre Alexandre, Thomas Cranmer's secretary. In the Winter of 1550 he wrote to Martin Bucer at Cambridge, reassuring him that the German stove would soon be arriving in the town (Corpus Christi College, Cambridge, Ms 119, p. 303; pers. comm. John Cherry).

90. Rackham 1939a, pl. IVa, for cistern with arms of Henry VII and his consort Elizabeth of York; Gaimster 1988b, pl. XXIVc, cat. II.3, for candle-sconce moulded with the arms of Elizabeth I.

91. Gaimster 1988b for full corpus of finds; see Cowell 1988; and Cowell and Gaimster 1995, for scientific studies (NAA) of source of manufacture.

92. Gaimster 1988b, appendix I and postscript. Recent additions include the Earls of Stafford (later Buck-ingham's) manor house at Place Farm, near Bletch-ingly, Surrey (pers. comm. Michael Russell, Bourne Society); a previously unrecorded mould-type with the royal arms of Henry VIII supported by the motto 'DIEU ET MON DROIT' found on the Thames foreshore at Bankside, Southwark (private col-lection); and the stove-tiles from Greenwich Palace, found in the rubble of the royal manor house demolished in 1499 (Dixon 1972, 10).

93. Gaimster forthcoming (e).

94. See ceramic stoves in the centre of public bathhouse scenes by Hans Sebald Beham dating to the 1540s in Strauss 1968, figs 29 & 30.

95. Dixon 1972, 10.

96. Rowlands 1988, cat. 210, pl. XXXI; Gaimster forthcoming (e) for full discussion.

97. Howard 1991.

98. Hollestelle 1970; Hollestelle 1981; Massing 1990.

99. Cruden 1825; Borg *et al.* 1980, 40–4; Hurst *et al.* 1986, 144, fig. 65, no. 225. For Durham, see *Pro-ceedings of the Society of Antiquaries of Newcastle-upon-Tyne*, IX (1890), 103.

100. Rackham 1926. The tiles were laid in the chapel after being found in the grounds of the house during the 19th century, and are thus not in their original position.

101. Rackham 1926, 71.

102. *Ibid.* 61–71.

103. Laurent 1922.

104. Hurst in prep.

105. Gaimster forthcoming (a).

106. Rackham 1959, 186–7, fig. 21, nos. 1–16.

107. See Rackham 1926, 75.

108. Dawson 1979, 51–53, fig. 11, no. 204. See also Britton 1987, 170–1, cat. nos. 180–4.

109. Michael Russell, Bourne Society, pers. comm.; Nenk forthcoming (b). The house belonged to the Duke of Buckingham until his execution in 1521, then to Sir Nicholas Carew, executed in 1539, and, in 1540, was granted by Henry VIII to Anne of Cleves; see Saaler 1995, 71, 79, 86–90, 104–6.

110. Eames 1980, 97; Norton 1981, 117; Norton 1992, 146–147, fig.135, nos.210–11; Nenk forthcoming (c).

111. Milet 1904, 95–96; Knecht 1994, 371. See also Ickowicz 1988, 122–3, for examples found during excavations in Dieppe castle.

112. Eames 1980, ch. 13.

113. *Ibid.* 239–47; Williams 1974.

114. Horton 1981.

115. *Ibid.* 243.

116. Eames 1980, 266. See also C. Norton, 'The medieval floor-tiles of Christchurch Priory', *Proc. Dorset Nat. Hist. Archaeol. Soc.*, 102 (1980), 61–3.

117. Eames 1980, 123–6; Keen 1969.

118. Britton 1987.

119. Dyer 1982, 36 for England; Boockmann 1994, 7–10 for the Continent.

120. Dyer 1982, 36, 38–9; and 1990, 210. See also Courtney this volume.

121. Gaimster 1997b.

Bibliography

Allan, J.P, 1984, *Medieval and Post-Medieval Finds from Exeter, 1971–1980*, Exeter Archaeological Reports, III, Exeter

Appuhn, H. & Wittstock, J. 1982, 'Mittelalterliche Hausmöbel in Norddeutschland', in J. Wittstock ed., *Aus dem Alltag der Mittelalterlichen Stadt*, Hefte des Focke Museums, 62, Helms Museum, Hamburg-Harburg, 43–54

Barker, D. 1986, 'North Staffordshire post-medieval ceramics – a type-series. part one: Cistercian Ware', *Staffordshire Archaeological Studies*, Museum Archaeological Society Report, new series, 3, Stoke-on-Tent, 52–7

Barton, K. 1992, 'Ceramic changes in the western European littoral at the end of the Middle Ages. A personal view', in D.R.M. Gaimster & M. Redknap (eds) 1992, 246–55

Behling, L. 1957, *Die Pflanze in der Mittelalterliche Tafelmalerei*, Weimar

Blackmore, L. 1994, 'Pottery, port and the populace: the imported pottery of London 1300–1600 (Part 1), *Medieval Ceramics* 18, 29–44.

Blackmore, L. forthcoming, 'The imported pottery', in D. Whipp, 'Excavations at the Tower Postern 1976', Museum of London Archaeology Service

Blake, H. 1980, 'Technology, supply or demand?', *Medieval Ceramics* 4, 3–12

Boockmann, H. 1994, *Fürsten, Bürger, Edelleute. Lebensbilder aus dem späten Mittelalter*, Munich

Borg, A., Franklin, J., Sekules, V., Sims, T. & Thomson, D. 1980, *Medieval Sculpture from Norwich Cathedral*, University of East Anglia, Norwich

Braudel, F. 1984, *Civilisation and Capitalism 15th-18th Century, Vol. III. The Perspective of the World*

Britton, F. 1987, *London Delftware*

Brown, D. 1993, 'The imported pottery of late medieval Southampton', *Medieval Ceramics* 17, 77–82

Carus-Wilson, E.M. 1967, *Medieval Merchant Venturers*, (2nd edition)

Carus-Wilson, E.M. 1973, 'Die Hanse in England', in *Hanse und Europa. Brücke zwischen den Märkten, 12. bis 17. Jahrhundert*, Cologne, 87–106

Clevis, H. 1992, 'Juggling Jacobakannen', *Medieval Ceramics*, 16, 55–63

Cotter, J. 1993, 'Continental stove-tiles from collections in Canterbury', *Medieval Ceramics* 17, 86–9

Cotter, J. 1997, *Post-Roman Pottery from Excavations in Colchester 1971–85*, Colchester Archaeological Report 7, Colchester Archaeological Trust, Colchester

Cowell, M.R. 1988, 'A provenance study of English armorial stove-tiles', in D.R.M. Gaimster (1988b), 338–40

Cowell, M. 1990, ' Report on the analysis of nine post-medieval stove-tile fragments from St Mary Graces', in Gaimster *et al.* 1990, 40–44

Cowell, M.R. & Gaimster, D.R.M. 1995, 'Post-medieval ceramic stove-tiles bearing the royal arms of England: further scientific investigations into their manufacture and source in southern England', in D.R. Hook & D.R.M. Gaimster (eds), *Trade and Discovery: the Scientific Study of Artefacts from Post-Medieval Europe and Beyond*, British Museum Occasional Paper, 109, 105–16

[Cruden, R. P.] 1825, *A Description of Three Ancient Ornamental Bricks, Found at Different Periods, in London and Gravesend*

Cunningham, C.M. and Drury, P.J. 1985, *Post-medieval sites and their pottery: Moulsham Street, Chelmsford*, CBA Research Report 54, Chelmsford Archaeological Trust Rep 5

Dawson, G. 1976, *The Black Prince's Palace at Kennington, Surrey*, British Archaeological Reports (British Series), 26, Oxford

Dawson, G. 1979, 'Excavations at Guy's Hospital, 1967', *Surrey Archaeological Society Research Volume 7*, 27–65

Dixon, P. 1972, *Excavations at Greenwich Palace 1970–1971. An Interim Report*, Greenwich and Lewisham Antiquarian Society, Greenwich

Dollinger, 1989, *Die Hanse*, Stuttgart (4th edition)

Dubbe, B. 1980, 'Import van kacheltegels in de zestiende euuw', *Antiek* 14, no. 8, 519–22

Dubbe, B. 1987, 'Een vondst van gotische kacheltegels in de Deventer binnenstad', *Antiek* 21, no. 6, 329–36

Dyer, C. 1982, 'The social and economic changes of the later Middle Ages, and the pottery of the period', *Medieval Ceramics* 6, 33–42

Dyer, C. 1990, *Standards of Living in the later Middle Ages. Social Change in England c.1200–1520*, Cambridge (2nd edition)

Eames, E.S. 1980, *Catalogue of Medieval Lead-glazed Earthenware Tiles*, British Museum

Eames, E.S. 1992, *English Tilers*, British Museum

Edwards, R. 1974a, 'London Potters circa 1570–1710', *Journal Ceramic History* 6

Edwards, R. 1974b, 'Documentary sources in relation to the excavation', in Sheldon 1992, 3–8

Evans, D. H. 1985, 'The Pottery' in M. Atkin, A. Carter & D.H. Evans (eds), *Excavations in Norwich 1971–*

78, Part 2, East Anglian Archaeology, 26, Norwich, 27–36

Evans, D.H. 1987, 'Reflections on the study of imported ceramics', in B.E. Vyner & S. Wrathmell (eds), *Studies in Medieval and Later Pottery in Wales presented to J.M. Lewis*, Cardiff, 199–224

Felgenhauer-Schmiedt, S. 1995, *Die Sachkukltur des Mittelalters im Lichte der Archäologischen Funde*, Europäische Hochschulschriften, Reihe XXXVIII, Archäologie 42, Frankfurt-am-Main

Gaimster, D.R.M. 1987, 'The supply of Rhenish stoneware to London, 1350–1600', *London Archaelogist* 5, no.13, 339–47

Gaimster, D.R.M. 1988a, 'A survey of Cologne-type stove-tiles found in Britain', in I. Unger (ed.), *Kölner Ofenkacheln. Die Bestände des Museums für Angewandte Kunst und des Kölnischen Stadtmuseums*, Cologne, 44–54

Gaimster, D.R.M. 1988b, 'Post-medieval stove-tiles bearing the Royal arms: evidence for their manufacture and use in southern Britain', *Archaeological Journal* 145, 314–43

Gaimster, D.R.M. 1989, 'An imported Renaissance stove-tile from Dover in the collections of the Society of Antiquaries', *Antiquaries Journal* 69, pt. II, 298–306

Gaimster, D.R.M. 1993a, 'Cross-Channel ceramic trade in the late Middle Ages: evidence for the spread of Hanseatic culture to Britain', in M. Gläser-Muhrenberg (ed.), *Archäologie des Mittelalters und Bauforschung in Hanseraum. Eine Festschrift für Günter Fehring*, Schriften des Kulturhistorischen Museums in Rostock, I, Rostock, 251–260

Gaimster, D.R.M. 1993b, 'Imported stove-tile fragments' in Margeson 1993, 168–170

Gaimster, D.R.M. 1994, 'The archaeology of post-medieval society, c.1450–1750: material culture studies in Britain since the War', in B. Vyner (ed.), *Building on the Past. Papers Celebrating 150 Years of the Royal Archaeological Institute*, London, 283–312

Gaimster, D.R.M. 1997a, *German Stoneware 1200–1900. Archaeology and Cultural History*, British Museum

Gaimster, D.R.M. 1997b, 'London's Tudor palaces revisited: a user's guide the backlog', *London Archaeologist* 8, no. 5, 122–6

Gaimster, D.R.M., Goffin, R. & Blackmore, L. 1990, 'The Continental stove-tile fragments from St Mary Graces, London, in their British and European context', *Post-Medieval Archaeology* 24, 1–49

Gaimster, D.R.M. & Verhaeghe, F. 1992, 'Handles with face-masks: a cross-Channel type of late medieval

highly decorated basin', in Gaimster & Redknap 1992, 303–323

Gaimster, D.R.M. & Redknap, M. (eds) 1992, *Everyday and Exotic Pottery in Europe c.600–1900, Studies in Honour of J.G. Hurst*, Oxford

Gaimster, D.R.M. forthcoming (a), 'A late-medieval stove-tile and a group of 16th-century painted maiolica floor-tiles', in Parnell forthcoming

Gaimster, D.R.M. forthcoming (b), '"Distant Voices, still-lifes". Late medieval religious panel-painting as a context for archaeological ceramics', in *Medieval Europe Bruges 1997*, Session on Method and Theory in Historical Archaeology (pre-printed papers, Bruges, 1997)

Gaimster, D.R.M. forthcoming (c), *Angebot und Nachfrage von Keramik am Niederrhein im 15.–18. Jahrhundert*, Rheinische Ausgrabungen (Bonn, 1998)

Gaimster, D.R.M. forthcoming d, 'Rhenish stonewares from shipwrecks: contexts for the study of ceramic function and lifespan', in M. Redknap (ed.), *Artefacts from Wrecks. The Archaeology of Material Culture from Shipwrecks of the late Middle Ages to the Industrial Revolution*, Nautical Archaeology Society and Society for Post-Medieval Archaeology (Oxford, 1997)

Gaimster, D.R.M., forthcoming (e), 'The armorial stove-tiles from the King's Privy Gallery', in Thurley forthcoming

Gaimster, D.R.M. & Nenk, B.S. (eds) forthcoming, *Maiolica in the North. The Production of Tin-Glazed Ceramics in North-West Europe c.1500–1600*, British Museum Occasional Paper (1998)

Goldthwaite, R.A. 1989, 'The economic and social world of Italian Renaissance maiolica', *Renaissance Quarterly* 42, 1–32

Gras, N.S.B. 1918, *The Early English Customs System*

Haslam, J. 1975, 'The Saxon and the Tudor Pottery from the Cesspit', in M.J. Hammerson, 'Excavations on the Site of Arundel House in the Strand, WC2, in 1972', *Transactions of the London and Middlesex Archaeological Society* 26, 221–31

Hirschfelder, G. 1996, *Kölner Fernhandel im Spätmittelalter*, Geschichtlicher Atlas der Rheinlande, Beiheft VII/7, Cologne

Hollestelle, J. 1970, 'Herkomst en verspreiding van haardstenen in de Nederlanden', *Antiek* 5, no. 5, 316–28

Hollestelle, J. 1981, 'Haardstenen in enkele Gelderse Kastelen', in T.L. Hoekstra, H.L. Janssen & I.W.L. Moerman (eds), *Liber Castellorum: 40 Variaties op het Thema Kasteel*, 360–66

Holling, F. 1977, 'Reflections on Tudor Green', *Post-Medieval Archaeology* 11, 61–66

Horton, M. 1981, 'Imported Motto Tiles: a Group of Sixteenth-century Slip-Decorated Dutch Floor Tiles in England', in A. Detsicas (ed.), *Collectanea Historica: Essays in Memory of Stuart Rigold*, 235–46

Howard, M. 1991, 'Laughton Place: the Tudor house and its terracottas', in J. Farrant, M. Howard, D. Rudling, J. Warren, & C. Whittock, 'Laughton Place: A manorial and architectural history, with an account of recent restoration and excavation', *Sussex Archaeological Collections* 129, 99–164

Huggins, R.M. forthcoming, 'Pottery, The Tudor Palace period', in H.J.M. Green, 'Excavations on the West Side of Whitehall 1960–62', Part 3: The Finds, *Transactions of the London and Middlesex Archaeological Society*

Hughes, M.J. forthcoming, 'Neutron activation analysis of maiolica from London, Norwich and the Low Countries', in Gaimster & Nenk (eds)

Hundsbichler, 1986a, '"Innovation" und "Kontinuität" als Determinanten von Alltag und Fortschritt', in *Alltag und Fortschritt im Mittelalter*, Veröffentlichungen des Instituts für Mirttelalterliche Relalienkunde Österreichs 8, Vienna, 65–81

Hundsbichler, H. 1986b, 'Nahrung, Kleidung, Wohnen', in H. Kühnel (ed.), *Alltag im Spätmittelalter*, Graz (3rd edition), 196–270

Hurst, J.G. 1971, 'South Netherlands maiolica', in G. Beresford, 'The Old Manor, Askett', *Records of Buckinghamshire* 18, 343–366

Hurst, J.G. 1978, 'Imported pottery', in D. Andrews & G. Milne (eds), *Wharram: a study of settlement on the Yorkshire Wolds I. Domestic Settlement: Areas 10 and 6*, Society for Medieval Archaeology Monograph Series, vol. 7

Hurst, J.G. in prep. 'A note on the maiolica floor-tiles from Whitehall Palace', in Gaimster & Nenk (eds) forthcoming

Hurst, J.G., Neal, D.S. & van Beuningen, H.J.E. 1986, *Pottery produced and traded in north-west Europe 1350–1650*, Rotterdam Papers VI, Rotterdam

Ickowicz, P. 1988, 'Céramiques du Chateau de Dieppe des XVIe et XVIIe siècles', *Bulletin du Groupe de Recherches et d'Etudes de la Céramique du Beauvaisis* 10, 57–153

Kashden, M. 1988, 'Some notes on a collection of excavated lids', *Journal of the Pewter Society* 6, 88–92

Keen, L. 1969, 'A series of seventeenth- and eighteenth-century lead-glazed relief tiles from North Devon', *Journal of the British Archaeological Association* 32, 144–70

Knecht, R.J. 1994, *Renaissance Warrior and Patron: The Reign of Francis I*

Laurent, M. 1922, 'Guido di Savino and the Earthenware of Antwerp', *Burlington Magazine* 41 (December 1922), 288–97

Le Patourel, J. 1983, 'Documentary evidence for the pottery trade in North-West Europe', in P. Davey & R. Hodges (eds), *Ceramics and Trade. The Production and Distribution of Later Medieval Pottery in North-West Europe*, Sheffield, 27–35

Margeson, S.M. 1993, *Norwich Households: Medieval and Post-Medieval Finds from Norwich Survey Excavations 1971–1978*, East Anglian Archaeology 58, Norwich

Massing, J.M. 1990, 'Veleda, Susanna, Boadicea or Dorothy: Antiquarian Discussions on some Sixteenth-Century Ornamental Bricks', in E.Chaney & P.Mack (eds), *England and the Continental Renaissance. Essays in Honour of J.B.Trapp*, Woodbridge, 283–94

Matthews, L.G. & Green, H.J.M. 1969, 'Post-medieval pottery of the Inns of Court', *Post-Medieval Archaeology* 3, 1–17

Mellor, M. forthcoming, 'The pottery' in M.R. Roberts, 'The tenement of Roger of Cremnar and other investigations in North Oseney, Oxford', *Oxoniensia* (1996)

Milet, A. 1904, *Catalogue du Musée de Dieppe*, Dieppe

Mohrmann, R.-E. 1985, 'Wohnen und Wohnkultur in nordwestdeutschen Städten in Spätmittelater und in der frühen Neuzeit', in *Stadt im Wandel. Kunst und Kultur des Bürgertums in Norddeutschland 1150–1650*, Landesausstellung Niedersachsen, Braunschweig, 3, 513–525

Moorhouse, S. 1972, 'Medieval distilling apparatus of glass and pottery', *Medieval Archaeology* 16, 79–121

Moorhouse, S. 1979, 'Tudor Green: some further thoughts', *Medieval Ceramics* 3, 61

Moorhouse, S. 1983, 'The medieval pottery', in P. Mayes & L.A.S. Butler (eds), *Sandal Castle Excavations 1964–73: a detailed archaeological report*, Wakefield, 83–212.

Moorhouse, S. 1984, 'Late medieval finewares', *West Midlands Pottery Research Group Newsletter* 3, 1–6

Nelson, S. forthcoming, 'The pottery', in Parnell forthcoming

Nenk, B.S. 1992, 'Ceramic Culinary Moulds', in Gaimster and Redknap (eds) 1992, 290–302

Nenk, B.S. forthcoming (a), Post-medieval redware pottery from London in the British Museum

Nenk, B.S. forthcoming (b), 'Maiolica floor tiles in

England', in Gaimster & Nenk (eds), forthcoming

Nenk, B.S. forthcoming (c), 'A group of imported early Renaissance floor tiles from Brémontier-Massy, near Neufchâtel-en-Bray, northern France'

Norton, C. 1981, 'The British Museum Collection of Medieval Tiles', *Journal of the British Archaeological Association* 134, 107–119

Norton, C. 1992, *Carreaux de Pavement du Moyen Age et de la Renaissance. Collections du musée Carnavalet*, Paris

Orton, C.R. 1982, 'The Excavation of a Late Medieval/Transitional Pottery Site at Cheam, Surrey', *Surrey Archaeological Collections* 73, 49–92

Orton, C.R. 1985, 'Diffusion or impedence – obstacles to innovation in medieval ceramics, *Medieval Ceramics* 9, 21–34

Orton, C.R. 1988, 'Post-Roman Pottery', in P. Hinton (ed.), *Excavations in Southwark 1973–1976, Lambeth 1973–1979*, London and Middlesex Archaeological Society and Surrey Archaeological Society Joint Publication 3, 293–365

Orton, C.R., Orton, J. & Evans, P. 1974, 'Medieval and Tudor pottery', in Sheldon 1974, 293–365

Parnell, G. forthcoming, 'Excavations at the Broad Arrow Tower, Tower of London', *Transactions of the London and Middlesex Archaeological Society*

Pearce, J. 1992, *Border Wares*, Post-Medieval Pottery in London, 1500–1700, vol. 1

Pettegree, A. 1986, *Foreign Protestant Communities in Sixteenth-Century London*, Oxford

Pollard, S. & Crossley, D. 1968, *The Wealth of Britain, 1085–1966*

Power, E. & Postan, M.M. (eds) 1953, *Studies in English Trade in the 15th Century*

Pryor, S. and Blockley, K. 1978, 'A 17th-century Kiln Site at Woolwich', *Post-Medieval Archaeology* 12, 30–85

Rackham, B. 1926, *Early Netherlands Maiolica, with Special Reference to the tiles at The Vyne in Hampshire*

Rackham, B. 1939a, 'Early Tudor Pottery', *Transactions of the English Ceramic Circle* 2, no. 6, 15–25

Rackham, B. 1939b, 'A Netherlands maiolica vase from the Tower of London, *Antiquaries Journal* 19, 285–90

Rackham, B. 1959, 'Netherlands Maiolica Tiles', in M. Biddle, L. Barfield & A. Millard, 'The Excavation of

the Manor of the More, Rickmansworth, Hertfordshire', *Archaeological Journal* 116, 186–87

Ramsey, G.D. 1975, *The City of London in International Politics at the Accession of Elizabeth Tudor*, Manchester

Rowlands, J. 1988, *The Age of Dürer and Holbein. German Drawings 1400–1500*, British Museum

Saaler, M. 1996, *Anne of Cleves*

Sheldon, H. 1974, 'Excavations at Toppings and Sun Wharves, Southwark, 1970–1972', *Transactions of the London and Middlesex Archaeological Society* 25, 1–116

Schofield, J. 1995, *Medieval London Houses*

Southampton, 1976, *Luxury Goods from a Medieval Household*, Southampton Archaeological Research Committee

Stephenson, R. 1991, 'Post-medieval ceramic bird-pots from excavations in Greater London', *London Archaeologist* 6, no. 12, 320–21

Strauss, K. 1968, 'Der Kachelofen in der graphischen Darstellung des 15. und 16. Jahrhunderts', *Keramos* 39, 22–36

Thrupp, S. 1969, 'Aliens in and around London in the fifteenth century', in A.E.J. Hollaender & W. Kellaway (eds), *Studies in London History*, 251–72

Thurley, S. forthcoming, *Whitehall Palace: An Architectural History*, Historic Royal Places

Vince, A. 1985, 'The Saxon and Medieval Pottery of London: a review', *Medieval Archaeology* 29, 25–93

Vince, A. 1988, 'The date and frequency of German imports in the City of London from the 10th to 15th centuries', in D.R.M. Gaimster, M. Redknap & H.-H. Wegner (eds), *Zur Keramik des Mittelalters und der beginnenden Neuzeit im Rheinland. Medieval and Later Pottery from the Rhineland and its Markets*, British Archaeological Reports International Series 440, Oxford, 241–42

Vince, A. & Bell, R. 1992, 'Sixteenth Century Pottery from Acton Court, Avon', in Gaimster & Redknap (eds) 1992, 101–12

Webber, M. 1991, 'Excavations on the site of Norfolk House, Lambeth Road, SE1', *London Archaeologist* 6, no. 13, 343–50

Williams, B. 1979, 'Late Medieval Floor Tiles from Acton Court, Iron Acton, Avon, 1974', *Rescue Archaeology in the Bristol Area: 1*, City of Bristol Museum and Art Gallery Monograph No. 2, 61–76

14 Diet in Late Medieval and Early Modern London: the archaeobotanical evidence

John Giorgi

Introduction

During the late medieval and early modern period, London underwent great economic, social and cultural change as a result of topographical expansion, rapid population growth, inclusion of new immigrant groups and the development of global trade. A large body of archaeobotanical data, collected over the last twenty years from medieval and post-medieval deposits from sites within the City and Greater London, has been used for the study of continuity or change in the use of different food plants during this period.

The following discussion is based on the study of plant remains recovered from 14th- to 18th-century deposits, most of which are represented by seeds (in the broadest sense) and fruits, as these are usually the only parts of the plants that survive. The more fragile parts such as stem, leaf fragments, mosses and cereal bran are sometimes found in the better preserved deposits although they are often difficult to identify.

Preservation

Plant remains may be preserved in archaeological deposits in one of three ways. Preservation by waterlogging occurs as a result of an anoxic environment and consequent prevention of bacterial decomposition. The survival of plant remains by waterlogging can be exceptionally good in London owing to the location of the City on the River Thames and the steadily rising river level since the end of the last Ice Age. Large amounts of well-preserved waterlogged plant remains are found in waterfront dumps, where past land reclamation from the river has resulted in the dumping of various forms of debris from locations across the City. Away from the river, waterlogged plant remains are also found in pits, wells and other deep, or well-sealed features.

Secondly, plant remains may become mineralised when they are deposited in features which are damp and contain calcium and phosphate salts, with the calcium phosphate replacing the cell tissue of the fossil.[1] Sources of calcium phosphate include faecal deposits and bones; therefore such remains are often found in rubbish pits and cesspits.

Finally, plant remains may also be preserved by charring. This occurs when material is burnt but not reduced to mineral ash: for example, charred plant remains on the edges of fires, or during the preparation, cleaning, or cooking of certain foodstuffs, e.g. cereals.

Limitations of the Evidence

The nature of preservation is such that certain categories of plant material have a greater chance of surviving than others. For example, with regard to waterlogged remains, fluctuations in the watertable and the periodic drying out of deposits often results in only the preservation of the more robust parts of plants. Mineralised remains tend to consist mainly of fruit seeds deposited in cesspits and rubbish pits,

site	site type	sample nos
Cutler Street, E1 (CUT78)	industrial/domestic	20
Finsbury Island Pavement, EC2 (FIP92)	refuse dumps	37
Abbey of St Mary Graces/The Royal Navy Victualling Yard, E1 (MIN86)	monastic/manor/navy supplies	197
St John's Clerkenwell, EC1 (JAN90)	monastic/manor	46
St Mary Spital, 4–12 Norton Folgate, E1 (NRF88)	monastic/manor	26
The Fleet Valley, EC4 (PWB88/VAL88)	mixed features	7
Winchester Palace, SE1 (WP83)	manor	36
total		369

a) Main sites

Abbots Lane, SE1 (ABO92)	
2–16 Bevis Marks, EC3 (BEV80)	* (3)
Battle Bridge Lane (BAB95)	* (6)
Billingsgate Market Lorry Park, EC3 (BIG82)	* (1)
28–34 Bishopsgate, EC2 (BOP82)	* (2)
Baynards Castle, EC4 (BYD81)	* (1)
Chatsworth House, EC3 (HOU78)	* (5)
129 Lambeth Road, SE1 (LAM129/73)	
Lambeth Palace Gardens, SE1 (LAM525/85)	
1–6 Ludgate Circus Buildings, EC4 (LAT82)	* (1)
119–121 Cannon Street, EC4 (LIB82)	* (1)
54 Lombard Street, EC3 (LOA90)	
Liverpool Street and Broad Street Stations, EC2 (LSS85)	
Milk Street, EC2 (MLK76)	
Peninsular House, EC3 (PEN79)	* (1)
1–12 Rangoon Street, EC3 (RAG82)	* (1)
Swan Lane Car Park, EC4 (SWA81)	* (1)
Trig Lane, EC4 (TL74)	* (1)
Watling Court, EC4 (WAT78)	* (1)
15–29 Liverpool Road, N1 (LIV93)	* (6)
Platform Wharf, SE16 (PW90/91)	
283 Tooley Street, SE1 (TOS93)	* (2)
15–17,20,155–6 High Street, Uxbridge (UX88IX)	
Corney Reach, Chiswick (VCR95)	

(see figure 3 for location of sites in italics)

b) Other sites (* sites used in analysis with number of samples selected in brackets)

Fig. 14.1 *The Sites (see figs 14.2 and 14.3 for location)*

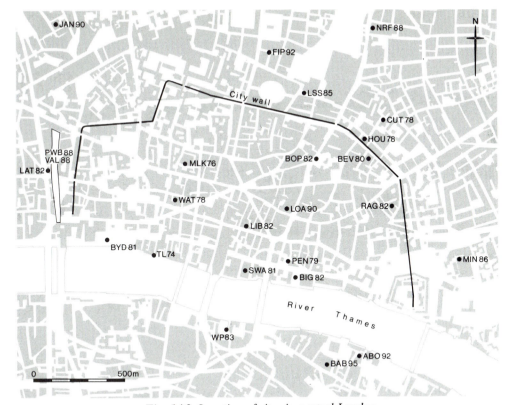

Fig. 14.2 *Location of sites in central London.*

Fig. 14.3 *Location of sites in Greater London.*

while charred remains tend to consist of cereal grains and occasional weed seeds. Furthermore, owing to the variable and often fragmentary condition of the plant material, which may also be affected by pre- and post-depositional processes, a large part of the botanical assemblage may either be impossible or difficult to identify.

Most plant remains recovered from urban sites are found in mixed seed assemblages, often with a high species diversity. These include seeds from plants that may have been growing *in situ*, either cultivated or as weeds, and plants that were deliberately or accidentally imported into the London by humans, animals or through natural processes, such as by wind or water. The variation in both seed production of different plants and their ability to disperse also means that certain plants may be over-represented in a sample. Perhaps the biggest problem in interpreting urban plant assemblages for evidence on diet is distinguishing the residues of native food plants from their wild relatives which grow commonly as weeds.

Sampling opportunities for the recovery of plant remains are also limited for this period. The continual redevelopment of the City has resulted in the truncation of late medieval and post-medieval deposits. This is particularly true of the post-medieval period, where the only surviving features on a site, other than structures, are usually deep pits and cellars, as a result of 19th-century basement construction and recent commercial development. Moreover, deposits which do survive may be contaminated by residual and intrusive material. This effects the City to a far greater extent than those areas outside the City walls, where the archaeological sequence has often escaped truncation.

At the present time there is a disparity in the quantity of recovered data from the medieval and post-medieval periods in London with less material from the latter period, particularly from the 18th century. While this is partly due to limited sampling opportunities, archaeological research programmes have often tended to ignore or give a low priority to post-medieval deposits on the basis that little could be gained from excavation of such a recent, well documented period.

The Current Data

For the following discussion, plant remains from 402 samples from 22 sites were considered (Fig. 14.1). The data were assembled from a number of different projects carried out by members of the Greater London Environmental Archaeology Service (GLEAS), and, from 1991, the Environmental Archaeology Section of the Museum of London Archaeology Service (MoLAS). Most of the plant remains were recovered from sites just outside the City walls, while botanical material from the City sites was collected mainly from isolated features, such as deep pits. The locations of the sites are shown in Figures 14.2 and 14.3. The majority of the samples used in this survey were from 16th- and 17th-century deposits; the best sampled features were rubbish pits and cesspits followed by dump deposits (Fig. 14.4).

Virtually all the plant remains were recovered from bulk soil samples, collected from well-stratified and datable deposits, with a sample size of between 10 and 40 litres for the recovery of charred (and mineralised) remains, and up to 10 litres for plant remains preserved by waterlogging. Much of the botanical material was separated from the soil samples by processing in a flotation machine although deposits with a high organic content were wet-sieved; both processes used a sieve size of 0.25mm for collecting the plant remains.

The botanical data have been used collectively to examine continuity or change in food plants from the late medieval through to the early modern period rather than on a site by site basis, partly because deposits from only one of the two periods may have been analysed for a particular site and also because the change in the character of the site often makes comparisons difficult, for example where monastic sites gave way to private residences. This was the case at St Mary Spital, 4–12 Norton Folgate, just north of the City, and the Abbey of St Mary Graces/ the Royal Navy Victualling Yard, immediately outside the City walls, to the east of the Tower of London.

	14th C	15th C	16th C	17th C	18th C	total
dump deposits*	2	1	75	5	2	= 85
layers	4	9	3	2	4	= 22
gully/drain fills	2	12	4	20	4	= 42
well fills	–	1	19	1	4	= 25
rubbish/cesspits	4	9	55	100	17	= 185
fills	1	10	23	6	3	= 43
total	13	42	179	134	34	= 402

* this includes waterfront dumps

Fig. 14.4 *Number of samples by feature and period.*

Results

Cereals (Fig. 14.5)

Cereals are occasionally represented on sites, but usually by only small numbers of charred grains. Sometimes mineralised grains and cereal bran fragments (preserved by waterlogging) are found in faecal deposits. The most common species in both late medieval and post-medieval samples are free-threshing wheat (*Triticum aestivum* s.l.), barley (*Hordeum sativum*), rye (*Secale cereale*), and oats (*Avena* spp.).

The paucity of evidence for cereals in this period means that it is neither possible to establish the relative importance of the different types nor how this picture may have changed over time. The main reason for so few cereal remains is that by the medieval period cereals were mainly processed and milled into flour outside central London. Cereals imported as flour would leave little recognisable trace as plant remains in archaeological deposits except sometimes as bran. The majority of cereals imported into London as whole grain would have been for animal fodder or for malting in the brewing industry.

During the late medieval and early post-medieval period cereals would have been used for bread, biscuit-making, cakes, pastry and in pottages, which were stews made from a mix of cereals, root veget-ables and sometimes meat (the national dish of all classes until at least the late 17th century).[2] White wheaten bread was popular in London from the late medieval period onwards,[3] reflected in the increasing number of bakers of white bread as opposed to those of brown bread,[4] although barley, rye and oats, as well as mixes of cereals, were also used for bread in southern and eastern England. The affluent classes could afford the whitest bread, 'wastel', while the poor consumed the cheaper coarse brown varieties, e.g. 'treat'.[5]

Wholemeal and white bread may sometimes be distinguished by bran fragments in human faecal deposits. Thus, large quantities of sizeable bran fragments in human waste would indicate wholemeal bread, while it has been suggested that smaller fragments of bran in well-preserved contexts might be interpreted as well-processed cereals, as was the case with wheat/rye bran in 16th-century cess deposits at 54 Lombard Street in the City.[6]

Barley was also used for making ale and beer. Germinated barley may be evidence of the cereal being prepared for malting although germination may also occur naturally in damp conditions. Seven large assemblages of six-row barley which included germinated grain were found in post-medieval deposits at Platform Wharf, Rotherhithe, one possible use of which could have been for brewing.[7] An extensive deposit of barley grain, burnt *in situ*, was

	14th C	15th C	16th C	17th C	18th C	nos of samples
bread wheat	+	+	+	+	+	43
wheat	+	+	+	+	+	14
barley	+	+	+	+		46
rye	+	+	+	+	+	20
oat	+	+	+	+		31
cereal grains	+	+	+	+		48
cereal bran	+	+	+	+		12
rice				+		1

Fig. 14.5 Cereals.

also uncovered on a warehouse floor within a 17th- to mid 19th-century building complex at Abbots Lane, Southwark.[8] This grain was probably intended for the production of malt for brewing, a use confirmed by documentary sources which record the presence of breweries in the area from 1418 onwards.[9]

Vegetables (Fig. 14.6)

Pulses, such as peas and beans, are occasionally found in late medieval and post-medieval deposits, usually as charred remains. For example, a small charred assemblage including pea (*Pisum sativum*), common vetch (*Vicia sativa*), lentil (*Lens culinaris*) and ?horsebean (cf. *Vicia faba*) was found in a 14th- to 15th-century burnt deposit at the site of St John's

Clerkenwell.[10] Seeds from the *Brassica/Sinapis* group, which includes a number of common vegetables, such as cabbage, swede and turnip, are often recovered, although the problem of identifying seeds of the individual species and varieties within these two genera means that it is usually not possible to establish whether the seeds are from cultivated species or their wild relatives. This problem also extends to other common vegetables such as carrot (*Daucus carota*), several seeds of which were found at Finsbury Island Pavement[11] on the site of Moorfields just outside the City walls. A major reason for the scarcity of archaeobotanical evidence for vegetables is that most of these plants are harvested and eaten before they set seed.

The documentary sources suggest that vegetables

	14th C	15th C	16th C	17th C	18th C	nos. of samples
lentil		+		+		2
pea		+				1
?horsebean		+				1
common vetch		+				1
legume frags	+	+	+	+		15
Brassica/Sinapis	+	+	+	+	+	95
carrot	+	+	+			6

Fig. 14.6 Pulses and other vegetables.

were an important part of the diet during this period. Pulses were sown in gardens and in fields everywhere about London according to the 16th-century herbalist John Gerrard (1545–1612). Vegetables were considered to be food of the poor,[12] with a traditional use in pottage, although they were sometimes mixed with cereals for bread, particularly following poor cereal harvests.[13] From the end of the 17th century vegetables also began to be used as an accompaniment to meat.[14] The development of intensive market gardening and the cultivation of common vegetables around London from the mid 17th century onwards[15] radically increased the availability of cheap food for Londoners. Bedding trenches associated with 17th-century market gardens have been found at 129 Lambeth Road[16] and within the grounds of Lambeth Palace and Corney Reach, Chiswick.[17]

Fruits (Fig. 14.7)

Fruits and nuts are the most commonly found food remains in both late medieval and post-medieval deposits in London, with a wide range of species being represented as waterlogged, mineralised and occasionally charred remains. This is due to the high number of cesspits and rubbish pits found on sites of these periods and the robust woody nature of many of the fruit pips and fruit stones. Mineralised remains of fruit in human faecal deposits provide direct evidence for consumption.

The most frequently found fruit pips are fig (*Ficus carica*), grape (*Vitis vinifera*), elder (*Sambucus nigra*) and blackberry/raspberry (*Rubus fruticosus/idaeus*), often represented by large numbers of seeds, partly by virtue of being abundant seed producers. Fairly common fruit pips are strawberry (*Fragaria vesca*), apple/crab apple (*Malus domestica/sylvestris*) and mulberry (*Morus* spp.). These fruits have all been represented in earlier deposits from sites in the City, from Saxo-Norman levels, for example in a 12th-century cesspit from Milk Street,[18] and from medieval waterfront dumps, also in the City.[19] Seeds of barberry (*Berberis vulgaris*), ?bilberry (cf. *Vaccinium myrtillus*), ?redcurrant (*Ribes* cf. *rubrum*)[20] and ?blackcurrant (*Ribes* cf. *nigrum*)[21] have occasionally been found, but only in deposits from the 16th century onwards.

The most common fruit stones that have been recovered belong to plum/bullace (*Prunus domestica* s.l.), sloe/blackthorn (*Prunus spinosa*), and cherry (*Prunus avium/cerasus*), all found in earlier medieval deposits from London,[22] with the variation in the size of the plum stones suggesting that a number of different varieties were present during this period. Indeed, in 1629 John Parkinson, in *Paridisi in Sole Paradisus Terrestris*, listed 61 different types of plums (including bullaces).[23] Less frequent finds are peach (*Prunus persica*) stones from 16th-century contexts[24] (also found in a 13th-century deposit from Billingsgate),[25] and an ?apricot (*Prunus* cf. *Armeniaca*) stone in an 18th-century deposit from Cutler Street in east London.[26] Shell fragments of hazelnut (*Corylus avellana*) appear on many sites while shell fragments of walnut (*Juglans regia*) are also sometimes found.[27]

Occasionally, archaeobotanical evidence for exotic fruits is found. A ?date (cf. *Phoenix dactylifera*) stone and a seed of *Citrus* (orange, lemon, lime) fruit were recovered from 18th-century deposits at 4–12 Norton Folgate, while a ?quince (cf. *Cydonia oblonga*) seed was found in mid 16th- to 17th-century deposits from the same site.[28] A *Citrus* seed was also found in a 15th-century deposit from Trig lane.[29] At 283 Tooley Street in Southwark, three small virtually complete coconuts (*Cocos nucifera*) were recovered from probable 17th-century deposits.[30] Broken seals at the top of each nut suggests that they might have been used for transporting some commodity. In deposits broadly dated to the post-medieval period, two barbasu (*Orbignya* sp.) palm nuts, an oil producing plant from Brazil, were found in Thames foreshore deposits, and a brazil nut (*Bertholletia excelsa*) identified in a pit fill from Uxbridge in west London.[31]

Documentary records suggest that all the common fruit species listed above were used for food and drink during this period.[32] The records of the Carpenters' Company of the City of London, which cover the period 1438–1516, mention apples, pears, cherries and mulberries, as well as some of the more exotic fruits which are only occasionally recovered as archaeobotanical remains, for example, quinces (first record 1505), oranges (1500), and dates (1492). To this list may be added barberries, figs and lemons from later records of the Carpenters' Company covering the period 1571–1591.[33] Little fruit was consumed fresh in the medieval and early post-medieval period, as it was considered unhealthy and associated with common illnesses such as diarrhoea and dysentery.[34] Instead, fruit was mainly cooked with sugar and spices and often prepared in pies, pastries and puddings,[35] or used in pottage.[36] Figs, barberries, hazels and walnuts were sometimes preserved or stored for later consumption, while soft fruits were made into conserves. Attitudes changed during the 18th century and fresh fruit became regarded as an essential part of a healthy diet.[37]

With regard to drink, wine was made from elderberries as an adulterant of more expensive foreign wines or to disguise English raisin wine.[38] Other fruits, such as cherries, blackberries and raspberries, were fermented with sugar from the late 17th century onwards to produce alcoholic drinks,[39] while apples were used for cider.[40]

The cultivation of English grapes had declined by the Elizabethan period,[41] partly due to cheap wine imports, possibly also climatic change, and the Dissolution of the monasteries. Figs were grown in some gardens in sheltered places[42] although it was difficult to obtain good crops from home grown figs.[43] Therefore, many of the fig and grape seeds found in London deposits were probably from imported dried fruit. Customs accounts for London between 1480 and 1481 record the import of figs and grapes as dried fruits from Spain, Portugal and Italy.[44]

Many of the fruits found as archaeobotanical remains were listed by the horticulturalist Thomas Tusser (c.1524–1580) in *Five Hundreth Pointes of Good Husbandrie* (1590).[45] His work mentions some of the rarer finds, such as bilberry, redcurrant, blackcurrant, apricot, and *Citrus* fruits. In the late medieval and early post-medieval periods many fruits were grown in London in private gardens and gardens attached to monastic houses while others, such as sloe, blackberries, elderberries, and strawberries, may have been collected from the wild. The expansion and increased urbanisation of London, however, restricted fruit growing and led to the development of new areas of cultivation around the City.

Increasing imports of fruits during this period makes it difficult to establish from the archaeobotanical record which were imported and which were home grown. However, one may speculate on the likely origin of the archaeobotanical material if dates of introduction can be established from the documentary records. For example, the earliest documented orange trees in England are those grown on the Beddington estate in Croydon by Sir Frances Carew, sometime before 1562.[46] In the 17th century orangeries were built by the wealthy to protect the fruit trees from British winters,[47] although oranges were still a rare commodity by the time of Pepys.[48] The seed of *Citrus* sp. from 4–12 Norton Folgate[49] was from an 18th-century context and thus may be from a home grown specimen, although an earlier 15th-century find from Trig Lane[50] was probably from an import. The customs accounts for London for the late 15th century show that oranges were imported from Spain and Portugal and lemons from Italy.

The cost of native fresh fruit was high in the late medieval and early post-medieval period because of the relatively short season of availability, although in the first half of the 18th century prices did fall, probably as a result of increased commercialism and the expansion of fruit growing around London. The archaeobotanical results show an increase in the range of fruits present in the early modern period, with the appearance of more exotic fruits, although usually some time after the first historical record. The large number of fruits represented in the samples, even allowing for an obvious preservation bias, does suggest that some fruits (e.g. grapes and figs) were consumed by much of London society.

Cucurbits (Fig. 14.7)

Seeds of cucurbits, which include pumpkins, cucumber, squashes and gourds, are occasionally found in late medieval and post-medieval deposits, although they are often difficult to identify to species because of cross fertilisation and hence a large number of hybrids. Finds in London have included seeds of cucumber (*Cucumis sativus*), melon (*C. melo*), watermelon (*Citrullus lanatus*) and New World *Cucurbita* species, a group which includes marrows,

	14th C	15th C	16th C	17th C	18th C	nos of samples
barberry			+	+	+	8
grape	+	+	+	+	+	182
fig	+	+	+	+	+	302
blackberry/raspberry	+	+	+	+	+	220
elder	+	+	+	+	+	179
mulberry			+	+	+	24
strawberry	+	+	+	+	+	96
sloe/blackthorn	+	+	+	+	+	36
plum/bullace	+	+	+	+	+	62
cherry	+	+	+	+	+	33
peach			+			3
?apricot					+	1
Prunus spp.	+	+	+	+	+	48
apple/crab apple			+	+	+	35
pear				+	+	2
apple/pear	+	+	+	+	+	88
walnut		+	+	+		9
hazel	+	+	+	+	+	42
?redcurrant			+		+	4
?blackcurrant				+		1
currant (*Ribes* sp.)			+	+	+	3
?bilberry			+			1
?date					+	1
orange, lemon (*Citrus* sp)		+			+	2
?quince			+			1
melon		+	+	+		4
watermelon			+			2
marrows etc. (*Cucurbita* sp.)			+	+		3
cucumber			+	+	+	16
coconut				+		2

Fig. 14.7 Fruits and cucurbits.

pumpkins, squashes and gourds. The earliest finds of seeds belonging to both Old World and New World cucurbits in London date to the 16th century (with the exception of cucumber seeds in Roman deposits).[51] For example, cucumber, watermelon, melon and *Cucurbita* sp. were represented in 16th- to 17th-century deposits from the Royal Navy Victualling Yard.[52]

Cucumber was the only cucurbit commonly grown in Britain by the 16th century, with the purchase of cucumber seeds by Lambeth Palace mentioned in 1321–22.[53] Thus seeds of this species, found in 16th- to 18th-century deposits, may represent home grown produce. Cultivars of melon and watermelon suitable for greenhouse production in a British climate, however, were not developed until the 17th century.[54] Hence, 16th-century finds of these species in London, for instance, in dump deposits at Finsbury Island Pavement,[55] might represent imported fruits, probably from southern Europe.

The New World cucurbits were introduced into western Europe in the early contact period and are described in 16th- and 17th-century herbals. In the mid 16th century Thomas Tusser, in *A Hundreth Good Pointes of Husbandrie* (1557) mentions that 'pompions' (marrows) were commonly grown.[56] If Tusser is reliable, it suggests that the earliest *Cucurbita* seeds found in deposits dating from between 1560 and 1635 at the Royal Navy Victualling Yard,[57] and in 17th-century contexts from Cutler Street[58] and Baynard's Castle in the City,[59] might represent home grown produce.

Cucumber, watermelon and melon were used mainly for their edible flesh although oil could also be extracted from the seeds for cooking. Cucumbers were probably used as a vegetable salad in summer and pickled as gherkins for winter food.[60] The New World species, such as marrows and pumpkins, were eaten as a mature vegetable in baking, jam or pies, while as an immature plant, they were consumed fresh or stewed, boiled or fried.

Herbs and Spices (Fig. 14.8)

Seeds of the following herbs and spices have been found in medieval and post-medieval deposits in London: caraway (*Carum carvi*), coriander (*Coriandrum sativum*), dill (*Anethum graveolens*), fennel (*Foeniculum vulgare*), garden parsley (*Petroselinum crispum*), summer savoury (*Satureja hortensis*), rosemary (*Rosmarinus officinalis*), opium poppy (*Papaver somniferum*), white mustard (*Sinapis alba*), black mustard (*Brassica nigra*), allspice (*Pimenta dioica*) and pepper (*Piper nigrum*).[61] These plants are usually represented by only small numbers of seeds although occasionally large numbers of seeds of one species are found. For example, many coriander seeds were recovered from several late 16th- to early 17th-century deposits at the Royal Navy Victualling Yard.[62] For the more common species however, which can also grow as weeds, e.g. opium poppy and mustard, their use as flavourings may only be implied when large numbers of seeds of one species are found. For instance, large numbers of black mustard seeds were recovered from an 18th-century pit fill at 4–12 Norton Folgate.[63]

Culinary herbs and spices were used for flavouring, both fresh and dried. Black and white mustard seeds were ground together to produce mustard flour

	14th C	15th C	16th C	17th C	18th C	nos. samples
opium poppy	+	+	+	+	+	19
black mustard	+	+	+	+	+	12
white mustard		+	+			4
summer savoury			+			2
coriander	+	+	+	+	+	17
fennel		+	+	+		18
dill	+	+	+	+		12
garden parsley			+	+		3
caraway			+	+	+	6
rosemary			+			1
pepper			+		+	5
allspice					+	1

Fig. 14.8 Herbs and spices.

and used as a condiment.[64] Allspice, found on just one occasion in an 18th-century pit fill at 4–12 Norton Folgate,[65] and black pepper, had many culinary uses, the latter as a preservative in curing meats and for overcoming the smell of putrefying food. Pepper has been used in this country since at least the 11th century, when it was mentioned in the Billingsgate Tolls.[66] It was apparently already one of the cheaper spices by the late medieval period[67] and is mentioned in a number of entries from the Carpenters' accounts for the 1490s. Peppercorns have been recovered from several sites although the earliest post-Roman find from London is from a 16th-century cesspit on 54 Lombard Street.[68] It is perhaps not surprising that pepper is rarely found in archaeological deposits as it would have been ground up before being used.

Other Food Plants (Fig. 14.9)

Other possible food plants recovered as archaeobotanical remains include flax/linseed (*Linum usitatissimum*), and hop (*Humulus lupulus*), both of which are occasionally represented by large numbers of seeds. For instance, large numbers of flax seeds were recovered from a 16th-century waterfront dump at Winchester Palace, Southwark[69] (although these could represent the residues of the plant used for making fibres). Large quantities of waterlogged hop seeds and bracts were found in the fills of several large early 17th- to mid 18th-century cut features at 15–29 Liverpool Road, Islington,[70] and large amounts of hop seeds were recovered from several 16th- to 17th-century deposits both at the Royal Navy Victualling Yard[71] and at Battle Bridge Lane in Southwark.[72] Rice (*Oryza sativa*) has been found on one occasion in a late 17th-century cesspit at Billingsgate.[73]

Documentary records show that flax and hops were grown in gardens,[74] while the field cultivation of hops as a preservative and flavouring in brewing[75] was developed in Kent by the Huguenots in the early 16th century. Seeds of the flax plant were used in bread and stews[76] and oil from the seeds used for cooking, although the main use of flax would have been as a fibre plant. Documentary sources show that beer and ale were widely consumed because of their low cost and brewed both commercially and at home. By 1688 public houses were selling 12 million barrels a year, the equivalent of 36 gallons for every person in the country.[77]

Wild Plants

Many wild plants, now thought of as weeds and represented in archaeological deposits, may also have been exploited for food from time to time. Thus, the leaves of many plants, such as fat hen (*Chenopodium album*), nettles (*Urtica* spp.), corn spurrey (*Spergula arvensis*), docks (*Rumex* spp.), and goosefoots/oraches (*Chenopodium/Atriplex* spp.), may have been picked from gardens, fields and woods and added to pottage or eaten as green vegetables. The seeds of these plants are frequently found in late medieval and post-medieval deposits in London. However, as they are common weeds of disturbed ground and waste places, high seed producers, and usually recovered in mixed assemblages, it is virtually impossible to establish whether or not they were actually used as food.

Exotic Introductions and Global Trade

The development of global trade and its effect on the plant food diet of Londoners during this period is

	14th C	15th C	16th C	17th C	18th C	nos samples
flax	+	+	+	+	+	17
hop	+	+	+	+	+	41

Fig. 14.9 Other food plants.

Fig. 14.10a–d *Photographs of plant remains:* **a**, *curcubits – cucumber/melon (top), marrow/pumpkin etc. (bottom);* **b**, *allspice;* **c**, *fruit pips including grape, fig, elder, apple/pear, mulberry, blackberry/raspberry;* **d**, *fruit stones and nutshell fragments including peach and walnut (Scale on photographs in mm).*

indicated by traces of exotic plants in archaeological deposits. It is also interesting to compare the first historical record with the first archaeobotanical record to establish how quickly and widespread the use of some of these exotic food plants may have become. The presence of exotic plants, however, may not imply direct trading links with the country of origin, as they may have arrived in London indirectly through an intermediate trader. For example, the customs accounts for London in 1480–81 show that dates from North Africa were imported via Italy.

Contacts and trade with the New World are shown by *Cucurbita* seeds, such as marrow and pumpkins, found in 16th-century deposits in London soon after the initial settlement of North America. The 18th-century find of allspice is evidence of trade between Britain and the West Indies, although the first record of the import of allspice to Europe is much earlier, dating to 1601.[78]

Evidence of contact or trade with South America includes the finds of brazil nut and barbasu palm nut. These finds, as noted above, however, could only be broadly dated to the post-medieval period. The coconuts from 283 Tooley Street in probable 17th-century deposits, indicate trading links with tropical countries, coconuts growing at low altitudes in Asia, Africa and South America.

Trading links with the Far East are suggested by finds of pepper in 16th- to 18th-century deposits although the documentary evidence shows that pepper had already arrived in Britain in the medieval period via trade with other countries. Nevertheless, the demand for black pepper played a major part in the search for new trade routes to south-east Asia in the 15th and 16th centuries.[79] Other species indicative of trade include the 17th-century rice husks from Billingsgate (although rice is mentioned as early as 1510 in the Carpenters' records).

Other exotic commodities which first appeared in London during this period, such as tea, sugar, cocoa and tobacco, are unlikely to be found as archaeobotanical remains, because many of these plants would have been part or fully processed before being exported.[80] Documentary records, however, show that London was the dominant importer and consumer of such exotic goods,[81] being at the heart of colonial expansion and trade, with the high levels of wealth and income in the capital, even among the labouring classes, giving Londoners a purchasing power at least twice that of the rest of the country.[82]

Discussion

The archaeobotanical evidence collected from late medieval and post medieval deposits in London has shown that a wide range of plant foods was available, with an increase in the range of certain foodstuffs, for instance, fruits, and continuity in the use of others during this period. Occasionally, archaeobotanical evidence for exotic food plants has been found. The finds of these plants often appear only several centuries after the first historical records for their introduction, presumably a reflection of the initial scarcity of such goods, and probably gives some indication of when they became more widespread.

However, on the strength of the current archaeobotanical data, it is difficult either to quantify or establish the relative importance of different categories of plant foods in the diet of Londoners and how this may have changed over time. Thus, the plant remains present a rather conservative picture of diet during this period, with the data limited in a number of ways. The biggest problem is the relative survival of different plant foods in the archaeological record with little evidence for pre-processed foods or plants which are harvested and eaten before setting seed. Thus, there is an abundance of fruit species, which are probably over-represented, although this does allow us to examine the relative frequency of different species, the appearance of new ones and how this picture may have changed over time. On the other hand, there is little evidence for cereals, pulses and common vegetables, despite being staple foods during this period according to the documentary records.

Many of the problems outlined above may simply be addressed by the collection of more data, particularly from areas with well-preserved plant remains, e.g. areas near the river, and also from sites with low intrusive activity, for example outside the City walls. Also, much of the evidence currently available comes from high status sites; thus it is important to obtain, if possible, botanical data from low status sites to examine possible variations in diet. It may also be possible to use the plant remains, in conjunction with faunal and artefactual data, to establish dietary variation based on cultural and ethnic differences.

The inability to identify some plant remains may in future be addressed by the application of recent identification techniques to leaf and stem epidermis,[83] bran fragments[84] and possibly charred roots and tuber fragments.[85] Some of these techniques may help in the recognition of vegetables for which there is presently little other archaeobotanical evidence.

Other biological, artefactual and structural evidence from features/areas from which plant remains are recovered, may aid the interpretation of the botanical remains, and establish whether they represent the residues of used plants or simply weeds, as well as providing information on foodstuffs for which there is an absence of archaeobotanical data due to the problems of preservation. For instance, the appearance of exotic pre-processed plant foods on the London market may be detected from associated artefactual evidence, for example from sugar refining vessels, recovered from 18 sites in London, and tobacco pipes, found on many sites, from 1620 onwards.[86] Osteological data may also provide evidence on the changing use of foodstuffs, e.g. increases in dental disease due to a higher sugar intake.[87]

Certainly, a multi-disciplinary approach is necessary when considering the complexity of diet during this period in London and the effects of social, economic and cultural developments in the City. Consumer choice would have been based on a multitude of factors, including economic status, social class, occupation, ethnic group and contemporary ideas on diet, health and nutrition. The status of food was inextricably linked with market availability, and as particular foods became more common, so their status diminished accordingly.

The archaeobotanical evidence, presented above, has shown that that there is both continuity and change in the use of different food plants during the late medieval and early modern period. It is therefore important that future research programmes on archaeological sites, which include the recovery of archaeobotanical remains, should consider this period as one rather than divide it along historical lines.

Notes

1. Green 1979, 279–84.
2. Wilson 1976, 191.
3. *Ibid.* 234.
4. Dyer 1989, 199.
5. *Ibid.* 199.
6. Holden 1992.
7. Giorgi, Rackham & Sidell 1993.
8. Giorgi & Sidell 1993.
9. Bluer 1993, 59–66.
10. Davis, forthcoming (a).
11. Giorgi, forthcoming (a).
12. Weinstein 1990, 96.
13. Wilson 1976, 221.
14. Weinstein 1990, 97.
15. *Ibid.* 95.
16. Hinton 1988, 159–67.
17. Derek Seeley pers. comm.
18. Jones, Straker & Davis 1991.
19. Pearson, in prep.
20. For example, in Davis, forthcoming (b).
21. For example, in a 17th-century cesspit at Billingsgate Market Lorry Park, Lower Thames Street: Armitage *et al* 1987, 279.
22. Jones *et al.,* 1991, 18; Pearson in prep.
23. Wilson 1976, 305.
24. For example, in deposits associated with the Royal Navy Victualling Yard: Giorgi, in prep. (a).
25. Pearson, in prep.
26. Giorgi 1995a.
27. Giorgi, in prep (a).
28. Davis, forthcoming (b).
29. Pearson, in prep.
30. Giorgi, Sidell & Wilkinson 1994.
31. Davis 1993.
32. Wilson 1976.
33. Marsh (ed.) 1914; Ainsworth (ed.) 1937. The second and fifth volumes of the accounts of the Carpenters' Company are used here as an illustration; several other companies have equally full records of their food purchases from 1500 to the 19th century.
34. Weinstein 1990, 82.
35. Wilson 1976, 312.
36. *Ibid.* 299.
37. Weinstein 1990, 99.
38. Grieve 1992, 268.
39. Wilson 1976, 352.
40. *Ibid.* 360.
41. *Ibid.* 349.
42. Thomas Fairchild in the *City Gardener* (1722) mentions figs growing in Rolls Garden in Chancery

Lane and Dr Bennet's garden in Cripplegate: Rohde 1932, 189.

43. *Ibid*. 296.
44. Cobb (ed.) 1990. All references to the customs records are to this volume.
45. Wilson 1976, 305–6.
46. *Ibid*. 308.
47. Haliwell 1991, 71.
48. Wilson 1976, 308.
49. Davis, forthcoming (b).
50. Pearson, in prep.
51. Willcox 1977.
52. Giorgi, in prep. (a).
53. Stott 1990, 37.
54. Letts 1991.
55. Giorgi, forthcoming (a).
56. Rohde 1932, 106.
57. Giorgi, in prep. (a).
58. Giorgi 1995a.
59. Giorgi 1995b.
60. Weinstein 1990, 84.
61. Allspice, pepper and black mustard were all identified in 18th-century deposits at 4–12 Norton Folgate: Davis, forthcoming (b).
62. Giorgi, in prep. (a).
63. Davis, forthcoming (b).
64. Mabey 1972.
65. Davis, forthcoming (b).
66. Greig 1988, 126.
67. Wilson 1976, 254.
68. Holden 1992. Pepper was also found in a 17th-century drainfill at Baynards Castle and in a 18th-century context at the Royal Navy Victualling Yard.
69. Giorgi, forthcoming (b).
70. Giorgi 1994.
71. Giorgi, in prep. (a).
72. Giorgi, in prep. (b).
73. Armitage *et al.* 1987, 279.
74. Greig 1988, 114.
75. *Ibid*. 115.
76. *Ibid*. 122.
77. Hibbert 1987, 288.
78. *New Encyclopaedia Brittanica Micropaedia* vol. 1 (15th edition, 1990), 260.
79. Zeven 1976, 234.
80. Outside London, coffee (*Coffea arabica*) beans were recovered from a bronze cannon from the seabed off Padstow, in Clapham unpublished, cited in Greig, 1991, 329. Possible finds of cocoa (*Theobroma cacao*) were identified in Dublin: Geraghty, pers. comm. cited in Greig, *ibid*. 33.

81. London had by far the greatest number of licensed dealers in coffee and tea in England and Wales during the 18th century: Chartres 1986, 176.
82. *Ibid*. 191. Brandon & Short 1990, 157.
83. Tomlinson 1985, 1985a.
84. Dickson 1987, 95–102.
85. Hather 1991, 661–75.
86. G. Egan, pers. comm.
87. For example, a study of 400 human skeletons studied from the New Churchyard, Broad Street, in use between 1569 until the early 1700s, provided indirect information on the changing use of foodstuffs, with an increase in dental disease and tooth loss in the skeletons compared to medieval examples, attributed to the growing use of sugar in the diet in the post-medieval period: Malt 1991, 37.

Bibliography

Ainsworth, J. (ed.) 1937, *Records of the Worshipful Company of Carpenters Vol V. Warden's Account Book 1571–1591*, Oxford

Armitage, P., Locker, A. & Straker, V. 1987, 'Environmental Archaeology in London. A Review', in Keeley (ed.) 1987, 252–331

Astill, G. & Grant, A. (eds) 1988, *The Countryside of Medieval England*, Oxford

Beier, A.L. & Finlay, R. (eds) 1986, *The Making of the Metropolis, London 1500–1700,* London & New York

Bluer, R. 1993, 'Excavations at Abbots Lane, Southwark', *London Archaeologist* 7 (3), 59–66

Blatherwick, S., Stephenson, R., Betts, I. & Malt, D. (eds) 1993, 'Platform Wharf. A Post-Excavation Assessment Report and Updated Research Design' (MOLAS Archive Report)

Bluer, R. (ed.) 1993, 'Abbots Lane, London SE1. London Borough of Southwark. An Assessment of the 1992 Archaeological Excavations' (MOLAS Archive Report)

Brandon, P. & Short, B. 1990 , *The South East from AD 1000*

Chartres, J. 1986, 'Food consumption and internal trade', in Beier & Finlay (eds) 1986, 168–96

Cobb, H.S. (ed.) 1990, *The Overseas Trade of London. Exchequer Customs Accounts 1480–1*, London Record Society Publications 27

Davis, A. 1993, 'Uxbridge Market Town: Assessment of Environmental Material from Soil Samples' (MoLAS Environmental Archive Report)

Davis A. forthcoming (a), 'The Plant Remains from St John's Clerkenwell'

Davis A. forthcoming (b), 'The Plant Remains', in Thomas *et al.* (eds) forthcoming

Dickson, C.A. 1987, 'The identification of cereals from ancient bran fragments', *Circaea* 4, 95–102

Dyer, C. 1989, *Standards of Living in the Later Middle Ages. Social Change in the Later Middle Ages*, Cambridge

Forsyth, H. 1990, 'Medicinal and Kitchen Gardening', in Galinou (ed.), 56–65

Galinou, M. (ed.) 1990, *London's Pride. The Glorious History of the Capital's Gardens*

Giorgi, J. 1994, 'Liverpool Road (LIV93): The Environmental Evidence' (MoLAS Environmental Archive Report)

Giorgi, J. 1995a, 'The Environmental Samples from Post-Medieval Deposits at Cutler Street (CUT78)' (MoLAS Environmental Archive Report 13/96)

Giorgi, J. 1995b, 'An Environmental Sample from a Post-Medieval Sewage System at Baynards Castle (BYD81)' (MoLAS Environmental Archive Report 08/96)

Giorgi J. forthcoming (a), 'The Plant Remains', in Malcolm (ed.) forthcoming

Giorgi, J. forthcoming (b), 'The Plant Remains', in Seeley *et al* (eds) forthcoming

Giorgi, J. in prep., 'Environmental Evidence in Post-Medieval London: A Review of the Evidence and Considerations for Future Research'

Giorgi, J. in prep. (a), 'The Plant Remains', in Grainger (ed.) in prep. (a)

Giorgi, J. in prep. (b), 'The Plant Remains', in Grainger (ed.) in prep. (b)

Giorgi J. & Sidell J. 1993, 'The Environmental Evidence', in Bluer (ed.) 1993, 164–73

Giorgi, J., Rackham, D.J. & Sidell, J. 1993, 'Environmental Assessment', in Blatherwick *et al.* (eds) 1993, 20–4

Giorgi, J., Sidell, J. & Wilkinson, K. 1994, Appendix 5, 'The Environmental Evidence', in Saxby (ed.) 1994

Grainger, I. (ed.) in prep. (a), 'Excavations at the Abbey of St Mary Graces'

Grainger, I. (ed.) in prep. (b), 'Excavations at Battle Bridge Lane, Southwark'

Green, F. 1979, 'Phosphatic mineralisation of seeds from archaeological sites', *Journal of Archaeological Science* 6, 279–84

Greig, J. 1988, 'Plant Resources', in Astill & Grant (eds) 1988, 108–127

Greig J. 1991, 'The British Isles', in van Zeist *et al.* (eds) 1991, 299–334

Grieve, M. 1992, *A Modern Herbal*, Harmondsworth

Hather, J.G. 1991, 'The Identification of Charred Archaeological Remains of Vegetative Parenchymous Tissue', *Journal of Archaeological Science* 18, 661–75

Haliwell, B. 1990, 'Flowers and Plants in the Seventeenth Century', in Galinou (ed.), 66–77

Hibbert, C. 1987, *The English. A Social History 1066–1945*

Hinton, P. 1988, '129 Lambeth Road', in Hinton (ed.) 1988, 159–67

Hinton, P. (ed.) 1988, *Excavations in Southwark 1973–76; Lambeth 1973–79* (Joint Publication No. 3, London & Middlesex Archaeological Society and Surrey Archaeological Society)

Holden, T. 1992, 'The Plant Remains from a Cesspit on 54 Lombard Street (LOA90)' (Museum of London GLEAS Environmental Archive Report PLA 03/92)

Jones, G., Straker, V. & Davis, A. 1991, 'Early Medieval Plant Use and Ecology', in Vince (ed.) 1991, 347–379

Keeley, H. (ed.) 1987, *Environmental Archaeology. A Regional Review* Vol II (Historic Buildings and Monuments Commission for England, Occasional Paper No. 1)

Letts, J. 1991, Cucurbits (unpublished report)

Mabey, R. 1972, *Food for Free. A guide to the edible wild plants of Britain,* Glasgow

Malcolm, G. (ed.) forthcoming, 'Excavations at Finsbury Island Pavement', *London and Middlesex Archaeological Society Transactions*

Malt, D. 1991, *The New Churchyard, in Broadgate and Liverpool Station*

Marsh, B. (ed.) 1914, *Records of the Worshipful Company of Carpenters Vol II. Warden's Account Book 1438–1516*, Oxford

New Encyclopaedia Brittanica Micropaedia vol. 1 (15th edition, 1990)

Pearson, E., in prep. 'Plant Remains from Medieval waterfront dumps'

Rohde, E.S. 1932, *The Story of the Garden*

Saxby, D. (ed.) 1994, '283 Tooley Street, London, SE1. An Archaeological Excavation' (MOLAS Archive Report)

Seeley, D., Carlin, M. & Philpotts, C. (eds) forthcoming, *The palace in Southwark of the medieval bishops of Winchester: excavations at Winchester Palace, London, 1983–90, Part 2*

Simmonds, N.W. (ed.) 1976, *Evolution of Crop Plants*

Stott, P. 1990, 'The Medieval Garden', in Galinou (ed.) 1990, 30–41

Thomas, C., Sloane, B. & Phillpotts, C. (eds) forthcoming, *St Mary Spital, London. Excavations at the Priory and Hospital 1935–1991*

Tomlinson, P. 1985, 'Use of vegetative plant remains in the identification of dye plants from waterlogged 9th-10th century A.D. deposits at York', *Journal of Archaeological Science* 12, 269–83

Tomlinson, P. 1985a, 'An aid to the identification of fossil buds, bud scales, and catkin bracts of British trees and shrubs', *Circaea* 3, 45–130

Weinstein, R., 1990, 'London's market gradens in the early modern period', in Galinou (ed.) 1990, 80–99

Willcox, G. 1977, 'Exotic plants from Roman waterlogged sites in London', *Journal of Archaeological Science* 4, 269–282

Wilson, C.A. 1976, *Food and Drink in Britain. From the Stone Age to Recent Times*, Harmondsworth

Vince, A.G. (ed.) 1991, *Aspects of Saxon and Norman London 2: Finds and Environmental evidence*, London and Middlesex Archaeological Society Special Paper 12

van Zeist, W., Wasylikowa, K. & Behre, K. (eds) 1991, *Progress in Old World Palaeoethnobotany. A retrospective view on the occasion of 20 years of the International Work Group for Palaeoethnobotany*, Rotterdam

Zeven, A.C. 1976, 'Black Pepper *Piper nigrum* (Piperaceae)', in Simmonds (ed.) 1976, 234

15 Wound Wire and Silver Gilt: changing fashions in dress accessories c.1400 – c.1600

Geoff Egan and Hazel Forsyth

Introduction (GE & HF)

The periods termed 'medieval and 'post-medieval' saw a constant transformation and modification of decorative motifs and other stylistic traits as well as of the forms and usage of whole categories of dress accessories. While plain versions of some basic items such as aglets remained remarkably constant, many archaeological finds – the primary source for information on mass-produced fashions at the lower end of the social scale – clearly illustrate this fluidity. Relatively few finds are of precious metal and only a tiny proportion of the excavated material features even oblique reference to mainstream artistic motifs. It has proved impossible to define any satisfactory chronological watershed which saw 'medieval' fashions superseded by 'later' ones.

There are at present great problems in dating accurately finds assemblages from the mid 15th to the mid 16th centuries, partly through a marked lack of tightly dated reference material, but mainly because this century has, across the country, tended to fall into neglect between the two period stools. The continuing diversity in fashions does, however, give scope to begin to define a few subtle shifts and perhaps some major trends too within this time bracket. The following discussion largely deals with London finds, reflecting the workplace of the writers; where appropriate, published material from else-where is mentioned.

The abundance of finds in the capital of dress accessories attributed to c.1150 – c.1450[1] might suggest that a synthesis dealing with the subsequent century and a half should have plenty of excavated material to draw on. The chronological biases of the capital's archaeological record, however, mean that the sites which for that first 300–year period produced almost 500 buckles,[2] furnished fewer than 20 attributable to the next century and a half.[3] The explanation lies in the cessation of setting down finds-rich, land-reclamation dumps of rubbish (and hence a lack or buried foreshores too), together with a much more widespread phenomenon, observed in several towns, of the ending by the 15th century of the general accumulation of deposits which had gradually raised the ground surface. In addition, the increasing insertion over the next five centuries of deep foundations, cellars and services inevitably removed first the vulnerable uppermost deposits. The overall effect in many urban areas across the country is that late 15th- and 16th-century features tend to have a relatively poor survival rate. The most profitable opportunities in the future for investigation of the material culture of these elusive centuries in London, and possibly in the country as a whole, seem (from from finds assemblages already recovered there but not yet fully assimilated) to lie in the strip of land alongside the Thames on the south side, especially eastwards of the Metropolitan centre.

Although the Museum of London's collections in this field are the most extensive in existence for this difficult period, few of the finds come from securely dated contexts. Many of the accessories within the Museum's reserve collection were recovered by chance and most have been retrieved from the

Thames foreshore, or from the sites of 16th-century rubbish dumps located around the northern perimeter of the City. On the whole provenance is vague and for some finds unknown. The vagaries of the evidence are such, that definitive statements about the major artefact groups of dress accessories can only be made with utmost caution. Whilst some groups are extremely plentiful, such as pins, plain aglets, buckles and hook fasteners, others are significantly under-represented. Only a dozen head-dress frames have been identified for example, although there may be others as yet unrecognised amongst assemblages of copper wire waste. Within the chance find corpus there are also a few accessories which are unparalleled elsewhere, and yet their very survival must surely indicate a certain abundance in the 16th century.

Furthermore, the impressive array of pins, dress hooks, fasteners, buttons, hooks and eyes, aglets, head-dress frames and so on recovered to date, does not correlate particularly well with documentary evidence. Manuscripts provide a wealth of quantitative evidence, but little descriptive detail to help with attribution or the identification of types. In addition, there are classes of material which contemporaries described but which cannot be identified within the archaeological corpus, such as the cheap rings, chains and trinkets of 'counterfeit' precious metal purchased at St Martin's fair during the 15th and 16th century. The popularity of these tawdry goods is well attested in literature, and it would appear that many Londoners would 'rather wear a Martin chain, the price of 8 pence, than they would be unchained,'[4] even though this meant that they had purchased an item which was 'fair to the eye and rich outside, but if a man should break them asunder and look into them, they are nothing but brass and copper'.[5] But although many of the archaeological and chance-find dress accessories are of poor quality, and are apparently similar to goods sold at St Martin's fair, they cannot be assigned to a particular trading district or production site. There is archaeological evidence for dress accessory manufacture in London, which includes an important group of cheaply made strap ends and buckles from the Blossoms Inn site,[6] and tentative evidence of aglet production in Coventry,[7] but on the whole it is unclear whether dress acces-

ories were made here or abroad. Where documentary evidence for domestic manufacture does exist, it is not currently possible to attribute finds to the production site.

Portraits provide a useful source of information, but most reflect higher status products which rarely correspond with surviving artefacts, and the garments usually conceal methods of attachment, especially of the most basic and functional kind. When dress accessories are depicted the scale is often misleading, and items are often slightly enlarged for effect. Furthermore, it is difficult to formulate ideas about what people were actually wearing, because although artists took reasonable care to portray their subject as accurately as possible, the subtle, and for us diagnostic details, are not always clearly delineated. To compound the difficulty, most 15th- and 16th-century portraits of English men and women were painted by foreigners and it is possible that the cultural background of these artists may have influenced their representation; they may have painted what they knew rather than what they saw. Although useful information can be obtained from monumental effigies and brasses, there are very few portraits of 15th-century date, and those that survive mostly depict immediate members of the court circle. Furthermore, 15th-century images tend to be somewhat stylised, whereas those of the 16th are far more representational. The partial view of the portrait also conceals useful information about the quantities of dress accessories worn; thus for example, the portrait of Edward, Prince of Wales c.1538 by Holbein,[8] shows just three pairs of gold aglets on his coat, and yet surviving accounts from the Royal Wardrobe state that eight pairs were attached to this garment.[9] The posture of the sitter can also conceal important evidence, and buckles and belt fittings are often hidden by the artist's strategic positioning of arms, hands, weapons, gloves, and even furniture.

Wherever possible, analysis of dress accessories should be studied in conjunction with extant costume, but little clothing for this period survives and even when it does, most of the accessories are missing. Aglets and buttons tend to be the sole survivors, but these are generally so damaged or corroded as to be of little use. So it is extremely difficult to know how the dress accessories were used, and by whom.

Buckles (GE)

Buckles, a form of accessory owned by virtually everyone, are very frequently excavated. Their prominence in assemblages helps highlight a number of trends that can be seen, though they are less readily apparent, in other categories of metal dress fittings. It is possible, with some of the more distinctive forms, to define specific styles that were current across England.[10] Parallels inevitably impress the researcher, so the similarities can be overstated, and far more well-dated finds are needed throughout the country to establish a fuller picture.

A range of fashions in copper-alloy buckles which had lasted 100 years or more seem to have come to an end c.1400, though the composite forked-spacer type[11] continued probably well into the 15th century, if not the early 16th, with slightly differing frame shapes. Some buckles, including ones specifically of latten, were being imported into London in 1480–1[12] but no indication of their shapes or place of origin is given. Several apparently new styles were current during the early 16th century, including frames in the patriotic form of heraldic roses[13] and others which seem to imitate conventional heraldic knots with two loose cord ends[14] (Fig. 15.1). Possibly around the same time composite double frames in copper alloy, consisting of two opposed C-shaped parts riveted to a central bar of iron come into the record[15] (Fig. 15.1); presumably it was cheaper to assemble these components than to make a single casting.

An innovation by 1500 is a cheaply produced series of buckles with frames and pins as well as plates ingeniously made entirely of folded copper-alloy sheeting. These accessories are exemplified by a large manufacturing assemblage found in a well in London.[16] The technique eliminated the need for mould-making and casting skills and also for a fuel-consuming workshop and permanent foundry plant – some clippers and a pair of pliers were probably the only investment required apart from the raw materials. Accessories of this series often retain traces of a now-black coating thought to be similar to the *vernis brun* of the Norman period (when it was used on items other than dress accessories); the original colour may have been a warm reddish-brown. The characteristic limited repertoire of stamped motifs on the buckle plates of this series have been widely recognised in finds recovered in Coventry, Northampton, Norwich (fitted to a cast frame), Salisbury and the Isle of Man.[17] It appears that the marketing nationwide and into the North-

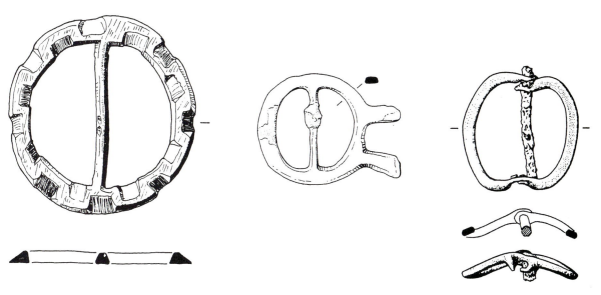

Fig. 15.1 *Common forms of 15th- and 16th-century buckles (drawings 1:1, from Margeson 1993, fig. 15 no. 159, Williams 1996, fig. 12 no. 84, and Moir forthcoming) .*

Sea province even of a cheap line of novel but basic dress accessories presented no significant problem in this period of economic growth. The fashion for coatings seems to have continued to the late 16th or early 17th century (appearing on iron accessories for bladed weapons etc. perhaps particularly towards the end of the this period).

Cast frames continued in use throughout the 16th century, especially double ones, which often feature moulded floral or other motifs at the extreme ends.[18] A poor standard of finishing is evident in some of the plainer frames from this time, with sprues and mould seams unfiled[19] – such finds seem too frequent all to be losses prior to preparation for the customer.

Remarkably, it is not possible to point to a single excavated buckle in mainstream Renaissance style – a contrast with a sizeable number of earlier ones in the late gothic tradition (ogival frames were common and others even appear to imitate Lombardic style lettering,[20] though by the 15th century mass production of ones with figurative decoration such as heraldic lions and engraved monsters on the plate seems to have been a thing of the past). Renaissance style has been claimed for one London find, which, like others in the same vein, actually features the 'daggers' of gothic tracery.[21] What appear to be absent from excavated material are mass-produced frames with arabesques or strapwork, let alone grotesques and other representational motifs.

The elaborate, openwork frames now known as 'lyre-shaped' seem to have been a new fashion in the late 15th/early 16th century, but there is little tight dating yet for what could have been a short-lived fad for these and related spectacular accessories.[22] Lead/tin sleeved buckles[23] had probably disappeared by 1500, or 1550 at the latest, and there is no obvious continuation of the tradition of ornate strap accessories in the same alloys. Usage of buckle plates, common since the Roman period appears to have declined markedly from around this time, with decoration of the flat surface virtually disappearing by the 17th century as personal ornamentation came to be emphasised elsewhere on dress. The long-standing small, circular buckles of lead/tin or iron for shoes were also gone or well on their way out by the early 17th century.[24] Strap buckles of iron, usually of simple forms, continued throughout the period considered.

Strap ends   (GE)

There was apparent continuity of prevailing styles in copper alloy and lead/tin from around the turn of the 15th century into the early 16th, with development of large, ornate openwork varieties (the equivalents of the 'lyre-shaped' buckles).[25] Engraved decoration continued on some of the plainer strap ends, including for the first time a few of lead/tin. Brief inscriptions, often of a religious character, were engraved on several late 15th-/early 16th-century strap ends of copper alloy[26] – these appear to end with the Reformation (Fig. 15.2). A black coating on some strap ends made of sheet copper alloy marks these accessories out as products of the metalworkers who were making the folded sheet buckles. The forked-spacer type of strap end, also in copper alloy, probably came to an end around the mid 16th century, after a fashion for a loop at the lower end became common (Fig. 15.2).[27] It is uncertain whether one strap end with a simple sheet bell attached represents a popular practice or was an unusual adaptation.[28]

A chance find silver-gilt strap end was recovered from the Thames foreshore in 1989. Although its form is unparalleled in British collections and is not represented within the archaeological corpus, it does compare in general style and size to a strap end on the belt of St George in Jan van Eyck's Van de Paele altarpiece of 1436. The cast relief figure of St Barbara occupies central place, and on either side within the chased border are incised motifs of a rose and pomegranate and an engraved inverse inscription 'RAF. FELMIGAM'. The inscription is an abbreviated form of the name Ralph Felmingham, identifiable from documentary evidence as a Sergeant-at-Arms under Henry VII.[29] Although the circumstances of the strap end's deposition are unknown, the function, material value and location of the find suggest accidental loss, and the apparent absence of any secure method of attachment may well have been a contributory factor. Were it not for the inscription, however, we would never have been able to give this dress accessory such a precise and fascinating historical context. The conjunction of the badges of Henry VIII and Katherine of Aragon would suggest that the strap end was made between 1509 and 1520s; and as a member of the royal household it is unlikely

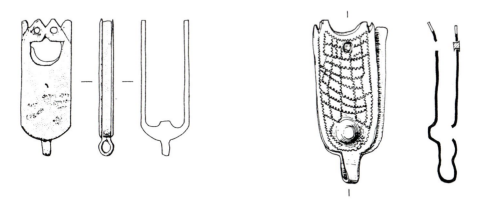

Fig. 15.2 *Strap ends with engraved 'IHC' (from London Museum 1940, fig. 85 no. 6) and with terminal loops (drawings 1:1, from Moir forthcoming and Margeson 1993, fig. 20 no. 238).*

that Felmingham would have continued to wear an object with obvious Aragon association after Henry's divorce (see discussion below – badges).

To judge from archaeology, despite their appearance on men's sword belts in later portraits of the upper classes, by the 17th century mass-produced, decorative strap ends were as much a thing of the past as the central pendant girdles which had probably given them their prominence as fashion accessories in the first place.

Mounts (GE)

The prolific use of mounts of increasingly elaborate and varied forms in all of the main metals in the 15th century[30] seems to end by the early 16th century, and here too any obvious Renaissance style is virtually absent among excavated assemblages (Fig. 15.3). What may be the last traces of the old tradition comes with a series of copper-alloy mounts (new, lens-shaped outlines, for example, as well as more-elaborate motifs), which for some reason very often have two integral, sharply pointed rivets (this variety

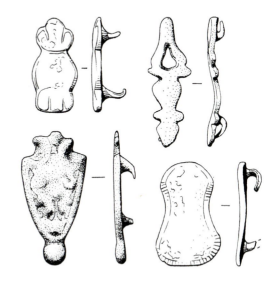

Fig. 15.3 *Mounts with two sharp prongs – a late 16th-century development? (1:1, from Williams 1996, fig. 13 nos. 95–98).*

lasted long enough to feature among the earliest assemblages recovered from permanent European settlement in America[31]). Some of these, particularly the larger ones, could be from horse harnesses.

By the early 1600s the popular tradition that had, from archaeological evidence, lasted virtually half a millennium of showy mounts on waist belts was almost at an end. Far more closely dated finds from the late 15th/16th centuries are required before the course of its final decline can be traced in detail and more fully understood. The familiar sexfoil and octofoil mounts that were so popular on belts and elsewhere in dress through much of the medieval period continued, though seemingly less prolific, into the 17th century,[32] some with a slightly changed role as decorations on armour and saddles.

Brooches (including badges)   (GE)

The longstanding fashion for frame brooches with separate pins, worn to secure garments at the neck as much as for their decorative possibilities, had ceased or virtually ceased to figure among excavated assemblages, in London at least, by c.1400, presumably because their function was gradually taken over by buttons. The few brooches of that style from later contexts in the capital may be residual rather than the latest manifestation of the tradition. There was regional continuity elsewhere, with frame brooches lasting in rural Gloucestershire into the 18th century.[33]

The other main form of popular brooch, of lead/ tin and with an integral pin, which had begun in the 12th or early 13th century with pilgrims' souvenirs, enjoyed a last flourishing in the early 15th century and then declined as pilgrimage itself waned in popularity in the face of increasing scepticism. A gradual blurring of the political and religious spheres has long been held to be one of the characteristics of the end of the Middle Ages[34] and clear evidence of this trend at street level is found among these lead/ tin brooches, with some pilgrim souvenirs from Walsingham from c.1400–25 including a rose into which political significance might be read,[35] and a whole series of rebus badges of allegiance to civic dignitaries and factional leaders, several from the time of the Wars of the Roses.[36] This blending is at its most prominent in the archaeological record in

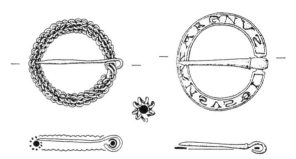

Fig. 15.4 *Medieval frame brooches (1:1, from Egan & Pritchard 1991, fig. 164 nos. 1337 and 1340).*

the hundreds of badges recovered, mainly but not exclusively in the capital, from visits to the Windsor shrine of the 'martyred' Lancastrian king and claimed saint, Henry VI (Fig. 15.5), whose cult was created and fostered under Henry VII as propaganda to blacken the Yorkist cause during the early years of the new Tudor dynasty.[37] The sheer number and variety of badges connected with this cult indicates just how popular a political cause could be made by giving it religious undertones, even when belief in the most fantastic legends connected with saints and the institution of pilgrimage itself were waning. Genuinely religious accessories diversified, perhaps trying to distance themselves from the fashion which was becoming sullied, with the introduction in the 15th century of a series of stamped, brass-foil, sew-on badges at a number of saints' shrines,[38] though inspiration is often lacking in the designs compared with earlier ones – a further sign, perhaps, of declining interest. In religious souvenirs of lead/tin the ornate openwork gothic tracery, which in the 14th and early 15th century on these trinkets at their best had been a vibrant manifestation of the availability of the predominant artistic styles of the day among the less well-off, had disappeared. There was, it seems, no development of Renaissance style for this sector of the market. By the end of Henry VIII's reign the usefulness of the cult of Henry VI was long over. A political strand is evident, nevertheless, in what may be the latest of all the badges of the traditional form, which feature a conjoined rose of England and Spanish pomegranate, signifying the marriage of Katherine of Aragon either with Prince Arthur or

Fig. 15.5 Top: Souvenir badge from a pilgrimage with political overtones – Henry VI of Windsor standing on his heraldic beast, an antelope (1:1, Museum of London collection). Bottom: The end of a tradition – a brooch commemorating Katherine of Aragon's marriage to Prince Arthur or Henry VIII (slightly enlarged, MoL collection). (Photographs MoL).

subsequently with Henry VIII (Fig. 15.5). These dynastic favours, presumably celebratory and free of controversy when first produced, would have become highly politicised statements if they had been worn on the streets in the late 1520s, when divorce proceedings were under way. It is quite probable that the tradition which these brooches represented was

seen as so inextricably tied to the Catholic Church that they became completely beyond the pale with the Reformation. Certainly this centuries-old tradition ends sharply in the archaeological record around that time. Their makers might briefly have persevered with a few Mayday and Plough-Sunday brooches,[39] but there is so far no recognised trace in finds assemblages of any revival under Queen Mary, and Shakespeare is disparaging about lead brooches in the last scene of *Love's Labours Lost*, where the head of a schoolmaster who is wearing a helmet to play Judas Maccabaeus before an unsympathetic audience is ridiculed by being likened, among other things, to a profile of St George 'in a brooch of lead'.[40]

Brooches of some kind were brought into London in ships of Antwerp and Middelburg in 1480–1,[41] specifically 'lead brooches' are recorded among imports of foreign goods into London in 1568[42] and 'brooches of latten or copper' appear in lists from 1582 and (?)1609 of imports liable for customs duty[43] – there seems so far to be nothing from archaeological sources to elucidate what any of these may have looked like.

Some brooches, along with other accessories of course, continued to express allegiance to the monarch among the wealthier classes at Court and elsewhere, as the Cheapside Hoard clearly attests,[44] but mass-produced favours to express such feelings, at least in durable form, had seemingly disappeared. Even with the change of dynasty in 1603, when it might have been expected that brooches with thistles or other Scottish/Stuart motifs would have been produced, no archaeological trace has been recognised (copper-alloy pins with thistle-like heads[45] were made from the mid 16th century and have nothing to do with the accession of James I).

Buttons (GE)

These had been in use since at least the early 13th century,[46] but they seem to have come into their own, probably displacing frame brooches from the main repertoire of accessories, by the early 15th century. The majority that have come down from the Middle Ages are very plain, though a few have glass stones or decorative motifs. The simplest, with heads consisting of two hemispheres of sheet copper alloy

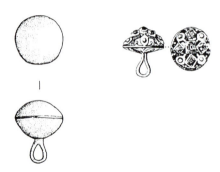

Fig. 15.6 *Left: Medieval button of a long-lasting form, probably early 14th century (from Egan & Pritchard 1991, fig. 179 no. 1404).* **Right:** *Button from the Cheapside Hoard, an unusual find of a dress accessory in gold (from Wheeler 1928, fig. 4), both 1:1.*

(Fig. 15.6), continued unchanged from the early 14th to the mid 17th centuries.[47] Some buttons of unspecified material were imported into London in ships of Antwerp in the late 15th century.[48] A small number of late lead/tin pilgrim badges are in button form, with the saint occupying most of the disc,[49] presumably intended to be worn singly. Several buttons, in different metals, with the crowned maiden from the arms of the Mercers' Company, seem to be early livery buttons from the 16th century. The fashion for dark coatings on brassy alloys appears on a few late 15th-/early 16th-century fairly plain buttons as an almost glassy addition.[50] The rose is one among the many decorative motifs that proliferated on metal buttons in the 1500s. There are also a few dark (black?) glass button heads from the late 16th century,[51] some painted with flower-like details (these ones are not yet closely dated). Dutiable goods listed in 1582 and (?)1609 include imported buttons of copper, latten and steel (all for jerkins) and also ones of silk, brass, crystal and glass and thread only in the later list.[52] The gold versions with coloured enamel from the Cheapside Hoard are the finest to have come from the ground (Fig. 15.6, right).

Pins   (HF)

Pins are recovered in abundance from almost all sites yielding 15th- and 16th-century material. They were indispensable and vast quantities were used in England for fastening clothing and paper and for sewing. A number of contemporary documents allude to the problem that English pin makers 'could not produce all the different types of pins ... in sufficient quantity and the same cheap price as the Dutch'.[53] Thus although iron and copper pins had been made in England since the late 13th century,[54] most were imported from the Netherlands and the Rate Books show for example that 23,473 dozen thousand, worth £4,693, were received in London in the year from Michaelmas 1587.[55] Similar quantities were imported during the 15th century,[56] the majority in bulk consignments, but others in smaller packages for particular customers. Thus the Petty Customs Accounts for 1480–1 list pins amongst imported goods into London, but these were mostly received in fairly small consignments of three or four dozen, and some are specifically described as 'dressying pins'.[57] Throughout the 15th and 16th centuries the sheer quantity of imported pins into England was such that legislative measures were introduced to protect both the consumer and the interests of domestic producers. But the legislation had little effect. Thus Sir Thomas Smith includes the pin in his long list of imported foreign knick-knacks in his treatise of 1549, which deals with the imbalance of trade to the detriment of domestic manufacture and employment.[58]

Although vast numbers of pins have been recovered from excavation in London, by far the largest corpus in the country, only a very small sample from the 14th and early 15th century has been analysed.[59] None of the late 15th- or 16th-century pins have been evaluated and this important corpus needs to be studied before any conclusions can be drawn. Nationwide, the situation is different, for although pins are generally the most plentiful category of 'dress' accessory find within this period, the national corpus is remarkably small given the enormous quantities recorded in documents and literature. A total of 132 was recovered from excavation in Northampton for example, and of these 54 were from 15th-century and 43 from 16th- and 17th-century contexts.[60] There are four pins of post-medieval date from King's Lynn[61] and only 400 (from the 12th to 18th centuries) from Exeter.[62]

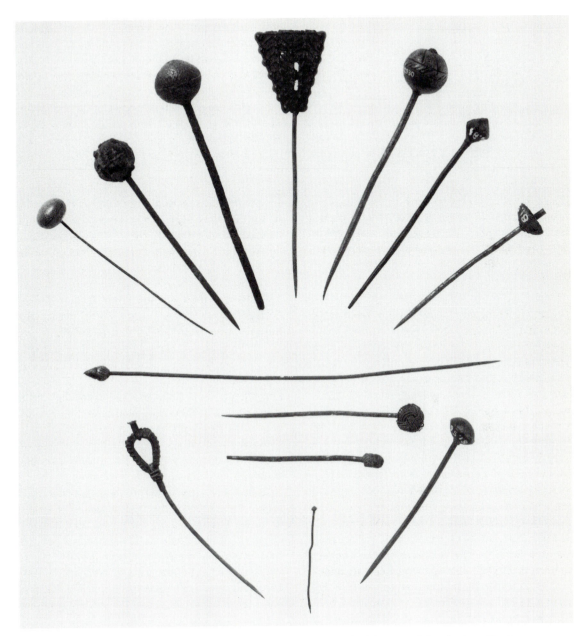

Fig. 15.7 *Group of 15th- and 16th-century pins from the Museum of London's collection*
(length of largest 120mm).

The general paucity of archaeological evidence presents one difficulty and the lack of analysis another. But nomenclature is also a problem. Documents and literature refer to white pins, black pins, angel pins, red pins and red number pins, white pins, double cawkins, pins made from brass, pins coated with tin, and iron pins.[63] White pins may be synonymous with tinned pins, as red pins with copper and black pins with iron pins. But even contemporaries had difficulty distinguishing particular types and materials.[64] It is also possible that the black pins may have been copper with a black coating, of the kind described earlier in this paper. Pins came in different sizes and weights, they were packaged in variable quantities and the quality and price ranged considerably. How does the material evidence compare with that provided in document form?

Pins could not be sold unless 'they be double-headed and all the heads soldered fast to the shank of the pinne, well smoothed, the shank well shaven, the point well and round filed, cauted and sharpened.'[65] Spherical wound wire or 'double-headed' headed pins were made throughout the 15th[66] and 16th centuries. Hemispherical or polygonal-headed pins with stamped decoration occur in early 15th-century contexts[67] and some of these forms and designs may have continued into the early 16th century. One can only suppose that the large headed hemispherical or globular pins on short, thick shanks were used as hat or decorative dress pins, and from the scant evidence available, they seem to have been a fashionable accessory from perhaps the mid to the late 16th century. These are far more robust than the early 15th-century decorative pins which tend to have long thin shanks. The average length of the 16th-century decorative headed pin is 60mm. The shanks vary in thickness, with some measuring 3mm, but the gauge of wire does not seem to correspond to the size and weight of the head or the overall length. On the whole the decorative repertoire of the globular headed pin is fairly limited: the lower hemisphere is usually plain and the upper face has either radial grooves or bosses. But there are remarkable exceptions, including a small corpus with finely attenuated, twisted and plaited wire heads, and one or two unique finds with lead/tin alloy decorative heads (Fig. 15.7). The most spectacular type of globular headed pin seems to be a higher status artefact, and Sue Margeson has made a really valuable contribution to the study of these pins with filigree and granular decoration, comprising two groups, stylistically similar, but of mid-Saxon and 16th-century date.[68] As she has argued, metallurgical analysis of a wide sample from securely dated contexts is required in order to test stylistic hypothesis. More work needs to be done, not least in a careful analysis of the

methods of construction as well as material. Can we distinguish, for example, between foreign pins and those of domestic manufacture? The Dutch developed a technique whereby two men could point more pins than a hundred working with a file had done previously,[69] and one might expect differing production methods to show in the quality of the finished article.

Aglets[70]   (HF)

In its most simple form, a sheet of copper alloy folded to form the tag of a lace or ribbon, these useful accessories are known from the 13th century. Whilst aglets served a functional purpose throughout the 15th and 16th centuries, from the early 1500s they were also used for decorative effect, and ornamental aglets were employed to dangle from caps and decoratively slashed garments. Thus Spenser describes Belphoebe in the *Faerie Queen* (1590)

> with golden aygulets, that glistened bright
> like twinckling starres.[71]

Documentary and pictorial evidence indicate that many of these ornamental aglets were bejewelled, enamelled and composed from precious metals. Pictorial evidence also suggests that many of the decorative aglets must have been made from cast metals in contrast to the cheaper mass produced, plain and purely functional product made from sheet metal. The shape of the ornamental aglet is also different. Decorative aglets seem to have a wider diameter and rectangular outline, whereas the plainer functional types seem to be thinner, mostly tapering to a point to make threading easier. Although lavishly decorated aglets are frequently depicted in portraits, none have been recovered from archaeological contexts in Britain. An ornamental aglet has been excavated in Virginia[72] and a chance find from the Thames appears to be the sole representative in England.[73] The foreshore aglet (Fig. 15.8) is constructed from sheet copper alloy wrapped around upon itself to form a cylinder, with incised diaper decoration and two holes near the aperture for a rivet. The square base has four slits from the centre to the corners, thereby ensuring a neat and flat fold at the end. But even this unique find is a poor cousin of the

Fig. 15.8 Ornamental aglet, (28×7mm), Thames foreshore, probably 16th century (Private collection).

elaborate ornaments depicted in portraits; a much cheaper version of the high fashion article.

Although higher status products are virtually unknown within the archaeological corpus, a number of aglets have been recovered with simple punched decoration. The small group of chance finds within the Museum of London's collection includes a number with stamped decoration, and within this corpus, fleurs-de-lys and diaper patterns predominate.[74] One unique foreshore find, in a private collection, is marked with the letters RH above a diaper and fleurs-de-lys design (Fig. 15.9). If the letters are the initials of the maker, the aglet is the first example known with a maker's mark. This aglet is probably of 16th-century date, even though it cannot be ascribed to a specific place of origin or definite context, and may therefore, within the corpus of mass-produced accessories, be the earliest to be marked in this way.

Another chance find from the Thames, also unparalleled, is folded along its length with a straight longitudinal seam, but is composed of two sheet metals, copper alloy at the top and lead/tin alloy

tapering to the point. Other examples include straight sided aglets with circumferential lines in relief of small repousse bosses. But none of these match the elaborate products described in literature and depicted in portraits and very few are known within the archaeological corpus.

Aglets were used in vast numbers during the 15th and 16th centuries and yet the quantity recovered from systematic excavation is extremely small. Only 47 have been recovered from Exeter and these range from late 13th- to mid 17th-century date.[75] Excavations in Northampton have produced 18 examples of 15th-century date and nine aglets from deposits of the 16th to 17th century,[76] and excavations in Beverley have produced two finds for the 1400–

Fig. 15.9 Aglet with 'RH' mark (45×3mm), probably 16th century.

1600 period.[77] Although substantial quantities have been recovered from excavations in London, and some of the pre-1450 material has been published,[78] no analysis of aglets from late 15th- or 16th-century assemblages has been undertaken to date. Huge numbers of aglets were imported into London during the 15th and late 16th century,[79] and the stamped aglets may be imports. Bristol was the principal centre for domestic manufacture, with Manchester a close second,[80] but as yet no archaeological evidence for this activity has been recognised.[81] Analysis of sheet copper alloy waste from sites may yield evidence of production. Most of the aglets within the archaeological corpus are plain and may correspond to the purely functional type alluded to in Henry IV pt 1.

> Their points being broken
> Down fell their hose.[82]

The sizes and lengths vary considerably and a close analysis of surviving examples attached to garments provides much valuable information with regard to their functional application.[83] The longest, at 47mm, seem to have been used for tying breeches to the waist of a doublet, and from about 1560–1610 these points were hidden beneath the doublet skirts. Slightly shorter aglets 38mm long were employed as decorative points on the doublet, of the sort depicted in the full length portrait by Cornelius Ketel of Sir Martin Frobisher, dated 1577.[84] The longest, plain aglet so far recorded, and again a chance find from the Thames foreshore, is 90mm in length. Both wrapped and folded forms are known throughout the 1400–1600s, although the folded aglets seem to predominate towards the end of the 16th century. But much more analysis needs to be undertaken before any typological conclusions can be drawn. The largest assemblage of aglets still attached to their laces was recovered from rubbish deposits of the 16th century along the north of the City wall adjacent to Moorfields in London. The pairs of plain aglets are folded around lengths of plaited silk.[85]

Head-dress and hair ornaments   (HF)

In his *Anatomie of Abuses* of 1583, Stubbes vigorously condemns contemporary hair fashions 'which of force must be curled, frisled and crisped, laid out

in wreaths and borders from one ear to another' and 'thus wreathed and crested, are hanged with bugles... gewgawes and trinkets besides.'[86] Few bugles (glass beads) have been recovered from archaeological contexts, although vast numbers were imported during the latter half of the 16th century.[87] Those that do survive are mostly associated with bizarre ornaments of uncertain attribution (Fig. 15.10). These ornaments are generally circular or oval, and are composed of thick copper wires with recurving hooks at each end. None have been identified from 15th- or early 16th-century contexts and all seem to date from the second half of the 16th and early 17th century.[88] Tightly coiled fine wire is wrapped around the circumference to provide a decorative frame. The interstice is either filled with a square of sheet copper alloy, each corner folded over into the centre, or with decoratively twisted wires of different gauge. Beads of bone and glass are usually attached, either below the hooks or on each side of the frame. These ornaments may be components from an elaborate head-dress of the type described below, but it is difficult to see how they could be applied without endangering the wearer or her dress.

Head-dresses afforded ample opportunity for rich display, and the ornate fillets worn by fashionable ladies are described by Stubbes: 'Then on the edges of their bolstred hair (for it standeth crested round about their frontiers, and hanging over their faces like pendices with glass windows on every side) there is laid great wreathes of gold and silver, curiously wrought and cunningly applied to the temples of their heads.'[89] The most complete surviving head-dress of elaborate construction is thought to date to the late 16th or early 17th century and was recovered from the Thames foreshore.[90] This object is constructed from twisted copper alloy wire and sheet metal with bone and glass bead embellishments. Unlike the functional plain wire frames which were hidden beneath fabric, this elaborate adornment was designed as an item of jewellery.

A wire accessory of copper alloy, with traces of gilding and flowers of white glass, was recovered from excavations at Nonsuch Palace.[91] This bauble, arranged in three tiers and supported on spiral springs of tightly twisted wire is inherently unstable, a deliberate structural device which enables the trinket

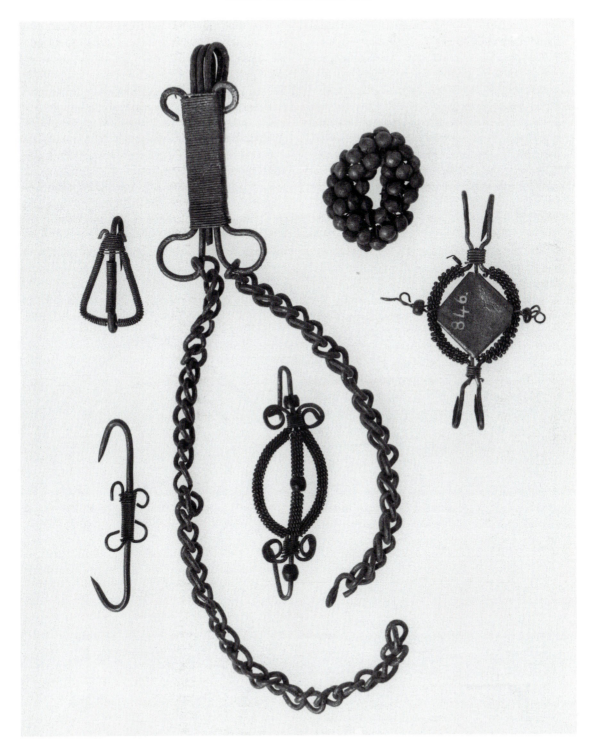

Fig. 15.10 *Assorted wire-work accessories: all chance finds in the Museum of London's collection, probably 16th century. The large hook (58×29mm) with lengths of chain is the belt attachment from a chatelaine.*

to oscillate and catch the light. Numerous portraits of the late 16th century depict similar ornaments, worn in the hair or sewn on to garments. The monumental brass of Dame Margaret Chute (d.1614)[92] also presents intriguing evidence: her hair is brushed up into pinnacles, presumably supported by invisible wire-work, and interspersed throughout this creation are round ornaments, possibly of the Nonsuch type. Similar fragments have been recovered from the Thames foreshore, although these are less sophisticated and are composed entirely of base metal. The most striking consists of bunched beads of copper alloy. Each bead is made from two hemispheres, joined by solder, with looped shanks of wire on the underside for attachment (Fig. 15.11). These gewgaws seem to be a phenomenon of 16th-century dress and hair decoration.

Most of the elaborate head-dress fittings are chance finds, and very few have been recovered from excavation. However, excavations have produced a number of plain head-dress frames, of the kind concealed under fabric and worn by all but the poorest. The diversity of head-dress design is evident from contemporary illustrations, engravings, tapestries, ivory and wood carvings, and monumental brasses and effigies, but although the external appearance is clearly defined, little is known of the internal supporting structure. Contemporary descriptions of ladies head-gear provide helpful, although somewhat confusing detail, suggesting that there were subtle variations of basic designs, as well as standard shapes.[93] Head-dress wires from early 15th-century contexts in London have been analysed[94] but no systematic study of the later archaeological material has been undertaken. Short lengths of shaped copper wire, particularly those that have been deliberately bent and waved, should be re-examined and evaluated since this material could yield crucial evidence for head-dress study. Examples from Temple Street in Bristol,[95] of thick copper wire, with a wire of finer gauge wrapped around one end, and Austin Friars, Leicester,[96] with wrapped wire, may be possible contenders.

In spite of the comparative paucity of archaeological evidence, several distinct forms of head-dress can be identified from extant frames: the diamond, angular, pediment and curved.[97] Head-

dresses with diamond, and pediment profiles, were especially fashionable at the end of the 15th century and during the first quarter of the 16th century, and these can be seen in many contemporary portraits and monumental effigies.[98] Holbein's drawings of Lady Butts, Lady Barkley and Lady Eliot[99] amongst others, provide very clear details of these gable or 'gothic' forms of head-dress. Both the high pediment, diamond and slightly more angular head-dress were worn concurrently, as portraits of Margaret, Countess of Salisbury, dated 1532/5[100] and Queen Jane Seymour[101] c.1536 reveal. The curved frame or French hood seems to have been worn concurrently with the gable types throughout the 1520s and 1530s, but features more prominently in portraits from perhaps the fourth decade, gradually superseding the gable form and remaining popular until well into the 1560s. One might expect to find fragments from the

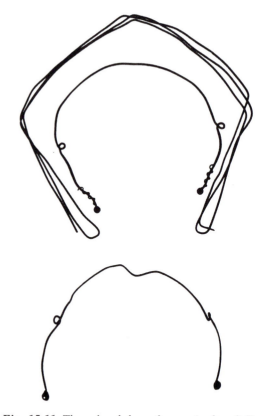

Fig. 15.11 Three head-dress frames (reduced). **Top:** *Museum of London acc. no. NN55.28;* **Middle:** *MoL acc. no. A27909;* **Bottom:** *MoL acc. no. A27910.*

popular 'horned head-dress' of the 15th century as worn for example by Lady Shernbourn (d. 1458),[102] and yet so far none have been recognised from archaeological assemblages. The so-called 'butterfly head-dress' with flamboyant 'wings' of fabric supported by thin wires was extremely popular from the 1430s to 1490s,[103] and it is possible that some of the very thin copper or iron wires with textile wrappings may have originated from just such an adornment.

Some of the simple curved frames have round terminals of lead/tin or spiral wire, presumably placed to protect the wearer from the rough ends and to facilitate attachment.[104] In addition, the curved frames are often composed of several separate lengths of wire; the main support and wire of thickest gauge is usually looped on itself, one loop on each side of the head, presumably for attachment. The smaller wires, which may have had a decorative and/ or functional purpose, are then wrapped around this frame.[105] By contrast, the angular, pediment and diamond forms consist of single lengths of folded wire. The method of construction is very precise and entirely symmetrical, with equal numbers of folds on each side.[106] The frame was probably secured to the head with ribbon or perhaps held in place by lateral pressure (Fig. 15.11).

In addition to the frames and head-dress adornments, hair was also covered with a cawl, as Stubbes comments, 'made Net-wyse, to th'ende, as I thinke, that the clothes of gold, cloth of filver or els tinsell (for that is the worst) wherwith their heads are covered and attyred withall'. A few fragments of fine copper wire net have been recovered from the foreshore[107] and it is possible that these may be cheaper versions of the nets described above, which would have certainly glistened and shined 'Soe that a man that seethe them... wold thinke them to have golden heads.'[108] Cauls were fashionable accessories from 1400[109] through to the early 1600s[110] and the sizes and shapes were almost infinitely variable and often greatly enriched with jewels.

Ruff supports or supportasse   (HF)

The oft quoted phrase from Stubbes is worth repeating: 'They have great and monstrous ruffes...

whereof some be a quarter of a yard deep, yea some more... But if Aeolus with his blasts, or Neptune with his stormes chaunce to hit uppon the crasie bark of their brused ruffes, then they goe flip flap in the winde, like rags flying abroad, and lye upon their shoulders like the dishcloute.'[111] Ruffs were starched and the largest were supported with wires or supportasse, especially crested for the purpose, and these were wrapped in thread of gold, silver or silk. As yet no supportasse has been identified from an archaeological site, but fragments of wire with traces of textile adhering have been recovered from the Thames foreshore. Besides these, vast amounts of copper wire, sometimes with loops and finer wires attached, have been recovered from sites yielding early modern material, and these warrant further investigation.[112] Ruffs were fashionable from the mid 16th to first quarter of the 17th century. But the largest and most extreme forms, of the type described above, seem to feature prominently during the latter half of the 16th century, and one would expect to find supportasse from assemblages of this date.

Finger rings   (GE)

Finger rings, especially those of precious metals, have received considerable attention in the literature[113] and archaeology has produced too few of the finest ones to add significantly to the established picture for these. It has, on the other hand, a considerable contribution to make from the many excavated rings of base metals, which include many with initials, personal marks and other devices, used for sealing documents.

Archaeological finds suggest that the long-standing tradition of cheap, relief-decorated lead/tin rings[114] had apparently ended by the 15th century, as too had the gold (?marriage) rings with wire-thin hoops and stones barely the size of a medium contemporary pinhead (Fig. 15.12 left).[115] Both of these changes may be because increasing affluence in society in general meant that better-quality rings were affordable more widely – and with precious metals better was larger. There seems from casual finds to be an increase, by the end date of this present survey, in silver (including silver-gilt) for finger rings after a period during which it was not commonly

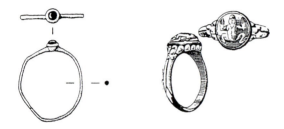

Fig. 15.12 *Finger rings. **Left**: 1:1, medieval gold marriage ring using minimal precious metal; **Right**: slightly reduced, post-medieval ring with 'toadstone' from Cheapside Hoard (drawings from Egan & Pritchard 1991, fig. 215 no. 1610 and Wheeler 1928, fig. 2).*

used for them. It would be helpful to know whether gold in rings was tending to become more alloyed at the same time, as this might indicate an erosion of the attitude that only the purest gold, with all its symbolism for marriage, was suitable for the one expensive piece of jewellery that was purchased in a lifetime by many people. Perhaps a choice of rings for wearing was becoming a more potent fashion statement than the continual usage of a single one as a token of wedlock.

Rings of copper with stones and ones of tin and other metals were being imported into London in 1480–1.[116] Wound-wire finger rings became popular at the lower end of the market in the 15th or 16th century, and at least one large pin was bent into a circle, the spherical head serving as a stone,[117] as a novel variation of this style (doubtless some contemporaries would have been struck more by the cheapness of the product than by the ingenuity of the maker).

While rings featuring saints dramatically fell out of fashion with the Reformation, mottoes, particularly amatory ones, continued.[118] The folklore surrounding different stones also survived the new scepticism relatively well (the latest English lapidary was written in the late 16th century[119]) to last in some cases to the present day, though arguably it became for most wearers a secondary consideration to the decorative qualities. The Cheapside Hoard illustrates some the continuity, particularly evident in inherently non-attractive 'stones' like the fossilised fish teeth believed to be toad stones (Fig. 15.12 right).[120]

The finest finger rings excavated, in contrast with

most other categories of dress accessories, include a significant proportion in which mainstream Renaissance motifs are prominent, e.g. in a gold ring with an intaglio of a Classical head, found in the City ditch in London[121] – the Cheapside Hoard again features a number of comparable quality, and also an unset cameo with the head of Elizabeth I.[122] The reason remained, as with the medieval marriage ring, that for many people in Tudor times a finger ring was the most expensive piece of jewellery acquired, and purchases of fine rings just about reached the level of market penetration that meant they would be lost often enough to figure occasionally during latter-day retrieval from the ground.

Neckchains (GE)

Necklaces in the form of long, elaborate collar chains of precious metal became fashionable for the upper classes and the aristocracy in the 15th century following a long period when this sort of accessory was apparently not in favour. A complete silver collar with links in the form of the Lancastrian S motif has been unearthed in London.[123] Various decorations like this appear in contemporary paintings, but archaeology has shown that there were also lower-class versions, formerly unsuspected, in base metals. Several joined links from a lead/tin chain probably of this category have been found in London and there is a possible fragment from Northampton.[124] Versions in elaborately twisted copper-alloy wire as well as ones with thicker links of this metal are known from London and elsewhere.[125] A few in gold with enamel from the Cheapside Hoard give an indication of more expensive neckchains.[126]

Hook fasteners (HF)

Hooks of this type (Fig. 15.13) are found fairly frequently on archaeological sites in England and on the Continent, particularly the Netherlands.[127] Most are cast in one piece from copper alloy, and seem to come from securely dated contexts of the late 16th or early 17th century. Hook fasteners are also made from combinations of lead and copper alloy, and some are gilded or tin-coated. More rarely examples are found in silver.[128] Although the basic structure is

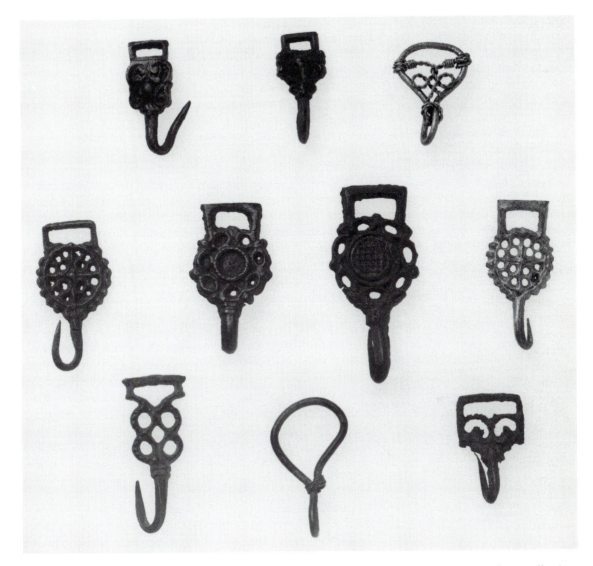

Fig. 15.13 *Group of hook fasteners (top left 24×10mm); chance finds in the Museum of London's collection; late 16th- / early 17th-century.*

fairly standard, consisting of three parts: an angular or trapezoidal loop, a central plate and a recurving hook, the decoration varies considerably.[129] The plates are usually geometric: rectilinear, square, round, oval, diamond, heart or trefoil, although other shapes are known. Most have pierced and relief ornamentation of simple geometric or foliate design, arranged within contiguous beaded circles or a sexfoil or octofoil framework. Yet others are decor-

ated with incised lines, hatching and raised bumps. The decorative repertoire also includes, but more rarely, flower heads (roses or auricle) bird heads and lion masks, human figures, fleurs-de-lys, monograms, initials, shells, heraldic and true-lovers' knots, and emblems such as the cross saltire (perhaps for St Andrew) and the Sacred Monogram IHS. The full range of motifs seems to occur throughout the period of production, with no obvious concentrations of design or pattern. Apart from a few examples with figural motifs, the designs are mainly those of the abstract world of form and shape rather than the antique pictorial art of the Renaissance. The average size is 35×18mm, with the smallest at 20×9mm and largest up to 60×20mm. Size variation seems to be constant and there is no apparent metamorphosis of form within the period of production.

The hooks are similar to those dating from the 7th – 12th centuries, although none have been found in intervening periods. Dutch archaeologists suggest that the hooks were used in conjunction with a length of chain to keep loose hanging clothes together,[130] and indeed a number of pairs have been found with chain or ribbon fastened to the loops. Whilst this interpretation of function is entirely possible, the hook element is generally extremely large and vicious, and it is difficult to see how such barbarous items actually worked without damaging the cloth and the wearer. Furthermore, there is no pictorial evidence to support this hypothesis, and most of the excavated hook fasteners are not associated with a chain or cord. None have been found with a chain in this country. There are two alternative explanations: first, strikingly similar examples are shown in portraits, and these are attached to the belt and sword-hanger. The loop is sewn on to the belt and the hook links into another attached to the strap end of the hanger. The Hans Eworth portrait of Gregory Fiennes, 10th Baron Dacre, 1599[131] provides a very clear example. Second, surviving costume evidence of the early 17th century suggests that such hooks may have been sewn to the waistband of breeches for eyelets attached to a reinforced strip inside the doublet waist.[132] None of these interpretations are mutually exclusive, and a careful of study is required before any firm conclusions can be drawn.

The distribution of hook fasteners was widespread, and examples have been recovered as far afield as the Isle of Man,[133] Yorkshire, Wiltshire, Avon, Oxfordshire, the Midlands, East Anglia and Hampshire.[134] However, the largest concentration of finds is from London, and large numbers have been recovered from archaeological sites in the capital. In addition, the Museum of London has 135 hook fasteners recovered by chance. Taken together, the relative proportion of hook fasteners within the

corpus of late 16th- and early 17th-century dress accessory finds both in the metropolis and nation-wide is high, a clear indication of their importance during this period. Equivalent types of fastener have not been identified from 15th- or early 16th-century contexts.

Belt clasps *(HF)*

Sixteenth-century dress hooks also include cast copper alloy girdle clasps of S-shape with bird or dragon head terminals (Fig. 15.14).[135] The central section usually consists of a relief pattern of swirling lines and circumferential dots. This particular form of clasp appears in many paintings by Fresian masters of the period 1598–1621, and examples are found on archaeological sites in England, especially the Home Counties and on the Continent.[136] Essentially a variant of the Romano-Celtic dragonesque brooch,[137] the decorative S-shape was adopted in the 16th century to join the two hooks or strap loops at each end of the belt. This accessory is clearly depicted in the portraits

Fig. 15.14 *S-shaped belt clasp; (30×14 mm), 16th-century (Museum of London acc. no. 86.398/95).*

of Sir Peter Carew (1549)[138] and the 1st Earl of Leicester, Robert Dudley (c.1575).[139]

Hooks and eyes   (HF)

Hooks and eyes are much in evidence in clothing of the mid 16th century, but they were not a major method of fastening until the early 17th.[140] Very few are found on archaeological sites, and as yet no systematic study has been undertaken. Surviving examples in clothing need to be examined and analysis undertaken of those recovered from excavation before any definitive statements can be made.

Beads   (GE)

The majority of these recovered from the ground are quite plain in form, though the materials are extremely varied. There are a couple made of tin from the early 15th century.[141] Imports to London in the early 1480s include ones of bone, boxwood, jet, coral, glass and mistletoe (the last include some described as 'counterfeit'[142]). Amber and jet are fairly common among finds up to the mid 16th century,[143] when glass – previously unusual if archaeological retrieval gives an accurate picture[144] – appears to come into its own with a range of colours, including a striking turquoise. Beads of bone, crystal, box and other woods are still listed, along with 'jasper stones for beads square', among dutiable import goods in 1582.[145] The mention of jasper may refer to fairly large, multifaceted oval beads of dark stone with red streaks that have occasionally been recovered in London (private collections). Most finds from the pre-Reformation period probably come from rosaries. Bone beads, though not common finds in themselves (they are very difficult to spot in the soil) are widely attested by waste panels from which they were cut (Fig. 15.15).

These panels fall sharply out of the archaeological record around the middle of the 16th century.[146]

Purses   (GE)

Excavated purses of the 14th/early 15th centuries seem with few exceptions to have been entirely of leather or textile and only very occasionally to have had decorative metal mounts.[147] Metal bars and frames came into widespread usage during the late 1400s for a relatively brief period of popular fashion up to the mid 16th century.[148] The small, twisted loops of copper alloy wire that seem to be ubiquitous on sites from the 16th century could be the 'pouch rings' of the books of customs import duty rates[149] if a find of textile covered with these loops from Southampton is indicative of their main use; this has been interpreted as a purse and it has the rings sewn all over one face, presumably to act as a defence against cut purses in the street.[150] 'Pouch rings' might alternately have described the more robust ones now usually thought to be for curtains (these have occasionally been found wound with textile[151]), or the ring frame or support of the pouch. It is not clear that the previous range of metal accessories for purses lasted into the 17th century.

Conclusions   (GE & HF)

Summing up such diverse evidence is no easy task, particularly in view of the major limitations indicated above. The study of dress accessories for this period is not helped by the vagueness of much of the documentary evidence: categories or specific types are concealed within, to use contemporary parlance, 'haberdashery or small wares', and the descriptions, when they exist tend to be minimal or non-specific. The corpus of 15th- and 16th-century dress access-

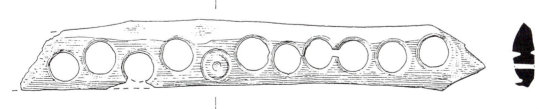

Fig. 15.15 *Bone panel from which beads have been turned (1:1, from Egan & Pritchard 1991, fig. 207 no. 1567).*

ories recovered by systematic excavation or chance finds is extremely small, and this paucity of artefactual evidence is at variance with the documentary record. Even the most abundant finds, pins and aglets, are rarely found in sufficient numbers from securely dated contexts to permit intensive analysis.

Around 1500 a fresh line in cheaply-made buckles made entirely of copper alloy sheeting, along with the novel employment on these and other sheet accessories of a distinctive coating, probably a vegetable oil, suggests that a new group of manufacturers with little capital had entered the market. Wound-wire jewellery, which has been mentioned under several headings, was also easily manufactured, normally using cheap materials (Figs 15.4 left and 15.10). It probably required no more than a simple tool to produce accessories that sometimes look very complicated. The main popularity of the technique, which goes right back to the Roman period, came in the early 16th century, when it was used in a wide variety of clasps, pins, rings, headdresses and chains worn by a broad spectrum of society.[152] Coiled-wire jewellery, while by no means universally worn, was nonetheless a prominent characteristic of personal adornment in the Tudor period.

From the evidence available, dress accessories for the period 1400–1600 demonstrate a wide variety of fashionable self-expression and the emergence of popular conspicuous consumption. As yet it is not possible to establish the full significance of typological variations and transition among the excavated material. References to mainstream art, politics and religion, all present among late medieval dress accessories, fade out from the usual range of finds halfway through the second of the two centuries considered here. The complete absence of obvious Renaissance motifs in several categories is particularly surprising and has no ready explanation. These changes seem to occur around the time of the Reformation, and in these shifts of fashion it is perhaps possible to see a major transition. There are, nevertheless, many other changes, many no more than the whims of design, which cannot be related to traditional historical preoccupations. As with much archaeological evidence, it is possible to emphasise either continuity or diversity, depending on the perspective from which these complicated issues are considered. Several trends are emerging for dress accessories in the 15th and 16th centuries, but a fuller understanding requires further, closely dated evidence from the ground.

Acknowledgements

Thanks for help on a variety of fronts to: Janet Arnold, Torla Evans, the late Sue Margeson (who provided fresh information especially for this paper), Andrew Russel, Roz Sherris, Brian Spencer, Judy Stevenson, Bly Straube, David Williams and members of the Society of Thames Mudlarks.

Notes

1. Egan & Pritchard 1991.
2. *Ibid.*
3. Moir forthcoming.
4. Becon ?1550, 438.
5. *The Compter's Commonwealth* 1617.
6. Egan forthcoming (a).
7. Egan forthcoming (b).
8. Hans Holbein the Younger, National Gallery of Art, Washington.
9. PRO E315/456 f.33.
10. See note 17; cf. Egan 1996, 109 for accessories similar to ones recovered across England found in the Isle of Man.
11. Egan & Prichard 1991, 76–82.
12. Cobb 1990, 176 index nos.
13. Margeson 1993, 28–9, fig. 15, no. 157.
14. Moir forthcoming; Woodfield 1981, 89 & 92 no. 29.
15. London Museum 1940, 278–9 and pl. 77 nos. 13 & 14.
16. J. Clark in Murdoch 1991, 11 and 156–7 no. 413; the assemblage is Museum of London acc. no. 21111.
17. Woodfield 1981, 95–6 nos 71 & 67, reconsidered in Egan forthcoming (b); Oakley 1979, 257–8 fig. 111 no. 88; Margeson 1993, 25, pl. 9; Goodall forthcoming; Egan 1996, 30–31 fig. 15 no. 2. This coating is used in reserve to decorative effect on one buckle plate (MoL acc. no. 88.9/19).
18. For example Hinton 1988a, 402–3 fig. 184 no. 190.
19. Egan forthcoming (a).
20. Egan & Pritchard 1991, 71–2 nos 284–5.
21. Blackmore 1981; cf Egan & Pritchard 1991, 84–5 no. 344 and 87–8 no. 377, both attributed to the early 15th century.

22. London Museum 1940, 270 fig. 85 no. 1; 266 fig. 84 no. 16 is from a tomb brass dated to 1391.
23. Egan & Pritchard 1991, 13 and 162ff.
24. *Ibid.* 60–64 nos. 60–210.
25. London Museum 1940, 270 and 272 fig. 85 no. 1.
26. *Ibid.* 269–70 and 272 fig. 85 nos. 2 and 6 pl. 76 no. 10.
27. Moir forthcoming.
28. Museum of London acc. no. O2203.
29. Forsyth 1996 and forthcoming.
30. Egan & Pritchard 1991, 162–235 *passim*.
31. Goodall 1984, 339 and 342 fig. 191 no. 114; Harvey 1975, 265 and 267 fig. 245 no. 1867; one in the form of a lion has been found in America in the course of excavations at the early 17th-century Jamestown colony by the Association for the Preservation of Virginia Antiquities.
32. Egan & Pritchard 1991, 247–60 and 269–71.
33. Evans 1921, 40.
34. Huizinga 1937.
35. Spencer forthcoming, no. 151.
36. *Ibid.* nos. 270ff.
37. *Idem* 1978.
38. For example *idem* forthcoming, nos. 151a–f.
39. *Ibid.* nos. 306b and 307a.
40. Cited in *idem* 1969, 34.
41. Cobb 1990, 7 no. 23 (twelve dozen) and 53 no. 165 (one pound).
42. Dietz 1972, 71 no. 458, a consignment of 12 gross.
43. Willan 1962, 10; also Anon 1969.
44. Wheeler 1928, 26 and 29 fig. 4.
45. For example Margeson 1993, 12–13 fig. 5 no. 44; Moir forthcoming.
46. Egan & Pritchard 1991, 276–7 nos. 1397–1404.
47. *Ibid.* 274 nos. 1376–9.
48. Cobb 1990, 6 no. 20 and 33 no. 103.
49. Spencer 1990, 15–6 and 69 fig. 7 no. 11, a souvenir of St Osmund.
50. MoL collection.
51. Woodfield 1981, 92 and 94 no. 41; head recognised as glass in Egan forthcoming (b).
52. Willan 1962, 12; also Anon 1969.
53. BL Landsdowne MS 152, ff. 322–4 and 332.
54. Brinklow 1975.
55. PRO E190/7/8.
56. Cobb 1961, 77–80.
57. *Ibid.* no. 152.
58. Smith 1549.
59. Egan & Pritchard 1991, 297–304.
60. Oakley 1979, 260–62.
61. Clarke & Carter 1977, 289.
62. Goodall 1984, 345 fig. 193.
63. PRO SP 39/9 no. 6; BL Cotton MS; Titus BIV, f. 60.
64. Guildhall Muniment Room LM1331/36.
65. PRO Statute 37 Henry VIII cap. 13.
66. Egan & Pritchard 1991.
67. *Ibid.* 297–304.
68. Margeson 1995, 161–5.
69. BL Cotton MS Titus BV, f.304 (n.d.).
70. The orthography of this word varies considerably, but 'aglet' seems to have been the most popular version in the 16th century.
71. Spenser 1590, II.iii.26.
72. Hume forthcoming.
73. Private collection.
74. MoL acc. nos. 91.123/6; 95.195; 86.361/15.
75. Allan 1984, 339 M125–9 fig. 191 nos. 128 and 129.
76. Oakley 1979, 263–4.
77. Armstrong 1991, 152.
78. Egan & Pritchard 1991, 281–90.
79. PRO E190 Port Books: 37/4; 37/8; 38/1; 41/1; 41/5; 42/1; 44/3; and E351/910 and SP12/8/31.
80. Stratford 1581, 'Bristow had a great trade by the making of points and that was the chief mystery that was exercised in the town'.
81. Apparently unfinished ones have been found at Coventry – Egan forthcoming (b).
82. Shakespeare, Henry VI pt 1, II.iv.238.
83. Arnold 1985, 12 fig. 60; 14 fig. 74; 30 fig. 205; 46 fig. 327; 53 fig. 1A and B; 55–6; 77.
84. Cornelius Ketel, The Curators of the Boldeian Library, Oxford.
85. Egan & Pritchard 1991, 281 fig. 181 and 285.
86. Stubbes 1583, 67.
87. PRO E190/7/8 and 8/1.
88. Baart 1977, 154 nos. 161 and 164.
89. Stubbes 1583, 67.
90. Weinstein 1989.
91. Biddle forthcoming.
92. Macklin 1907, 282–3.
93. Repton 1836, 29–76.
94. Egan & Pritchard 1991, 291–6.
95. M. W. Ponsford pers. comm..
96. Clay 1981, 136–7 nos. 42 and 57.
97. Museum of London acc. nos. A2993; A26764; NN55.28; A7309; A9910.
98. Planché 1867.
99. Parker 1945.
100. English School, National Portrait Gallery.
101. Holbein, Kunsthistorisches Museum, Vienna.
102. Boutell 1847, 91.
103. PRO Calendar of State Papers (Venetian) 15 (1909),

270, written in 1618, but applicable to fashions of dress in the 16th century. Also Boutell 1847, 75 and 92.

104. MoL acc. nos. A27309; A9910.

105. MoL acc. no. A27909.

106. MoL acc. nos. NN55.28; A2993.

107. Stubbes 1583, 69 leaf 35.B.

108. Private collection, recovered from Bull Wharf; Stubbes *ibid.*

109. Boutell 1847, 85–90.

110. Repton 1836, 29–76.

111. Stubbes 1583, 51–2.

112. MoL acc. no. 81.564/104 (a possible contender).

113. For example Dalton 1912, Oman 1930, Cherry 1981, Gere 1981.

114. Egan & Pritchard 1991, 332–5.

115. For example *ibid.* 326–7 nos 1610–11.

116. Cobb 1990, index under rings 185.

117. MoL acc. no. 86.109/18.

118. Evans 1931.

119. Evans & Serjeantson 1933, 11 and 119–30; cf. Evans 1922, 167–83; this tradition continued in alchemical writings into the late 17th century e.g. in the philosophical transactions of the Royal Society of London.

120. Wheeler 1928, 32; cf. 17–18 and pl. III, MoL acc. no. A14243 and cf. Evans 1922, 170 and 181.

121. MoL acc. no. CAP86 acc. no. 11.

122. Wheeler 1928, 30 and pl. XI 2.

123. Spencer 1985.

124. The most complete London find is VHA89 acc. no. 854; for the Northampton fragment see Oakley 1979, 265–6 fig. 115 no. Pb2.

125. Margeson 1993, 18–19 fig. 9 nos 76–8; Murdoch 1991, 110–11 no. 208, thought to be 16th century, illustrates the technique at its most elaborate, though this particular accessory could have been worn at the waist.

126. Wheeler 1928, 14–16.

127. Baart 1977, 249–70; Enlart 1916, 242–3; Janssen 1983, 109.

128. Sotheby Parke Bernet Monaco SA, 1981 lot no. 88.

129. Clevis & Smit 1990, 343 fig. 376 shows a similar hooked fastening but with a concealed loop attachment.

130. Baart 1977, 154 figs. 162–4.

131. Hans Eworth, private collection, cf. Hearn 1995, cat. 25.

132. Arnold 1985, 87.

133. Egan 1996, 109–11.

134. Goodall 1984, 232–3 fig. 1 no. 30 and pers. comm.

135. MoL acc. no. 86.398/95 and Murdoch 1993, 109 fig. 205. Hooks with zoomorphic head terminals also appear on sword belt fittings (Gaimster 1988).

136. Pain, pers. comm. (Farnborough, Kent) and Baart 1977, 163 nos. 194–5.

137. Bulmer 1938, 146–53 and Feachen 1951, 32–44.

138. Hampton Court.

139. Unknown, National Portrait Gallery.

140. Arnold 1985.

141. Egan & Pritchard 1991, 315–16 nos. 1584–5.

142. Cobb 1990, index under beads, 'bead stones' (bede stones) and misletoe beads 175 and 183.

143. Egan & Pritchard 1991, 305–9 and 316; Moir forthcoming.

144. Egan & Pritchard 1991, 315–16 fig. 209 nos. 1586–7.

145. Willan 1962, 4 and 34.

146. Egan & Pritchard 1991, 310–15; the BOY86 site in London produced them in large numbers from the late 15th to early 16th century; cf Murdoch 1991, 88 no. 97 for part of a bone-bead rosary from a late 16th-century deposit. Several beads, presumably for rosaries, were found on the wreck of the *Mary Rose* a decade after the Reformation.

147. For example Egan & Pritchard 1991, 351 and 356 no. 1701; cf Goodall 1984, 345–6 no. 218 dated (with reservations) to the 11th/12th century.

148. London Museum 1940, 158–71; bars were found on the wreck of the *Mary Rose* from 1545.

149. Willan 1962, 48; pouch rings also appear among imports to London at the start of the 1480s, Cobb 1990, index 184.

150. Egan in Moir forthcoming – the Southampton parallel is in the collections of Southampton City Council Heritage Services, site SOU105; similar twisted loops have been claimed as early as the late 13th century and into the late 17th century: Goodall 1984, 347.

151. Margeson 1993, 6 and 8 fig. 2 and pl. 1 no. 17 from the late 15th to early 16th century.

152. Murdoch 1991, 105 no. 108; Egan & Pritchard 1991, 254 and 256 fig. 164 nos. 1339–40 are brooches with wound-wire decoration dated to the late 12th century or slightly later, and see also the portrait called Duchess of Chandos, 1578 (or 1579) attributed to John Bettes the Younger, French & Co Inc, New York.

Bibliography

Allan, J.P. *et al.* 1984, *Medieval and Post-Medieval finds from Exeter, 1971–1980*, Exeter Archaeological Report 3, Exeter

Anon. 1969, *The Rates of Marchandises*, [?1609] da Capo reprint, Amsterdam/New York

Armstrong, P. *et al.* 1991, *Excavations at Lurk Lane Beverley, 1979–82*, Sheffield Excavation Reports 1, Humberside Archaeology Unit

Arnold, J. 1985, *Patterns of Fashion: The Cut and Construction of Clothes for Men and Women c.1560–1620*

Baart, J. 1977, *Opgravingen in Amsterdam; 20 jaar Stadskernonderzock*, Amsterdam

Becon ?1550, 'Jewel of Joy', in Parker Society 1844

Biddle, M. forthcoming, *Excavations at Nonsuch Palace*

Bird, J., Chapman, H. & Clark, J. (eds) 1978, *Collectanea Londiniensia: Studies in London Archaeology and History Presented to Ralph Merrifield*, London Middlesex Archaeol Soc Special Paper 2

Boutell, C. 1847, *Monumental Brasses and Slabs an Historical and Descriptive Notice of the Incised Monumental Memorials of the Middle Ages*

Blackmore, L. 1981, 'A 16th–17th-century bronze buckle', in Robertson-MacKay 1981, 129

Brinklow, D.A. 1975, *An Examination of Copper Alloy Metalworking in Medieval York*. Unpublished, MA Dissertation, University of Bristol.

Bulmer, W. 1983, 'Dragonesque brooches and their development', *Antiquaries Journal* 18, 146–53

Cherry, J. 1981, 'Medieval rings, 1100–1500', in Ward 1981, 51–86

Clarke H. & Carter A. 1977, *Excavations in King's Lynn 1963–1970*, Soc for Medieval Archaeol Monograph Series 7

Clay, P. 1981, 'The small finds', in Mellor & Pearce (eds) 1981, 130, 136–7

Clevis H. & Smit M. 1990, *Verscholen in vuil: archaeologische vondsten uit Kampen 1375–1925* Stichting Archaeologie IJssel/Vechtstreek

Cobb, H.S. (ed.) 1961, *The Local Port of Southampton for 1430–40*, Southampton University

Cobb, H.S. (ed.) 1990, *The Overseas Trade of London: Exchequer Customs Accounts 1480–1*, London Record Society 27

Courtney, P. 1993, 'Medieval and post medieval objects', in Ellis 1993, 134–61

Dalton, O.M. 1912, *Franks Bequest, Catalogue of the Finger Rings, Early Christian, Byzantine, Teutonic, Medieval and Later*, British Museum

Davey, P.J. *et al.* (eds) 1996, *Excavations in Castletown, Isle of Man 1989–1992*, Liverpool

Dietz, B. 1972, *The Port and Trade of Elizabethan London*, London Record Soc 8

Donald, M.B. 1961, *Elizabethan Monopolies: The History of the Company of Mineral and Battery Works from 1565 to 1604*, Edinburgh and London

Egan, G. 1996, 'Non ferrous metal', in Davey 1986, 29–35

Egan, G. forthcoming (a), 'Some archaeological evidence for metalworking in London c.1050 – c.1700 AD', *Historical Metallurgy*

Egan, G. forthcoming (b), report on finds from Coventry Whitefriars site (includes a reassessment of some items published in Woodfield 1981)

Egan, G. & Pritchard, F. 1991, *Medieval Finds from Excavations in London 3: Dress Accessories*, HMSO

Ellis, P. 1993, *Beeston Castle, Cheshire, Excavations 1968–85*, HBMC(E) Archaeological Report 23

Enlart, C. 1916, 'Le Costume', in *Manuel D'archéologie Française depuis les temps Merovingiens jusqu'a la Renaissance* Tome III, Paris

Evans, J. 1921, *English Jewellery from the 5th Century AD to 1800*

Evans, J. 1922, *Magical Jewels*, Oxford

Evans, J. 1931, *English Posies and Posy Rings*, Oxford

Evans, J. & Serjeantson, M. 1933, *Medieval English Lapidaries*, Early English Text Society 190

Fingerlin, I. 1971, *Gürtel des hohen und späten Mittelalters*, Berlin

Forsyth, H.R. 1996, 'An inscribed silver-gilt chape of the 16th century' *Burlington Mag*, June 1996, 392–3

Forsyth, H.R. forthcoming 'An inscribed silver-gilt chape of the 16th century', *Trans London Middlesex Archaeol. Soc.* 46 (1995)

Feachen, R.W. de F. 1951, 'Dragonesque fibulae' *Antiq J* 31, 32–44

Gaimster, D.R.M. 1988, 'Archaeological Notes: Two post-medieval sword-belt fittings from Pyecombe, West Sussex' *Sussex Archaeol Collect* 126, 245–7

Gere, C. 1981, 'Rings from 1500 to 1900', in Ward *et al.* 1981, 87–133

Goodall, A.R. 1984, 'Objects of metal' in Allan *et al.* 1984, 337–48

Goodall, A.R. forthcoming, 'Copper alloy objects', in *Salisbury and South Wiltshire Museum Medieval Catalogue 3*

Grew, F. 1984, 'Small finds', in Thompson *et al.* 1984, 91–128

Harvey, Y. 1975, 'The bronze', in Platt & Coleman Smith 1975, 254–68

Hearn, K. 1995, *Dynasties: Painting in Tudor and Jacobean England 1530–1630*, Tate Gallery

Hinton, P. 1988a, 'The small finds', in Hinton (ed) 1988b,

385–416

Hinton, P. (ed.) 1988b, *Excavations in Southwark 1973–76, Lambeth 1973–79*, London Middlesex Archaeol Soc/Surrey Archaeol Soc Joint Paper 3

Huizinga, J. 1937, *The Waning of the Middle Ages*

Hume, I.N. forthcoming, *Excavations at Martin's Hundred*

Janssen, H.L. 1983, 'Metaal' in *Van Bos tot Stad: opgravingen in s'Hertogenbosch,* s'Hertogenbosch

Lodge, E. 1812, *Portraits of Illustrious Personages of the Court of Henry VIII Engravings from Holbein in the Royal Collection*

London Museum 1940, *Medieval Catalogue,* London Museum Catalogue 7

Longcroft A. & Joby, K. (eds) 1995, *East Anglian Studies, essays presented to J. C. Barringer*, University of East Anglia

Macklin, H.W. 1907, *The Brasses of England* 2nd edn

Margeson, S, 1993, *Norwich Households: Medieval and Post-Medieval Finds from Norwich Survey Excavations 1971–78*, East Anglian Archaeology 58, Norwich Survey

Margeson, S. 1995, 'Ball-headed pins: a typological puzzle,' in Longcroft & Joby (eds) 1995, 161–165

Mellor J.E. & Pearce T. (eds) 1981, *The Austin Friars, Leicester*, CBA Research Report 35, Leicestershire

Moir, D. forthcoming, 'Post medieval finds c.1450 – c.1700 – a selection from City of London sites 1972–1982', in *Post-Medieval Archaeol*

Murdoch, T. (ed.) 1991, *Treasures & Trinkets: Jewellery in London from pre-Roman times to the 1930s*, Museum of London

Oakley, G.E. 1979, 'The copper alloy objects and the lead alloy objects', in Williams (ed.) 1979, 248–67

Oman, C.C. 1930, *Catalogue of Finger Rings*, Victoria & Albert Museum Department of Metalwork

Parker, K.T. 1945, *The Drawings of Hans Holbein in the Collection of His Majesty the King at Windsor Castle*, Oxford and London

Parker Society (ed.) 1844, *The Catechism*

Planché, J.R. 1876, *Encyclopaedia of Costume or Dictionary of Dress.* Vol. I

Platt, C. & Coleman Smith, R. (eds) 1975, *Excavations in Medieval Southampton, 1953–1969*, vol. 2, Leicester

Repton, J.A. 1836, 'Observations on female head-dress in England, chiefly subsequent to the date of Mr Strutt's remarks in his "Habits of the people of England"' *Archaeologia* 27, 1838, 29–76

Robertson-MacKay, R. *et al.* 1981, 'A group of Saxon and medieval finds from the site of the Neolithic causewayed enclosure at Staines Surrey, with a note on the topography of the area', *Trans London Middle-*

sex Archaeol Soc 32, 107–131

Smith, Sir T. 1549, *A Discourse of the Common Weal of this Realm of England*, Lamond, E. (ed.) 1954, Cambridge

Spencer, B. 1969, 'London – Saint Albans return', *London Archaeol* 1.2, 34–5

Spencer, B. 1978, 'King Henry of Windsor and the London pilgrim' in Bird, Chapman & Clark (eds) 1978, 235–64

Spencer, B. 1985, '15th century collar of Ss', *Antiquaries Journal* 65.2, 449–51

Spencer, B. forthcoming, *Medieval Finds from Excavations in London 7: Pilgrim Souvenirs and Secular Badges*, HMSO

Spenser, E. 1590, *Faerie Queene* Smith, J.C. & de Selincourt, E. (eds) *The Poetical Works*, London 1912

Stratford, W. ?1581, *A Briefe Conceipte Touching the Commonwealth of this Realme of England.* Treatise by 'WS' assigned to William Stratford, Furnivall, F.J. (ed.) 1876, New Shakespeare Society

Strong, R. 1969, *Tudor and Jacobean Portraits*, 2 vols HMSO London

Stubbes, P. 1583, *The Anatomie of Abuses: Containing a discourse, or brief summarie of such notable vices and corruptions as nowe raigne in many Christian Countreys of the worlde*

Thompson, A. *et al.* 1984, 'Excavations at Aldgate, 1974' *Post-Medieval Archaeol* 18, 91–128

Tylecote, R.F. 1972, 'A contribution to the metallurgy of 18th and 19th century: Brass pins', *Post-Medieval Archaeology* 6, 183–90

Ward, A. *et al.* 1981, *The Ring from Antiquity to the Twentieth Century*

Waterhouse, E. 1953, *Painting in Britain 1530–1790*

Weinstein, R. 1989, 'Exhibits at Ballots: An early seventeenth-century head-dress fragment – a further remarkable chance find from the Thames foreshore' *Antiquaries Jnl* 69.2, 323–4

[Wheeler, R.E.M.] 1928, *The Cheapside Hoard of Elizabethan and Jacobean Jewellery*, London Museum Catalogue 2

Willan, T.S. 1962, *A Tudor Book of Rates* [1582], Manchester

Williams, D. 1996, 'Some recent finds from east Surrey', *Surrey Archaeol Collect* 83, 165–86

Williams, J.H. (ed.) 1979, *St Peter's Street Northampton, Excavations 1973–1976*, Northampton Development Corporation

Woodfield, C. 1981, 'Finds from the Free Grammar School site, at the Whitefriars, Coventry, c.1545 – c.1557/58', *Post Medieval Archaeology* 15, 81–159

16   Getting There, Got It: archaeological textiles and tailoring in London, 1330–1580

Kay Staniland

Clothing styles have always been in a state of transition. In retrospect some of the changes can seem to have been revolutionary, radical breaks in long-established fashionable outlines. However, it can always be shown that these changes were part of a continuous process of development, that essentially the new line was a logical progression from the old. This argument is as true of the Middle Ages as it is of the 20th century: it is simply that different social and economic forces have prevailed.

The period 1400 to 1600 witnessed many changes in the clothing of both sexes, changes which can be shown to be a natural development from 'medieval' dress through styles readily recognisable as typical of the Tudor and Elizabethan periods. Dress historians habitually commentate on these changes as they are revealed by such sources as manuscript illuminations, portraits or sculpture. Less often, however, do they explore beyond these images, questioning why or how such changes came about, searching documentary sources or literature for further evidence, or considering what changes in contemporary society may have resulted in changes in dress. Surviving garments (or fragments thereof), preserved above or below the ground, have yet to be cajoled into yielding all the facts or clues they certainly hold. Received wisdom has been accepted and repeated without question; observations have failed to be made, questions have sometimes been neither asked nor answered; publication of vital information has, until recently, often been lamentable. As a result our insight into the nature of the changes observed in the clothing recorded in visual sources continues to be inadequate. So, too, is our understanding of the circumstances which brought about these changes.

Does the theme of this conference 'The Age of Transition 1400–1600' adequately describe the period in terms of the development of European dress? It is certainly true that these two centuries witnessed the metamorphosis of the simpler 'medieval' form of dress into the considerably more complex and lavishly ornate edifaces of the Tudor reigns. However, if any span of two centuries were selected it would be possible for me to demonstrate that fashionable dress experienced a major 'transition'.

The more profound period of change, as far as dress historians are concerned, was the century before 1400. This is often classified in textbooks as the age of the tailoring 'revolution' because of the radical nature of the changes which appear to have taken place in the shaping of clothing, seemingly within a comparatively short time-span. These changes produced the developments after 1400 which can be traced through Italian and Flemish paintings, sculpture and tomb effigies. For my contribution to this conference I have adopted a broader time-span to enable me to offer an assessment of the formative earlier period, followed by an overview of the evolution in styles which grew out of it; the contribution of excavated textiles in the City of London is interwoven into these two sections.

London has indeed been most fortunate in the quantities of excavated medieval and Tudor textiles discovered on demolition and archaeological sites within the City, and my broader time-span was selected precisely to allow some of the 14th-century finds to be incorporated into my contribution. They are mostly too fragmentary to demonstrate much about either the cut or the extent of the changes which took place in clothing during this earlier period, but nevertheless form a valuable and tangible starting point for an investigation of early tailoring practices, and are therefore relevant to my theme of change and improvement.[1]

In essence tailoring is the cutting up of a length of cloth and the shaping of it, by cut and stitch, to fit the contours of the human frame. The so-called 'tailoring revolution' of the 14th century, implying the introduction of tailoring practices, needs to be approached with caution: it is relatively easy to show how cloth was cut to create 'fitted' clothing for a century and more before 1300. One argument has suggested that there was a reticence in the Middle Ages about cutting into a length of cloth and thereby 'wasting' some of it. After all, it had been produced by a succession of painstaking and highly-skilled manual processes. It may also have been transported considerable distances, passing through the hands of several middlemen. The end product was often enormously expensive and was certainly much prized. There can be no doubt that every scrap of any textile was indeed put to practical use during the Middle Ages: strips could always be used as facings or bindings, or as contrasting decorative borders on other garments. But it is true that powerful considerations of practice and 'economy' came to be challenged and, gradually, overturned during the course of the 14th century. Was this in reality the result of pressures within an increasingly affluent society seeking 'fashionable' dress at any cost? The issue demands more detailed investigation, on an inter-disciplinary basis.

However, it is a fact that the skilful manipulation of rectangles, squares and triangles ('gores'), cut from a length of material without involving any 'waste' at all, did at first provide effective shaping for tunics and over-garments.[2] An undeniable interest in form and outline can be observed in both male and female clothing of the 12th century, and could almost certainly be traced in earlier centuries. The sidelacing

so ostentatiously portrayed on the tunic of a devil in a manuscript illumination of the period suggests that such a means of fitting a garment close to the torso was already known.[3] How widely it may have been employed at the time is not known. But this simple device was to enable a garment to be pulled on over the head and then laced close to the body. This did away with the need for much looseness in the garment. It is clear, too, that both tailors and their customers well understood the qualities of fine cloths. Certainly during the 13th century there began to be an exploration and exploitation of these qualities as well as a very obvious shift to more shapely clothing. The swing of a hem which the simple insertion of gores afforded to skirted garments, for example, must have been a potent element in medieval dress, difficult for the sophisticated modern eye to appreciate to the full. The elegance so apparent in contemporary manuscript illuminations and sculptures cannot be attributed solely to the imaginations and artistic skills of their creators: they were, surely, reflecting the essential nature of the clothing worn by those about them? It is a trend noted in 13th-century literature too.[4]

Judicious use of cloth doubtless remained an important consideration, but for those wealthy enough to be able to indulge in such luxuries the cost of an extra metre or two of an expensive cloth – or silk, or fur – was surely of small consequence? Constituting one the few vehicles for demonstrating status and wealth, clothing was accorded far greater significance and outlay than has been the case in more recent times. The use of increasing quantities of fabric (and furs) in medieval garments had long been a major factor in this social practice. The adoption of circular capes and mantles – or those based on a segment of a circle – is well demonstrated in Giotto's frescos in Padua and Assisi, painted around the turn of the 13th and 14th centures. These shaped garments certainly necessitated some 'waste', but it is equally certain that offcuts, when not employed elsewhere in the construction of the same garment, could be put to all manner of other uses and therefore did not actually constitute 'wasted' cloth. Even under the modern factory system offcuts are put to all sorts of ingenious uses, and it is reasonable to infer that in the Middle Ages spare pieces of cloth were similarly used elsewhere by the tailor or by his customer.[5]

It has been suggested that the catalyst for the radical changes in dress of the mid 14th century was the readoption of plate body-armour in the late 13th and early 14th centuries. If it is accepted that the shaping of clothing was already well-established before this innovation, we need to be cautious before adopting this thesis. It is an intriguing suggestion which needs to be explored much more thoroughly. Plate would certainly impose modifications on the garments worn beneath it. Padded linen armour was already widely worn; it was an effective defensive garment in its own right when nothing more was available to the wearer, and could be further reinforced with internal metal plates.[6] Padded tunics could also form additional protection under the extremely weighty mail shirts, but were not, it seems, always worn. It is suggested that the padded and reinforced tunics were gradually remodelled to form much more closely fitting defensive garments, and that their new form in turn influenced the shaping of the tunics worn in conjunction with them – 'aketons', 'pourpoints', 'gambesons'.

It could therefore be claimed that it was the linen-armourers who led the way in the 'tailoring revolution' rather than their close associates the tailors, who concentrated their efforts solely upon civilian dress. What kind of links might we expect there to have been between the linen-armourers and the tailors? Did the trends in armour percolate through their customers to tailors or vice-versa? Today the huge clothing and media industries have such a grip on choice and change that it is less easy to comprehend the very different forces active in the Middle Ages. Then royal and ducal courts were the main arenas for the display of rich and 'fashionable' knightly dress where novelties would have been tried out and, if they found approval, copied. Improvements and changes in knights' military equipment would similarly have been conspicuous here, as well as on the battlefield. Plate was expensive and therefore limited to the wealthy. This inter-relationship between martial and civilian spheres, both with regard to those commissioning and wearing armour and the combinations of craftsmen creating it, is a fascinating one which demands further exploration

in conjunction with armour historians. Only then can we be clearer about the part changes in armour may have played in the so-called tailoring revolution.[7]

The new tailored garments did not wholly supplant the older form of tunic in civilian dress. This continued in widespread use throughout Europe and can be recognised, little altered, even in the 16th century. The cut can be detected in men's shirts and women's chemises throughout the 17th and 18th century until changes in coats and dresses finally made it obsolete. This older economically cut medieval tunic is best exemplified by that found on the body of the medieval traveller (thought to be a merchant) discovered at Bocksten in southern Sweden in 1936, currently dated at between the early 14th century and c.1360.[8] It offers no assistance with the problems connected with the introduction of tailoring elsewhere in Europe and merely prompts questions about the time lapse involved in the transmission of fashions from courts to country, or throughout society. In contrast the London textile finds of the 14th century are fragmentary, offering little information about cut but many valuable insights into cloths, and sewing and constructional techniques. They have now been published in some detail and I will therefore refer to just a few relevant pieces.[9] The group is invaluable as an entity because it demonstrates the remarkably large and varied range of cloths employed in clothing in 14th century London: from heavyweight to lightweight, from coarse to very fine, from plain to patterned. This diversity is just one facet of the sophisticated nature of metropolitan society in northern Europe and the culture which was in the process of undergoing a profound change, sartorially speaking. It seems very likely that such cloth and clothing were limited in distribution: the Bocksten merchant, for example, certainly did not have access to fine cloth or to the most up-to-the-minute tailoring skills.

These same London fragments reveal high levels of sewing skills and the presence of sophisticated finishing techniques. For example, the lower portion of a finely checked red and white sleeve of c.1320–30 has neatly worked silk buttonholes and small buttons made of the same material; already tailors placed a silk facing behind the buttonholes to strengthen them.[10] The evenness and fineness of the buttonholing itself can today only be equalled by the best couture houses. Such evidence as now exists suggests that buttons had only replaced other fastening methods on clothing in the mid 13th century and, if this can be shown to be so, it is all the more remarkable that the skills associated with this small accessory had been mastered in little more than half a century.

Of even greater significance is the existence of a tablet-woven silk braid worked directly onto the buttonhole edge of the sleeve opening. This was at the same time a practical and yet elegant finishing device not previously expected in medieval dress because it is not shown in visual sources. Such small details, which many would dismiss as insignificant, are particularly valuable for the light they throw upon the refinements of dress and the skills which existed within tailors' workrooms in large medieval con-nurbations like London. Skills in working silk seem usually to have been a woman's preserve in the 14th century – and probably earlier – and it is likely that there was a mixture of male and female workers in tailoring workrooms. The accounts of Edward III's armourers suggest that such mixed workrooms did survive in London, but no similarly detailed accounts exist to reveal whether similar conditions prevailed in the workrooms of the royal tailors.

This important new evidence confirms that in their sewing skills at least – in the numerous methods of sewing seams and hems, for example, or of finishing raw edges of cloth or silk, or providing decorative features – medieval tailors in London were already extremely competent. We know far less about tailoring skills in the 13th century, or even 12th century, although the embroidery commonly referred to as *opus anglicanum* relied upon remarkably fine sewing skills which could just as easily have been applied to secular clothing: it probably was, at the highest levels. The London fragments demonstrate that for those in the 14th century who could afford to pay for this skilled labour – City merchants and their like – clothing was already becoming a refined possession, manipulated to convey its owner's wealth and taste. The finishing touches, like the buttonholes or tablet-woven edgings, furthermore suggest that some of the finer points of dress would only be apparent to those who came close enough to see such

discreet detail. We can justifiably claim that by the mid 14th century London tailors at least were well and truly 'getting there'.

The shortage of information about the shaping of clothes in the London finds is regrettable, particularly as it seems unlikely that any further comparable discoveries will be made in London. Therefore, to help determine the changes occurring in men's clothing during the second and third quarters of the 14th century, visual sources must be re-examined. The speed with which these changes happened, as well as the details of all the individual developments, have yet to be ascertained and are beyond the scope of this paper. At present it seems reasonable to accept the hypothesis that innovations in armour could well have provided one impetus for the considerable changes in civilian dress. However, it seems likely that other factors were at work too. Complex and changing economic and social factors must also have been influential in stimulating changes and increasing luxury in dress; there certainly appears to be evidence of an increase in such luxuries as finer and more expensive cloths, silks and furs. These were mostly imports which had previously been limited to the wealthy classes of medieval society. Contemporary references, sumptuary legislation and inventories show that people owned larger quantities of clothing. Another aspect, as yet unexplored to my knowledge, is the identification of national variants. Visual sources from all European countries can provide valuable details for a common pool of information, but it is necessary to separate those which have a truly international perspective from those which clearly relate to specific localities.

Similar changes are reflected in contemporary women's dress: figure-hugging torsos with widening hems to help accentuate this curvaceous new body-line. It is assumed – but not proven – that female dress followed male dress rather than led it at this particular time. The way that these changes took place and the effect that this had on the cut and styling of dresses has not been studied in any depth. At some point, for example, it became helpful to introduce a seam at the waist to aid the shaping process and thus the form of dress which was to establish itself as recognisably 'Tudor' emerged.

The ingenuity of tailors now began to be put to a

severe test. The accumulated cutting and sewing skills touched upon earlier indubitably helped the changes to come into being. Presumably the tailoring developments in the workshops of the linen armourers were transferred to those of the civilian tailors. The latter began to apply a considerable inventiveness to the problem of fitting flat pieces of cloth round torsos and arms, and different solutions are to be found scattered in visual sources throughout Europe; I am not aware that these have been collected together and examined by anyone interested in the evolution of cut. The jupon associated with Charles de Blois – not an excavated example but one cherished since it left its owner's back – reveals only one of what must have been many solutions to the cutting of the 'new' tailored tunics or doublets. A diagram showing the construction of this garment reveals that the older principle of employing rectangles and triangular gores had mostly to be completely abandoned for these extremely tailored garments.[11] If other doublets of this date had survived I am sure that we would have been examining some very different approaches to construction. This was truly an 'age of transition' as far as male clothing was concerned.

At this point accusations of wastefulness surface in the acidic writings of chroniclers, inhabitants of monasteries who reacted with considerable vehemence to the radical changes confronting them on civilians. Their own dress was prescribed, traditional and ultra-conservative. This much has to be taken into account when these comments on the 'new' styles of dress are used as evidence. In fact the older tunic was by no means abandoned. It continued in widespread use throughout Europe and for long formed the habitual wear of manual labourers. The changes in the styling of fashionable dress dispersed quickly throughout urban and then rural communities. The constant peregrinations of the English court coupled with the movement of the aristocracy between the court, their estates and Westminster and the City facilitated the speed of this change.

From having been responsible for producing what we might view as relatively straightforward clothing in previous centuries, making only modest 'improvements' to their products as the decades passed, tailors seem to have emerged in the mid 14th century as a radically innovative force in metropolitan society. Is this an accurate reading of what happened and of those responsible for bringing about the transformation of men's clothing? Did the changes take place quite as rapidly as historians have inferred from visual sources? The accurate dating of many manuscripts, paintings, sculptures and brasses has yet to be accomplished before dress historians can establish a sound chronology of developments in European clothing. The processes of creation, influence and diffusion must have been very different in court and connurbation. And furthermore several generations of tailors must have been involved in pushing forward the boundaries; the same could be said of their clients too. There seems every reason to accept that then, as now, it was the young who were more receptive to the new and extreme forms of dress. Many issues must be examined before the existence of a 'tailoring revolution' can be accepted with assurance.

Thus by the last two decades of the 14th century tailors had experienced *their* age of transition. Well-trained apprentices were now suitably equipped to confront the challenges of *our* Age of Transition, 1400–1600. Four centuries of consecutive transitions in dress styles were to follow before anything equalling the seemingly revolutionary changes of the 14th century were to reappear in European dress. From the end of the 14th century tailors' workshops began to feature in manuscripts, and this may be no mere coincidence.[12] Does this relate to to the changes we have just been considering or is it part of an expansion of artists' subject? I would be most grateful if anyone can lead me to such illustrations earlier than the late 14th century.

English fashions of the 15th century have been ratherly thinly researched.[13] Visual sources are, generally speaking, not so abundant and dress historians have instead turned their attention to the infinitely richer fields of Burgundian, Flemish and Italian works of art. With good reason too. For works like the famous *Trés Riches Heures,* or Jan van Eyck's *Arnolfini Marriage,* portray so well the fine flowing cloths which were such an integral part of north European dress, the rich silks now available in increasing quantities as the result of considerable expansion in the Italian silk industry, and the quantities of fine furs imported from northern

Scandinavia and Russia. There is a great deal of documentary evidence but this has been little explored, whilst a lack of contemporary excavated textile finds has again meant that research into the textiles and clothing of the century has not been stimulated.

Since space demands generalisations I would admit that we can yet see the 15th century as a sort of age of transition in the field of tailoring history: the transition between 'medieval' and Tudor clothing. For having 'invented' and established the abbreviated and close-fitting men's tunic – and reintroduced warmer and more practical long, loose overgarments (the 'houppelande' and its successors) – the fashions of this century might be summed up as variations on this theme. Did tailoring tend to rest on its laurels – or was it that customers, innately conservative, needed a period of adjustment before embarking upon the next sequence of sartorial challenges? Tomb effigies and engraved brasses seem to confirm this point. It appears that we in Britain were content on the whole to be influenced by continental fashions rather than to initiate our own fashions. Having mastered the art of fitting cloth closely to the human body – in the form of tunic and tights – tailors turned their attention to the generously cut fur lined over garments where the fullness was diverted into elegant vertical pleats. This sumptuous style was echoed in women's dress too, and the headwear of both sexes grew in height and width to balance the new outline. By the end of the century it is perfectly clear that tailors were fully competant in the arts of cutting and shaping cloth. The stiff padded outline of male dress had given way to a much softer line, whilst women's dresses had already taken on the fitted form of bodice with wide square neckline so much associated with the Tudor period.

A second sizeable accumulation of excavated textiles, dating to the 16th century, is preserved in the Museum of London. Regrettably this group of finds is mostly unresearched, unpublished and unphotographed, although several pieces have been conserved for exhibition, and a very few have been illustrated in publications. The full value of these finds has yet to be demonstrated. Although they contain less varied examples of cloths, they do have a greater proportion of clothing fragments, numerous

Fig. 16.1 *Sleeve of tabby woven cloth, found in Moorfields, London; probably 1540–60 (Museum of London accession no. 22444b).*

fragments of ribbons, braids and laces and, most importantly, a considerable quantity of examples of knitting in wool. Like the 14th-century excavated textiles, only a few pieces are of a size to provide information about the shaping and sewing of clothing in Tudor London. A complete cloth sleeve, for example, cut in one piece and with an additional triangular gore inserted at the inner elbow for flexibility, is a valuable link with earlier shaping practices (Fig. 16.1).[14] Ingenuity was required from tailors for the construction of cod-pieces, those false male genitalia so unique to the Tudor age (Fig. 16.2). These prosaic London versions do not compare with the magnificent examples shown in many portraits, but they do reveal how tailors went about creating them – and that they were commonly worn on the dress of less affluent citizens of London. Manipulation of cloth to provide an ingenious finish on a

Fig. 16.2 *Three cod-pieces formed from layers of twill woven cloth, found in Worship Street, London; probably 1540–60 (Museum of London accession nos. A26604, A26757, A26858).*

garment is demonstrated by several strips of cloth (Fig. 16.3).[15] These show how a long narrow strip of cloth could have a series of regular slits made along its length so that when the resulting 'tongues' were turned in on themselves, in a manner recalling similar manipulation of parchment to hold seals in place, the end product created a most satisfactory and cost effective surface decoration for the doublet of a less affluent citizen of London. Associated fragments of stamped and pierced leather from men's doublets hint at the diverse and ornate nature of men's dress in the mid 16th century; these can frequently be seen in contemporary portraits.

These London fragments were discovered on various City redevelopment sites earlier in the present century by workmen and antiquarians and mostly cannot now be related to associated finds. Therefore accurate dating is not a possibility. They do, however, have much to reveal about the clothing of London's citizens, whilst the large quantity of knitted items is without parallel; indeed many examples made their way from the London sites directly into a number of other collections in Britain and North America.

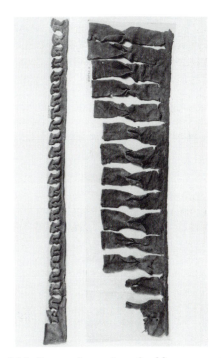

Fig. 16.3 *Decorative strips of tabby woven cloth, found in Worship Street, London; probably 1540–60 (Museum of London accession nos. A26808–9).*

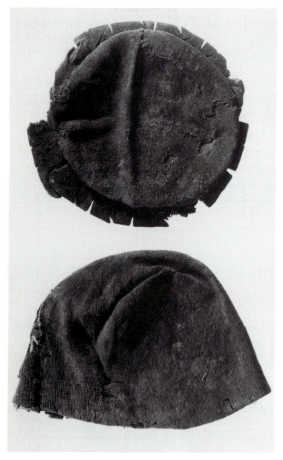

Fig. 16.4 *Caps of knitted wool, the brimmed cap found in Finsbury, London; late 15th to mid-16th century (Museum of London accession nos. 13,049 and A6340).*

The knitted wool caps are the largest and best known group amongst these finds (Fig. 16.4). They embrace styles fashionable between the late 15th century and the third quarter of the 16th century, but the lack of adequate stratigraphy makes it impossible to know whether all were deposited at the same time or over a period of time. Recent carefully conducted excavations have yielded fragments of knitted wool from late 14th-century London levels, possibly the remains of a cap and a stocking.[16] Much has yet to be learned about the introduction and early history of knitting in London, as well as of the subsequent development of a thriving local knitting industry.

These finds are therefore of some consequence.

A brimless cap from an unidentified London site is of a type fashionable in the last quarter of the 15th century, and may have been discarded in favour of the brimmed caps so ubiquitous in Tudor portraits.[17] Cloth and felt examples of these later caps also survive, whilst the variety of styles represented by the knitted versions suggests a deposit period embracing some fifty years. Smaller brimmed caps, some ornamented with ribbons or slashes through the heavily felted knitting, seem to be exactly contemporary with examples found more recently on the ship *The Mary Rose*. Some 15–20 successive stages were involved in the production of these caps, turning them into felted waterproof head-coverings, the forerunner of the modern beret. Already a small-scale industrial process was at work although the caps, so ubiquitous in contemporary portraits, were undoubtedly the product of individual households. Once more there seems to be little background information about this industry, its organisation and growth.

As well as caps this group of finds includes stockings, sleeves, and a child's 'vest' and mitten. The stockings again show a transition, but in construction technique rather than fashionable style. Cloth leg coverings were still in use in Tudor London and a complete example has survived (Fig. 16.5a): fragments of less ably tailored versions from the 14th-century excavations reveal that the construction of these articles of clothing had improved by the later period. But this ancient form of leg covering was now fast disappearing and its place was being taken by knitted versions which, created using the significantly named, and elastic, *stocking stitch*, were a considerable improvement. The finds include a primitive form, little more than a tube drawn together at the toes, and heavily reinforced at that familiar weak point, the heel (Fig. 16.5c). The transition taking place is apparent in the foot section of a further example (Fig. 16.5b). This demonstrates the art of manipulating stitches, by decreasing or increasing stitches in selected areas, to shape that tube more nearly to the natural form of the foot and ankle; what was apparently developed at this period has continued little altered to the present day. Exactly how that transition came about has yet to be studied. The

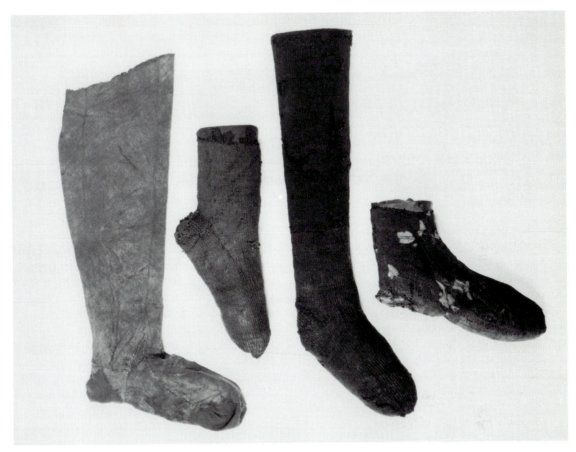

Fig. 16.5 *Leg coverings from left to right of a) twilled cloth, b) & c) knitted wool and d) silk, the latter found in Whitecross Street, London; probably 1540–60 (Museum of London accession nos. 22407, 22401, A26851, A13833).*

foot of a silk stocking – the only example of knitted silk, or indeed of a skilfully constructed fashionable piece of clothing, amongst the London finds – perhaps a discarded luxury import from Italy or Spain, is extremely finely knitted and suggests a source of inspiration for the much clumsier northern wool versions (Fig. 16.5d). Some elaborately patterned knitted silk stockings have recently been found in the Medici tombs in Florence and these echo those worn by Sir Christopher Hatton, Elizabeth I's Lord Chancellor, in the famous miniature by Nicholas Hilliard.[18] Finally there is a humbler piece of knitting in the London finds which should be mentioned. This is a knitted garter, certainly the earliest knitted example to survive and unique in its

way (Fig. 16.6). This must be the origin of the term 'garter stitch', the most basic knitting stitch and one with an elasticity perfect for the purpose of holding stockings in place. As yet such pieces have received little or no attention, but the recent formation of a specialist study group suggests that the origins and history of knitting in Western Europe will now encourage work on this neglected area.[19]

The important and varied nature of these archaeological finds has lured me away from my central theme of London tailors, their collective expertise and achievements. There is something of a cyclical quality to fashion, and the less padded flowing male fashions of the late 15th century gradually gave way to a new stiffening and elaboration. No better

Fig. 16.6 *Fragment of a garter knitted in wool, findsite not known, probably 1540–60
(Museum of London accession no NN18752).*

prototype could be found for Tudor tailoring than Henry VIII himself. His portraits well demonstrate the quantities of padding, shaping and elaborate surface decoration necessary for these imposing masterpieces of the Tudor tailor's art.

This end of our timescale is infinitely better supplied with source material. Not only is there a profusion of visual sources but also a number of complete men's suits have been preserved in Europe and Scandinavia and these have been studied in detail and published, together with many isolated or fragmentary garments.[20] Furthermore, there are still in existence a number of 16th-century manuscript tailors' pattern books of this period from Germany and some printed versions from Spain.[21] These books embrace both men's and women's garments, and the diversity of the patterns reveals just how complex the world of professional tailoring had become. In order to qualify as masters, journeymen in Germany were required to make a number of these garments ('masterpieces') to a satisfactory standard. One of the Spanish books is now available in translation.[22] Juan de Alcega's *Book of the Practice of Tailoring*, originally printed in Madrid in 1589, not only illustrates the pattern pieces laid out on lengths of material, as an economical cutting guide. It also advises readers how much material would be required for making up each pattern, and provides instructions about the cutting and making of each example. Whether anything of their like existed in England is not known, but practises probably did not vary greatly and even if manuscript versions did not exist, these continental books demonstrate how far tailoring had progressed since the Middle Ages.

Tailors, they prove, had certainly 'got there'.

John Stow (1525?–1605), himself a qualified London tailor, preferred to pour his energies into investigating and recording the capital's history rather than documenting his own trade. What an incalculable loss to history! By the time Samuel Pepys (1633–1703), the famous son of another London tailor, was responsible for his own attire it could be claimed that the whole complex art of tailoring had passed its first major peak. Already much softer and less elaborate clothing had become established in the world of fashion. The art of tailoring would never again face such a period of challenge and achievement.[23]

Notes

1. See Crowfoot, Pritchard & Staniland 1992.
2. *Ibid.* 177.
3. The Winchester Psalter, c.1160–70 (Cathedral Library, Winchester); illustrated and discussed Staniland 1969, 12.
4. Evans 1952, 16.
5. Offcuts could have been used to make smaller accessories (purses, for example), seal bags, ornamental borders for garments, and cut up into motifs for appliqué embroidery. The undamaged areas of cast-off clothing were probably often reused in this way.
6. Blair 1958, 32–35, 40, 75–6.
7. I am grateful to Claude Blair for reading and commenting upon an early draft of this paper.
8. Nockert 1985, 47–52.
9. Crowfoot, Pritchard & Staniland 1992, 150–198.
10. *Ibid.* 162–3, 168. It is very likely that there were,

additionally, linen facings which have almost completely disappeared.

11. Evans 1952, 30.
12. See the series of Italian MSS relating to health matters (e.g. Vienna, Nationalbibliotek, MS Cod. Ser. n. 2644).
13. Cunnington 1952; Scott 1980; Houston 1939.
14. Museum of London accession no. 22444b, found in the Moorfields area; illustrated Hunnisett 1996, 46–47.
15. Museum of London accession nos. A26807–10, found in Worship Street.
16. Crowfoot, Pritchard & Staniland 1992, 72–5.
17. Museum of London accession no. 13049 'found in London' (ex Guildhall Museum collection); a similar cap is shown in Antonello da Messina's *Young Man* of 1474–9 (National Gallery).
18. Rutt 1987, 71–2; Victoria and Albert Museum, P.138–1910.
19. The Early Knitting History Group; garter, Museum of London accession no. NN 18752.
20. Arnold 1985.
21. Petrascheck-Heim 1969.
22. de Alcega 1979, facsimile pages 13–88.
23. I am grateful to the editors for allowing me to revise this paper. It was heavily supported by illustrative material when originally delivered, and has been rewritten to incorporate these visual aspects of my argument.

Bibliography

Arnold, J. 1985, *Patterns of Fashion: The cut and construction of clothes for men and women c.1560–1620*

Blair, C. 1958, *European Armour c.1066 – c.1700*

Crowfoot, E., Pritchard, F. & Staniland, K. 1992, *Medieval Finds from Excavations in London: Textiles and Clothing*

Cunnington, C.W. & P. 1952, *Handbook of English Medieval Costume*

de Alcega J. 1979 facsimile [trans. Pain, J. and Bainton, C., intro. Nevinson, J.L.], *Tailor's Pattern Book 1589*, Carlton, Bedford

Evans, J. 1952, *Dress in Medieval France*, Oxford

Houston, M. 1939, *Medieval Costume in England and France*

Hunnisett, J. 1996, *Period Costume for Stage and Screen: Patterns for Women's Dress, Medieval – 1500*, Studio City, California

Nockert, M. 1985, *Bockstensmannen och Hans Drakt*, Falkenberg, Sweden

Petrascheck-Heim, I. 1969, 'Tailors' Masterpiece-books' *Costume: The Journal of the Costume Society* 3, 6–9

Rutt, R. 1987, *A History of Knitting*

Scott, M. 1980, *Late Gothic Europe 1400–1500*

Staniland, K. 1969, 'The Medieval "Corset"' *Costume: The Journal of the Costume Society* 3, 10–13

17   Seals and Heraldry, 1400–1600: public policy and private post

John Cherry

Introduction

Seals through their use of inscription and image define the nature of the person or institution for which they provide legal identification. The increased importance given to heraldry on seals and changes in the iconography of seals reflect the age of transition.[1]

Michael Clanchy saw the development of heraldry in the 12th century as co-incidental with the growth of literacy and also as an alternative series of signs which was peculiar to the knightly order and distinguished their names by symbols.[2] In the period marked by the title *The Age of Transition* heraldry is increasingly seen as an aspect of the display of magnificence. 'For a visitor to an early Tudor royal house the new elements of design would have been virtually submerged beneath the tidal wave of heraldic devices, mottoes and badges. Indeed it is the welter of heraldry that strikingly predominates'[3] And 'It is often stressed what a significant part the display of heraldry played in the status of the powerful in Tudor England. Heraldry often engaged in a double allusion to the owner, his family ties and his chief local connections on the one hand, and to his allegiance to the King on the other'.[4]

One of the most impressive illustrations of the political effectiveness of heraldry is the wooden screen in King's College, Cambridge, that was put up by Dr Edward Foxe, the Provost of King's, in the 1530s. It is covered in emblems and initials celebrating the successful end of the King's great matter, his divorce of Queen Katherine of Aragon. It is almost as if these badges represent a statement of the new heraldic display.[5]

Another illustration of the importance of heraldry is the execution of the Earl of Surrey in 1547 for, among other things, his use of arms which were too close to the royal arms. Ever since 1543, Surrey had vaunted his royal descent from Edward I through Thomas of Brotherton and had professed a right through the Mowbray family to the arms of Edward the Confessor. Although the College of Heralds had found against him, he had not hesitated to emblazon on a panel at Kenninghall, Norfolk, an escutcheon displaying the leopards and the cross along with his own arms. It was for this heraldic example of high treason that he lost his head.[6]

This article will consider how far seals and heraldry in the 15th/16th centuries were affected by the religious and economic changes by examining the great seal, the introduction of Italian designs, the changes to religious seals, and the increased use of the signet ring.

The great seal

The medieval great seal is often held up as one of the elements of conservatism in sigillography.[7] It is true that the form of the great seal has remained much the same since the double great seal of William the Conqueror to the present day with the seated monarch on one side and the equestrian figure on the other. If we compare the enthroned figure of the

Fig. 17.1 *Second great seal of Henry IV, engraved between 1408 and 1413. Society of Antiquaries casts. Diameter 12.5cm.*

Fig. 17.2 *Second great seal of Queen Elizabeth engraved in 1586. Society of Antiquaries casts. Diameter 14.6cm.*

monarch on the first and last great seals of our period there are clearly considerable changes. The second or 'gold' seal of Henry IV, which was engraved between 1408 and 1413 (Fig. 17.1) shows the enthroned King in the middle of an elaborate Perpendicular screen with niches. To the King's left and right are St Edmund with St Michael above, and Saint Edward the Confessor with St George above. To their left and right are standard bearers with the standards of Lancaster and England and France modern quarterly. In projections at the side are the symbols of the evangelists, and the Virgin and Child is shown above the head of the King. The King is presented in the middle of saints and the representation of the royal saints, Edward and Edmund, may indicate his claim to the throne through his descent from Henry III. The presence of the Virgin and Child and the evangelists' symbols stress the importance of divine protection.

Compared with the second great seal of Elizabeth which was engraved in 1586 (Fig. 17.2), the enthroned figure of the Queen is much larger and dominates the seal, to such an extent that the top of the throne rises up into the surrounding inscription.

The appearance of a hand from clouds on each side to gently lift her cloak is the only gesture towards divine protection. These hands are less prominent than the roses above or the royal arms surrounded by the Garter with crowns above which flank the queen in place of saints. On the equestrian side her horse raises his feet above a rose bush and the three symbols of countries – rose, fleur-de-lis and harp – are all surmounted by crowns. The principal change between the two seals is the elimination of the religious figures on the first which is replaced by heraldry. The authority that was given to the seal of Henry IV by the saints, from whom Henry saw his descent, is replaced by heraldry and badges.

In addition to this change in authority there was also a change on the great seal from Gothic to a northern Renaissance style. This occurred when the third great seal of Henry VIII was made in 1542. It was presumably the change in Henry's style to include the title of head of the Church in England that caused the new seal to be made by Morgan Wolff, goldsmith. It is not known who designed the seal but it has been suggested that it was Lucas Hornebolte since the portrait of the King on the obverse is similar to those on manuscripts illuminated by Hornebolte, and he sits on a throne in the Renaissance style.[8] This stylistic change can be detected much earlier in the seals of Cardinal Wolsey.

Italian style

The seals of Cardinal Wolsey illustrate both the traditional devotion on the eve of the Reformation and the change to Renaissance style. The seal for the college that he founded in Ipswich in 1528 which shows the Virgin in Glory (*Maria in Sole*) in the centre provides a good example of this. The image may be an imitation of the seal of Eton College, founded by Henry VI.[9]

Wolsey played an important part in the introduction of the Italian style into seals.[10] This subject needs more study than can be given here, and in particular the interrelationship of English and Italian seals still has to be studied. Wolsey was created a Cardinal in 1516. Sir Hilary Jenkinson has pointed out that Lautizio di Meo de Rotelli may have designed the golden bull for the document of Clement VII confirming the title *Fidei Defensor* on Henry VIII of 1524.[11] The earliest occurence of Italian influence on the seals of Wolsey is on his seal as Archbishop of York, first known in 1524, which he changed two years later in 1526. Wolsey was also clearly influential in the engraving of the great seal of 1525 and the seal of 1527 for the Treaty of Amiens. The seal of Cardinal College of 1528 (Fig. 17.3) is a final example of his influence. This has a peculiar representation of the Trinity since the Almighty wears a large full robe embracing three small figures

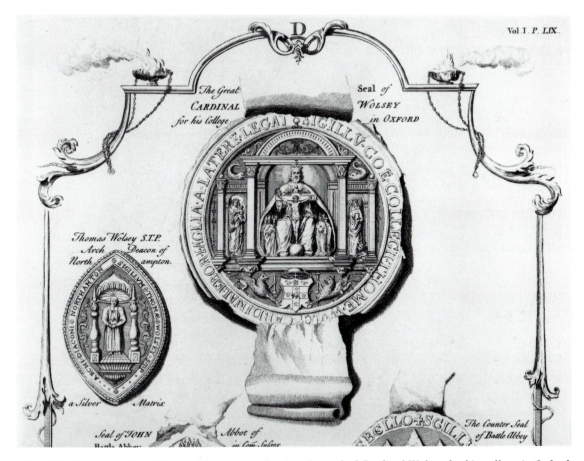

Fig. 17.3 *Engraving from* Vetusta Monumenta *showing the seal of Cardinal Wolsey for his college in Oxford.*

Fig. 17.4 *Cast of the seal of John Kite, Bishop of Carlisle 1521–37. Society of Antiquaries casts. Height 8.7cm.*

on each side. He is placed within a Renaissance niche surmounted by a double arch filled with Renaissance ornament and dolphins.[12] This Italian influence may also be seen in seals of the Wolsey circle such as that of John Kite, Bishop of Carlisle, who held the see from 1521 to 1537 (Fig. 17.4).[13]

Episcopal seals

The tradition of devotion, for which England was noted in the early 16th century, can be seen in other seals. For instance the seal of the Crutched Friars (or Brethren of the Holy Cross) of London, engraved in 1526, shows the Crucifixion with five brethren on each side.[14]

Religious reform in the 1530s and 1540s affected seals in three ways. The first and most obvious was in changes to institutions of which the disappearance of the monastic seals and the creation of seals of new bishoprics are the most obvious, secondly the replacement of unsuitable religious scenes, and thirdly, the replacement of religion by heraldry.

The seals of the bishoprics created in 1540 show an interesting change. There were seven refoundations of old cathedrals (Carlisle, Durham, Ely, Norwich, Rochester, Winchester, and Worcester) and six new foundations (Bristol, Chester, Gloucester, Oxford, Peterborough and Westminster).[15]

Some of the changes were relatively minor, or at least economical, such as that at Norwich Cathedral where the Annunciation has been removed to make place for a deeply cut ornamental shield of arms.[16] Where completely new seals had to be engraved, the main type (represented by Chester, Worcester, and Oxford) shows a religious scene on the obverse and the King in majesty on the reverse, a representation derived from the reverse of the great seal. The double seal of the Dean and Chapter of Oxford that replaced that of the Augustinian canons of St Frideswides in 1546 provides a good example (Fig. 17.5). On the reverse Henry VIII is shown seated against a shell niche while on the obverse Christ is shown standing with five cherubim on either side.[17] The reverse reflects the great seal, and so asserts royal power. The legend on the reverse *Servire : deo : reg .... est : factum : anno : gracie : 1546 : anno : regis : henrico : 8 : 38:* stresses the role that Henry VIII thought the college should have in serving the King and perhaps becoming the means by which the Crown controlled Oxford University.[18]

The second change is the replacement of unacceptable religious scenes. This may be illustrated by the seals of Thomas Cranmer, Archbishop of Canterbury (1533–53). His first seal followed closely that of his predecessor William Wareham.[19] His second (Fig. 17.6) shows the scene of the martyrdom of Thomas Becket that had been traditional on the seals of the Archbishops of Canterbury since that of Archbishop Arundel in 1396. For his third seal the martyrdom was cut out and replaced by the Crucifixion (Fig. 17.7). This change was made between 1533 and 1539, most probably in 1538 when the

Fig. 17.5 *Casts of the obverse and reverse of the seal for the Dean and Chapter of Oxford. Society of Antiquaries casts. Diameter 8.4cm.*

Fig. 17.6 *Cast of the second seal of Thomas Cranmer, Archbishop of Canterbury, showing the martyrdom of Becket. Society of Antiquaries casts. Ht 9.6cm.*

Fig. 17.7 *Cast of the third seal of Thomas Cranmer, Archbishop of Canterbury, showing the crucifixion. Society of Antiquaries casts. Probably 1538. Ht9.6cm.*

shrine of Becket at Canterbury was broken up.[20] Ever since Henry had discovered he was Supreme Head of the Church of England, he had detested the memory of Becket, whose cult represented the triumph of the Church over the King of England. At much the same time, the scene of Becket's martyrdom was cut out of Cranmer's prerogative seal and replaced by the scourging of Christ.[21]

The deletion was paralleled on the city seal of Canterbury where in 1541–2 the scene of the martyrdom was cut away and replaced by a poor shield of the city arms. In the city accounts for 1541–2 is the entry recording the alteration:

> Paid to William Oldfeld, Belfounder, for puttyng out of Thomas Bekket in the comen seale, and gravyng agayn of the same. iis. viiid.[22]

The process was reversed when the scene of the martyrdom of Becket was reinstituted on the seal engraved for the Prerogative court of Canterbury during the incarceration of Cranmer in 1555 and also on the seal of Archbishop Pole for the prerogative court of Canterbury in use in 1557.[23]

Later episcopal seals in the 16th century ignore episcopal insignia and saints. The seal of John Scory, Bishop of Rochester, (1551–2), attests to the virtues of preaching, by showing the bishop in a pulpit.[24] The seal of Richard Barnes, Bishop of Durham from 1577–87, shows the bishop seated and his right hand instead of blessing grasps a birch rod – for discipline – as a scroll on his chancery seal says and his left hand, instead of a crosier, holds the open bible, inscribed *verbum dei*.[25] Sometimes the device on episcopal seals is banal. The seal of Thomas Dove, (1555–1630), which contains an emblematic design with dovecote and male figures fowling, emphasises the loss of nerve in major episcopal seal design.[26]

The third major change provoked by Reform was the replacement of traditional Christian images in churches such as the rood with its statues of the Virgin and St John by displays of the royal arms. There is clear documentary evidence for this process. Cautley quotes examples from 1541 onwards and a considerable number from 1552. In Wandsworth, Surrey, in 1552: 'Paid for pulling down the roodloft and setting up the scriptures... and ... the King's Majesty's Arms £4.12s.6d.'[27] This change signified

the abolition of Papal power and the exaltation of the Tudor monarchy. Those hostile to the Reformation in England had no doubt as to the significance of this development. As the famous controversialist, Nicholas Sander, wrote:

> In the place of the cross of Christ, which they threw down, they put up the arms of the King of England namely three leopards and three lilies, having for supporters the outstretched feet of a serpent and dog. It was a declaration that they were worshippers not of our Lord but of an earthly King whose armorial barings they had substituted for it.[28]

Many ordinary folk may have shared the contempt expressed by Thomas Martin at Cranmer's examination: 'Down with the sacraments! Down with the Mass! Down with the altars! Down with the arms of Christ and up with a lion and dog!'

There are two examples surviving. The first is at Rushbrooke in Suffolk, which was dated by Cautley to the reign of Henry VIII (though it must be said that it has been suggested that this is a Victorian fake).[29] The second is at Westerham, Kent, which may be dated to the reign of Edward VI.[30]

On seals the replacement of religion by heraldry is shown most clearly by the seals for ecclesiastical jurisdiction. At the highest level Henry VIII created the Court of Delegates which provided in ecclesiastical causes a substitute for for the court of appeal hitherto furnished by the court of Rome. Seals of Henry VIII and Edward VI exist for this.[31] Local seals were made after the Statute of Edward VI in 1547 which ordained that ecclesiastical jurisdiction was to be exercised in the name of the Crown, and that the seals of several jurisdictions were to bear the royal arms with the name of that particular jurisdiction in characters beneath the arms. The Statute was repealed in the first year of Mary's reign 1553. There are fifteen seals known that were made as a result of these Acts. Of the fourteen matrices known, thirteen are from England and one from Wales.[32]

The characteristic of these seals, illustrated by that for the deanery of Hereford (Fig. 17.8), is the crown above the royal arms with lion and dragon supporters.[33] All the seals are similar in their upper parts but have a different inscription beneath to indicate the area or court for which the seal was to

Fig. 17.8 Modern impression of the seal for ecclesiastical causes of the Deanery of Hereford. BM MLA Tonnochy no. 800. Height 7.3cm.

be illustrated by the early 15th-century seal matrix of the confraternity of the gild at Knowle in Warwickshire which shows Saints Anne teaching the Virgin to read, John the Baptist and St Laurence, with their names indicated in Latin in the inscription.[34] The effect of the dissolution of the monasteries is seen in the mid 16th-century seal matrix of the hospital of St Stephen in Norwich. This was previously subject to the priory of St Faith at Horsham and the seal was presumably made shortly after the dissolution of the priory in 1536. On the seal the crowned rose appears like a great stone ready to crush the saint and the inscription announces in English 'This seael belonge to the hospetal of saint stevens in Norwich'.[35] A more drastic change was made at the hospital at Shoreham in Sussex where the title 'our saviour jesus Christ' replaces St Catherine and her representation on the

be used. This inscription usually beginning *pro* is struck with individual letter dies and is not engraved. In this series of seals the bureaucratic similarity of intention and execution is impressive. The seals are notable not only for the assertion of the primacy of the royal arms but also for the assertion of the name being spelt out in letters rather than alluded to by a symbol. Here the name itself becomes a symbol.

Lesser religious institutions

The seals of lesser religious institutions, such as gilds, confraternities and hospitals, reveal a similar story, although we lack a comprehensive survey of this area. The late medieval devotion to saints may

Fig. 17.9 Modern impression of the seal of Lord Hastings of Loughborough BM MLA Tonnochy no. 857. Height 5.8cm.

seal is reduced to a Catherine wheel beneath the crucifixion.[36] Perhaps the the clearest example of the intrusion of the growth of secular in place of religious philanthropy is the development of private foundations such as the Hospital of Stoke Poges, Buckinghamshire, founded by Lord Hastings of Loughborough in 1557–8.[37] On this seal the crucifixion is about the same size as the bull's head badge of Lord Hastings encircled with the Garter (Fig. 17.9).

Reaction against reform

In contrast the reaction against reform that occurred in the reign of Queen Mary (1553–8) can be detected in the seal of the almost the only monastic house recreated in her short reign. This is the seal matrix of the Carthusian Priory of Sheen, which was refounded in November 1555, and lasted until her death. The charter of incorporation is dated 26th January 1557 and it allowed the new house to have a seal. This seal may only have been in use in England from 1557 to 1558, when it appears to have been taken abroad. The seal shows the Nativity, in a form similar to the way that it was depicted on the 15th-century seal of the Priory.[38]

Secular seals

Schools

Tha abolition of monasteries may be seen as having led to a greater concentration on the founding of schools. Education became a matter of public policy, a matter of concern to the spiritual power and, more suprisingly, to the civil power. For instance, Henry VIII's first act as Supreme Head of the Church of England was to order the publication of his title by parish priests to their congregations and by schoolmasters to their pupils.[39] School seals are therefore more common in the 16th century, and by their choice of heraldry, scenes of schooling, enthroned headmasters with birch, depictions of Queen Elizabeth or scenes of local significance they provide an interesting field for study which has not been surveyed since T.J. Pettigrew published his articles in the early 19th century.[40] Queen Elizabeth appears

on a number of seals, notably those of Wimborne Minster, Dorset (refounded 1563), Faversham, Kent (founded 1576), Cranbrooke, Kent (founded 1574), and Darlington, Durham (founded 1567). The most impressive of these school seals showing Queen Elizabeth is that of Ashbourne Grammar School of 1585. This shows, in the upper part, Queen Elizabeth enthroned, with two lions as supporters and holding a sceptre and globe, surrounded by petitioners, an image based on her Great seal. In the lower part there is an assembly of teachers and their pupils ready to receive instruction.

Administrative seals

If we turn now to official seals, the changes in government made in the reign of Henry VIII and their effect on seals have been considered in detail by Hilary Jenkinson.[41] Although the main legal courts of King's Bench and Common Pleas had new seals, other new courts such as the Requests, First Fruits and Tenths, did not. One of the new courts that did obtain a new seal was the Court of Wards and Liveries, created in 1541. This produced a distinctly unmedieval touch by introducing two children to uphold the royal arms. New seals were also engraved for the Welsh counties created by the Act of 1542. These have been well catalogued by Alan Wyon, and the main new feature is the distinctive supporters used for each of the four groups of counties.[42] Indeed the increasing use of supporters for arms is a feature of the 16th century that distinguishes it from the earlier century of the Age of Transition.

Admirals' seals provide another instructive instance of change. These are interesting not only for information on the archaeology of ships but also for the use of the heraldry on the sails. The change from official to personal is demonstrated most clearly by the imposition of the shield on the mainsail. The seal matrix of Richard Cletherowe of 1406 shows a three-masted ship which flies the flag of England, the cross of St George, from the stern post, while the mainsail bears the royal arms.[43] Soon this was to be replaced by the Admiral's own arms and it appears in this manner on Admiral's seals in the late 15th and 16th century. A notable example of the mainsail bearing the Admiral's arms is the ivory seal matrix

Fig. 17.10 *Modern impression from the seal matrix of the Muscovy Company. BM MLA Tonnochy no. 158. Diameter 5.1cm.*

Fig. 17.11 *Ivory seal matrix of Sir George Carey, showing the ship with his shield on the sail. BM MLA Tonnochy no. 952. Diameter 8.8cm.*

of Sir George Carey of c.1586 as Captain of the Isle of Wight and Admiral of Southampton (Fig. 17.11). His seal has two ivory faces perhaps indicating his two different official positions. One face has a shield of arms with twenty quarterings reflecting that inflation of quartering that was so characteristic of the heraldry of the 16th century. On the other end, Carey places his own arms (here with nine quarterings) on the mainsail of the ship, and flies the royal arms from the main mast and the flag of St George fore and aft. At the very end of our period, possibly dating from 1585, the seal of Charles, Lord Howard of Effingham, is a double seal on one side of which is the shield of arms of Howard and on the reverse is an equestrian version of the Earl, rather than a ship. This double seal is perhaps modelled on the royal great seal. But here the indication of his role as Admiral is reduced to an anchor depicted on the caparison of his horse, a sad decline from the splendid ships that had graced the earlier seals of Admirals.[44]

Commercial seals

The seal and arms of commercial companies presented a new opportunity for heraldry and seals. The seals of trading companies and fraternities of craftsmen in the later Middle Ages often show saints. The seal, dated c.1475, of the Fraternity of Tailors in the city of Exeter shows St John the Baptist with the Agnus Dei between two shields showing open shears and the 15th-century seal of the English merchants trading to Flanders, Brabant, Holland and Zeeland shows the figure of St Thomas of Canterbury in a ship.[45] In contrast the seal of the Muscovy merchants, founded in 1555 to further maritime trade with Russia, has a shield composed of a ship with royal badges of a lion and two roses above. The inscription, still in Latin *refugium nostrum in deo est*, refers to God (Fig. 17.10).[46] However, the Eastland Company, founded in 1579 to regularise the Baltic trade in opposition to the Hanse, has a shield with a three-masted ship in full sail with a lion above. There are two bears as supporters and the motto is in English *Dispair not*.[47]

260 *John Cherry*

The merchant's mark was not a new type of signifier in the 15th century, but its use greatly expanded in the period. Part of its popularity may have been that it was a sign that could be read without any knowledge of language.[48] The merchants personal or business mark was also used for labelling and so indicated the signification of possession. It is noticeable how many portraits of merchants show seal matrices and documents. For instance, the painting by Hans Holbein of the merchant George Gisze shows him opening a letter, while in front of him there is shown an ivory-handled seal and a signet ring, and another (older?) seal matrix behind him.[49] The painting of Pieter Bicker Gerritsz, dated 1529, by Maerten van Heemskerk (1498–1574) in the Rijksmuseum Amsterdam, shows two ivory-handled seal matrices with spherical ends. It is clear that business was becoming more bureaucratic, which may be an indication of the age of transition. Merchants' marks were increasingly used as if they

were heraldic signs since they were often inherited and used by the sons of merchants.[50]

Correspondence and rings

In the 15th century and 16th century the amount of personal correspondence that has survived shows a considerable increase. This is shown by such collections as the Paston, Stonor, and Lisle letters as well as the huge official correspondence in the 16th century. The relationship of this to the methods of authentication, particularly to the growth in the number of signet rings, has yet to be assessed. Many letters were authenticated by signature, also known as the sign manual, and this practice had spread rapidly in the early 15th century.[51] The seal or signet ring was often used to seal the outside of the folded letter. It is clear that in the 16th century there was a considerable growth in the postal system.[52]

The use of the desk seal and the ring for sealing

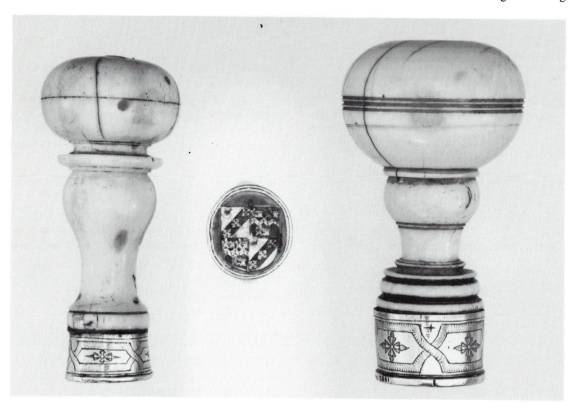

Fig. 17.12 *The two seal matrices and ring of Sir Thomas Smith. BM MLA 1982,7–1,1–3. Height of the taller matrix (right) is 9.2cm.*

letters and documents can be illustrated by the seals of Sir Thomas Smith (BM MLA 1982,7–3,1–3) whose two desk seals and ring have been preserved (Fig. 17.12). He was Secretary of State to Edward IV and Elizabeth and Chancellor of the Order of the Garter. His circular armorial desk seal, with turned ivory handle, shows his shield of arms surmounted by his crest of a salamander, while his lesser desk seal, also with a turned ivory handle, shows only his crest of a salamander. Documents exist sealed with these seals and both appear to have made between 1571 and 1573 and were used both together and separately. It is less clear when he would have sealed with his ring, whose bezel is shown in Fig. 17.12, though this may have primarily been used for letters. The ring does not show a device but his complete shield, though without mantling and crest.[53]

Another group of seals that shows the distinction between personal and official are the three silver seal matrices of Sir Walter Raleigh. His seal as Warden of the Stannaries and Governor of the Isle of Jersey, of around 1600, shows a mounted knight, his seal as Governor of Virginia of 1584 shows the arms of Raleigh alone while his private seal shows a shield of arms with sixteen quarterings.[54]

Conclusion

The study of seals is one of those subjects that became a subject of antiquarian interest even during the period of transition with which we are concerned. It was the first topic on which Francis Tate, Secretary of the Elizabethan Society of Antiquaries, collected notes for a lecture to the Society entitled 'Of the Antiquity of seales etc', and a lecture delivered on 23rd June 1591 was 'Of thoriginal of sealing here in England with armes or otherwise', which brings seals and heraldry neatly together.[55]

The transition in the use of heraldry and seals in the period is both simple and subtle. At one level it replaced the depiction of saints, and became an aspect of secular and royal propaganda. It was also used to bolster an emphasis on genealogy for those in power who were often of recent origin. This archaeology of communication can be appreciated on at least two levels – the practical nature of communication and the communication of ideas and attitudes. Here tradition and change are inextricably intermingled.

Notes

1. For a general introduction to the use of medieval seals see Harvey & McGuinness 1996. The inter-relationship of heraldry and seals is discussed in Pastoureau 1979.
2. Clanchy 1979, 229.
3. Thurley 1993, 98.
4. Howard 1987, 42.
5. RCHM *City of Cambridge* 1959, 128–30 says between 1533 and 6. See also MacCulloch 1996, 45.
6. Anglo 1992, 38–9. Sara Stevenson 'The Heraldic idea in England 1560–1610', an unpublished thesis in the Warburg Institute (University of London), 1972, discusses the use of heraldry in the latter part of the period. I owe this reference to Tim Wilson.
7. Wyon & Wyon 1887, 43–6 and 77–8. For a later survey see Birch 1907, 20–60 and Jenkinson 1952–3, 550–63. There is no modern survey of all the great seals of England.
8. Strong 1983, p. 41 and no. 19.
9. The seal for the Ipswich college is discussed in Gunn & Lindley 1991, p. 39.
10. Partial studies of Wolseys's seals are Gunn & Lindley 1991, 39 and Auerbach 1954, 38–9. There is no complete study.
11. Jenkinson 1968, 63.
12. Birch 1887, no. 5280 where it is wrongly dated to 1547. The seal is attached to PRO E24/5/2 and L and P iv, iii, no. 5345 of 5 March 1528.
13. Birch 1887, no. 2409.
14. Tonnochy 1952, no. 880. *VCH London,* vol. 1, 1909, 515–6.
15. For Durham see Birch 1887, no. 2517, Norwich Birch 1887, no. 2102, Worcester Birch 1887, no. 2298, Chester Birch 1887, no. 2432, and for Oxford Birch 1887, nos. 2138 and 9.
16. *Ibid.* no. 2093 and its revision in 1544?, no. 2102.
17. *Ibid.* nos. 2138 and 9.
18. Haigh 1996, 7 and 15. The seal cost £4.
19. Birch 1887, no. 1259.
20. MacCulloch 1996, 228–9, especially footnotes 195 and 196.
21. *Ibid.* 228 and pl. 18. A similar change occurs in the Cranmer's prerogative seals in 1538, see Mac-Culloch 1996, pl. 19, though here it is the scourging of Christ rather than the crucifixion that replaces the martyrdom.

22. Jewitt and Hope 1895, 320 quoting *Hist Mss Comm Appendix to 9th Report*, part i., 153.
23. Birch 1887, nos. 1280 and 1281.
24. *Ibid*. no. 2157, and Society of Antiquaries casts C34. John Scory (d.1585) was one of the six preachers whom Cranmer appointed at Canterbury in 1541. In 1551 he was appointed to Rochester, in 1552 to Chichester, and in 1559 he became bishop of Hereford. See *D.N.B.*
25. Birch 1887, no. 2484. Hunter Blair 1928, pl. xiv, no. 2. Richard Barnes (1532–87) was elected bishop of Carlisle in 1570 and bishop of Durham in 1577. See *D.N.B.*
26. Birch 1887, no. 2141. Thomas Dove was elected bishop of Peterborough in 1601. He was formerly chaplain to Queen Elizabeth, who is said to have admired his eloquence in preaching, and to have observed that this Dove was a dove with silver wings, who must have been inspired by the grace of him who had once assumed the form of a dove. See *D.N.B.*
27. Cautley 1934 provides the best survey of this, but the criticisms made by Hasler 1980 should be noted.
28. Sander 1877, 172.
29. Cautley 1934, p. 18 and pl. 2. Pevsner 1974, 409 accepts it as genuine. Hasler refers to the views of those who think that it is a Victorian fake, based on King's College Chapel, Cambridge. The controversy may be followed in the pages of *Country Life*, after Cautley restated his views on 22 October 1953.
30. Cautley 1934, p. 23, and pl. 3.
31. For the seal of Henry VIII see Society of Antiquaries casts and for Edward VI see *Durham seals* ii, pp. 416, 429.
32. The only survey of the whole group is by Perceval 1882, 39.
33. Tonnochy 1952, no. 800.
34. *Ibid*. no. 884.
35. *Ibid*. no 849. Also Knowles & Hadcock 1971, 54 and 68.
36. Tonnochy 1952, no. 855 and *VCH Sussex*, 1907, vol. ii, 106.
37. Tonnochy 1952, no. 857.
38. *Ibid*. no. 862. *VCH Surrey*, 1905, vol. ii, p. 89. Knowles 1959, p. 439. There is a full and documented account of the refoundation of Sheen in Thompson 1930, 500–9.
39. Orme 1973, 256.
40. Pettigrew 1856, 55–72, 145–155, and 223–234.
41. Jenkinson 1936, 293–338.
42. Wyon 1893, 1.

43. Tonnochy 1952, no. 26. For the use of flags and pennants on ships see Wilson 1986 and Perrin, 1922, 46, 78.
44. Birch 1887, nos. 1042–56 has a good series of descriptions of admirals' seals in the period. For the seal of Charles, Lord Howard of Effingham, see no. 1056. This is attached to a charter dated 1601, but he was appointed in 1585. For the seal of Sir George Carey see Tonnochy 1952, no. 952.
45. Tonochy 1952, nos. 177 and 156.
46. *Ibid*. no. 158.
47. *Ibid*. no. 155.
48. The best surveys of merchants' marks are by Elmhirst 1959 & Girling 1962.
49. The picture is in the Gemäldegalerie, Staatliche Museum Preussischer Kulturbesitz, Berlin.
50. Elmhirst 1959, 226.
51. For the use of the sign manual see Harvey & McGuinness 1996, 2.
52. Hurcomb, 1914, 92, 144, 208, 304. For original evidence of the postal system see Sir Brian Tuke's memorandum 'On the state of the posts' in 1533 to Thomas Cromwell see *State Papers Henry VIII* vol. 1, p. 405.
53. These comments are based on the notes of Timothy Wilson preserved in the relevant file in Medieval and Later Antiquities, British Museum.
54. Tonnochy 1952, nos. 346–8.
55. Harvey & McGuinness 1996, 22.

Bibliography

Anglo, S. 1992, *Images of Tudor Kingship*

Auerbach, E. 1954, *Tudor Artists*

Birch, W. de G. 1887, *Catalogue of seals in the British Museum*

Birch, W de G. 1907, *Seals*

Cautley, H.M. 1974, *Royal Arms and Commandments in Our Churches*, Ipswich

Clanchy, M. 1979, *From Memory to Written Record*

Dalton, O.M. 1912, *Catalogue of finger rings in the British Museum*

Elmhirst, E.M., 1959, *Merchant's Marks*

Elmhirst, E. 1954/5 'Merchants Marks and Heraldry Problems of Kinship', *Coat of Arms*, vol. 3, pp. 226–8

Girling, F.A. 1962, *English Merchants Marks*

Gunn, S.J. & Lindley, P. (eds) 1991, *Wolsey: church, state and art*

Haigh, C. 1996, *1546 Before and After the Making of Christ Church, a commemorative lecture given on 2 November 1996*, Oxford

Harvey, P.D.A. & McGuinness A. 1996, *A guide to British Medieval Seals*

Howard, M. 1987, *The Early Tudor Country House, Architecture and politics 1490–1550*

Hunter Blair, C.H. 1924, 'Medieval Seals of the Bishops of Durham', *Archaeologia* 77, 1–24

Hurcomb, C. 1914 'Posts under the Tudors', *The Antiquary* 50, 92, 144, 208, 304

Jenkinson, Hilary. 1936, 'The great seal of England: Deputed or Departmental seals', *Archaeologia* 85, 293–338

Jenkinson, Sir Hilary. 1952–3, 'The Great Seal of England', *Journal of the Royal Society of Arts* 101, 550–563

Jenkinson, Sir Hilary. 1968, *Guide to seals in the Public Record Office*

Jewitt, L. & St. John Hope, W.H. 1895, *The Corporation Plate and insignia of office of the cities and corporate towns in England and Wales*

Knowles, D. 1959, *The Religious Orders in England*, Cambridge

Knowles, D. & Hadcock, R.N. 1971, *Medieval Religious Houses, England and Wales*

MacCulloch, D. 1996, *Thomas Cranmer*

Orme, N. 1973, *English Schools in the Middle Ages*

Pastoureau, M. 1979, *Traite d'Heraldique*, Paris

Perceval, C.S. 1882 'Notes on the collection of seals formed by the late Mr Tyssen', *Proceedings of the Society of Antiquaries of London,* series 2, 9, 36–54 but especially 38–41

Pettigrew, T.J. 1856 'Notes on the Seals of the Endowed Grammar Schools in England and Wales', *Journal of the British Archaeological Association* 12, 55–72, 145–55, and 223–234

Pevsner, N. 1974, *Suffolk*, Harmondsworth

Sander, N. 1877, *Rise and Growth of the Anglican Schism*

Starkey, D. (ed.) 1991, *Henry VIII, A European Court in England,* catalogue

Strong, R. 1977, *The Cult of Elizabeth*

Strong, R. (ed.) 1983, *Artists of the Tudor Court*

Thompson, E.M. 1930, *The English Carthusians*

Thurley, S. 1993, *The Royal Palaces of Tudor England*, London and New Haven

Tonnochy, A.B. 1952, *Catalogue of British Seal-dies in the British Museum*

Trapp, J.B. & Herbruggen, H.S. (eds) 1977, *'The King's Good Servant' Sir Thomas More, 1477/8–1535*

Wilson, T. 1986, *Flags at Sea,* Greenwich

Wyon, A.B. & Wyon, A. 1887, *The Great Seals of England*

Wyon, A. 1893, 'The Royal Judicial Seals of the King's Great Sessions in Wales' *Journal of the British Archaeological Association* 49, 1–15

List of Contributors

JOHN CHERRY
Medieval and Later Antiquities
British Museum
London WC1B 3DG

JONATHAN COAD
English Heritage
Historic Properties South East
1 High Street
Tonbridge
Kent TN9 1SG

NICHOLAS COOPER
Royal Commission on the Historical Monuments of
England
55 Blandford Street
London W1H 3AF

DR PAUL COURTNEY
20 Lytton Road
Clarendon Park
Leicester LE2 1WJ

PROFESSOR CHRISTOPHER DYER
School of History
University of Birmingham
Edgbaston
Birmingham B15 2TT

DR GEOFF EGAN
Museum of London Archaeological Service
Walker House
87 Queen Victoria Street
London EC4V 4AB

HAZEL FORSYTH
Early Collections
Museum of London
London Wall
London EC2Y 5HN

PROFESSOR DR FRANS VERHAEGHE
Department of Art History and Archaeology
Faculty of Letters
Free University of Brussels
Pleinlaan 2
B-1050 Brussels
Belgium

DR DAVID GAIMSTER
Medieval and Later Antiquities
British Museum
London WC1B 3DG

JOHN GIORGI
Museum of London Archaeology Service
Walker House
87 Queen Victoria Street
London EC4V 4AB

DR MAURICE HOWARD
School of Cultural and Community Studies
Arts Building
University of Sussex
Falmer
Brighton BN1 9QN

DR HELMUT HUNDSBICHLER
Institut für Realienkunde des Mittelalters und der
frühen Neuzeit
Körnermarkt 13
A-3500 Krems
Austria

DR MATTHEW JOHNSON
Department of Archaeology
University of Durham
South Road
Durham DH1 3LE

Dr Philip Lindley
Department of Art History
University of Leicester
Leicester LE1 7RH

Beverley Nenk
Medieval and Later Antiquities
British Museum
London WC1B 3DG

Dr John Schofield
Museum of London Archaeology Service
Walker House
87 Queen Victoria Street
London EC4V 4AB

Dr Paul Stamper
English Heritage
Gardens and Landscape
429 Oxford Street
London W1R 2HD

Kay Staniland
Later Collections
Museum of London
London Wall
London EC2Y 5HN

Hugh Tait
46 Malborough Mansions
Cannon Hill
London NW6

Dr Simon Thurley
Museum of London
London Wall
London EC2Y 5HN